UNBINDING
Gentility

MUSIC IN AMERICAN LIFE

*A list of books in the series appears
at the end of this book.*

UNBINDING

Gentility

WOMEN MAKING MUSIC IN THE
NINETEENTH-CENTURY SOUTH

CANDACE BAILEY

**UNIVERSITY OF
ILLINOIS PRESS**
Urbana, Chicago, and Springfield

This book is accompanied by a web page, https://www.press.uillinois.edu/books/bailey/unbinding/, that features supplemental text.

Publication supported by grants from the Henry and Edna Binkele Classical Music Fund and from the Donna Cardamone Jackson Fund, Joseph Kerman Fund, and General Fund of the American Musicological Society, supported in part by the National Endowment for the Humanities and the Andrew W. Mellon Foundation.

Library of Congress Cataloging-in-Publication Data
Names: Bailey, Candace, 1963– author.
Title: Unbinding gentility: women making music in the nineteenth-century South / Candace Bailey.
Description: Urbana: University of Illinois Press, 2021. | Series: Music in American life | Includes bibliographical references and index. |
Identifiers: LCCN 2020045521 (print) | LCCN 2020045522 (ebook) | ISBN 9780252043758 (cloth) | ISBN 9780252085741 (paperback) | ISBN 9780252052651 (ebook)
Subjects: LCSH: Women musicians—Southern States—History—19th century. | Musicians—Southern States—History—19th century. | Women—Southern States—History—19th century. | Women—Southern States—Social conditions—19th century. | Music—Social aspects—Southern States—History—19th century. | Music and race—Southern States—History—19th century. | Binder's volumes (Music)—Southern States—History—19th century.
Classification: LCC ML82 .B27 2021 (print) | LCC ML82 (ebook) | DDC 780.975082—dc23
LC record available at https://lccn.loc.gov/2020045521
LC ebook record available at https://lccn.loc.gov/2020045522

To Julian

Contents

List of Illustrations

FIGURES

TABLES

Acknowledgments

Unbinding Gentility: Women Making Music in the Nineteenth-Century South has been a long time in the making, and throughout the process I have been honored with support from a wide-ranging body of people and organizations. Over the years that I have spent traipsing through archives, libraries, historic estates, antique bookstores, private collections, and online booksellers, I have been assisted by wonderful people whose generosity frequently extended well beyond what their positions required. Without them, this book would be incomplete. Space prohibits naming them all, but a few deserve special recognition. Lucinda Cockrell (Center for Popular Music at MTSU), Diane Steinhaus (Music Library at UNC), Germain Bienvenue and Tara Laver (Hill Collection, LSU), and Jennifer McCormick (Charleston Museum) allowed me unfettered access to materials in their collections, and this has meant so much to the end product, for as of yet no standard method exists for cataloguing this repertory. The uncatalogued or simply boxed materials put at my disposal at the Georgia Historical Society, the Athenaeum (Columbia, Tennessee), the Houghton (Harvard), and other places have yielded treasure troves of information concerning the lives of women in the South. Paul Allen Sommerfield at the Library of Congress has assisted me in locating materials there, both in research trips and online. I owe special gratitude to Andrea Cawelti (Houghton Library, Harvard and Sheet Music Consortium) for her ineffable support, advice, and direction.

In addition to these archives, librarians at Duke University (Rubenstein Rare Book and Manuscript Library, and Music Library) have continually assisted my research. In Columbia, South Carolina, Graham Duncan searched through uncatalogued items to find music for me. Mark Brown (Executive Director of the Belmont Mansion in Nashville), Matt Davis (Director of Historic Museums at

Georgia College), and several other managers of historical properties kindly opened their doors so that I could not only view their music collections but also get a feel for performance spaces themselves.

Undertaking a project of this magnitude requires the help, advice, and friendship of scholars whose encouragement has been unending. Katherine Preston has been and remains a stalwart supporter of my endeavors, writing letters of support, offering advice, and inviting me to Williamsburg to work with materials at William & Mary. Lucinda and Dale Cockrell have been stars: their knowledge of music, society, and local history have pointed me in new directions and challenged me to think more carefully about social position and class in this period. Denise Von Glahn graciously lent me Wiley Housewright's information on music in Florida and later offered that last bit of encouragement that pushed this work to completion. Others whose letters of support have further enhanced the final product include Annegret Fauser, Sandra Graham, and Thomas Riis. I cannot thank these scholars enough for their continued assistance and encouragement.

My research has been graciously supported by several organizations—an indispensable boost for a scholar at a teaching university. An HBCU Faculty Award (2015–16) from the National Endowment for the Humanities (NEH) made possible the time to plan and organize my research materials, and to complete the first draft of the manuscript. The Judith Tick Fellowship from the Society for American Music funded a trip to Baton Rouge to work with the William Johnson Papers and other materials at LSU, as well as a visit to the Historic New Orleans Collection. As a recipient of one of the inaugural Project Development Grants from the American Council of Learned Societies, I have been able to examine materials at the Library of Congress, the Newberry Library, the American Antiquarian Society, the Houghton Library, and the Boston Public Library. The opportunity to work with scholars at the NEH Summer Institute Visual Cultures of the Civil War and Its Aftermath allowed me to spend time with a community of experts from areas of research that differed substantially from my own. The final phase of writing was made possible through a fellowship at the National Humanities Center in 2019–2020, supported by the Andrew W. Mellon Foundation. My dean at NCCU, Carlton Wilson, has unfailingly supported my time away from campus and championed my research.

Conferences large and small have encouraged conversation and enriched my perspective of the social and cultural worlds covered in *Unbinding Gentility*. I wish to acknowledge "Early American Music and the Construction of Race," organized by Glenda Goodman and Rhae Lynn Barnes, which has provided insightful discussions impacting my questions concerning race and women in the South. The meaningful and encouraging relationships that I have made in the Society for American Music have proven invaluable. The anonymous readers of this manuscript contributed insightful comments that have deepened my interrogation of materials and substantially reshaped the final version. I appreciate the time and effort they expended toward its publication. My editor at the University of Illinois Press, Laurie Matheson, continues to amaze with her thoughtful questions and gentle encouragement.

Beyond traditional assistance, numerous friends and colleagues have offered suggestions, listened to frustrations, and encouraged me through difficult times. At the risk of accidentally omitting someone, I wish to express my gratitude to Amanda Eubanks Winkler, Catherine Gordon, Kendra Leonard, Mona Kreitner, Kristen Turner, and Charles McGuire for their kindness and support. These friends make life as a musicologist all the better.

Finally, my family. This book could not have been written without their support. My mother, Brenda Bailey, remains my most stalwart supporter, followed closely by my two children, Emma and Graham Renfrow. My father, J. W. Bailey, who died while I was writing, impressed upon me the importance of family and place. He never quite understood what I did, but he was proud nonetheless. Julian Prosser has read every word several times, provided a quiet retreat to unwind and breathe, and been a stalwart traveling companion. This book is dedicated to him.

Abbreviations

CBA	Bailey, *Charleston Belles Abroad*
CPM	Center for Popular Music, Middle Tennessee State University
GDL	*Godey's Lady's Book*
LSU	Louisiana State University
MFL	Mary Fenwick Lewis
MSB	Bailey, *Music and the Southern Belle*
MTSU	Middle Tennessee State University
SCHS	South Carolina Historical Society
SHC	Southern Historical Collection, University of North Carolina at Chapel Hill
SMB	Sheet Music Bound, Charleston Museum
SMJ	*Southern Musical Journal*
SWEM	Swem Library, College of William and Mary
UK	United Kingdom
UNC	University of North Carolina at Chapel Hill
US	United States
VMHC	Virginia Museum of History and Culture

Author's Note

First, a word of caution concerning binder's volumes. Rarely can we know exactly who decided what music a young woman would own or what would be included when sheet music went to the binder. Fathers who traveled, brothers at school, friends, relatives, and teachers could have provided music that found its way into a binder's volume. Thus, Nannie McMorris's copy of "I'll Be No Submissive Wife" does not necessarily indicate Nannie's personal view of marriage. It might, but most of the time we cannot be sure. In other cases, the connection is clear, such as Kate Berry's writing many notes on her music. These are facts to keep in mind when contextualizing music in any particular collection.

Any history of women must address how to refer to them. I have used "Miss" and "Mrs." to denote marital status only when relevant. Married names are often given in brackets [] to aid researchers who may have only those. First names are used to connote amateurs; last names for professionals. Women married, many more than once, and southerners were notorious for reusing names, which complicates the issue further. Within a section, I have used the given (or preferred) name of amateurs in lieu of their last names, after the first mention. Professionals, on the other hand, are referenced by their last name. For women professionals, I have used the name that appears in print most often. (Henrietta Maria Dillon Kowalewski Poetz, therefore, is Kowalewski.)

Well-known cities and towns do not have states associated with them, except in the case where another southern town could be mistaken for it. Spellings are given as they appear in the sources. Capitalization has been regularized for song titles, even though nineteenth-century sources followed no rules, and many titles were printed in all capitals. Foreign-language titles follow the conventions of the language in which they appear. The United States census records have been used to calculate approximate family assets.

The current locations of the binder's volumes to which I refer can be found online. Similarly, biographical information that is not relevant to a particular point in the text but that could be useful in future research has also been placed on the book's website (https://www.press.uillinois.edu/books/Bailey/Unbinding Gentility). English titles of operatic arias and appendices A and B are also available there. The author's website (clbaileymusicologist.com) provides much more information on the provenance of nineteenth-century binder's volumes.

UNBINDING
Gentility

INTRODUCTION

"One would like to know"

As long ago as 1909, an anonymous writer in a New Orleans newspaper recognized the neglect of the city's earlier music history and attempted to reconstruct its connection to the present. Not only did this author include composers and performers, but even young women of the city whom composers (or publishers) flattered with dedications: "It may be called New Orleans music, for it is all identified with this city in some intimate way. It was composed here, or published here, or was dedicated to some one who lived here." This intimate connection underpins the ideas presented in *Unbinding Gentility: Women Making Music in the Nineteenth-Century South*.[1] Like this author, I seek to recover silent voices and position them within the social world of which they were so much a part.

Silent they were in 1909, and silent they have remained. Consider, for example, how the writer emphasizes the importance of Rose Kennedy, a debutante of renown, instead of the composer, when describing a composition: "'Norma, Grande Fantaisie Brilliante,' by "Georges Schmitt (Pianiste de sa Majeste le Reine d'Espagne),' is also localized by being dedicated to Mlle. Rose Kennedy of New Orleans. The date is 1849, and Mlle. Rose Kennedy has passed to the land of the forgotten. . . . Doubtless she was a beauty and a belle in that old time. . . . One would like to know."[2] Yes—one *would* like to know more about Rose Kennedy. Did she actually play this virtuoso piano composition? Did she perform in public? How did Georges Schmitt and William Vincent Wallace come to dedicate pieces to her? Why did she spend time practicing? Did her colleagues also play like this? Did women outside of New Orleans study such music? The tenor of the 1909 article highlights the amateur women who performed in New Orleans. How have we, as musicologists, ignored them for so long?

Interpreting the role amateur women played in American music history re-quires consideration of class, culture, and society through a combination of methodologies. Dominant themes grounding the work of historians of the South (material, cultural, social, literature, and visual) have yet to figure prominently in musicological research.[3] On the other hand, the implications of circulation, repertory, and musical practice have not been examined by non-music scholars, even though the sister arts of visual art and theater have.[4] To examine women's music, however, they must.

Unbinding Gentility addresses these issues and other assumptions about music in the United States. Scholars have traditionally populated it with generic white middle-class women who performed simple music in their parlors; overlooking specific practices, regions, and even class distinctions. Such books rarely inspire readers to delve further into women's musical artifacts, many of which remain under the category of "ephemera"—items that were never intended to last but rather to be discarded when they had outworn their usefulness. Visual historian Michael Wilson's observation that "the presumption that visual is 'trivial' becomes self-fulfilling" can be applied with equal measure to women's ephemera, in this case substituting "sheet music" for "visual."[5] Furthermore, gender and race as top-ics within this history become silenced because preservation practices prejudice composer and title over circulation and performance. The history emanating from these materials as presented belongs almost exclusively to white men.

Recasting southern musical practices from the point of view of women's history results in a study entirely at odds with most modern literature. For example, in *America's Musical Life: A History*, Richard Crawford asserts that "American parlor culture was not much concerned with issues of art or musical substance." He reads the "repackaging" of familiar melodies "as a way to create communities of feeling, common especially among women," presumably the repertory of arrangements of popular songs and opera excerpts that dominated both women's binder's volumes and men's public recitals. Phrases such as these linguistically brand their experi-ences as feminine and therefore ephemeral and unartistic. His claim that "in the nineteenth-century parlor, music's purpose was more social than artistic" does not acknowledge the prevalence of these works on the concert stage nor does it honor the hours of practice and preparation needed to play large-scale transcrip-tions such as Ferdinand Beyer's *Les Huguenots* or sing bel canto arias ranging from "Una voce poco fa" to "Casta diva" as published by the composer.[6] These probably did provoke "feeling," but not simply heartwarming sentimentality.

Admittedly, much of women's musical experience was social, and it was not always artistic. But why social should continue to be cast in opposition to artistic is puzzling. The programs highlighted in this study prove that professionals and amateurs often performed the same pieces. How do we differentiate amateur and professional performances if both musicians sang "Casta diva" in the same key from the same score? Similarly, piano arrangements could require much more of the performer than many have assumed. Far from easy, they are not demure, gentle, delicate, or any other qualities southern women were taught to project, yet they can be found in binder's volumes that include other physically demanding compositions, such as Gottschalk's invocations of African cultures, notably "Bamboula" and "Banjo." The time has come to dismantle assumptions that underpin much of the scholarship on this period. We cannot divorce music from its social and cultural uses; we must treat it within them.

Marcia Citron asserts that the words we use highlight this discrimination: men create, women re-create.[7] Re-creation, like ephemera, lacks historical gravitas. As one archivist recently quipped when offered a substantial collection: "it's only old sheet music."[8] What happened after a composition's creation typically has been measured by its popularity or even its familiarity today. How it circulated, what meaning it held for those who performed or heard it, and related questions remain unasked. Furthermore, the dismissal of women's music collections as ephemera has led writers to lump women together, with little regard for social status or cultural class except race—and even here there are problems.[9] These attitudes have resulted in the representation of antebellum music by the songs of Stephen Foster or minstrelsy. Neither of these, Foster nor minstrel songs, figures prominently in women's musical practices of the antebellum South.

At a recent conference I happened to dine with a respected musicologist—an Americanist—who kindly enquired about progress on this book, and, as the conversation developed, I offered examples of new information I had uncovered in its research. As I recounted proof of remunerated women musicians, repertory belonging to women of color, difficult opera arias sung in their original keys and languages by amateurs, she repeatedly responded "I've been lied to!" Her meaning lay in the fact that even though she has studied music in the United States for decades, no one mentioned that these practices existed in the South, especially before the Civil War.[10] Jenny Lind and Amy Beach still remain the face of women and music in the United States.[11]

Acknowledging the one-sidedness of social expectation *vis-a-vis* real-life practice is at the heart of *Unbinding Gentility*, but I am far from the first to suggest this. In his study of music and society in Paris, London, and Vienna, William Weber recommends that "studying musical life" permits the comprehension of differences in both class structure and cultures.[12] This methodology reveals much more than earlier approaches, but the present book demonstrates the need to map the cultural geography across an alternative space and time.

My research encompasses music's transmission, education, circulation, and repertory in order to understand music's meaning in women's culture of the South.

It is a sizable topic, and I do not claim to cover every type of music performed over the entire mid-nineteenth century. The concentration here is music read from notation. Spending the time and money to learn to read music implies a tangible appreciation for its undertaking, and it indicates that those who paid for the education saw a benefit in doing so. It conferred value, in this case cultural capital, on those who have learned how to read music and to perform it. This value served in the performance of gentility in the mid-nineteenth century. I draw on information gleaned from over fifteen hundred binder's volumes, numerous nineteenth-century magazines and journals, newspapers, letters and diaries, official records, and similar documents. As an ethnographic reading of archival sources, this study crafts new and vital interpretations of music in southern culture.

First and foremost, this book is a history of women in the nineteenth-century US South told through the medium of music. I happily admit being influenced by Ruth Solie's *Music in Other Words: Victorian Conversations*. She sought to recover what lies in the blank, unwritten, and unspoken, spaces of women's history in the nineteenth century, as do I. Indirect references to musicking in musical and nonmusical sources inform this discourse, and little of my work touches the traditional narrative for this era.[13] Instead, I make vivid the repertory consumed by southerners and mark the existence and influence of professional women. Solie asserts that "musical practices help to make social realities what they are," people's experiences and beliefs about music impact, and I add reflect, other aspects of their lives.[14] Cultural expectations in the South sharply defined women from various social classes, but the degree to which music figured in this delineation has yet to be fully understood. Scholars in nonmusic disciplines, Catherine Kerrison and Susan Harris for example, have looked at other aspects of women's culture in order to incorporate a wider source of data by which to contextualize class, gender, and culture in this period.[15] What is less familiar, and what this project seeks to uncover, is how scientific music functioned in women's culture throughout the population.

Persistent Binaries

In *Music and the Southern Belle: From Accomplished Lady to Confederate Composer*, I examined music in the context of elite southern women during the Civil War, arguing that their self-perception changed during the war years. This study expands the data to include nonelite women—a higher percentage of the population—who lived in the South during the mid-nineteenth century and extends the time to 1880. I measure music as an "ideal" accomplishment or "real" practice, probing the space between what people expected women to do and what they truly did.

Two persistent binaries mislead how we read women and music in the ante-bellum South and hence any meaningful developments in that culture through the Civil War and Reconstruction. One is the view, purposely engraved in the common collective by *Birth of a Nation, Jezebel,* and *Gone with the Wind,* that women in the South were either white plantation daughters (or wives) or they were enslaved Black women. Few novels, films, or television dramas portray southern middle-class women in this era. This dichotomy, however, distorts our histories: people obviously existed between these two socioeconomic extremes. The nonexistence of middle-class women in the common narrative also derives from the deliberate rewriting of southern history around the turn of the twenti-eth century, which created the belle/mammy binary at the expense of all others. *Unbinding Gentility* aims to rectify this lacuna by including women between these two social bookends and providing information on women's musical practices that mirrors the society itself. Gentility, as we shall see, carries mixed interpreta-tions of class status.

The second binary ties loosely to the first. Modern publications tend to present women's music of the mid-century in one of two contexts: 1) white middle-class women performed Stephen Foster's songs in the parlor; and 2) Black women sang spirituals and work songs.[16] This, too, is deceptive. First is the shift of class status, from elite belle to middle-class woman. Then there is the problem of rep-ertory. Two common melodies that surface in southern binder's volumes are the "Last Rose of Summer" and "Home! Sweet Home!" This seems logical; after all, how many times does one need to ponder "The Last Rose of Summer" before acknowledging its simplicity, elegance, and undeniable tunefulness? These are also traits identified in some of Foster's songs. Suppose, however, that we question the validity of using Foster's music as the most popular and representative samples and actually seek the data from the collections of women engaged in music prac-tice. Such an inquiry reveals that these assumptions belie musical practices and challenge prevailing ideas about who performed what during the mid-century. Women from various classes learned music ranging from demanding French and Italian arias to simple ballads in English, from elaborate waltzes in five-four time to time-honored quadrilles. Furthermore, not all of these women were white, a fact that opens the door to another realm of questions.[17]

Gentility

Locating women's musical practices in the performance of gentility provides one path forward in reconciling the evidence and the narrative. Unlike social status, gentility belonged to no single group of people. The use of music as a sign of prestige extended across a wide spectrum, from enslaved Black women to the daughters of affluent white planters. Wealthier young women set the standards for gentility, and those lower on the social scale employed it to disguise their status or to move into higher circles. Gentility enabled women to blur lines between classes.

In her highly influential *Confidence Men and Painted Women: A Study of Middle-Class Culture in America, 1830–1870*, Karen Halttunen asserts that "the social stamp of success was that elusive quality of gentility which aspiring middle-class men and especially women sought to achieve by studying the art of politeness." She equates etiquette to fashionable clothing, both of which became authoritative markers in the middle-class parlor between 1830 and 1860.[18] To this end, American etiquette manuals flooded the market, and one stands out for its direct correlation with gentility: Emily Thornwell's *Lady's Guide to Perfect Gentility: In Manners, Dress, and Conversation, in the Family, in Company, at the Piano Forte, the Table, in the Street, and in Gentlemen's Society* (1856). The title also explicitly ties music to gentility.

Two parts of Halttunen's work find repeated application. First, she asserts that genteel performance consisted of "a system of polite conduct that demanded flawless self-discipline practiced with an apparently easy, natural sincere manner." It served to ameliorate tensions between sentimental sincerity and self-restraint, and from the beginning helped construct ideologies of gender. Second, her emphasis on the rules that helped determine true gentility from false finds resonance in discussions of southern women and their limited sphere of power. She divides the rules into three classes: the laws of polite social geography, the laws of tact, and the laws of acquaintanceship.[19] These guidelines manifest rules governing control of bodily and facial expression (including physicality), the parlor, and those who witness the genteel performance.

Halttunen's work exerts its greatest impact on a broader period when amplified by Richard Bushman's explanation of the spread of genteel refinement in the first half of the nineteenth century.[20] His conclusions prove the more convincing when looking at women's musical culture because gentility extended across the same groups of people that owned music. In the years of Jacksonian Democracy, many Americans prided themselves on a lack of aristocracy, but the inculcation of this idea did not extend to all in the South. Early-nineteenth-century anxieties over displacement and a fluid social order received reassurance by markers of hierarchy and distinction.[21] Nonelite aspirational Americans sought to better themselves by acquiring gentility. In addition to making money, this goal necessitated strict self-discipline, as well as "the correct practice of a repertoire of values, tastes and habits, in other words, cultural capital to match financial capital."[22] Here we must introduce music. As this book will demonstrate, one of the most visible signs of refinement was music. Being able to play the piano, guitar, harp, or sing, and knowledge of the most current operas and dances was a signifier of a young woman's suitability—for what is a matter for much lengthier discussion and will be examined throughout the book.

Bushman's cultural system extends downward from the aristocracy; Halttunen deals only with those in the middle, identifying an "emergent middle-class culture of social mobility" after 1830, people who believed themselves on a "social escalator to greater wealth and prestige."[23] The seeming conflict between these understandings of gentility is keenest in the decade before the war. It does not have to be, however. Prestige is the important variable here; wealth, being tangible and accessible (theoretically but not in reality) to all, could not encapsulate all the necessary facets of gentility. Linda Young acknowledges the problem with weighing affluence too heavily as a social marker, noting that both wealth and poverty can coexist with refinement or uncouthness. Her conclusion that "the range of permutations in between generates a society composed of a multitude of small gradations of difference, where internal conviction and taste mark the distinction of one stratum from another" affords a thoughtful framework by which to interpret music in this period.[24] Music signified some of these gradations.

The republican egalitarianism that underpins Halttunen's concept of gentility did not apply to all parts of the nation equally, particularly the South, where class divisions remained in place longer. But her work finds resonance in underresearched facets of southern society: burgeoning middle classes and culturally engaged lower classes that remain practically nonexistent in most scholarly literature on art music. Their influence on southern culture grew significantly by 1860, and the activities of women in this segment of the population—both white and of color—greatly expand our knowledge of women and music in the South, as well as the nation as a whole.

In the 1950s, sociologist Erving Goffman analyzed the way we perform a socially desirable self by constructing fronts, both personal and of setting. Since then, Milette Shamir, Carolyn Sorisio, and Halttunen have applied Goffman's ideas to the parlor as a space for the performance of a consciously constructed self.[25] The parlor provided a setting for women to perform their refinement, and in its purest *antebellum* sense, to be genteel meant to be sincere. A woman's genteel image expressed her inner values, made visible by her performance. During the midcentury, the environment changed, and so did the performance: the connection between "ideology and behavior made explicit."[26] Americans, acknowledging the paradox that constructed fronts could not simply reveal the true self, began to shed the prescribed ideal of transparency and truth, and adopted a front that allowed their personal preferences to shine more fully. Southern women followed this trend—a few before the war but most after it. The necessities for transgressing boundaries of femininity as constructed under gentility opened the door for newly conceived ideas about women's work after it.

The concept of gentility does not account for every aspect of music and women in the South; no single term can. I have adopted it because no other term suffices when contextualizing how music fit into the performance of culture by so many disparate women. Halttunen's definition and description of gentility, and genteel performance, have influenced many studies on culture in the nineteenth-century United States since the 1980s. Employed in studies of Black aristocrats (Willard B. Gatewood) to white parlor theatricals (Alan Louis Ackerman Jr), and from women as different as Rose Greenhow Lee (Sheila Phipps) to Elizabeth Keckley (Sorisio), her approach has been proven beneficial in understanding how diverse individuals manipulated accepted social intercourse procedures—etiquette—to situate themselves in mid-century society.[27] As cultural historian John Kasson writes at the beginning of a chapter entitled "Etiquette Books and the Spread of Gentility," "'genteel' and 'gentility' are words with notable shifts in meaning."[28] With its vast size and diverse population, the nineteenth-century South is a model case study for this idea.[29]

Gentility and the Parlor

During the nineteenth century, sites of musical practice functioned as spaces of cultural production for women musicians. Women used musical practice as a form of cultural capital that allowed them to define or redefine their status during a time of great social change.[30] "Cultural capital" here connotes the acquisition of signifiers that demonstrate education in modes of behavior that collectively represent expectations of a particular class. Women with more economic means employed music in their efforts to constantly redefine gentility and reinforce class distinctions. Less wealthy women manipulated music as a form of cultural capital and transformed their social positions, gaining power within and without their own circles.

The space within which antebellum women displayed their cultivation was the parlor, a "comfortable theater" for the middle-class presentation of values. The parlor was also the stage on which women performed culture, because it served as a space to navigate a growing populace in American cities. It provided the physical place for southern women to confirm their cultural status: the place-ment of binder's volumes on the piano in the parlor helped assure guests of the hostess's suitability. Many writers have recognized the parlor as the appropri-ate place for young women to sing or play musical instruments. It represented the stage on which southern women presented music rather than performed it, and these are important distinctions. Here they maintained their distance from the public gaze while nonetheless being on display. In contrast, the public stage functioned as an area where southern women viewed women performers (often singing the same songs) but did not appear there themselves. Genteel girls were to have some knowledge of concert repertories and etiquette, but they should also know where to draw the line between how professional musicians performed and how they should appear when presenting music. Understanding this contrast is prerequisite to appreciating performance in the parlor versus performance on the stage. More than any other space, the parlor and its materials symbolized the inner qualities of gentility.[31]

Women used the parlor to display the family's refinement to their visitors. In 1878, Clarence Cook wrote that this "room ought to represent the culture of the family,—what is their taste, what feeling they have for art; it should represent themselves, and not other people; and the troublesome fact is, that it will and must represent them, whether its owners would let it or not."[32] The physicality of the room itself varied according to economic capital. The wealthy often had double parlors, some had only a single room designated as the parlor, and for many it doubled as a family sitting room. In this, too, it showed the admitted audience the owner's place in society.

Class

Questions of class loom large in this study. My current inquiries began with the apparent contradiction between the common association of parlor music with middle-class women and my own previous book on elite white women. Investigation into the backgrounds of students in schools reveals that their populations included young women across the economic spectrum, rich and poor alike in the same rooms but mostly those from the "middling classes."[33] Sheet music forms the most prevalent source of data, but it can be found in collections from extremely divergent households. Since the repertory overlaps significantly, class itself cannot be the sole indicator of how women participated in musical practice if women whose inheritance figured over one million dollars and those worth only a small fraction of that amount played or sang the same music.

In her study of Charleston, Maurie Dee McInnis finds "shared communal values dictated loyalty to certain principles and affiliations" that marked southern aristocracy. It was not something one could personally achieve—the aristocrats were not self-made. Only those born into aristocratic families, or those who married into them, could claim such status.[34] At the top stood the white planter, his wife's position a lady. Peggy Whitman Prenshaw interprets the role of the "lady" in southern literature of this period as both representative of genteel refinement and requisite to the aristocratic social structure. She cites the repeated invocation of Walter Scott's medieval fair lady to represent southern aristocratic values. Such distinction contradicts those who rely on US Republicanism to formulate theories about the structure of antebellum society, yet it reflects southern positioning and must be considered. It challenges those who assign gentility to the middle class alone and constitutes another justification for treating the South as an entity.[35] Much of the extant music in archives today belonged to women from this very group.

This fact substantiates including more than just the middle class among those who performed gentility. Southern author Augusta Jane Evans confirmed that gentility could be associated with upper-class families when she wrote in *St. Elmo* (1866) that "[Edna] shrank from meeting people whose standard of gentility was confined to high birth and handsome fortunes."[36] I, too, apply it to a much wider group, with gradations within. In this I interpret gentility as Lawrence does when she writes that it is "helpful to recognize that gentility is not fixed and absolute, but highly sensitive to environmental circumstances, therein lies its strength, and is a process, not an entity."[37] The concept of "process" is particularly applicable for understanding how gentility changed during and after the war.

To some degree, southerners identified class by birth, but income and material display could also be markers of social circles. In this, individual practices warrant investigation because some spent a higher proportion and some saved: numerous or expensive objects in a woman's parlor might affirm comfortable wealth or be a sign of profligacy for someone who could ill afford it. Another alternative to the term *class* is to identify a woman by her husband's occupation. We can thus read the pair as a single entity because her success was tied to his. Markers such as status and occupation invited competition to move into a higher set or to keep people out of one's own circle. A hierarchy of material and cultural circumstances, familiar at any given moment to those at the height of society and as well as those significantly lower down contributed to the fluidity of gentility. These gradations depended not only on financial capital but also on cultural capital, the latter which admittedly usually required a degree of the former.[38]

Race

It is my desire to impress upon its readers that we have neglected much of women's social history through our focus on men, composers, grand performances, and related aspects of historiography. The participation of people whose ancestry does not trace directly to Europe has traditionally been omitted because we have assumed people of color did not take active roles in musicking that required the ability to read music. Furthermore, the material evidence (chiefly from binder's volumes) points to the majority of scientific music being associated with whites in the United States. On the other hand, the fact that women in the Caribbean, Central, and South America participated in the same musical practices combined with the rich ethnic diversity of places like Florida, Louisiana, and other regions makes obvious the reality that music education and presentation were not the purview of whites alone. As I introduce readers to alternative views of who made music under what circumstances, I employ both "Black" and "women of color." The choices are deliberate ones. To use "Black" only would erase the ancestry of many women in places like New Orleans, a city populated by immigrants from the Caribbean and Central America, indigenous people, and others whose lineage traces to regions other than or in addition to Africa. Nonetheless, almost all of the women whose biographies have been discovered thus far (and therefore included here) are Black. I have no doubt, however, that in time we will uncover more information that will expand our view of who performed scientific music in the United States in the nineteenth century.

Material Culture and the Paraphernalia of Gentility

This study relies on material culture—binder's volumes—as evidence of genteel aspiration. The expansion of the southern economy throughout the second quarter of the century impacted women's musical experiences in the years leading up to the Civil War. The subsequent increase in income spurred a rise in the number of families who could afford the material goods associated with gentility and therefore a diverse population who sought it. The resulting fluidity in social boundaries reinforced a need for class distinctions to maintain order, and, as the 1850s progressed, southern women increasingly intensified their aspirations in attempts to define these boundaries. It can be felt through many different groups. The wealthiest planters wished to be distanced from the less fortunate, the old middle class (associated with lawyers and doctors) from the new (businessmen and technocrats), and so on down the ladder.[39] The middle-class expression of gentility in the 1840s necessarily involved contingency, competition, and compromise, among its own and with those above and below it.[40] By the end of the decade, however, traditional divisions began to crack, foreshadowing the dramatic social changes effected by the Civil War.

Gentility not only demanded purity, transparency, and restraint, it also required, in degrees, the correct tangible measures of taste and refinement. It required visible expression through the accoutrements associated with it. Modest bonnets that shaped the face (and therefore the personality), self-improving literature, and music education exemplified by bound collections of sheet music all contributed to the presentation of gentility.[41] Material culture, expressed through both objects and the practices associated with those objects, empowered women's agency. Considering the sites in which objects are situated permits an examination of their networks and meanings, including utility, powers of evocation, symbols and signifiers, and new affiliations. Because objects such as pianos, sheet music, binder's volumes, and other paraphernalia of music performance represented and evoked a complexity of meanings, the refinement necessary for gentility gave these objects a real power and provides an opportunity to frame cultural values.[42]

Binder's Volumes

In her work on gender and the Civil War, Susan Powell Witt contends that various forms of visual culture functioned as participants in the cultural phenomenon of the parlor.[43] Equally representative is the binder's volume: a collection of sheet music bound into a single volume placed on the piano in the parlor. The binder's volume was a material symbol of gentility, its foremost musical artifact. Binder's volumes constitute yet another object that operated similarly to Witt's objects and at times can be interpreted themselves as visual culture. A binder's volume standing on a piano desk or even lying on a piece of furniture proclaimed that a young woman had been properly brought up. In the second third of the century, the growth of the sheet music industry and piano manufacturing filled an expanding need for music materials that complemented the adaptation of gentility throughout an increasingly wealthy population.[44] Thousands of these survive from the American South, and many others have been deliberately disbound (a practice that destroys the owner's agency in the item's creation). They range from the exquisitely bound collection of Charlestonian Jane E. Schmidt—a volume so beautiful it now belongs in the Leach Binding group of the American Antiquarian Society—to cheaply created unnamed books or even Civil War–era manuscripts. These items constitute a major data source for many women whose stories do not otherwise endure. They represent the performance of culture as understood at a given time and place, and thus serve as meaningful documents in microhistories whose sum in turn contributes to a fuller understanding of a broader narrative.

Binder's volumes are surprisingly uniform on the outside because sheet music in the mid-nineteenth century ran approximately the same size. This has probably contributed to their being lumped into boxes as inconsequential data. The primary difference is how many pages have been bound into each, and here they vary tremendously. The heyday of the binder's volume, 1830–1880, provides the chronological boundaries for the study. Bound collections of music (manuscripts or printed sheets) certainly existed long before 1830 and after 1880. However, binder's volumes were not as ubiquitous before 1830 as they became in the mid-nineteenth -century, driven by technological improvements in printing as well as rising incomes. Around 1880, publishers began offering printed collections of music that could serve the same purpose as an individual's binder's volume, hence initiating its slow decline.

The South

I choose to look only at southern women and women who worked in the South for a number of reasons. That whole groups of academics, from college departments to scholarly organizations, have formed to interrogate the South and that publishers devote entire series to its history in various guises provides enough rationale to add music to this ever-growing body of scholarship. But southern music, especially before the twentieth century, has not held the significance to warrant such consideration. This situation partially derives from a Eurocentric vision of the period and those who see confirmation in its biases, but even Americanists tend to overlook the South unless their interest lies in music of the Civil War.

The region itself was expansive by nineteenth-century standards, and therefore geographical location figured as much in musical culture as other factors. Simple issues of sheet music circulation depended on accessibility of roads, postal service, importers, travel, towns, etc. How far one lived from the ports of the Atlantic, Gulf, or Mississippi River considerably impacted both the contents of binder's volumes and opportunities to hear professional performers. It also affected social standing: to be at the top of the social ladder in Mobile did not mean the same as being at the top in Charleston, and the best families in North Carolina's piedmont region may not have been acceptable in the finest homes of New Orleans.

The vast number of southern studies by historians of different emphases (literary, cultural, social, and so forth) demonstrate that people living in the United States in the nineteenth century recognized distinct cultures on both sides of the Mason-Dixon line. In light of this wealth of scholarly literature on southern culture, it seems reasonable to view music through the same lens. The impact of a society whose economy grew on the backs of the enslaved, whose patriarchal system of governance touched on everyone living in the area, and whose cultural codes grew more stringent up to the Civil War justifies an investigation of the South as a separate geographic construct. Whether these findings hold true in the North has not been tested; I do not claim that the South necessarily treated women's musical experiences differently, although I strongly suspect that it did.[45]

Unbinding Gentility

To unsilence women's voices, numerous microhistories dot this volume. In this, *Unbinding Gentility* expands significantly on the data in *Music and the Southern Belle*. The numbers of people considered substantiate the conclusions presented here, and the details are necessary to counter many current assumptions about music in the South. Many names appear throughout; they are here to assist further research into social networks and musical relationships. I have not cross-referenced names in footnotes, but the Index will aid the reader in following a particular woman's journey across time. The book's website includes a list of those who owned binder's volumes and another that provides biographical information on many of the people mentioned in the text.

Some cities receive repeated references, especially Charleston, Mobile, and New Orleans; others less so. In these cases, I have deliberately chosen to provide context for life in these locations so that change can be better observed. Many others receive mention, too, as do rural areas. Occasionally, many places have been listed under a single composition or even person. These provide the extent of circulation for particular pieces or composers. Most locations can still be found on modern maps, and for those no longer intact, I have included nearby towns and cities.

Because the majority of binder's volumes and other archival material belonged to white women, I have not declared their race in every mention. Documentary evidence from other women, on the other hand, does not exist in the same proportions—to date only one antebellum music collection can be connected to a Black family. In the initial discussion of the antebellum demographics of music sources, I have deliberately separated white women and Black women. This serves several purposes. First, it reflects cultural divisions that keenly defined social groups in the South. Social circles subdivided into myriad subsections between 1830 and 1861, but race cleaved a deep chasm on the sides of which other groups proliferated. Second, it recognizes music's role in the construction of whiteness and proves a rich starting point to contemplate why Black women pursued music literacy in a world that would never accept or acknowledge their practice. And then there is the real problem of the lack of source material. If white women's musical culture has been silenced, the musical experiences of Black women have been virtually obliterated from the historiography, much like the women themselves.

I intend a narrative shape for the book, although each part or even chapter of *Unbinding Gentility* stands as a distinct study. A few women's stories appear across more than one chapter, and those figuring across more than one of the three chronological divisions (antebellum, Civil War, Reconstruction) underscore the impact of the destruction of the South's social hierarchy on musicking. The first three parts establish the norms for southern society of the antebellum period in order to demonstrate how the Civil War upset expectations and thereby the performance of gentility according to preestablished standards. Individual chapters within each part concentrate on specific aspects of women's musical practices in this period. Part 1 examines the plethora of participants, from the wealthiest planter's daughters to enslaved Black women and their descendants.

To show the ubiquity of music in society, it necessarily includes many names and places. A chronological orientation affords the opportunity to observe how the economic growth of the 1840s and 1850s impacted who partook of musical accomplishment as a means to gentility. Binder's volumes reveal a much more widespread literate music practice than has been previously acknowledged and also provide robust data on music circulation, including gifting, sharing, and inheriting.

Part 2 interrogates the repertory employed to signify gentility. It does not describe all of the pieces or even types of pieces heard in the antebellum United States. In chapter 3, I contextualize prominent genres, focusing on music for dancing, the types of songs that women preferred (which varies chronologically), and instrumental adaptations of favorite melodies. Chapter 4 deals solely with opera. The significance of operatic tunes across a wide spectrum of people and places has yet to be properly acknowledged in broad studies of this period, despite Katherine Preston's efforts to verify its status across the nineteenth-century United States.[46]

If Parts 1 and 2 nuance somewhat familiar information with new interpretations, Part 3 presents entirely new material. For this reason, it consists of three chapters. The first (chapter 5) deals with the term *scientific music*, a code word that informs the listener/reader that the music is the type required for a genteel education. Here, I investigate the use and definition of the term, its marker as a status symbol, the people charged with imparting this science to young women, and the variety of circumstances that they represented. Chapter 6 looks specifically at the teachers, particularly how qualified were they to instruct a gentle science to young women whose positions often placed them socially above the instructors. The final chapter in this part introduces a new concept into American music history narratives, remunerated women musicians that did not belong to the stage, as well as professional performers. Tensions surrounding the public gaze and gentility come to the fore here, and these prepare the reader for changes in these concepts in the last half of the book.

The Civil War and Reconstruction are covered in single parts, although these are longer than the earlier ones. In Part 4, chapter 8 illustrates southerners' attempts to maintain life as before, in spite of the difficulties facing them during the war. Chapter 9 addresses real changes in how society moved, shifting interpretations of ideal womanhood and the public gaze, and the role of professional women. Part 5 looks at the Reconstruction (ending with the final withdrawal of Federal troops in 1878) from two different perspectives. The first (chapter 10) largely concerns women who had established themselves as musicians before the Civil War and brings to light their critical bearing on civic performances. These are women who took on leadership roles and who were publicly lauded for doing so. The final chapter focuses on the group that historian Jane Turner Censer's labels the "third generation" of southern women in her *Reconstruction of White Southern Womanhood*; she asserts that young women born just before or during the war held strikingly different attitudes toward femininity and rules of conduct.[47] I develop this idea further by contextualizing the repertory they performed in public and what this tells us about new ideas of the self in the 1870s. That one of the most famous composers in western history frames the final chapter verifies the cultural shifts that mark the mid-nineteenth century.

PART 1

Social Diversity among Amateur Women Musicians

1

"The circle in which you move"

Gentility, Music, and White Women

During the 1850s, Sarah Ponleva "Eva" Berrien Eve (1841–90), the daughter of an affluent planter living near Augusta, played and sang music from popular operas as well as simple ballads and had her music collection bound into at least ten volumes. In the same decade, Mary Owen Stedman (b. 1840) of Fayetteville (North Carolina), also learned music from European operas and American collections, and owned a binder's volume. Her father, an unsuccessful businessman, died during this decade, leaving his widow with eleven children. Eva and Mary, born within a year of each other, exemplify some of the diversity found in southern homes in the years leading up to the war. Their musical lives correspond in several aspects. Both attended boarding schools where music figured in the curriculum. Their binder's volumes included music previously belonging to relatives. Both owned "Kathleen Mavourneen," an unpretentious song reflecting Old World sentiments and stylistic features, but they also sang versions of Italian bel canto arias.

Here, however, the similarities end. Mary, along with three of her sisters, attended the Burwell School in their home state. Eva, on the other hand, traveled to Bethlehem, Pennsylvania, and Washington, DC, for her studies.[1] Mary owned one binder's volume, which she shared with her sisters and mother; Eva had at least ten for herself alone. Mary sang "Where Are Now the Hopes I Cherished," a watered-down arrangement of "In mia man alfin tu sei" from Bellini's *Norma*, and her piano versions of operatic music consist of abridged dances from Auber's *Le dieu et le bayadére*. English did not suffice for Eva, and she (or an instructor) added the original-language texts to English-language versions of European arias (Italian and French). Her music from *Norma* was Ferdinand Beyer's grandiloquent arrangement of the opera's melodies; one of several from his op. 42 that she owned.

These two collections encapsulate aspects of 1850s gentility and highlight the distinctions that social status maintained as economic and cultural capital blurred the lines between classes. The differences in detail between the daughter of a successful planter and the daughter of a failed businessman justify the need for microhistories of women and their music because they emphasize the multiplicity of genteel music cultures before the Civil War. The opportunities to study music belonged neither to the elite nor the middle class alone but fell within the purview of many southerners. The practice of teaching women to read music (instructing them in "scientific music") encompassed a wide range of social and economic backgrounds from Black women in Natchez to poor white women in rural North Carolina, from the enslaved to the wealthiest in Charleston. Moreover, their stories anticipate new directions in southern society that tend to be acknowledged only after the war but that clearly surfaced before it.

Social Class and Cultural Aspirations

Through the course of the 1830s and 1840s, southern society changed dramatically, and writers of etiquette manuals ensured the growing middling classes that they, too, could claim gentility. The next decade saw the epitome of genteel performance in the parlor, but it drove the standards ever higher as women sought to move into superior social circles that themselves had ever-rising standards for admittance. Increasing economic stratification forced a drastic restructuring of social relations.[2]

Planters and their relations stood at the top of the social ladder. Mary Greenhow Lee labeled the relationship between these two "visitable connexions"—a term that neatly encapsulates the variety one might have within a single circle. Friends and acquaintances might be endorsed through family connections, through social status, or (to a degree) through class, as long as they adopted the behaviors of gentility, literate music skills being one of these.[3] The elite class and their visitable connexions constituted one divide, and their relationships confirm that southerners employed markers other than wealth to define their social parameters. As the bar between gentry and non-gentry dropped precipitously, gentility spread. Farmers in rural areas added parlors to their houses and furnished them with musical instruments, clerks in town read books on etiquette, and merchants of all sorts adopted prescribed manners in pursuit of gentility. Through this process, genteel culture cut across society as an independent variable social distinction that was not tied directly to ancestry or land.[4] Aristocratic gentility met democratic America, and outward signs of leisure became social measuring tools for working Americans. The elite continually refined the markers of genteel status, and their musical practices reflected their need to set themselves apart. How this played out in the South can be read through Michael O'Brien's assertion that southerners remained intellectually tethered to older European cultures, saw themselves as imperial, yet struggled against a "cultural anxiety" in determining how to create a prosperous empire, republic, and democracy on the backs of enslaved people.[5] Gentility was one means of establishing order in the confused world wrought by these competing ideals.

Commodification of Gentility

The performance of gentility at home required a piano in the parlor, preferably with a bound volume of music on it. Cultural historian Lisa Tolbert uses the example of Virginia Campbell of Murfreesboro (Tennessee) to illustrate that by the 1850s, the piano had taken the place of the spinning wheel in the parlor, thereby signifying the spread of conspicuous consumption and the role of music in narrowing the gap between social classes. A visitable connexion with powerful political relatives, she married William Shelton, a professor and part-time clergyman, and moved into a six-room house. Virginia wrote that her new parlor was "handsomely . . . painted and papered and furnished (all except a piano, which I must procure sometime soon)."[6] In other words, her parlor was not completely finished until she acquired a piano. Her acquaintances—the circle to which she wished to belong—would have judged Virginia by the public areas of her house and their presentation.[7] She required a piano as part of the accoutrements of gentility.

To earn money to buy an instrument, Virginia took in boarders and occasionally taught music at the Eaton Female College beginning in 1851. The gulf between being seen at a certain level on the social hierarchy and having to earn money placed women whose economic means fell short in a difficult position. Working outside the home positioned a woman lower socially, although economic need required many to do so: imagined ideal womanhood demanded real work. Nonetheless, the tension between ideal accomplishment and real practice was surmountable, as Virginia Shelton realized. Teaching was one of the most acceptable options; in 1843 the *Holly Springs Gazette* (Mississippi) urged parents to consider teaching music as an honorable way for their offspring to generate a living.[8] Virginia's efforts proved insufficient, however, and her parlor remained without a piano until 1853, when her uncle gave her a piano as an attempt to overcome grief after her baby died. As a gentleman, he had been taught music's power to soothe, and he enabled her social aspirations even while she worked to maintain her social station. Virginia and William traveled by train to Nashville to choose the piano, stool, and cover, spending $300. The piano arrived the next day, and Virginia played "several old scotch airs" for her family.[9]

The production of music in the parlor, rather than useful material goods such as homemade clothes, signaled a significant transformation in southern society.[10] This reshaping touched all facets of the culture, enabling women who previously lacked the means to aspire to a higher rank the possibility of doing so. Music was no exception. A growing economy meant that many more women had both the means and opportunity to buy—literally—musical accomplishment. The acquisition and display of material goods, including sheet music and instruments, contributed to southerners' cultural capital and legitimized how a young woman determined taste suitable to her station. In communities where the goods necessary for upward mobility were readily attainable, more was demanded. In less affluent areas, the continuum was smaller.

Etiquette Manuals: Guides to Gentility

Simply owning musical materials did not make one genteel: it was necessary to know how to perform gentility through music in the right manner. People claiming genteel status had to demonstrate their knowledge of the correct rules of engagement. Those with the highest social status defined the etiquette practices, and those beneath them adopted these behaviors to the extent that they could afford to do so. The production of etiquette manuals accelerated to meet the needs of a growing market that saw benefits in being able to draw boundaries between the socially acceptable and those less favored. Modern writers identify a middle-class audience for these books—a reasonable conclusion since those of the upper class would not have needed such advice because they set the rules by their own behaviors and styles.[11] The manuals recommended how one displayed good taste, in essence how one performed gentility, but their rules could not address all aspects of refinement.[12] No author could provide all of the necessary and explicit guidelines for appropriate style. One simply knew or didn't what was tasteful.[13]

Nevertheless, this elusiveness did not impede authors from trying to explain genteel behavior and presentation, and the data gleaned from them exposes taxonomies at variance with assumptions made by modern authors. Thornwell's aptly titled *Ladies Guide to Perfect Gentility: in manners, dress and conversation, in the family, in company, at the pianoforte, the table, in the street, and in gentlemen's society; also a useful instructor in letter writing, toilet preparations, fancy needlework, millinery, dressmaking, care of wardrobe, the hair, teeth, hands, lips, complexion, etc.* exemplifies the direct instruction that marked the influence of Jacksonian democracy on American etiquette manuals.[14] Initially published in 1856, Thornwell includes gentility at the piano on the title page and mentions music (and dancing) several times throughout the book.[15] Her book opens with an image of "Gentility" that embodies the rules: the woman is demure but not coy, tastefully dressed without extravagance, and holds her body in a passive stance,

Figure 1.1. "Gentility," Thornwell, 1856.

all of which confirms her place of genteel status (see Figure 1.1). She contrasts the image that opens "The Belle of the Opera: Essays upon a Woman's Accomplishment, Her Character and Her Mission" by Joseph Chandler in *Graham's Magazine* of 1846.[16] Both were intended as positive views of young women, but the differences between them are obvious.

Gentility personifies the characteristics that Thornwell recommends for her readers. *Belle* portrays an equally endorsed woman, albeit under different circumstances (see Figure 1.2). Belle performs her station in public, at the opera, within the bounds of taste. The space Gentility occupies is less specific, but her presence in a less-public space—the parlor—seems certain. Chandler clearly establishes that "the Belle at the Opera" is an ideal mother who knows how to sing in the nursery but also understands that only professionals perform in public. The parlor and musical performance in it is understood today as a ubiquitous part of the gentlewoman's cultural experience, but *how* it occurred, under what circumstances, escapes most explanations, as does why women who aspired to Gentility's personification and those who met Belle's often performed essentially the same music in the same space.

Answers to such queries exist in part in etiquette manuals. In Thornwell's section entitled "The Lady at the Piano-Forte," she includes two sections of note:

Figure 1.2. "The Belle of the Opera," *Graham's*, 1846.

"Invitations to sing or play" and "Kind of songs and style of singing." Like her contemporary authors, she insists that a lady should agree to perform when invited, if she intends to play or sing at all, without affectation or indecision. She allows that good singers "will add to the pleasure of your friends, and to their regard," and even poor ones will evince "the desire to amuse . . . and will be appreciated."[17] In other words, pleasing one's friends outweighs an immaculate performance.

Music Practices among the Classes

As they had done for decades, the women of white planters' families studied music as a prerequisite part of belonging to the elite class. Thus, musical practices associated with the parlor did not belong solely to the middle class. The expenditures of Thomas A. Person, a successful planter in Franklin County (North Carolina) on his daughter, Tempie, illustrate the investment those who could afford to do so made on music. Her Louisburg Female College tuition statement includes music lessons for $35, the use of an instrument for $10, and $6.79 for twenty-three pieces of music—this over the fees required for room, board, and general tuition.[18] Considering that several of Thomas's nine children were in school at that time, he spent a considerable amount on Tempie's musical education. It demonstrated that he had the means to invest in what he understood a young woman needed, including a substantial amount of music. Thomas directed his children's upbringing with specific social goals in mind, as indicated in an 1854 letter that he wrote to his two daughters (Tempie and Sallie), both at the College, urging them to "be such women as will adorn the circle in which you move."[19] He understood that music was a required accomplishment if his daughters were to mingle in the highest society in Franklin County.[20] Similarly, the Judson Female Institute catalog assures parents that a Judson student's "soul is imbued with love of the beautiful, the true and the pure; she becomes prepared to be a WOMAN— a woman fitted for the practical duties of life; fitted wisely, beautifully, to fill and adorn her appropriate sphere of society."[21] The anticipated circle or sphere in which they moved would be those of their own social class once they returned home and presumably married.

Precise divisions between social circles could not be easily drawn, yet everyone knew where they ranked. Binder's volumes that belonged to planters' daughters, such as Eva Eve and Mary Frances Moore, confirm that musical accomplishment remained a necessary part of an elite girl's education. Nowhere was this more apparent than in Charleston. The city reached its zenith as the epitome of southern culture at this time: its etiquette rules were strict, visible signs of refinement grand, and standards of amateur musical accomplishment high.[22] Henrietta Aiken, whose father was the governor of South Carolina and a US House Representative, collected a substantial number of music method books, anthologies, and sheet music that she did not have bound, probably as a sign that she could easily afford to replace any lost music. She traveled to Europe four times before her twentieth birthday and returned to Charleston with numerous French textbooks, individual sheets of music, piano and voice method books, and at least one complete music collection (the *Échos* [sic] *de France*). The young women of her acquaintance—Charleston's elite—all had binder's volumes that included a variety of music from home and abroad. Included in this group were women of the Middleton, Huger, Grimball, Alston, Allston, and Manigault families.[23] Their sheet music symbolizes their refinement in that a substantial portion of it is foreign—a measure used by those of the highest social position to distinguish themselves.[24]

Association with Paris bestowed a degree of cultural refinement—as sixteen-year-old Alabamian Mary Fenwick Lewis (1825–98) declared in 1844, "The French have the best taste in the fashionable world."[25] To position their children for the best society, some elite parents sent young women to France for an education.[26] Music frequently formed part of their experiences, either in private tutorials or lessons at school. Henriette Manigault, daughter of Charles Izard and Elizabeth Heyward Manigault, traveled with her entire family to Paris to attend school for two years (1846–47), at which time she took piano lessons with a Monsieur De-lue.[27] At about the same time, Henrietta Aiken received much of her education in Paris (not in school), and French method books for both voice and piano point to the likelihood that she also studied music while there.[28]

Firsthand experiences acquainted women with European musical traditions, at least those who could afford to make the journey. Mary Lewis spent two years at school in Paris (1842–44). There, she heard a professional woman violinist (not an instrument of choice for women in the South), listened to a cappella singing at the Madeleine, and saw the actress Rachel in Racine's *Polyenete* at the Théâtre-Français.[29] She wrote to her sister Ellen that the Opéra-comique was her favorite with its orchestra of fifty musicians: "what brilliant execution—the violins, violin-cellos, bugles, horns, flutes, drums, triangles, etc.—all form a splendid collection. I am enchanted with the overture of 'La Sirene.'"[30] She heard "Orthello," featuring "the divine 'Grise' warble," and "was perfectly enchanted." Music was only part of the attraction, and Mary found "the splendour of the theatre, the magnificence of the 'toilettes' and costumes all tended to complete the brilliant representation." Many elements of refinement combined in this single opera experience.[31]

Mary spent her time in Paris without her family. Though far from home, she reminded her sister Ellen to dust her piano daily and to practice her duets; she promised to buy "La Brigantine" and an accordion for her, which she would ei-ther send by Mr. Colhoun or bring home herself.[32] Her initial piano training, in Huntsville with Miss Howard (who lived with the family), and guitar preparation laid the foundation for more advanced study abroad, and her mother encouraged her to take lessons on piano, harp, voice, and guitar. The costs proved prohibi-tive, and eventually Mary reduced the frequency of lessons, omitting dancing altogether. She announced to her father that "I wish to teach all that I learn. . . . I would do nothing but practise music all the while and be the greatest dunce about other things in the world."[33] Music was her favorite accomplishment, and it would serve her well in later years when financial necessity after the Civil War forced her into teaching. Whether she meant teaching students for remuneration or her family members is unknown. Between her schooling in Paris and the war, she employed her musical training as many southern women did, by teaching her siblings.[34]

Exposure to European performances left some women critical of what they heard at home, and Mary was no exception. On several occasions she compared local musicians to those in Paris, and, predictably, those in Alabama never fared well. In 1843, her mother acknowledged Mary's superior cultural awareness and recommended that, after hearing it at the Opéra, she avoid renditions of excerpts from *Norma* by Madame Bode and Maria Walker (at Mr. B. Fearn's soirées) upon her return home. Mary herself had acknowledged Huntsville's disparity the previous year when she declared that her lessons there had taught her "nothing of the rudiments of music at all." Her mother conceded this problem and in hindsight thought Mrs. Bode would have been a better teacher for Mary than her husband because he essentially did not know how to teach. She defends the choice she made, however, writing "but you know how it is here."[35] Mrs. Bode offered a large class in vocal music, and Mary's sisters Myra and Sarah participated in it. The Bode household hosted musical soirées and tableaux vivants. Other events in Huntsville included a lecture on music and a brass band concert in April 1843. The band's repertory included "Love Waltz," "Marseilles Hymn," and the "Huntsville March" composed for the occasion by Mr. Catherens, who was also the speaker. At this time, he served as teacher to members of the Lewis family, and Mary's sister Ellen summarized his abilities thus: "he can play on all of the wind instruments, but not a note of the piano, but can teach on it elegantly."[36]

Huntsville afforded the usual sorts of occasions one expected in most American towns, but elite families sent their daughters away to boarding schools where they could learn the social graces and accomplishments to a higher degree. Some, like Eva Eve, went to Philadelphia; other Alabamians ventured to St. Mary's in Raleigh. Even these, however, could not compete with Paris, as Mary observed when she wrote that Sarah Fearn, Mary McClung, and Moll Coleman have been to New Orleans "but have come back the same old thing." The trio traveled to Louisiana for finishing, but the experience failed to improve them. The benefit of a French education, bestowed on Mary but not these three, resulted in her superior taste. It also positioned Mary to wed advantageously: she married John Withers Clay in 1847, son of the governor and brother of a senator, in 1847.[37]

Traveling also brought the opportunity to bring back music from abroad. From South Carolina, Louisa Rebecca McCord journeyed around the Continent (occasionally fleeing war on the Italian peninsula) and while in London in 1859 bought several pieces of sheet music at Novello's.[38] Sarah MacIntosh Crawford went farther, purchasing her copy of "Rimembranze di Montecchiari Polka-Mazurka" (Antonio Torriani) in Alexandria, Egypt.[39] Such opportunities lay out of the realm of possibility for the majority of southern women and positioned these elites socially above those who could afford private lessons, instruments, and substantial collections of music but remained at home.

Daughters of prominent politicians (often planters) in other states left binder's volumes that testify to their musical accomplishment, although few reached the number of technically challenging pieces contained in collections from Charleston. Governors' daughters Marie Louise Morehead (North Carolina) and Sarah MacIntosh Crawford (Georgia) both owned bound collections, fulfilling expectations of prominent families.[40] Some well-positioned young women owned several books of music: Louisa Rebecca McCord, the granddaughter of the noted politician Langdon Cheves, left four surviving volumes, and Ann Beaufort Sims, daughter of the State Librarian in Columbia (South Carolina), collected enough music for six binder's volumes through the 1850s and 1860s.

As the southern economy grew, many outside the planter class realized prospects for financial success. Some merchants surpassed southern planters in their accumulation of wealth and established themselves as influential citizens. Their daughters, as well as those of the older middle-class ranks (doctors and lawyers) such as Carrie Mallett in Chapel Hill and Sarah Morgan Dawson in New Orleans, aspired to the same standards of gentility demonstrated by elite families, guided by authors such as Emily Thornwell and Florence Hartley. Emilia Carriere, who moved with her parents from France to New Orleans, collected several binder's volumes of music through the mid-century. Her mother, Emma Marie de Cruzel, was the daughter of a marquis, and her father, Antoine Carriere, ran a highly profitable import business.

In some instances, these middle-class women had the same or better opportunities to obtain the latest domestic sheet music. In Nashville, for example, Kate and Ellen Berry collected the most up-to-date pieces, and often their copies were particularly expensive, having full-page color images.[41] Their father, William Berry, was a merchant of considerable wealth and influence who ran a bookstore on Union St., stocking hard-to-find, expensive volumes.[42] Undoubtedly William's access to printed materials complemented his daughters' enthusiasm for these miniature works of art. They did not, however, travel abroad, nor did they obtain their music directly from European publishers.

Binder's volumes used by poorer white women also survive, and these corroborate widespread music-making throughout the South. In this sense, Mary Stedman's binder's volume is exemplary. One of eleven children, Mary did not have the opportunity to acquire completely new music: her father (John), a failed merchant who became a steamboat captain on the Cape Fear River, drowned in 1858, and on the 1860 census, her mother was described as "insane."[43] Whether John brought music from Wilmington to the family remains unknown but is likely.[44] Mary's music initially belonged to someone else since she was only seven when the latest publication appeared, and the most likely people were her mother, Olivia (b. 1813, who joined the music faculty at Floral College in 1861 out of financial necessity), and a sister who taught music after the Civil War.[45]

Other women positioned lower socially found the means to study music, and their collections evince the same basic standards seen in volumes belonging to the upper classes. Lucy M. Brown, the daughter of a "mechanic" in Clinton (NC) owned a binder's volume with music dating from 1832–64, although most pieces were published in the 1840s. She was born ca. 1842, which suggests that the music may have belonged to her mother or another family member and been passed down to Lucy. Such practice was common among nonelite women, no doubt due to the cost of printed music. That many wealthier families followed the same custom, however, suggests it contributed to a broader practice in women's culture.

Another way in which classes shared musical practices was in school. The daughters of music teachers, both native-born and immigrant, learned music as they sat beside wealthier acquaintances in music classes at school. Their education, however, frequently came with the purpose of providing them with the skills to earn a living, in contrast to the basis for the education of their classmates. One group learned for the sake of gentility, the other to teach gentility. Fanny (Frances Armisted) Burwell, whose parents ran the Burwell School in Hillsborough (North Carolina), journeyed to New York City to further her musical education with the intention of teaching in Burwell's music room.[46] Felix Strawinski's daughter Bellini ("Bella") and William Orchard's daughter Lizzie both attended the South Carolina Female Collegiate Institute at Barhamville where Felix taught dancing and guitar and William taught piano.[47] Lizzie and Bella met in class with members of the Aiken, Calhoun, and Pickett families.[48] Even if they would not normally meet socially, they did so at school. They absorbed the genteel behaviors that they, in turn, could soon impart to others.

Circulation: Gifting

Sharing and gifting sheet music depict not only aspects of circulation but also the generous nature of a genteel young woman. The practice also assists modern researchers in re-creating social circles and rituals among friends. For example, on the first page of Bernard Viguerie's "Douze Preludes dans les tons les plus usités" (a set of pedagogical preludes in twelve keys) in Martha Dickinson's binder's volume, a now-anonymous acquaintance has written in pencil: "my dear Martha, I send you the only Music I can find belonging to you. I have not got 'We part forever.'"[49] This may have been an acquaintance from school (she traveled to Philadelphia for her education), and the circumstances seem to be that Martha was leaving town. Young women such as the Dickinsons not only shared music with their family but also with their friends. Such social use of music can be observed in several other collections, particularly from before 1850. Their volumes also exhibit circulation trends and customs in planters' families, those at the top of the social ladder who set the standards for proper behavior, polite interaction, and the performance of gentility.

The Dickinson-Murfree women's collection evinces gifting over the span of three generations. It consists of three volumes compiled in Middle Tennessee, MTSU CPM Vols. 85–87.[50] Volumes 85 and 86 belonged to "F. P. Dickinson," and some of the early repertory points to ownership by the first Frances "Fanny"

Priscilla Dickinson [Murfree] (1816–1902). She was in her teens when much of the music in these two binder's volumes was published. Fanny Priscilla shared the collection with her sister, Martha Elizabeth (1823–50). Both women wrote in the volumes, and Volume 87 includes notations by Martha. Her name appears on several pieces, and she (or a later owner) made other marks as well, such as coloring in the necklace, brooch, and lips with red ink on "Aileen Mavourneen."[51] The two binder's volumes later passed to Fanny Priscilla Dickinson Murfree (1846–1941), sister of the writer Mary Noailles Murfree.[52]

Similar examples exist in other collections. Some, like Mary Stedman, inherited and shared because they could not afford new sheet music. The volumes belonging to Eliza Fisk Harwood (1827–88) demonstrate circulation trends among family and friends, as well as fluid class connections in antebellum southern society. She manifests how exceptions to simple categorizations by class—upper, middle, lower—expose fallacies inherent in modern interpretations of women's music in the mid-nineteenth century. Many women who lived in the South defy such labels. Those related to elite families but without money themselves (visitable connexions) nonetheless tended to move within upper-class circles. Eliza Harwood's social status could represent many women. Because her family lineage includes some of the "first families" of Virginia, such as the Randolphs and Carters, she belonged to elite society.[53] She did not, however, grow up in surroundings similar to theirs. Born in Norfolk, Eliza was one of the youngest of eleven children. Her mother, Susan Harwood, sent Eliza to live with her niece, Mary Ann, and her husband Dickie Galt in Williamsburg. The Galts rented rooms to students at William and Mary, thus Eliza grew up in a comfortable boarding house, not a plantation big house or even grand mansion in town.

In spite of reduced circumstances, Eliza studied music, in all likelihood first with Mary Ann Galt or her sister Maria Harwood.[54] A precocious child in every way (engaged at age twelve), her music collection suggests that her accomplishments impressed those in her acquaintance. The numbering of items on the tops of pages in her three binder's volumes that survive suggests that earlier collections had been disbound and Eliza's culled from these previously owned volumes. She benefited from her visitable connexions and the expectations that accompanied belonging to the planter class (even as a poorer relation), such as music lessons and dancing. She married a planter (Tristram Skinner) from eastern North Carolina, whose father owned several estates in that area.

Eliza acquired her music by several different means. The sheet music came from a variety of stores, from local ones (J. Bamford in Norfolk), to George Willig in Philadelphia and Baltimore, or even from Boston and New York. Some, such as the "The Fall of Paris" were bought by her guardian, Dickie Galt. She studied at some point with Signor G. George, a band director and singing teacher working in Norfolk during the 1840s, and he may have brought some music to her. Eliza also received music from acquaintances (including young men), who wrote their names in the music. Other pieces came from a "well-wisher" and a "friend," who could have been her future husband. One of her three surviving binder's volumes includes Henry Beale's signature and a faint signature of Miss M. Harwood—Maria, Eliza's older sister and Henry's wife. The names of Julia Thompson and Margaret Beale, two friends of hers in Williamsburg, are found on pieces in Vol. 3. Three have "Julia" penciled at the top: "If I Speak to Thee in Friendship's Name," (Henry Bishop), "I Turn to Thee in Time of Need" (Thomas Haynes Bayly), and "March & Trio" (Ignaz Moscheles). These would be appropriate gifts from a friend. During this period, Eliza frequently could be found in the company of Montegu Thompson, whose sister Julia gave Eliza several pieces of music. Julia's binder's volume also survives, but its repertory is more up-to-date than is Eliza's, probably because her family's financial situation was better than that of the Galts.[55]

Eliza's binder's volumes invite the re-creation of social circles, functioning as a multi-nodal framework of circulation patterns. Similar groups can be discovered in other collections. In Knoxville, Hattie E. Smiley's friends, including Mrs. Wadsworth, Professor Erdomann, Henry Bathes, and Jimmie gave her music. Several other collections have similar indications. Such evidence could prove useful in the future for establishing social networks among women.

Transgressions of Taste: Octavia Walton Le Vert (1810–1877)

Etiquette writers positioned the women in wealthy families as the standard for gentility, as Thornwell makes explicit: "Taste, there can be little doubt, depends . . . on association. . . . And persons of superior cultivation have . . . established for themselves a higher standard of grace or excellence."[56] Even though she published her work in the 1850s, a connection with an 1836 book suggests that these ideas were in place long before Thornwell catalogued them. These social codes stemmed from the aristocracy of earlier generations and determined that social position was hierarchical, based on wealth and manner. This understanding underpinned nearly every aspect of gentility.[57]

Within this hierarchy, cultural position could be illusive, and social status did not always translate into acceptability. Octavia Walton Le Vert serves as case in point. Born on Belle Vue plantation near Augusta, she grew up among well-to-do, socially connected, and prominent politicians. Educated at home by her mother and later a Scottish tutor, Octavia mastered French and Spanish, becoming conversant in several languages. She moved with her family to Pensacola in 1821 and translated documents for her father, who was serving as Florida's first territorial secretary under Governor William Duval. In 1832, she toured the United States and she met Washington Irving, with whom she remained friends until his death in 1859. She recorded two trips to Europe in an extensive travel diary and series of letters and published them under her name in a two-volume set in 1857 as *Souvenirs of Travel*. In this she eschewed boundaries of taste and presented herself fully before the public gaze. Moreover, her intentions behind the publication do not align with the agentic, nation-building letters of other women, such as Catherine Maria Sedgwick's *Letters from Abroad to Kindred at Home* (1841) or Margaret Fuller's extensive work.[58] Although Octavia occasionally adopts a similar stance, most of her writing reveals a concern with the famous people she socialized with, Americans or Europeans.

Octavia married French physician Henry Strachey Levert after her family moved to Mobile in the early 1830s. As demonstrated in the flagrant printing of her full name on her books, she tended to overdo everything: to shine more brightly than was fashionable, to show off her first-rate intelligence and famous social skills, and to parade in an ostentatious display of costume. When *Godey's Lady's Book* reported on the "Dresses worn at the late 'Drawing-Room' of her majesty, Queen Victoria," the only American woman described was Octavia. For the occasion, she donned diamond jewelry and a perfect form-fitting white lace robe, "richly embroidered in silver."[59] Her pretense to refinement extended to all things, and she insisted on using the "correct" French version of the last name ("Le Vert"), even though her husband continued with an Americanized "Levert."

In Mobile, Octavia established herself socially with lavish entertaining; her renowned gracious manner assisted in a national rise to social prominence, and she was hailed as the "belle of the nation." She further acquired the name by which she was known throughout the city: "Madame," without surname. A writer in the *Memphis Daily Appeal* on February 3, 1859, summed up her reputation: "Madame Le Vert of Mobile, long an habitué of Washington, who for her *social genius* is pre-eminent above all American women. . . . She has traveled widely, has visited nearly all foreign courts, can carry on conversation in six different languages *at one time*, and be equally charming in all." Such notices abound in references to Octavia.

Octavia's interest in the arts and literature were notable. She maintained a box in the theater in Mobile. She corresponded with Edgar Allen Poe, whom she met in the late 1820s, and she was a close friend of Henry Clay. Caroline Lee Hentz dedicated *Eoline; or Magnolia Vale* (1852) to her. Several composers wrote works for her, such as John Sinclair's "Come Sit Thee Down" (1842) and E. S. Hoadley's "Welcome Me to Thy Sunny Home" (1857). Even more striking, she published a song, "Come Ye Forth to Our Revels by Moonlight, or Sans Souci" in 1849 and included her full name on the cover. In so doing she became one of only a handful of southern women to do so before the Civil War, deliberately placing herself before the public gaze as she had also done with her *Souvenirs of Travel*.[60] By dedicating it to her mother—to whom the letters were also addressed—Octavia may have thought to circumvent the rules against such public display, but it was a feeble attempt at modesty.

Her struggle with the standards for gentility in the South can be felt in a comment Octavia made while visiting the Countess of Jersey. She observed that in London women "enjoy life much more than our women," are better educated, and are "capable of greater exertion in the pursuits of literature and art."[61] Perhaps she alludes to the fact that women were making more strides as professionals than she had seen in the United States, particularly in her native South. In England, Octavia socialized with artists, writers, sculptors, and singers. The aristocracy with whom she spent time were also involved in such pursuits and, like herself, published. Unlike other southerners, she used her time in England to live outside the norms of southern society by experiencing all that was available to European women.

Octavia wrote about these difficulties on other occasions. She once noted that "like all intellectual women," she tended to be sociable, but half her life was "condemned to silence and seclusion." Whereas men had "a thousand ways of making their talents available," "a woman has but one sphere wherein to enjoy her talents—*society*." In another document, she complained that women accepted too easily the roles their husbands assigned them, adding that it was "much better to be fettered and bound than to seem free, yet not be."[62] Unquestionably, Octavia struggled against the values drawn from cultural production in the southern United States with rules that grew ever stricter as the South strove to maintain its way of life in the 1840s and '50s.

Shortly after her marriage, Le Vert began having events at her house on Government Street that were known locally as Mondays: "the nearest approach to a salon which America has known."[63] These social events, lasting from eleven to eleven, included writers, actors, musicians, and politicians. Her biographer finds that "she enjoyed discussing the plays [of actors] and their conversation in general. The musicians would play, sing, and entertain however they wished. Townspeople were invited to meet them."[64] Matthew Pratt Guterl sees these salon events as "the display of the stylized performance of Europe's old imperial 'project'" in the United States as reflection of the values of the master class.[65] They reflected Octavia's knowledge of European culture, a highly valued commodity for elite southerners. O'Brien's oft-quoted portrayal of southerners imagining themselves as the "custodians of empire" explains their need to use European cultural behaviors "to provide 'order' for their world and to establish their place in it."[66] Octavia desperately sought not only to emulate European salons but also to situate herself in elite circles at home.

Swedish writer Fredrika Bremer visited Octavia and wrote about the experience in her *Homes of the New World*. Bremer wrote that she met a number of members of a theatrical company at the Le Vert home, and "They all appear agreeable and

well-bred people. . . . It is evident that actors in the New World take a higher position in educated society than they have yet done in Europe. They do not here
form a caste." In reality, however, they did, as remonstrations against women who
imitated professionals while performing in the parlor testify. Bremer hastened
to add that she had also seen "a great number of the grandees of Mobile" while
visiting Octavia, and they were as lovely ladies as she had ever met.[67] These additional remarks assure her audience that her time in Mobile was spent with the
best society, not merely with actors. She confirms that Octavia drew visitors from
a variety of backgrounds and social classes, a more diverse society that perhaps
reflects the new-money classes of Mobile society.

Octavia Le Vert's overt display of education, her equal treatment of actors and
nobility, and her brash publication of her name on both a music composition
and two books signify an undisguised independent spirit that most southern
women born to planter families dared not exhibit. In an era when women were
expected to be an ornament and ostentatious display was disdained, Octavia
sparkled more brilliantly than etiquette writers recommended. Her costume at
Queen Victoria's ball, described in the papers, distinctly overstepped the restraint
shown in Thornwell's image of Gentility or even Chandler's Belle. During the Civil
War, Octavia's conspicuous display ultimately sabotaged her efforts to establish
herself within the South's highest social circles: to paraphrase one Mobilian, the
city's inhabitants ran her out of town at the end of the war.[68] Her transgressions
in this case descended from her entertaining Yankees during their occupation
of Mobile, but one senses that Octavia's comeuppance was overdue.

* * *

Nicholas Tawa attributes music's becoming "a necessary component of a genteel
education" in the 1830s to the influence of Jacksonian democracy, resulting in a
broad expectation that music education be available for all citizens.[69] Visitors from
Europe noted with astonishment or humor that Americans from all parts of society (women of color, grocers, ironmongers' wives) performed "parlor songs" and
owned pianos.[70] Immigrants, such as Sarah Bashworth Cunningham (1808–98),
born in Rutherglen, Scotland, and resident in Savannah in the 1830s, brought their
varying experiences and possibly music scores with them.[71] Daughters of mechan-
ics, yeoman farmers, merchants, lawyers, doctors, clergy, as well as planters and
politicians, participated in relatively similar musical practices across the region.
But these white practitioners were not the only women taking piano lessons and
learning opera arias—they could not prohibit others from performing gentility
through music in the parlor.

"*Colored* girls under the control of *colored* teachers"

Gentility, Music, and Women of Color

Most modern research into the musical experiences of women of color has been confined to oral traditions: Black women in the South sang spirituals, work songs, and other genres not associated with reading music. That situation does not mean, however, that women of color did not learn to read music even if the evidence countering this narrative remains largely hidden.[1] Whether the women were enslaved or free, married or not, or belonged to any number of circumstances does not discount their being included in the broader narrative. Enough women studied music to warrant a reconsideration of what music as accomplishment meant in women's culture as a whole, as well as a reevaluation of how it might have been conceived in the construction of race. In her work on Black women in Charleston, Amrita Chakrabarti Myers argues that freedom was "not a static legal construct or a simplistic binary of slavery but an experience."[2] Throughout the middle years of the nineteenth century, free Blacks were subjected to increasingly restrictive laws that curtailed attempts toward education and economic prosperity. Nonetheless, women of color who lived under a variety of social, cultural, and political constraints studied music.

In the nineteenth century, white print media reinforced the stereotypes of Black musicking.[3] These images contrasted dramatically with scenes of white musical practices, even when depicting the same basic acts or spaces. They sharpened boundaries between whiteness and blackness. A comparison of the images in Figure 2.1 provides clear lessons in Black women's lack of cultivation and white women's refinement as the figures engage in roughly the same activities (dancing as a soloist). These visual representations conveyed how white Americans literally viewed others, and they helped preserve social distinctions, at least among their presumed audiences. These portrayals acutely enforced white views of musical practices, distinguishing between "primitive" and "art."[4]

Figure 2.1a. Unknown performer dancing on a copy of Bancker's Troupe of Sable Brothers, "I'se gwin down de Ribber." Courtesy of the Library of Congress, LC-USZ62–26011.

Figure 2.1b. Professional dancer Fanny Elssler in "La Cachucha."

In 1878, James Trotter put forth an alternative view, citing many people of color who had achieved recognition in art music.[5] His acknowledgment of those who had obtained public approval as professional musicians, such as Elizabeth Taylor Greenfield, begs the question: how representative is she of musical practice among women of color? Julia Chybowski and others have raised awareness of professional Black women singers, whose repertory transgressed the color line by including opera and other signifiers of white musical practice.[6] That these women exhibited themselves in public, however, confers a degree of belief and acceptance because genteel ladies would never put themselves before the public gaze and acknowledge their actions with names printed in the paper, or even monikers (like "the Black Swan" or even "Swedish Nightingale").

Amateur women of color in the slaveholding South reading notation implies a value placed on a musical education. Whether the reasoning behind mastering this accomplishment aligns with those of white women (which were by no means single-minded) is difficult to ascertain. Women of color learned to read music and received lessons in the performance of gentility in the parlor. Herein lies a paradox. In her reading of Elizabeth Keckley's *Behind the Scenes*, Carolyn Sorisio highlights stark divisions that saw Black women as "ungenteel and publicly accessible."[7] Whites reserved gentility for whites alone. What was the meaning, then, of learning music among those whom a white-dominant society presumed to lack the capacity for gentility?

This research deals with subjects whose lives and experiences have long been silenced, but scattered sources reference individuals whose microhistories unsettle the received narrative of the history of music in the United States.[8] Mere vignettes, their existence reminds us of how much we have assumed about musical practices among women and people of color. Unsilencing these microhistories is crucial to interpreting music in the United States. As an ethnographic reading of archival material, this topic demands interdisciplinarity in culling together myriad secondary research that includes mention of music or instruments—if no more than notices in wills, inventory, and the like. To decode the meaning of music in the lives of women of color requires an intermingling of ideas concerning race, gender, and class. The social statuses of these women vacillate as widely as those of white women, and their evidence supports the premise that women of all classes sought to define themselves through the performance of gentility.

Schools

The accounts of several Black women who studied music before the war proves that scientific music was not only the purview of white women. Early in the century, a Miss Crandall taught music to Black children at the Canterbury School in Wilmington.[9] Before the Civil War, the Oblate Sisters of Providence Convent in Baltimore (the so-called "Nineteenth-Century Black Capital") allowed free women of color to board there and receive an education that embraced music (including guitar and piano).[10] The school, begun by three women from Santo Domingo, put on musical events as part of the regular term.[11] Four daughters of a Black musician, John Pembleton, attended this school, and it is reasonable to assume music was part of their coursework.[12] Another of their graduates, Arabella Jones, was deemed a proficient pianist, and Elizabeth Brown's qualities as a musician also commanded notice.[13] In 1859, a correspondent reported that he had witnessed their "exhibition"—"*colored* girls under the control of *colored* teachers"—and heard "sweet voices and charming music."[14] The repertory almost certainly was that of the parlor.

New Orleans, too, fostered similar educational opportunities. During the 1850s, Michael Ross attests that over one thousand children of color attended private Catholic schools in New Orleans.[15] I have been able to document that music constituted part of the curriculum in at least some of them. One particularly well-known example was the Sisters of the Holy Family, led by Henriette Delille.[16] Félicite Callioux, operated the Catholic Institution for Indigent Orphans (Institute Catholique) in 1847, a school for Black children in New Orleans.[17] Here Adrinette Bazanac taught music. She formed part of the household of Charles Lambert, a prominent musician of color in the city.[18] Her husband, Joseph, played bassoon and flute with the Société Philharmonique (an organization of Creoles of color) and taught music himself.[19] Mercedes Duhart also taught music at the Catholic Institution.[20] In 1852, Mercedes's husband, Adolphe, worked at the same establishment as another prominent musician of color, Samuel Snaër. These families affirm a thriving music scene in New Orleans among people of color—one that is not defined by minstrelsy or oral traditions. Extant compositions associated with members of this community attest that their repertory consisted of the same styles experienced by whites.[21]

Admittedly insufficient, evidence suggests that some young women of color attended schools for white children, yet this scant information raises the possibility that many more studied music. Nevertheless, what has been found to date opens the door for a much more exhaustive search for data confirming the musical education of women of color in the antebellum South. According to author Adele Logan Alexander, Susie (b. 1830) and Cherokee Mariah Lilly Hunt (1833–95), the children of Nathan Sayre (1795–1853), a white planter and judge, and Susan Hunt (ca. 1810–92), a free Black woman, studied music at Sparta Female Model School in Georgia as day students. The family lived together at Pomegranate Hall, a large Greek revival home in Sparta where Susan and the children lived in the back three stories of the house.[22]

Mary Ann Day, born at about the same time as the Hunt-Sayre girls (ca. 1831), moved to Salem (North Carolina) to study music; no records indicate that she matriculated at the academy there. Christian Friedrich Sussdorff, a Moravian piano tuner (and presumably teacher) agreed to teach Mary Ann Day, the daughter of Thomas Day, the famous cabinetmaker, architect, and free man of color who lived in Milton, North Carolina.[23] A reference from the *Moravian Records* for June 28, 1847, clearly specifies that his daughter sought music lessons with the Moravians in Salem: "A certain Mr. [Thomas] Day from Milton, a mulatto, would like to send his sixteen-year-old daughter, educated in the North, to Br. Sussdorf in order that he may give her music lessons. . . . The Collegium does not think it objectionable if Br. Sussdorff take the girl into his house for some time and gives her the requested music instruction."[24] Mary Ann may have taken music lessons while attending Wesleyan Academy in Massachusetts and wished to continue with her instruction when she returned to North Carolina. Her skin color might have mitigated the socially awkward fact that Mary Ann lived in her music teacher's house while in Salem because she might have been perceived as a slave. Those who defined gentility as a whites-only pursuit automatically excluded her from it; therefore, her participation in the culture—her reasons for seeking this accomplishment—didn't matter because, to a degree, she didn't exist.

Charleston

As the examples of Baltimore and New Orleans illustrate, place also matters. Early-nineteenth-century Charleston consisted of a rigidly hierarchical society comprised of many layers. In *The Politics of Taste in Antebellum Charleston*, Maurie

Dee McInnis finds that "at the heart of the city and at the heart of [Charlestonians'] sense of self was the border between free and slave and white and black. . . . The perpetuation of the free/slave dichotomy was dependent upon a tightly woven web that could tolerate only minor disturbances to the proscribed order. The result was a social order very different from the national model." Social mobility was not necessarily achieved through hard work (a fundamental concept underscoring ideas of advancement in the northeastern part of the country) but through association with the correct families (which, admittedly, could have been made possible through earning the money required to purchase the right materials and education).

Charleston is also associated with an aristocracy in both modern and nineteenth-century literature. Within the category of white "upper class," McInnis uses the terms *elite* and *aristocracy* to indicate subsets demarcated by shared values, principles, and affiliations in association with landed wealth. Aristocracy was not something one could actually achieve—the aristocrats were not self-made. Only those born into aristocratic families, or those who married into them, could claim such status.[25]

Such distinctions matter because many authors write of a "Black aristocracy" in Charleston throughout the nineteenth century. In the *Journal of Negro History*, Horace Fitchett describes a class-conscious Black aristocracy that molded its manner on those of the "upper caste . . . of society," organizing the Brown Fellowship Society in 1790, as a way of maintaining social hierarchies among Charleston's people of color.[26] With its admission fee of fifty dollars, the Brown Fellowship Society clearly placed membership out of the range of many Black Charlestonians. Similarly, Bernard Powers argues that upper-class Blacks emulated white social mores before and after the war. Their stories are the ones for which the most sources survive, but unfortunately the data rarely mention music. Some do, however, and these sparse references suggest patterns of performance that confirm Powers's assertion that upper-class Blacks adopted cultural behaviors from wealthy whites in the city.[27] Myers documents this strategy by noting that families such as the Bonneaus, Westons, and Dereefs attended balls and other types of social activities, and music could be heard in such spaces.[28] Whether it was the same heard in white spaces (which sometimes employed Black musicians) or differed remains unknown.

The example of Martha Moor verifies the pursuit of scientific music among Charleston's Black elite. She married the successful barber Thomas Inglis, a member of the Brown Fellowship Society, in 1820. Finding that "married life for wealthy free women of color was full of pressures to present a picture of perfection," Martha decorated their home with mirrors, gilded wallpaper, fine pictures, and wine glasses—all accoutrements of the wealthy and also deliberate, according to Rita Reynolds, associations with the family's white (i.e., European) connections.

The Inglis family owned a piano, which showed others that they not only could afford such expensive items, but they also were refined because they understood the need to acquire the accomplishments associated with gentility. Furthermore, all of the Inglis children had music lessons.[29] It is reasonable to expect that the repertory would have been the same as in white parlors because that was the music of the period, as well as what was available in Charleston.

But are we right to assume that such musical practice was merely part of an effort to imitate the standards of white culture? In her work on postwar southern schools for Black and white women, Sarah Case asserts that women refashioned antebellum femininity in the postwar era in order to protect the reputations of women in the public gaze. Proper behavior was more essential for women of color than for white women because of longheld myths of Black female sexual aggressiveness. She is correct to identify these issues in women's schools of the Reconstruction, but the ideas behind them extend back before the war. Was it a refashioning of antebellum femininity designed to meet the perceived space between white and Black, occupied by members of the Brown Fellowship Society? Martha Moor Inglis recognized the importance of respectability to protect her children against stereotypes and fitted them with the necessities of social progress as exhibited by white culture. Among other aspects of gentility, the ability to play the piano evinced personal refinement and the ability to please others. Moreover, music in the parlor constituted a "deliciously unproductive means of passing time" and exhibited the fact that the family could support such idle time, signs that fit Martha's aim for perfection.[30]

The Johnson Sisters

The weightiest evidence for the cultivation of a musical education by free Black women resides in the music collection of Anna and Catherine (Katherine, Kate) Johnson. Superficially, it resembles that of other women from the mid-nineteenth-century South whose family's worth measures in five figures, but that is only one of its revelations. They were the two eldest daughters of William Johnson, known as "the famous barber of Natchez" (among other soubriquets), and Ann Battles Johnson, a formerly enslaved woman. It consists of two binder's volumes (one that definitely belonged to Anna and one that might have been used by Anna and/or Catherine, six boxes containing multiple folders of sheet music in each, and a volume of Bertini's piano method book (no date or name). As is the case with several white owners, the Johnsons cared for their music: many of the single sheets have been sewn together or even pinned to preserve them. They used it, too, as fingerings, written-out ornaments, drawings, and notations on some of the pieces. The repertory, for solo piano, voice, and occasionally guitar, ranges from the simple folklike songs of the British Isles to arias and dances from popular operas. The Johnsons owned several musical instruments, including a piano (which may have been purchased when Lavinia Miller [McCrary] accompanied William Johnson to Mr. Myers's store in Natchez to shop for pianos on October 18, 1850.[31])

This collection testifies to the importance of music in this family, as does the music that belonged to their aunt (and Anna's godmother), Lavinia. Catherine and Anna received several pieces (at least) from her.[32] Having music that her aunt once claimed as her own illustrates another way in which Anna Johnson's musical experiences mirrored that of white women. The Johnsons performed the same behaviors as those with whom they shared class values—white women of equal economic status.[33]

Anna's name is the more prominent name in the collection, found in both binder's volumes and in the unbound sheet music. While her father was alive, Anna attended school in New Orleans and lodged with Lavinia.[34] The name of her school has yet to be identified, but it could have been one such as that run by Madame L. Dumagene, who advertised that she would teach music "pour les jeunes personnes de couleur" at 54 Bourbon Street in 1853.[35] After their father's murder in 1850, their mother oversaw Anna and Catherine's music education. In 1855, Ann's records indicate that she paid for music lessons for "the two girls" in October and November, and again on August 30 and September 30, 1855, and January 15, 1856. The records are not legible enough to determine the name of this teacher, but Ben Bailey speculates he was a white man who taught these young women of color.[36] That three music teachers of color ("mulattos") are listed in the 1850 New Orleans Census suggests the possibility, however, that the Johnsons' music teacher may have been a person of color.[37]

The Johnsons' music includes several operatic transcriptions that indicate substantial technical accomplishment. Anna owned Beyer's op. 42 arrangement of *Les Huguenots* (no. 6), the same version found in Mary Huger Lowndes's and Elizabeth Grimball's binder's volume. Both Anna and Kate Berry (the daughter of a white merchant, see earlier) played *Th. Oesten's Nine Amusements*, No. 2 (popular tunes from *L'elisir d'amore, Beatrice di Tenda*, and *I due foscari*). How did this infringement upon white women's musical prerogative play out? The cultural capital conveyed by familiarity with operas and their stars can be seen throughout southern culture: in casual references to famous singers, or to attendance at gala affairs on the arm of a former US president in Europe. This capital was employed by women to advance socially or to maintain their position on the top. Wilma King argues that throughout the South, a gulf existed between the rhetoric of "free" and the reality of freedom, between the ideal and the lived circumstances of freewomen. She includes the intellectual history of antebellum women of color in her efforts to understand how freewomen maintained their self-esteem. She examines the standards by which they judged themselves, concluding that women like Anna and Catherine Johnson employed aspects of genteel performance within and without their own circles.[38]

The image in Figure 2.2 appeared on several different compositions in the 1857 run of *Frank Leslie's Gazette of Fashion and the Beau Monde*. Anna Johnson preserved it, as did Eva Berrien Eve, the white daughter of a wealthy planter.[39] It emphasizes the practical use of music in the performance of gentility. It evokes an idealized scene in which music functions as a backdrop for courtship. The Johnsons exchanged music with friends and inherited music from older female family members. They played piano in the parlor for dancing, and potential suitors were aware of their accomplishments and requested such.

Along with other artifacts, chiefly sheet music images and Catherine's diary, the musical scene in Figure 2.2 substantiates that the Johnsons might have used their social training in ways similar to those of middle-class white women. We can only guess at the reasons Anna or Catherine preserved this page.[40] It evokes an idealized scene in which music functions as a backdrop for courtship. (The "Swinging Polka" cannot be the composition being played by such a languid pianist, and the listeners do not appear to be enticed to dance.) Were such scenes reenacted in the Johnson household? In her diary, Catherine describes not wanting to sing for a visitor, even though he asks several times. She hints that romance was his

Figure 2.2. Parlor image on "The Swinging Polka," *Frank Leslie's Gazette*, 1857. William T. Johnson Collection, Series V, Louisiana and Lower Mississippi Valley Collections, LSA Libraries, Baton Rouge, La.

intention because prior to his arrival she had asked her mother not to leave the room.[41] In *Forging Freedom*, Myers contends that, for free Black women, stylish clothing served as a visual symbol that they held a non-slave status. Expensive items such as beautiful fashions and jewels testified that they were ladies, equals of white women.[42] The Johnson women may have used music in a similar manner. As Black women, however, Anna and Catherine cannot be simply subsumed into gentility as practiced by white women. Their cultural experiences evince a Black gentility in the antebellum South—one based on many of the same criteria used by white women (accomplishments, physical display of appropriate accoutrements, taste, and so on) but developed from an altogether discrete perspective.

The provocative image of a belle from New Orleans on the "Five Belles Polka" raises other questions (see Figure 2.3). Anna went to school in New Orleans, but, as Case observes, affluent women of color carefully constructed identities that countered the Jezebel stereotype encountered in literature by white authors. It may have served as a warning against wanton behavior, of what not to look like. Case documents the importance of sexual purity for free women of color, which suggests that an immodest figure like the Belle from New Orleans

Figure 2.3. "Five Belles Polka," by T. J. Cook. (note the use of thread to keep the pages together). William T. Johnson Collection, Series V, Louisiana and Lower Mississippi Valley Collections, LSA Libraries, Baton Rouge, La.

would not be appropriate for Anna Johnson—nor would it have been for any southerners aspiring to "belle" status.[43] Moreover, the Johnsons were probably not the only people of color who owned music like this, who participated so regularly in social rituals that included music, and who used music as a marker of social status.

Virginia Gould makes the case that as an emancipated Black woman, Ann Battles Johnson was "incompatible with the ideals associated with white women," yet she and others like her structured their lives in answer to those ideals to avoid disdain and degradation. She asserts that women such as Ann Battles Johnson and Adelia Johnson Miller (Lavinia's mother) modeled their identities on the dominant white culture, to a degree, and concurrently maintained the traditions of their own communities. Their constructed identities were neither Black enslaved woman nor free white woman.[44] They both instilled the study of music as an expected accomplishment in their daughters; they performed gentility, it seems, by the same means as white women of equal economic capital. They personified Black gentility.

This approach nuances Powers's assertion that Black women imitated white women. Many southern women of lower status attempted to emulate those at the top of the social spectrum—white women who were the daughters of farmers, small-town merchants, clergy, and so forth, aspired to genteel status in part by acquiring musical accomplishment. For some it was a means of economic freedom (becoming teachers), as it was later for women such as Ella Sheppard in postwar Nashville. It may have been possible before the war as well—we simply lack the evidence at this time. Ann and William Johnson sent Anna to school in New Orleans, shopped for a piano with her aunt, Lavinia Miller, and hired a music teacher in Natchez. They pursued gentility as understood in their region and molded its meaning to suit their cultural environment.

Music Education and Enslaved Women

Two examples of white fathers financing music lessons for their daughters by enslaved Black women illustrate the idea that not everyone understood musical accomplishment along a rigid color line. The musical education of Amanda America Dickson (1849–93), who inherited her white father's piano, provides a poignant case in point. Her father was planter David Dickson, and her mother was his slave, Julia Frances Lewis Dickson. Raised by her white grandmother, Elizabeth Sholars Dickson, in the family home, Amanda learned to play the piano and other accomplishments associated with gentility. When her father died in 1885, she inherited 17,000 acres of land in Georgia. After the war, David built a home for all of his children by Julia, and it, too, included a piano in the parlor, and this home became evidence against his children of color when his white children challenged his will, and the piano was specifically cited as something against Amanda and her siblings. At issue was the fact that Clara Dickson, David's white wife, was an accomplished musician who did not have a piano in her house.[45] Her husband chose to bequeath the accoutrements of gentility on his children by Julia, not Clara.

In *Forging Freedom: Black Women and the Pursuit of Liberty in Antebellum Charleston*, Amrita Chakrabarti Myers uses the narratives of several women to revise modern conceptions of gender, race, and agency in antebellum Charleston. One of her examples, Sarah Martha Sanders (1815–50), personifies these intentions through music. Over the course of twenty years, Sarah had ten children with Richard Walpole Cogdell, the white man who purchased her in 1830. Their offspring attended school in Charleston and received music lessons. Richard had musical interests himself: during the birth of one child (1844), he was in Europe attending a concert in Her Majesty's concert rooms at Hanover Square. From there he traveled to Paris and heard at least one opera.

Richard purchased a piano in the spring of 1832, at about the same time as the birth of their first child.[46] Myers has located an entry in Cogdell's Receipt Book that states that "Miss Sarah will have received 29 lessons since our last settlement; Paid Mr. Garcia on the 25th."[47] This was James R. Garcia, a music teacher in Charleston in the 1830s who also spent time in Boston. These lessons were for the enslaved mother of the children, not the children themselves.[48] Twenty-nine lessons indicate a degree of frequency and undoubtedly considerable expense. Sarah Martha Sanders thus proves that women of color, even if enslaved, occasionally had the opportunity to acquire literate music skills.[49]

The place where the Sanders children lived, Charleston, permitted the same pursuit of gentility in the same space with the same physical objects as white women: the piano and music in the parlor. The cultural space mirrors that of white women but the social status differs. Myers notes that "Sarah tried to ensure that her children had every possible cultural advantage made available to them."[50] They could obtain the artifacts and abilities associated with gentility, and their children moved into respected middle-class circles, once Cogdell relocated them to Philadelphia in the 1850s. One daughter even performed in public music recitals.[51] The eldest, Julia, married into one of Philadelphia's wealthiest Black families, and her musical accomplishment may be seen as a facet in a course of social uplift. Their example leads Myers to conclude that, in South Carolina at least, both whiteness and blackness were socially constructed, and "the performance of respectability" depended on the individual and the community. Respectability constituted one facet of gentility—one could be respected without being genteel, but respectability was required for gentility. Music contributed to the Sanders women being seen as genteel by their social group and, most likely, those immediately above and below them. It helped position them higher along a cultural continuum designed to define femininity and whiteness through specific accomplishments. If it did not transcend racial boundaries forged by white Charlestonians, it situated them higher within their own community through the adoption of genteel behaviors. Black gentility offered opportunities to establish and enforce culture boundaries within the racialized society of the South.

*   *   *

The foregoing examples have presented evidence that at least some Black women had access to musical accomplishment in the slave-holding South. Their stories differ widely, as do those of white women, and the fact emerges that the musical culture of the South was far from homogeneous. Geographical location and attitudes toward people of color in given places, population density and dispersion, and, most of all, personal inclinations for those with direct power over young women (be they parents or owners) impacted the possibilities for and purposes behind a musical education. They were never equal to those of whites, however. Even in New Orleans, with a vibrant musical scene open to people of varied ethnicities, the opportunities remained circumscribed. There, the professional pianist Henri Herz encountered racial prejudices apparently hitherto unknown to him. In one instance, a free man of color asked Herz to play a concert for a Black audience, but his manager warned that if he did so, he would never be invited to play for a white one. Another account reinforced the South's racial laws in his experiences. Herz had taken on students while in New Orleans, and one, Ellen, stood out as a "great beauty, brought up by a rich American family with all the desirable luxuries." He found her an "almost ideal creature," gentle, witty, and talented. When Amantine Soulé admonished him for not playing the piano for Ellen when she requested he do so in a private setting, he queried why she did not attend one of his concerts. Mrs. Soulé explained that Ellen had "been accused of having Negro blood in her veins, although her skin is a striking purity and whiteness;" she could not, therefore, have attended. Herz found this ostracism "odious"—he could not believe that Creoles in Louisiana would not socialize women of color, "often whiter than the whites."[52]

An unspoken part of this story is Ellen's socializing with white musicians. She had been one of his students in New Orleans, meaning that someone arranged for her to study with Herz. In all likelihood, this was Amantine Soulé, who was present when Herz refused to play for Ellen. This further indicates that Ellen visited the Soulé household as a guest, and everyone else there knew that she was categorized a Black woman. The French Quarter of New Orleans probably witnessed many such interactions among musicians, and so, too, did other places dotted throughout the South.[53]

Samuel B. Floyd once wrote that "the responsible and appropriate approach to historicizing Black music before the nineteenth century would be to ask *theoretically interesting questions* that evolve in the exploration of the circumstantial evidence."[54] This statement retains its relevance for the nineteenth-century examples I have compiled. Even if the answers to the questions cannot be ascertained, the exercise of seeking information yields new conceptions of women's lives in the South. Inevitably, definitions of whiteness and blackness blur when scrutinized under the light of real data rather than received mythology. Many more questions remain. How we understand literacy, power, and agency can be shaped through considerations of reading music. Recent scholarship continues to argue that southern periodical readership and even education was a privilege of whiteness, but the evidence of the Johnsons offers a counter view.[55] Moreover, did women of color weaponize music literacy as a technology of power? Did music literacy serve as a way to defy gentility's assignment to white supremacy and patriarchal rule?[56] To what end did women of color seek genteel status in the slaveholding South? Does the mere act of genteel performance by those who defined gentility to exclude them indicate agency? Lori Merish reads Black women writers of the period as adopting masculine qualities as an agency of power, subverting gender roles and bypassing gentility entirely.[57] Nevertheless, the women discussed here were not writers, and their lives contrast greatly those of Merish's main subjects, Harriet Jacobs and Sojourner Truth. If for nothing more, this comparison demonstrates the individual variation—the significance of microhistories—in antebellum women's culture.

We do not have enough evidence, yet, to address all of the issues raised here. What is certain is that the microhistories of the women described in this chapter provide enough data to disrupt the traditional narrative of music in the United States and show the need for a more thorough-going investigation of the musical practices of people of color, of women, and of place. Antebellum parlors were the spaces where femininity was constructed, but too many Americans owned spaces designated as parlors to assert a monoculture. Moreover, race and gender are not discrete entities, and the subtleties inherent in each historical actor's story make plain this reality.[58] Until scholars focus on individual collections and their provenance, we cannot pretend to know the representative history of music in the antebellum United States. To understand the role scientific music played in lives of women of color, we must first acknowledge their existence. Contextualization must be seen through their experiences and not necessarily through those of white women, which themselves cannot be explained in a one-size-fits-all definition. Gentility was fluid.

Conclusion

In the antebellum period, the South's aristocracy controlled the rules that ordered society: taste as defined by clothing, furnishings, etiquette, and so forth. That did not mean, however, that others could not acquire the refinement these material goods signified. The *Southern Cultivator* admonished in 1843 that "it does not look well for farmers daughters to be always talking about piano playing and the trillings of Signor Cantanini; while they do not know how butter is made, and pretend to suppose a cow a rhinoceros."[59] Such a remark would not have been necessary had women—farmers' daughters—not been participating in a musically literate culture that demanded lessons, sheet music, and instruments. In so doing, they overstepped their class boundary.

Class lines strained as the southern economy grew during the 1850s, supporting new or expanding industries across the region and spreading financial capital among those whose social status ranked beneath the planter aristocracy. These families vied in wealth with the elite and encroached on their social position. Even women from households whose economic situations placed them much lower in society could aspire to a higher rung on the social ladder by inculcating qualities associated with genteel ladies. Disciplined adherence to the laws of tact coupled with the acquisition of the proper accoutrements made gentility an attainable objective. The upper-most section remained off limits for this group, but the elite also strove to outshine each other by increasingly raising the standards of refinement. Social class itself was a performance.[60] Musical accomplishment became part of the cultural capital that positioned one within one's own circle and, possibly, lifted one into a higher social group. Seeking the need for such capital is but one step in the journey to understanding the meaning of musical accomplishment among those for whom we have assumed it did not exist, especially people of color. Women employed this capital as a source of agency in a time and place that allowed them few sources of self-empowerment. The home, the parlor was their space, and within it, they organized the boundaries of class.

A growing middle class demanded recognition of its cultural refinement. This group attaches most obviously to standard definitions of gentility. It was for this section of society that authors prepared etiquette manuals to advise people the proper ways to behave in various situations. As Florence Hartley describes in her *Ladies' Book of Etiquette* (1860):

> In the present age, when education is within the reach of all, both rich and poor, every lady will endeavor to become, not only well educated, but accomplished. . . . A lady without her piano, or her pencil, her library of French, German, or Italian authors, her fancy work and tasteful embroideries, is now rarely met with, and it is right that such arts should be universal.[61]

Hartley is not writing for elite, aristocratic, wealthy planter families, but the expanding number of middle-class people who could afford to throw parties, hire servants to attend guests, follow a proscribed dress code, and study music—all to be fit for society. Connecting these accomplishments to universal rights ties them to contemporary tensions between Jacksonian democracy, the rights of "man" as defined in the US Constitution, and the beginnings of the suffragist movement. Hartley probably did not see these connections herself, but they reflect conversations prevalent in the United States during the late 1850s. At a baser level, her assumption that almost everyone needs to be accomplished is key to understanding the performance of gentility throughout a varied social landscape.

Hartley probably did not see herself writing for women of color—her "everyone" would not have extended to anyone but whites, much as the preservation of materials has done in the past. Saidiya Hartman's observation that the "power and authority of the archive and the limits it sets on what can be known, whose perspective matters, and who is endowed with the gravity and authority of historical actor" applies to all the matters of gentility as well.[62] The histories begun in here will hopefully inspire further research on Black women and other women of color, seeking their ephemera and bringing it to the fore in a manner that affords a fuller view of the broad category of "women's musical practices."

PART 2

Repertory

3

"'Home, Sweet Home!' with brilliant variations"

Melody

Numerous books in both scholarly and trade presses, articles in different types of journals, and recordings made by professionals and amateurs alike attest to the enduring popularity of tunes from the mid-nineteenth century.[1] There is much more to be said, however. Repertory is a topic that seems familiar but has yet to be sufficiently examined in its social contexts. Moreover, the gulf between what was popular in the nineteenth century and how we have valued music since then remains expansive, in part because of the generic use of the term *parlor music*. The idea that "parlor songs" or "parlor music" encapsulates musicking in this period effectively marginalizes a practice that ranged from the sublime to the ridiculous (on purpose) and extended from lengthy virtuoso piano arrangements, to simple ditties, to a pretty sentimental song. To clarify the contexts in which southern women employed different types of pieces, this chapter examines the types of music that could be heard in southern homes and considers regional, socioeconomic, and geographic influences on the genres, composers, and basic musical qualities preferred by women throughout the South.

The songs of Stephen Foster and music associated with minstrelsy do not figure prominently here, although many readers might expect them. Neither of these dominate binder's volumes, school programs, or local concert events equivalent to the extent media promotes them today. Foster's songs exist in antebellum binder's volumes, but the number falls well short of expectations driven by modern authors. One is more likely to encounter pieces by Francis H. Brown than Foster's songs. Similarly, the music of minstrelsy can be found in many collections, especially melodies associated with specific ensembles. But offensive dialects and outrageous imagery did not belong in genteel women's books. No etiquette writer and no voice method author sanctioned such choices for study or performance.[2] Some performers, such as "The Virginia Minstrels," cleaned up their acts (seeking profit among more genteel audiences), and music connected to them can be found more frequently in binder's volumes.[3]

Typical Repertory

Most of the surviving binder's volumes from the 1830s belonged to the circle of women whose families could claim elite status or had visitable connexions with it. With songs by Michael Balfe and Thomas Bayley and piano pieces by Herz and Moscheles, Eliza Harwood's repertory is typical of the period, but what exactly is typical?[4] In the 1830s, Amelia Nance included French music in her New Orleans collection, having purchased pieces by Mlle. De Laborde, Bussoni, and Beauplan that Benjamin Casey imported. At the same time, theater music of all sorts formed part of the repertory of touring artists such as Jane Shireff and the Seguins. Young women attended performances featuring these artists and purchased music that advertised a connection to the singers.[5] The vocal repertory that formed part of home performances ranged from simple English ballads to arias from contemporary operas. Local music groups offered programs that began with an "overture" (which could simply mean the piece that opened the concert or an actual overture from a larger work), introducing audiences to instrumental compositions of different styles. Dance music could be heard in public venues, private gatherings, and homes of infinite variety. Music for guitar, harp, or piano sounded from the parlors of those who could afford them.

Genres

Over the course of the nineteenth century, the women of Grantlands Plantation in Middle Tennessee collected, shared, and inherited at least three binder's volumes of music that reveal several aspects of antebellum music practices. For one, they encompass the stark dividing point between the styles of an older period and the newer preferences of the nineteenth century. The earliest volume (CPM vol. 85), initially belonging to Frances "Fanny" Priscilla Dickinson [Murfree] (1816–1902), contains suitable songs for well-bred young women (for example, "The Lay of the Wandr'g Arab" or "The Highland Minstrel Boy") and solo piano works by Dussek and Steibelt, including the latter's Two Sonatas, op. 33 (published in 1804–1807).[6] Concertos and sonatas fell out of fashion in the 1820s, so much so that by 1840, pieces entitled "sonata" rarely occur in southern binder's volumes. A preference for pieces based on familiar melodies removed the sonata from the amateur woman's repertory. These reworkings of popular melodies, often as sets of variations, dominated the repertory for several decades, as the other volumes of the Dickinson-Murfree family (CPM vols. 86–87) document.[7] Sonatas would return only as understandings of gentility shifted during the Civil War.

Character pieces with fanciful titles can be found throughout this period, too.[8] Margaret Wingfield's binder's volume (music mostly from the 1840s) contains representative examples, among them "La harpe éolienne reverie pour le piano" (W. Kruger), "Les Cloches du monastère / the monastery bell / nocturne pour piano" (Lefébure-Wély, op. 54), and "A Twilight Thought" (J. C. Engelbrecht). A favorite of these types of pieces was Gottschalk's "Last Hope," found in books owned by women such as Sarah Friedlander, Regina Buck, Belle McGehee, and Mrs. A. K. Worms.[9]

Religious music rarely made it into binder's volumes, probably because printed sacred music often came in complete books, which was not appropriate for binder's volumes. Occasionally songs can be found, such as Topliff's "Ruth and Naomi" in Eva Eve's binder's volume or Shrival's "Hark! I Hear an Angel Sing" in Anna Johnson's. A few anomalies surface, such as a manuscript book of sacred music for Catholic services that belonged to Elizabeth Welsh Horner (1835–1923) of Fauquier County, Virginia. It contains compositions for religious use, such as "O Salutoris! #1, At the benediction Evening Hymn to the Virgin // Duett adapted to the Catholic Service by R. T. Hughes"; the final composition is an "Evening Hymn in E flat for solo woman."[10] Sarah Cunningham's manuscript collection, ca. 1840, contains several examples, and Lizzie C. Smith's binder's volume includes "Watchman, Tell Us of the Night." Nonetheless, the repertory of the parlor as evinced in binder's volumes was decidedly secular.

Outside the parlor, women participated in public sacred concerts, almost always as vocalists. Sometimes newspaper notices identified them ("Mrs. Clark," for example), but little is known about these singers. The New Orleans Sacred Music Society performed works by Haydn, Mozart, and Beethoven from at least 1842, when Mrs. Franklin and amateurs received credit in cultivating musical taste in the city.[11] The Richmond Sacred Music Society worked to "promote the cultivation of the science in all the classes of the community," suggesting a wide social range of participants and audience members.[12] That same year, the Philharmonic Society in Charleston put on Rossini's Stabat Mater at the Cathedral, and, although none were named, the performance must have included women.[13] In 1850, a singing class presented a concert that featured music by Handel (from *Sampson, Theodora*) and Haydn (excerpts from *The Creation* and Mass in C).[14]

Southern women's music between 1825 and 1861 focused on familiar melodies, which could also factor in another prominent genre: dance music. Shifting styles in favorite tunes reveal aspects of southern culture that affected not only musical taste but discrimination among classes, most keenly in the manipulation of operatic melodies. Mary Harrison Randolph (1819–1904) compiled a binder's

Table 3.1. Contents of Mary Harrison Randolph's binder's volume, SWEM 41

No.	Title	Composer	Information
1	Overture to the Favourite Opera of Zampa on La fiancée de Marbre	Herold; arr. C. Chalieu	Duet
2	Fantaisie sur un Air Suisse "The Swiss Boy"	J. C. Viereck, student of C. M. de Weber[1]	Composée et dediée a son Éleve Mademoiselle Madeleine Phillips. 1833
3	The Storm Rondo	Steibelt	
4	Souvenir de la Suisse. Rondo … on Two Favorite Airs	Hünten	
5	Rondeau militaire du ballet Lòrgie	Caraffa, arr. Hünten	
6	When the Day with Rosy Light. Swiss Air arranged as a Rondoletto for the Piano Forte.	Henry Lemoine	Quatre Recreations Musicales, No. 4
8	O Give Me but My Arab Steed	[G. A. Hodson]; arr. T. A. Rawlings	
9	She Never Blamed Him, Arranged with an Introduction and Variations	Moore; arr. Kiallmark	From Moore's National Melodies
10	Petite fantasie pour un Air Frossais	Herz	
11	Cavatina Ode l' Opéra Beatrice di Tenda	Bellini; arr. Czerny	
12	Fantasie on Two Popular Airs "On Yonder Rock" & Tis Tomorrow from Auber's Celebrated Opera of Fra Diavolo	Auber; arr. Czerny	
13	Rondeau sur un Tema de l'Opéra La Sonnambula	Bellini; arr. Czerny	
14	Motif Favori De Rossini	Rossini; arr. Czerny	

15	Second Sett of the Mahon Waltzes & Contradanzas Peculiar to the Island of Minorca	An Officer of the United States Navy	Dedicated to the Ladies of Philadelphia
16	Jane's Waltz, March & Contradanzas	An Officer of the United States Navy	Respectfully dedicated to Mrs. John C. Craig
17	Constellation's Waltz.	An Officer of the United States Navy	
18	Cinderella Waltz & Contradanzas	An Officer of the United States Navy	
19	The Mahon Waltzes & Contradanzas Peculiar to the Island of Minorca	An Officer of the United States Navy	Dedicated to Miss Ellen R. Mcilvaine. No. 1 - Mahon Waltz & Contradance. No. 3. The Minorca Waltz. Ellen's Waltz & Contredance No. 4. No. 6. Venetian Waltz & Contredance No. 8. Orfila Waltz. No. 9
20	Leon Bianca's or Bryon's Waltz & Contredance. The New Year's Gift	Arr., M. Schoengen	A new Animal or Musical Souvenir, Formed of the most Favorite Gems of Melody and Harmony that have become popular, Collated, Arranged & Composed as a Fantasia. 1831
21	Weber's Last Waltz	Weber [Reissiger]	Composed by him a few hours before his death for the Piano Forte
22	Amaranth Waltz	J. F. Hance	Dedicated to Miss Amelia Graham
23	La Douleur … Waltz	Beethoven	
24	Le Desire … Waltz	Beethoven	
25	Village Band Baltimore Waltz	Alexander Duff	Dedicated to Miss Frances Hart
26	La Sonnambula Three Setts of Cotillions from that Favorite Opera	(Bellini); arr. Henry Lemoine	
27	Celebrated Cinderella Waltz	Rossini; arr. Herz	

1. Marked "Presented to his Pupil Miss M. Randolph as a mark of approbation at her untiring application and improvement in the study of [cut off] June 1837 by W. Daniell."

volume of piano music that evinces the growing weight given to both operatic arrangements and dances in southern binder's volumes (see Table 3.1).[15] Waltzes permeate the collection, and the sets of cotillions and contradanzas with instructions point to dancing in the Randolph home. In addition to these and some popular airs, Mary played arrangements from Hérold's *Zampa*, as well as several from operas by Rossini and Bellini, and Caraffa's ballet *L'Orgie*. The composers range from Steibelt (his famous "Storm Rondo") to Czerny, Kiallmark, Hünten, and Herz, and several by local musicians. It dates primarily from the 1830s and provides another glimpse of the influence of opera in American parlors.

Dance Music

Dances combined several elements of southern women's musical experiences. Knowing the proper steps for specific dances helped define one's social position, as Hartley observed: "No woman is fitted for society until she dances well."[16] Astute composers and publishers often combined this requisite social intercourse with familiar melodies, such as the "Ben Bolt Polka," based on the popular song "Ben Bolt" and played by Kate Berry in Nashville and women in the Thornton Family of Sussex (Virginia), thereby extending the dance repertory.[17] Even better were dance arrangements of excerpts from well-known operas, and some of these became more familiar than the operas themselves. The "Cinderella Waltz" from Rossini's *La cenerentola* is a perfect example: the opera itself was not one many young southern women would have seen, but this waltz is one of the most frequently encountered in binder's volumes.[18] The earliest of Eliza Harwood's volumes, for example, includes arrangements of this and other widely-circulating works by Rossini, such as the overture to *Il turco in Italia*.[19]

Scholars have long acknowledged Rossini's popularity in the early-nineteenth-century United States, but other opera composers had similar success, at least in the South. In particular, the stage works of François Adrien Boieldieu and Daniel Auber appear regularly in binder's volumes. Among the favorites from Boieldieu were pieces from *La dame blanche* and *Le calife de Bagdad* (both of which are represented in Eliza Harwood's volume 2.) Dances (styled as waltzes, gallops, marches, and others) from Auber's operas *La muette de Portici*, *Le dieu et la bayadère*, *L'ambassadrice*, *Le domino noir*, *Fra diavolo*, and *Les diamants et de la couronne* saw repeated publication. These often appeared in groups, such as the three waltzes used in Fayetteville by Olivia Stedman and her daughters (see Figure 3.1.). This collection opens with an unnamed waltz (in G major), followed by "Je suis content, je suis heureux" (in C major), and concludes with "The Favorite Hop Waltz" (in D major, but modulating back to G so the first waltz can end the performance). Fanny Priscilla Dickinson and her sister Martha owned

Figure 3.1. The "Waltzes from La Bayadère," by p. 1, Auber, from Mary Stedman's binder's volume. Courtesy of the Music Library, University of North Carolina at Chapel Hill.

dances from Auber's *Le dieu et le bayadère* (Paris, 1830), arranged by Tolbecque as "Three favorite setts of Quadrilles." Others, such as Eliza B. Lindsley in Nashville and Amelia Nance in New Orleans, included these arrangements in their binder's volumes. Another common operatic adaptation was Carl Maria von Weber's "Favorite Waltz from Oberon." These versions of Continental operas provided a means to demonstrate that a young woman not only knew the latest dances but also melodies that had been transformed from stage works into dances, thereby demonstrating her awareness of an appropriate repertory from the theater or music associated with a famous performer.[20]

Dancing occurred in many situations. When studying abroad, southern women were able to maintain their interests in dance because many educators on both sides of the Atlantic saw it as appropriate for socialization as well as entertainment while at school and as exercise. At Mlle. Blandin's school in Paris (where one of the resident teachers was a dance instructor), it served the latter. In the period before term began but girls arrived, Mary Fenwick Lewis enjoyed dancing "nearly all day while one girl plays the piano," praising the playing of one ten-year-old student.[21] Mary wrote to her mother that the most fashionable dances in Paris in 1843 were the contradanse, waltz, and gallop.[22]

Published music offers a comprehensive way to gauge women's music in southern homes because for many people it was the usual space for dancing. Lithographers captured this sort of activity on numerous pieces of sheet music. The "Cally Polka," a popular work performed by (Allen) Dodsworth's Band features a young couple dancing at home, dressed in elegant attire, with roses in the woman's hair (see Figure 3.2). Young women could easily see themselves in this image of dancing at home, even if dressed in less stylish clothing. Equally plausible is the scene on the "Three Sisters" (no. 3, "Clara")[23] (see Figure 3.3). Women playing while others danced, even women together, was a common phenomenon during the antebellum period.

Figure 3.2. "The Cally Polka," by Allen Dodsworth, from Lucy Brown's binder's volume. Courtesy of the Music Library, University of North Carolina at Chapel Hill

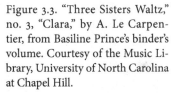

Figure 3.3. "Three Sisters Waltz," no. 3, "Clara," by A. Le Carpentier, from Basiline Prince's binder's volume. Courtesy of the Music Library, University of North Carolina at Chapel Hill.

Figure 3.3 communicates more than women's role in providing music for dancing. The pianist hardly studies the music, has a languid approach to the waltz, and wears modest attire appropriate for home (her hair is also worn loose, suggesting an intimate family-only gathering). It is difficult to imagine that she is really playing a waltz, which further suggests that the image is serving a visual purpose by demonstrating how something should happen. The picture also serves as a guide to proper control of the body while involved in physical activity.[24]

In addition to the "Cally Polka," Lucy Brown owned "The Social Waltzes, Being a Set of Simple Slow Movements Designed for the Use of Social Dancing Parties," a publication of waltzes that she could have played for her acquaintances while they danced, thereby testifying to their knowledge of what was required for genteel status. Perhaps in performing these waltzes, acquaintances in the Brown home saw themselves in the guise of the glamorously attired couples pictured on the first page. They would not have had access to a space such as the one depicted on the cover of "The Social Waltzes," but they could enact the ritual of genteel performance nonetheless (see Figure 3.4). Lucy's "Cally Polka" and its more intimate setting illustrates a more likely possibility for residents of Clinton (North Carolina). These and other dances in Lucy's collection demonstrate that women

Figure 3.4. "The Social Waltzes," by Frederick N. Palmer, from Lucy Brown's binder's volume. Courtesy of the Music Library, University of North Carolina at Chapel Hill.

of lesser means throughout the region cultivated social dances as part of their performance of gentility, just as wealthier women did.

Reading these sheet music pages as visual culture provides more clues about performance practices, including spaces, even if idealized for publication. For example, a Louisiana copy of the "Nouvelles Danses élégantes" (A. Wallerstein, op. 74, published by Schott in 1852 or 1853) shows a woman accompanying a large gathering for a dance. The majority of images, however, picture more intimate spaces. This could serve a twofold purpose: 1) dancing at home was the most common performance situation; and 2) the simple practicalities of producing an image of a room full of people dancing and an instrument.

Schools usually treated dancing not only as an important part of social interaction among peers, and therefore necessary to courtship, but also as exercise. At home, dancing served as an entertainment at all hours, which necessitated someone being able to accompany the dancers. An 1851 "Mems for Musical Misses" article from *Godey's Lady's Book* addresses how to accompany dancing: "Be above the vulgar folly of pretending that you can not play for dancing; for it proves only that if not disobliging, you are stupid. The chief rule in performing this species of music is to be strictly accurate as to time, loud enough to be heard amid the dancers' feet, and always particularly distinct marking the time. . . . In waltzes the first note in the bass of every bar must be strongly accented. In quadrilles the playing, like the dancing, must be gliding. In reels and strathspeys the bass must never be running, always octaves struck with a strong staccato touch; and beware of playing too quick."[25] In addition to instructing how to play different dance styles, such specific advice assumes that anyone who read this magazine would have the skills necessary to play the piano for dancing.[26]

Learning to dance demanded an expenditure of resources. One means of attaining perfection was to hire a dancing instructor, such as M. (or Señor) J. Vegas in New Orleans. If this prospect stood outside the realm of possibility because of location, cost, or other factors, many publications included instructions, enabling young women without a dance instructor the opportunity to learn new dances nonetheless.[27] Elizabeth Grimball's binder's volume (SMB 35) includes a publication intended to teach the reader how to dance the polka, without music. She and her sister were well-known debutantes in Charleston, where they experienced all of the pleasures deemed appropriate for women of the elite class.[28] Her binder's volumes are beautifully made with colorful endpapers and a harp embossed in gold under her name on the cover of SMB 35. She could have studied with a private teacher but kept these instructions in her binder's volume. Similarly, Eva Eve's "Christy Minstrel's Quadrilles" provides the steps for each of the dances in the collection.[29]

Susan Branch Bradford and Eliza C. Anderson both owned copies of Burgmüller's "La Redowa. Nouvelle valse bohémienne. Avec la Théorie de cette Danse d'après la Méthode Varin," which provided them with the procedure for this waltzlike dance.[30] The instructions in this copy are in French, which might limit its uses among southerners of lesser means, as does the fact that Schott published it in Mainz. The redowa, a dance of Czech origin, traveled from Paris to London to the United States in the late 1840s. When Jane Caroline "Carrie" North traveled to West Point, in 1852, she wrote in her diary that on August 23rd, she danced polkas, quadrilles, schottisches, and redowas.

On the other hand, some dances were likely not performed, or not performed well. Around 1850, a short-lived interest in waltzes in quintuple meter surfaced in a few southern cities.[31] In Baltimore, Mounsier M. Hlasko, "Maistre de dance polonaise" (who had been in Vienna for thirteen years), advertised dance lessons. He also was featured on at least two sets of dances published in the city. One of these, with music by C. A. Löpke, is the "Violet Waltz in Five Steps," in quintuple meter.[32] At about the same time, the French danseuse known as Mme. Angélina featured waltzing in the time of five in her performances in New Orleans; local composer

Robert Meyer, composed a set of waltzes "Valse à cinq tems" [sic] acknowledging this phenomenon. Mme. Angélina specialized in difficult dances and inspired amateurs across the city to attempt them. Eliza Ripley described her as "Mme. Angèlina, a new French importation, whose specialty was the new dances that nobody else could teach. . . . We pupils had to learn some new steps and flourishes to be able to make successful début, . . . [and] it was decreed 'L'Esmeralda' was to be most popular. Everybody, even some stout old ladies that did not mean to be relegated to back seats, and *passé beaux* who were fast becoming clumsy and awfully hard to dance with, took dancing lessons on the sly [with] Mme. Angélina, not to mention the young girls, débutantes and such, that went in small installments to her tiny room in Royal Street."[33] As a phenomenon, she figured among several artists competing in New Orleans for a musically-adept public. How this represented gentility is questionable since its overt display, which waltzing in five would have been, did not embody the characteristics of the gentlewoman, nor did showing off—as this most certainly did. In any case, oddities such as Meyer's dances in quintuple time or tricky footwork were atypical novelties.

Different places in the South viewed dances and their performance with varying degrees of acceptance. For example, dancing and tea parties were forbidden at the Robeson Institute, a coeducational school begun by Presbyterians in St. Paul (North Carolina) in 1851.[34] This prohibition corresponds with other bans on this activity espoused by white, Protestant evangelists and clergy, but it does not reflect trends in most southern schools.[35] Nonetheless, some dances held notoriety. Lizzie Brown, the daughter of a Florida governor, boasted that, around 1850, the waltz was not danced "in the United States," but she and her friends knew it long before others."[36] Perhaps their guardians did not sanction the dance: in "Christmas Eve at Pine Hill Plantation" [Florida], Susan Bradford remembered that, in addition to a hornpipe and other traditional tunes among "Mother's music," they danced quadrilles and reels, but not waltzes.[37] The polka fell beneath the standards of Jane North, who remarked that the dance was not the problem so much as "those who polked."[38] These lively dances, in which the dancers faced each other and embraced, tested the limits of propriety and good breeding. In spite of these rare prohibitions, images of dancers, even those associated with risqué foreign natives, figure with some regularity in southern binder's volumes.

Some women continued to dance long after their marriage, although their efforts did not always come across as genteel. Mary Withers wrote to her guardian, Francis Levert in 1858 that Octavia Le Vert (his sister-in-law), Octavia's mother (Mrs. Walton), and another woman "would you believe it, Uncle, all dancing together," as if their behavior shocked those present.[39] Evidently the sight was an unusual and unseemly one—another hint that Octavia's social circle vacillated between that which she wished to emulate and that to which she belonged.

Images of Dancing

Despite revealing costumes and questionable reputations, publishers used images of well-known dancers as a marketing tool. The popular "Sontag Polka" exemplifies how an arranger (Charles d'Albert) marketed his version with an image of Henriette Sontag as Adina dancing with LaBlache as Dr. Dulcarmo, dancing in *L'elisir d'amore*.[40] More common, however, were images of well-known dancers, such as the "Caradira Waltz as danced by Madame Taglioni" in Penelope Pugh's collection. Fanny Cerito (1817–1909), Fanny Elssler (1810–84), and Marie Taglioni (1804–84) reached a stardom resembling that of opera singers.[41]

Some of these compositions and their accompanying pictures can be construed as exotic—Native American, Asian, Arab, or some Other—and many of these were made acceptable through their association with famous performers whose cultural ties with European music validated potentially scandalous attire or nonwhite racial associations. Representative compositions include "Minnehaha" (from Longfellow's *Song of Hiawatha*) or Spanish names in the title. Another example is the Spanish song "La Naranjera" (1858), which appears among Eva Eve's pieces. She directly associates herself with the exotic by writing "Eva" near the woman's image.[42] While attending the Nash and Kollock school in Hillsborough, Ann Pettigrew wrote to her brother William that she had been assigned "La Gitana," one of Elssler's several dances with a Spanish connection.[43] Professional dancers needed to be able to perform ethnically different dances: in the course of a thirteen-night stand in Natchez, a group of French dancers performed eight different ethnically identified dances.

Costumes concealed the real person and, in its place, created a persona, but this false presentation was at odds with true and sincere gentility. An alternative reading of these disguises sees them through a lens of ethnicity. Ann Ostendorf interprets the preponderance of ethnically labeled dances "an attempt to organize diversity through partaking of difference in the form of ethnic genres." Among the examples she provides is "La Cachucha," popularized by Elssler. This dance can be found in many binder's volumes, including those of Margaret Wingfield and Lucy Williams, as well as on a concert program from Richmond, given by a group of men in 1843. C, when Bassini performed it as part of a "pot pourri" of melodies in a Soirée Musicale at the Exchange Hotel.[44] Anna Johnson included several such images in her collection, which could represent a connection with self-identification as Other, the space between occupied by a free woman of color exercising her self-styled gentility (see Figure 3.5).

The costumes worn by these women drew the attention of those observing them and not always with approval. Such exotic dances, especially when published with images of revealing costumes, could not have been models for gentility. Mary

Figure 3.5. "Elssler's Quadrilles," by Charles Jarvis, from the William T. Johnson Collection, Series V, Louisiana and Lower Mississippi Valley Collections, LSA Libraries, Baton Rouge, La.

Lewis saw Cerito dance in Liverpool but found her short costumes "immodest" as she understood proper dress codes for genteel women.[45]

Tunes Everyone Knows

The 1820s collection of Charlestonian Rose Butler Drayton (1806–86) conforms to the new style favoring simple songs in variation sets for the piano. Her binder's volume contains no abstract works for piano but rather pieces like Ross's popular variations on "Auld langsyne."[46] In fact, eleven of the first fifteen compositions in this book are variations, all on recognizable melodies such as "Robin Adair" (which Rose also owned in a version for voice and accompaniment). She also sang Bishop's "Home! Sweet Home!" and owned numerous waltzes. Charleston sellers, at least, provided—or guided, which came first is difficult to say—its consumers with music responding to the new penchant for variations on a popular melody. Rose's collection, like many others, documents an increasing market for musical works that rely heavily on tunes that everyone knows and marks a shift in repertory that remains largely unchallenged until the Reconstruction.

But this elusive quality—"tunes that everyone knows"—helps delineate class structures in the late antebellum period. As more young women became familiar with a repertory of popular songs, the emphasis shifted to new ones. This continual change afforded those with more disposable wealth the ability to distance themselves from the masses who still depended on cheaper, perhaps hand-me-down sheet music from family members.

At the beginning of the period under investigation here, the songs of Thomas Moore and Thomas Haynes Bayly appealed to many music consumers in the United States. They document the popularity of "old songs," especially those from, or seemingly associated with, Scotland and Ireland. They served as the musical equivalent to Walter Scott's popular novels, as a "gentleman of Philadelphia" who published the two artists' works together in 1826.[47] Moore's songs continuously appeared in print until after the mid-century, enjoying popularity with both men and women. Jane North recalled that while visiting in Quebec, George Joseph Webb sang and accompanied himself on the piano and included "some of Moore's melodies and some old Irish songs."[48] The "old Scotch airs" that Virginia Shelton entertained her family with in Murfreesboro might have included one of Moore's, such as "Oft in the Stilly Night," the "Scotch Air" from his *National Melodies*. His Irish melodies were very popular, especially "The Harp That Once Thro' Tara's Halls." That Mary Stedman had this song in her binder's volume is not surprising given that she culled together music published over several decades. But that it found a place in the up-to-date music collection of Kate Berry, who had access to the latest publications available, testifies to its enduring popularity. The widespread circulation of such pieces is shown by the fact that Kate included "Katy Darling" in one of her binder's volumes and Professor Folsom programmed it on a musical entertainment at Old Pisgah Church in Tallahassee in 1854.[49]

Not surprisingly, popular works from earlier decades continued to be sold throughout the 1850s, even as thousands of new ones appeared in print. Many of these were handed down from older relatives, but many more were newly purchased. Olivia Stedman probably gave her music to her daughter, Mary (b. 1813), including "Taglioni's Ghirlanda" of 1827 and Bayly's very popular "Gaily the Troubadour" of 1829, both published at about the time Olivia would have been studying music and performing for her family. On the other hand, Frances "Fannie" Morgandollar Riley (1834–72), a far wealthier woman from Coosawhatchie (South Carolina), included several older compositions in her volume of vocal music, among them Bayley's "I Turn to Thee in Time of Need." Similar songs remained in the repertory for decades, no doubt because of their limited range, lack of chromaticism, simple accompaniments, and overall tunefulness. Even though she would have sung the pieces in the 1850s, the stores that sold it (Zogbaum in Savannah and Richards in Macon) might have had a limited supply of new works, or Fanny (or her family) may have preferred the older style.

The simplicity of antique songs stimulated new fashioning by composers who sought to capitalize on their enduring popularity. Most of the William Vincent Wallace pieces in the Johnson collection belong to series such as *Gems of Scottish Melody, Fantaisie brillante de Salon pour piano sur des Mélodies Écossaises,* and *A Collection of Favorite Scotch Melodies.* The Wallace selections acknowledge the vogue for "antique" songs from the British Isles. Even if they do not reflect the predilection in binder's volumes for his most favored large-scale works (his "Grande Polka de Concert" or variations on "Le rêve"), they exemplify the continued influence of music associated with Scott's literature on southern parlor performance. They continue the tradition of Moore and others while they modernize the arrangements.

These types of pieces were not relegated to parlor performance only. When Henri Baseler directed a musical soirée at the Nash and Kollock school in Hillsborough in 1860, he programmed "Kathleen Mavourneen," as well as "Oft in the Stilly Night" and "The Last Rose of Summer."[50] These songs are natural candidates for such an occasion and for singing in the parlor, but they also figured in more auspicious performances, such as Anna Bishop's first concerts in Kansas City, Missouri (also 1860), which included "Oft in the Stilly Night" and "Home! Sweet Home!"[51] An opera singer (Bishop) performing these in public as a professional juxtaposed with Mary Fenwick Lewis's mother's comments on hearing excerpts from *Norma* in Huntsville soirées serve as cautions to simplistic categorization of vocal music by genre. Opera and simple song were fodder for the stage and parlor alike.

English Language Arias and Songs

The line between songs and ballads and pieces from English-language opera is difficult to draw. Simplified foreign-language arias with English texts further complicates the categorization because many of them resemble the arrangements of English operas. Composers deliberately modeled many of the tunes in English operas on songs favored by the public, so the two group together logically. Excerpts from Balfe's *Bohemian Girl,* especially "Then You'll Remember Me," made their way into binder's volumes, and nothing indicates that singers saw them as distinct from English songs. The binder's volumes of Eva Eve and Kate Berry exemplify the continued popularity of light songs in English.

Probably the best example of the close connection between simple songs and English-language melodies from popular operas is Henry Bishop's "Home! Sweet Home!" It first appeared in his *Melodies of Various Nations* in 1821 as a "Sicilian Air," and reached a larger audience after Bishop inserted it into the 1823 opera *Clari,* with lyrics by John Henry Payne.[52] Few melodies rivaled its status.[53] Siegling published an early arrangement for guitar by Eugène Guilbert, and Jenny Lind's association with the song helped keep it in vogue.[54]

The song was ubiquitous throughout the South, and the melody saw repeated arrangements in differing degrees of technical difficulty for instruments. When Melpominé Stella Bringier visited New Orleans in 1858, she and her family went to hear Thalberg and Vieuxtemps in concert at Odd Fellows Hall. Among the works performed were the pianist's "Sweet Home [*sic*]" and "Last Rose of Summer" for left hand alone. The audience demanded an encore for each piece, so she heard twice the concert that was advertised. Even so, she planned to return the next day for a repeat performance.[55] Belle McGehee played Thalberg's 1857 "Original Copy" (not the "Simplified Copy"). This arrangement included many of the popular figurations found in the "brilliant" piano music of the mid-century, such as simultaneous trills and melodic line in the right hand against a left-hand accompaniment (see Figure 3.6). Such technical feats tend to be found in the

Figure. 3.6. Thalberg, op. 72, p. 9, from Belle McGehee's binder's volume. Courtesy of the Music Library, University of North Carolina at Chapel Hill.

binder's volumes of women whose families ranked among the wealthiest, perhaps resulting from more leisure time to practice and better music teachers.

Not everyone reached the level of virtuoso technique demanded by Thalberg's setting. Simpler piano arrangements circulated throughout the South, and "Home! Sweet Home!" was no exception. Mary Stedman and Carrie Mallett owned the same modest setting ("Introduction & Variations") by William R. Coppock (1832).[56] In Georgia, Sarah Jackson played a version of the tune set with variations by Thomas Valentine and then handed it down to her daughter, Baseline Prince. Rebecca Norfleet Hill of Halifax (North Carolina) owned Valentine's work as well. In Marion, South Carolina, Mary Louisa Walker received J. H. Slack's "Home Sweet Home, with Brilliant Variations" (1850) from her "Cousin Joe."[57]

Shrewd composers acknowledged the continued popularity of older songs and consciously modeled new ones on them. Frederick Crouch's "Kathleen Mavourneen" (1837) is one such work, and it further serves to corroborate that women of varying social statuses frequently performed the same pieces. "Kathleen Mavourneen" formed part of the unbound collection of Henrietta Aiken, one of the most refined, musically gifted, and well-traveled women in Charleston; Louisa McCord, who studied voice in Paris and attended operas in England, France, and Italy; Mary Stedman, whose mother had to go to work to support the family; Carolyn "Carrie" Eliza Mallett, a physician's daughter in Chapel Hill; Mary Gibson in faraway Arkansas; Sarah Burton of Raleigh; Eva Eve, a planter's daughter educated in the North; Caroline B. McNairy with two copies in one binder's volume, and Sarah Crawford, a governor's daughter.[58] Another owner of "Kathleen Mavourneen" was Mary Eunice Copp (1833–1910) of Savannah. Her father was a moderately successful Yankee merchant. She would not have been part of Sarah Crawford's circle of friends. Nonetheless, Mary learned the latest songs that her peers—and those above her socially—would have been singing.

Crouch's "Kathleen Mavourneen" foreshadowed a substantial increase in the number of new parlor songs that coincided with a rise in American-born singers and composers.[59] The arrival of new repertory can be seen in Rachel Adeline ("Ada") Cannon's binder's volume. The daughter of a governor of Tennessee, Ada purchased at least some of her music at West's store in Nashville and marked pieces with her name and "1840." The repertory tends to simple songs, such as "Full Many an Hour I've Whiled Away" (marked "Ada Cannon, Asheby Hill 1840"), "The Maniac" ("Miss R.A. Cannon 1840"), and "Newport Polka" ("Miss R. Ada Cannon Rakeby Hall"). In other respects, however, her binder's volume is old-fashioned. Its operatic selections consist of earlier excerpts, such as "Oh! Soon Return," John Hill Hewitt's arrangement of an "Air" by Mozart.

At about the same time, Nashvillian Ada Clark added popular new and old Anglo-American pieces to her binder's volume. New works by William Henry Fry

("Affection Waltz"), William C. Peters ("Gentle Mary"), and dances with American titles (such as C. Hommann's "Monticello Waltz" and others from *Thirteen Popular Waltzes*) intermingle with "Oft in the Stilly Night," "Flow Gently, Sweet Afton," and "Believe Me, If All Your Endearing Young Charms." With a more direct nod to opera than seen in Ada Cannon's collection, the Clark volume finishes with several songs and dances from *The Bohemian Girl*.[60] Ada's copy of "Ethiopian Medley Overture" stands out as unusual because songs directly associated with people of color do not occur often in binder's volumes owned by antebellum white women.

Another example of women's music in Middle Tennessee is a manuscript that belonged to Adelicia Hayes, who at age twenty-nine was the wealthiest woman in Tennessee.[61] Adelicia's music book includes no sheet music, only manuscript entries, and bears the date "June 1833." Several hands wrote in this book, and it is likely that one of them is hers.[62] The music itself varies. Marches, popular songs, and dance music intermingle, and the copyists rarely included composer attributions. Identified exceptions are "Oh They March'd through the Town" by Nelson, "Away with Melancholy" by Mozart, "Auld Langsyne with Variations" by Ross, and "We Have Lived and Loved Together" by Herz. Some of the dance music has directions for performing the dance, which suggests that Adelicia may have used the music for recreation at home. The vocal music includes signs for ornamentation and written-out cadenzas, copied from prints.

German Music

Before 1850, southern women's familiarity with "classical" European music stemmed from a few sacred compositions by Mozart, Haydn, and Beethoven, but, in the main, excerpts from operas constituted the foreign repertory. Of the sixty-nine vocal pieces offered in 1858 at Henry Lord's American and European Music Emporium in Canton, sixteen derive from foreign operas (by Flotow, Weber, Verdi, Auber, Donizetti, and Bellini). The piano music features "pieces for Pianists of one year's practice," variation sets by Grobe and Thalberg, as well as several sets with "variations brilliant," including some polkas.[63]

Undoubtedly, the favorite songs (as opposed to arias) of the 1840s and 1850s that did not originate in English belonged to the composer Franz Abt. Lord stocked eleven of his songs, but by far the most common in antebellum binder's volumes is his "Agathe" (op. 39, no. 1), usually with its English title "When [the] Swallows Homeward Fly." By the Civil War, Beyer, Oesten, Viereck, and Brinley Richard's had published arrangements of this tune. Mary Hunt sang from George Willig's 1851 publication, which included the German text printed beneath the English. "Brightest Eyes" ("Die schönsten Augen") by the German opera singer Giorgio

Figure 3.7. "When the Swallows Homeward Fly,"
by Franz Abt, from Carrie Mallett's binder's volume. Courtesy of the Music Library, University
of North Carolina at Chapel Hill.

Stigelli also ranks among the most popular songs of this period. Similarly styled songs by Kücken, Weber, Spohr, and others can be found in collections such as *Gems of German Song*, published in the United States from at least the 1840s. In Portsmouth, Margaret Wingfield's 1854 copy of Heinrich Proch's "From the Alps the Horn Resounding" lists the pieces in the series *Gems of the German*, and by this time Mendelssohn's music appears in the series.

The title page of Carrie Mallett's version of "When the Swallows Homeward Fly" includes the name of the series, *Parlor Album*, and the compositions found in it (see Figure 3.7, p. 1). The components range from Italian opera arias in Italian ("Casta diva") or English ("It Is Better to Laugh Than Be Sighing"), and from Old World melodies ("Annie Laurie") to newer ones ("Kathleen Mavourneen"). Crouch is the favored composer. Two songs, "When the Swallows Homeward Fly" and Schubert's "Serenade," constitute the only German contributions. As in several other publications, the editor offered the German words under the English.

The appeal of Abt's song is undeniable. He imbued it with enough variety to keep the interest with flowing vocal lines that deliberately repeat only for emphasis. Its twenty-four measures are neither melodically repetitive nor harmonically stagnant. The second phrase moves immediately to the relative minor, expanding the tonal palette much faster than most songs of the period. Abt ends this phrase in the dominant and then switches the interest to the melodic line, which ascends to the seventh at the climax of the song. The return to the tonic fulfills expectations, and a final tag adds further interest. The range (an octave and a fourth) tends to the lower notes, rising for emphasis at the climax and as the final phrase begins. The placement of these pitches deliberately favors the singer, first in the repeated rising motive in the middle and then for the finishing touch at the end.

Schubert's music rarely occurs in southern sources of the 1830s, but soon thereafter his name appears frequently in lists of published series of songs. Looking again at Lord's advertisement, he listed these nine songs (some in French translation). The series *Gems of German Song* included Schubert's *Lieder*, on occasion, in the midst of songs by Abt, Reissiger, Kücken, and others. M. W. Wright sang the "Elf King" in English (#19), translated and sung by Charles Horn Jr. Slightly later, Sarah Lois Wadley borrowed a music book from Helen Underwood and found the "Erl King . . . beautiful."[64] "Ständchen" (usually "La serenade" or "Serenade") also met with approval across the region, from Pensacola to Canton.[65] Elizabeth Grimball, the daughter of a wealthy planter, had a copy of Schubert's "The Wanderer" with the German text handwritten under the printed English translation, and another Charlestonian, Henrietta Aiken owned a manuscript copy transposed down a half-step (to C minor).

Cynthia Beverly Tucker of Williamsburg was one of the first southern women to own some of Mendelssohn's *Lieder ohne Worte*, op. 53, in this case, the "Volkslied" (a gift from Mr. J. Smead). Her binder's volume is dated January 2, 1852, and was bound by Jos. B Keiningham on Broad St. in Richmond. A few other women played isolated pieces from this opus, almost always with an English title. His vocal music was rarer, although Louisa McCord purchased Mendelssohn's *Six Lieder for Voice and Piano* and Schubert's "Lebewohl" ("Last Greeting") while in London in 1858–59.

*   *   *

The primacy of a recognizable melody underpinned almost all of the music heard in southern parlors and on the stage during the antebellum period. The specific tunes that arrangers used depended on larger issues of style, such as the fashion for novels by Sir Walter Scott and songs associated with the worlds he evoked. Works by Moore, Stephenson, and Bayley also served as models for others, and opera excerpts by Bishop, and later Balfe, reflect these connections. At the same time, arias, dances, overtures, and other music from Continental Europe also influenced women's musical culture. Foreign-language opera, in many different guises, entered the purview of the rich and poor, and every singer in between.

4

"I have no time to tell you now half the enjoyment these operas have given us"

Opera as Cultural Capital

As Katherine Preston has argued, the impact of opera on American culture in the nineteenth century cannot be overestimated. Its imprint in the South can be detected early in Charleston and New Orleans, in both public performances and private collections.[1] In the 1820s and 1830s, southern women knew Italian arias as arrangements for piano that often included several variations on a principal theme or in simplified versions often adapted to English texts. In this regard, "Away with Melancholy," Mozart's "O dolce concento" from *Die Zauberflöte*, is representative (see Figure 4.1).[2] Professional harpists Septima Fayolle and her sister Adelaïde Giraud performed it in Charleston in 1823 (also under the English title).[3] It appears in numerous collections, in prints by Carr, Willig, Hewitt, and many others. In Nashville, Adelicia Hayes sang it from a manuscript copy. Another altered aria frequently encountered in southern binder's volumes is "Here We Meet Too Soon to Part," T. B. Phipps's version of Rossini's "Di tanti palpiti" from *Tancredi* (1813).

The binder's volume that belonged to Charlestonian Emma Middleton Huger (1813–1892) represents an early turn to Italian opera in Italian. Her friends called her "high-bred" and "imperial," placing her at the epitome of the cultured elite, and her music collection supports this characterization.[4] Like the Dickinson-Murfree women in Nashville, Emma gathered English-language songs for her binder's volume, featuring the same composers found in the collections of fellow Charlestonians Harriet Lowndes and Rose Butler Drayton. (All three sang music by Moore, Bishop, Wade, Horn, Barnett, Eckhard, and Stephenson.) Like Rose, she included Pucitta's popular "Strike the Cymbal." But the simpler, English-language pieces were placed in the latter part of her book.[5] Emma opened her binder's volume with Italian and French opera arias in the original languages.[6] Beginning with Paisiello's "Nel cor più non mi sento" (from his opera commonly known as *La molinara*), works by Mozart follow: "Batti, batti o bel Masetto" and

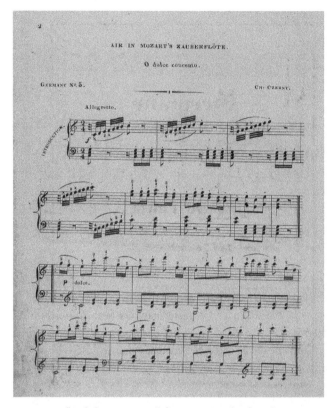

Figure 4.1. "O dolce concento," from *Die Zauberflöte*, by Mozart/
Czerny.

"Deh vieni, non tardar" from Mozart's *Il nozze di Figaro*; as well as "Madamina!"
"O statua gentilissima," and "Là ci darem la mano" from his *Don Giovanni*.[7] That
these last three pieces belong to male characters does not seem to have been an
issue, particularly when modified by the publishers to use treble clefs for the bass-
baritone vocal lines. ("Madamina!" is sung by Don Giovanni's servant Leporello,
a bass; "O statua gentilissima" is a duet for two basses; and "Là ci darem la mano"
is a duet for soprano and baritone.) Emma also sang Rossini's "Una voce poco
fa" from *Il barbiere di Siviglia*.

After other Italian works, her repertory turns to French, including opera arias
by Méhul and Dalayrac.[8] Weber's "Huntsmen's Chorus" from *Der Freischütz* (in
English) and Charles M. Sola's popular "Brûlant d'amour / A troubadour song"
also figure among her pieces.[9] The ordering points to a cultural hierarchy that
places foreign opera above simpler songs and ballads. Having this music first
might have been some attempt at showing off her modern music and familiarity
with a European repertory, a claim substantiated by the fact that some of these

pieces bear stamps from Weissenbruch's in Brussels. She may have bought them from a local publisher, or in New York, or they could have arrived with an émi-gré music teacher. Two New York firms that later specialized in imported music were Scharfenburg and Luis, and Breusing. Their stamps can be found on several pieces of sheet music in the Charleston Museum. By the early 1840s, Samuel Hart sold imported music in Charleston.[10]

In favoring non–Anglo-American music, Emma Huger's binder's volume offers an alternative to contemporary southern collections. A comparison with Lucia "Lucy" Cary Harrison (1808–42) in more rural Culpeper (Virginia) demonstrates the advantages that women from Charleston had over social equals in other southern communities. Lucy's grandparents belonged to one of the wealthiest and most powerful families in eighteenth-century Virginia; Thomas Jefferson was her not-too-distant cousin. She represented the elite class of Virginia. Her music helps gauge differences, however. Like Emma, she owned the same melody from *Der Freischütz* as well as "Di tanti palpiti," but unlike Emma, Lucy's collection depends heavily on English pieces, such as "Home! Sweet Home!" and "Oh Dear, What Can the Matter Be."

In Charleston, Emma Huger heard French musicians perform the latest melo-dies from operas in Paris, could easily purchase music at music stores, and visited acquaintances whose cultural knowledge of music rivaled her own. That there is overlap among the repertory in the binder's volumes of Rose Drayton, Emma Huger, and others of their circle is to be expected. As in other places, favorite airs in English by Moore/Stevenson—as well as popular tunes sung in Ameri-can theaters—figure prominently. Furthermore, music by Rossini began to take hold in both concerts by professionals and parlor entertainments by amateurs.[11] French music declined in favor of Italian opera. But Emma's miscellany of works in Italian, English, French, and Spanish typifies the music affluent young women who had a broad cultural exposure learned. Using mere economic success as the measure of class might indicate that Lucy Harrison and Emma Huger sought genteel refinement with the same musical tools, but the places in which they lived resulted in differences in what repertory they knew, which professionals they heard, and what knowledge they had of European musical styles.

Bel canto Opera

During the 1830s, bel canto opera excerpts became a common choice for south-ern binder's volumes and a necessary component in higher social circles. Martha Dickinson owned two Bellini arias in English ("Oh! Love, for Me Thy Power" from *La sonnambula*, and "Ah! Canst Thou Leave Me?" from *Norma*). Several women owned versions of the aria from *La sonnambula*; Leopold Meignen ar-ranged Martha's version for guitar. This extended cantabile-cabaletta includes high B's and a suggested high C at the end, even when transposed from Bellini's original key of E-flat to C. If Martha accompanied herself while singing this work, she must have possessed a considerable range and one that she could maneuver easily while simultaneously playing the guitar.

In Vicksburg, Mahala Eggleston performed another excerpt from *La sonnambula* ("Ah! Do Not Mingle, One Human Feeling") transposed down a third, as did Mary Gibson in Fort Smith (Arkansas). Such modifications to the original abound throughout the period. Other women, however, boldly attempted the works in original keys, languages, and with ornamentation. Marianne Porcher Smith Alston sang "Una voce poca fa," "Va crudele" (*Norma*), and arias by Meyerbeer and other mid-century opera composers in the original languages and keys. She included several pieces where someone, possibly herself, has added chord names, presumably for guitar accompaniment. Seeing such additions to arias such as "I'll Pray for Thee" from *Lucia di Lammermoor* prompts the conclusion that these works were accompanied by a guitarist or, less likely, an inexperienced pianist who needed the chords written in. Her copy of "Una voce poca fa," however, commands interest because of penciled-in ornaments in both the accompaniment and vocal part. Figure 4.2 illustrates one such addition for the vocalist (written in the piano part because there was space). Marianne must have been a decent singer indeed to require and then realize the rapid sixteenth-note ornamentation written into her score. As an elite woman, she had the time and

Figure 4.2. "Una voce poco fa," from *Barbiere di Siviglia* by Rossini, from Marianne Alston's binder's volume. Courtesy of The Charleston Museum, Charleston, South Carolina.

money to spend on extended music lessons, and she practiced this "air of all airs" with added embellishments.[12]

Bel canto opera permeated most collections of music by the 1850s, even if the versions were simpler, translated, and adapted for other uses (dances). Carrie Mallett's duet from *I Capuleti ed i Montecchi*, "The Hour of Parting," typifies how operatic melodies could be appropriated for parlor use, in this example adapting the opening chorus from Act 4 into a simple duet. Choruses were necessarily easier than arias and enabled less accomplished amateurs to sing something from a famous opera without taxing them with virtuoso passages.

The 1850s Opera Craze

As these examples demonstrate, Italian and French opera, as well as selections by Weber, enjoyed widespread appreciation throughout the American South, and this appreciation grew into a sort of culture of its own—an opera craze—during the 1850s. Opera was ingrained in American parlors.[13] Preston has drawn attention to this fact, singling out the 1850s as a time when foreign-language opera began to challenge English-language opera as a superior musical experience, particularly along the eastern seaboard. She writes of the move toward foreign-language opera, particularly Italian, in New York, Boston, and Philadelphia.[14] In the South, Italian *and* French opera figures in some way in many binder's volumes of the period, and in some it dominates entirely. The closer to New Orleans, the more French opera can be found in concert programs and binder's volumes. Familiarity with the operatic repertory—Bellini, Meyerbeer, Boieldieu, Auber, Donizetti, Rossini, and Verdi—was as commonplace as knowing which outfit to wear when. And, as in clothes, the wealthier one was, the more choices one had. Name-dropping was another means of showing off one's opera knowledge. Southern women spoke of Patti or Grisi as if they had heard them, and such references were not always complimentary: an anonymous critic in western Florida noted sarcastically in 1841 that a young woman who had "grown musical lately . . . warbles and quavers like a Sontag or Grisi."[15] Most, however, were positive. When Octavia Le Vert arrived in England in 1853, she wrote that nothing short of hearing Sontag sing compared to it. Since she wrote her letters with the intention of publication, her comment amounts to a public declaration of her refinement, and her audience knew of Sontag's name even if they themselves had not heard her perform.

As cultural capital, opera functioned as an umbrella for a multitude of uses— and probably abuses. The opera craze of the 1850s can be discerned from the music collections of wealthy belles in Charleston and Columbia who had attended performances in London, Paris, Venice, and Milan; to white women of lesser means who never heard the operas live but knew of their social cachet; to free women of color whose acquaintance with opera stemmed from the diverse musical culture of New Orleans. European opera infiltrated the southern parlor where culturally astute women across socioeconomic classes used it as a measure of sophistication. The music performed by these amateurs extended beyond Anglo-American favorites to a repertory that required robust musical skills: Bellini, Meyerbeer, Donizetti, and Verdi. Parlor performances of works by such composers embraced a wide range of techniques: simple dances crafted from popular tunes, to difficult piano arrangements (of single melodies or most of the main tunes from complete operas) by Beyer and Rosellen, or to transposed and simplified English-language settings to Italian arias as they appear in the original versions.

As women of the middle classes aspired to move into higher cultural positions, some did so by encroaching on a repertory once reserved for the elite. In response, those on the uppermost end of the social spectrum continued to distinguish themselves by raising the bar ever higher. Even if women from a variety of social classes owned the same repertory, the sheer numbers of opera pieces in wealthier collections testifies to its marker of social status. Often it was by more difficult piano arrangements or arias lifted straight from an opera. Some of those at the top of the social ladder both sang and played the piano. Elizabeth Grimball sang works such as Donizetti's famous aria, "Our Faith Then Fondly Plighting," from *Linda di Chamounix*, complete with only a slight modification to accommodate Elizabeth's apparent lack of a high C (see Figure 4.3). Eva Eve's binder's

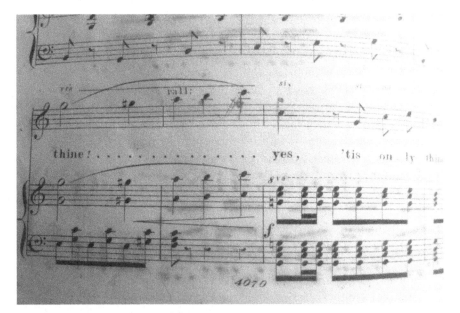

Figure 4.3. "Our Faith Then Fondly Plighting," from *Linda di Chamounix*, by Donizetti/Clare W. Beames, from Elizabeth Grimball's binder's volume. Courtesy of The Charleston Museum, Charleston, South Carolina.

volume includes pieces that are more modern and difficult, such as "The Beauties of Rigoletto" (a gift of a friend) and "Di provenza" from *La traviata*.[16]

Three binder's volumes originating in Richmond County, Georgia—ten that belonged to Eva Eve and another to her cousin, Ruth Berrien Whitehead—exemplify how music owned by close cousins can represent the popular repertory performed across the region but also distinguish them from those of lesser means.[17] Eva Eve showed her advantages by including operatic music that not only had English translations but also maintained the original languages. Her copy of Stigelli's popular "Brightest Eyes" provides both German and English texts, and several others in her collection have two languages as well. (There is an additional translation added above the vocal staff, with a note that it has been added by Eva.) Her versions of arias from Flotow's *Martha*; Bellini's *La sonnambula*; Donizetti's *La fille du régiment*, *La favorita*, *Linda di Chamounix*; Meyerbeer's *Le pardone de Ploërmel* (two); Verdi's *I lombardi*, *Il trovatore*; Mozart's *Don Giovanni*; and others have English and original texts underneath the vocal lines. Moreover, Eva played Beyer's challenging arrangements of *Lucia di Lammermoor*, *Norma*, *I puritani*, and *La fille du régiment*, as well as similarly difficult versions of popular tunes. She also owned Schulhoff's arrangement of the "Carnival of Venice"—a technically difficult setting of a popular melody that circulated widely. In fact, Eva owned a version from Ditson's that advertised four different arrangements, by Schulhoff, Cramer, Oesten, and Beyer—popular composers whom Americans recognized and appreciated.

Only one of Ruth's pieces has an English title ("Ocean Spray Polka"); the remainder includes mostly French titles, and four in German by Johann Strauss. Most of the compositions are dances, many culled from operas, such as "Polka-Mazurka L'Étoile du nord" (Meyerbeer). A few are character pieces, including Rosellen's "Trois Rêveries, Op. 31, No. 1." Even though all but two of Ruth's works were published in Europe, an overwhelming proportion came through Breusing's in New York before being sold. Ellen Cox's binder's volume, of uncertain provenance but almost certainly from the New Orleans area, contains a repertory similar to Ruth's, but Ellen's music came from Europe via New Orleans dealers.

The musical attainment of rich young women rose ever higher as the middle classes overran cultural markers of social status. The wealthiest planters' families employed opera to flaunt their refinement. The chief manifestation of this practice exists in the grand tour and its accompanying privileges: a seat at the Opéra, attendance at a gala affair, music lessons in Paris, shopping for sheet music abroad, and exposure to musical events beyond the scope of their poorer or poorly situated neighbors helped keep them in their places. Numerous southerners attended the opera at Covent Garden (London), the Opèra (Paris), La Scala (Milan), or La Fenice (Venice). The Aiken family saw *Le prophète* in Paris in 1857. Octavia Le Vert was present at the premiere of *Rigoletto* in London in 1853, also attended by

Queen Victoria, and she later attended an opera gala when Victoria and Albert were the guests of Napoleon III (an event famously depicted in a painting by Eugène Louis Lami).

Studying music abroad, as Louisa McCord and Mary Lewis were able to do, also heightened their cultural cachet. Purchasing music while overseas and including it in binder's volumes on display in the parlor assisted in promoting their station above the growing numbers of middle-class women who perhaps knew the same repertory but through a local perspective. Young finds a range of distinctions in the practice of gentility in 1840s Sydney, which in turn demonstrates the fluid and competitive character of the middle class.[18] Opera as part of a woman's musical practice can be interpreted in the same light and with equally distinctive markers of refinement. Louisa noted what music she purchased at Novello's store in London, and Sarah Crawford made sure to remember (and to inform others seeing it) that she acquired "Rimembranze di Montecchiari Polka-Mazurka" in Egypt. Finally, most often it is the women with the most leisure time—the wealthiest—who appear to have conquered the most challenging repertory, such as the extended compositions played by Mary Lowndes.

In spite of its pervasive presence throughout southern women's culture, the sheer number of opera pieces in wealthier collections (such as those of Elizabeth Grimball, Bessie Allston, or Mary Lowndes) testifies to its mark of social status. Everyone of elite status, it seems, knew of operas, and some were de rigueur as parlor repertory. Harriet Lowndes Aiken's request to a friend for an aria from *Il trovatore* to be sent to the family's plantation on Jehossee Island so that her daughter Henrietta could learn it exemplifies the emphasis placed on knowing the right operas and their music. Surviving correspondence tells us that Henrietta did indeed sing "Di due figli," and the score remains part of her music collection. Place, too, is a factor. It is no accident that many of the examples mentioned here hailed from Charleston or that much French opera stemmed from New Orleans.

Opera Arrangements for Piano, Varying Difficulties

Under the influence of European touring pianists such as Sigismund Thalberg, toward the mid-century arrangements played by southern women increased in technical difficulty.[19] Not surprisingly, the most virtuoso arias and piano reductions typically belonged to the wealthiest or most socially prominent, who used it as one measure of sophistication and refinement. Presumably those who could afford more time to practice or who had better teachers—the elite—had more opportunities to master the skills required of the more extensive arrangements. Elizabeth Grimball, for example, owned seven pieces from Beyer's substantial series of medleys, his *Boquets [sic] de Mélodies*, Op. 42. Her choices included

Les Huguenots (the same one owned by Mary Huger Lowndes), *La fille du régiment*, *Linda di Chamounix*, *Lucia di Lammermoor*, *La favorite* (all Donizetti), *I puritani* (Bellini), and *Ernani* (Verdi). Each of these has fingerings that suggest Grimball played them. *Les Huguenots* begins with an opening flourish, proceeds through "Plus blanche que la blanche herminé," a statement of "Ein feste berg," "Jeunes beautés" ("Bathers' Chorus"), "Rataplan," "Beauté divine, enchanteresse," "A vous et ma vie et mon âme," "Dans le nuit," "Toi, mon seul bien," "Tu l'as dit," "Pour cette cause sainte," and "Tu ne peux éprouver," and concludes with a bombastic restatement of "Ein feste berg." Such arrangements functioned as a sort of antebellum compact disc, introducing women to the latest popular melodies from operas—ones they would be expected to know. Elizabeth "Bessie" Waties Allston played Beyer's challenging arrangements of *La traviata* and *Il trovatore*. Her copies were imported by Breusing in New York, and her binder's volume of piano music was assembled in Charleston. She also sang while at school at the South Carolina Female Collegiate Institute during the Civil War.

Not everyone who performed the most demanding repertory descended from elite families, however.[20] The daughter of a Methodist minister, Mary Louisa Walker owned Beyer's most difficult version (op. 42) of melodies from *La sonnambula*, and Anna Johnson played his transcription of *Les Huguenots*. Similarly, Cynthia Beverly Tucker of Williamsburg played virtuoso arrangements of opera arias by Rosellen and Herz. The operas whose excerpts appear in her binder's volume are *Il crociato* and *Le prophète*, and some of her pieces were imported from Europe by Scharfenburg & Luis or Breusing in New York. Another Williamsburg citizen, Julia Thompson (Eliza Harwood's friend), learned Burgmüller's "Valse brillante" from *Le prophète* and excerpts from *Ernani* for four hands. *Ernani* features again in her binder's volume, along with several other titles from Henri Cramer's *Beauties of the Opera* (*La favorite*, *Lucrezia Borgia*, and *I puritani*). Markings in most of her pieces point to Julia's preparation of these scores.

Savvy arrangers capitalized on the need for simpler versions of opera melodies, often (but not always) performed by women who ranked lower in status. Beyer, for example, also arranged less demanding versions for the series *Fleurs Italiennes 12 Amusements pour le piano sur les motifs favoris des opéras* (op. 87). Margaret Wingfield owned this version of both *Lucia di Lammermoor* (no. 1) and *Beatrice di Tenda* (no. 2). In Fayetteville (North Carolina), Helen Huske played operatic melodies from Beyer's even easier arrangements of music from *Norma*, *I puritani*, and *La fille du régiment* in *Les progrès des jeunes élèves* (op. 88, two sets) and Duvernoy's *First Lessons . . . Beautiful & Easy Airs* by Rossini, Auber, Bellini, and others. Mary Mather in Louisiana played difficult versions as well as Beyer's op. 36, *Repertoire de jeunes pianistes / Petites Fantaisies Instructives pour le piano / Sur des motifs d'opéras favoris*. Similarly, Kate Berry owned a different composer's publication, *Th. Oesten's Nine Amusements*, No. 2, which consists of popular tunes from *L'elisir d'amore*, *Beatrice di Tenda*, and *I due foscari*. Lucy Williams (1826–1906) played from a simple four-hand arrangement of a march from *Norma*.

Lucy Brown owned the "Hernani Waltz from Verdi's Celebrated Opera of Hernani as performed by the Italian Company arranged for piano by W. Cooper Glynn," published in Boston in 1847 (the same year the opera premiered in the United States). How she acquired such a score is unknown, although there were music sellers not too far away in Goldsboro, Wilmington, and other places. Furthermore, the Clinton Female Institute had been established in 1826, only eight years after the town of Clinton itself, and became the Clinton Female Academy in 1852. The teacher there might have been the source of Lucy's music.[21]

Going "Opera Mad"

Anne Catherine Boykin Jones, the wife of a planter in Baldwin County who also traveled to Europe in the 1850s, provides an alternative view of European opera. Her diary furnishes more details about the trip than does Harriet Lowndes's scant travel diary (two mentions of music), presumably because it was Anne's only journey abroad (as opposed to Harriet's several). The Joneses had the economic capital to get the entire family to London and Paris, which points to upper-class status. Their social rank was on par with the Aikens, but her diary discloses a dissimilar stance to much of what she saw while abroad, certainly differing from the accounts of either Harriet Aiken or Octavia Le Vert.

Going to the opera and theater was a requirement for any trip abroad, and women's reactions to these experiences reflect their values. Rarely do any women mention instrumental music, and if they do it is not in a concert setting (usually in a park or a band performance). Anne's remarks on opera contrast those of the others examined here, perhaps because she spent most of her life in rural Georgia where the spirit of religious revival impacted many of the women in planters' families. Her naiveté shines in many entries in her diary. For example, she was surprised that at the Opéra all of Meyerbeer's *Le prophète* was performed in French. In Paris. And though a performance at the "Opera Comique" was better than one at the Opéra, she wrote that "I do not think, however, that I shall ever grow *Opera mad*. There is too much unnecessary & disgusting exposure, too much to tinge the cheek of the modest & refined woman with the blush of shame. Fine singing is not a sufficient palliative for all this, & the result most to be dreaded is the feeling of indifference to these shocks of delicacy." Her distaste for European culture extended to the ballet, which she compared to "our negroes at the camp-meetings and *corn shucking* particularly." She continues: "I have not *learned* to appreciate such music, call it splendid singing when the poor creature is laboring to carry her voice in continuous screams & shrieks to the highest pitch, & then from sheer exhaustion is compeled to trill it feebly down to the faintest whisper! Singing indeed! It is more like the hallowing of [a] jolly set of *fox hunters*." Opera-going was something she felt duty-bound to try but proclaimed herself too delicate and offended at the overt display of emotion, skin, and talent. To Anne, it represented the decadence that some Americans associated with Europe.[22]

Anne's views can be taken as gentility in the extreme and do not represent the majority of women from planter families, at least those who wrote about opera. Other southern women enjoyed attending the opera in Europe. Fourteen-year-old Louisa Rebecca McCord saw *Norma* in Paris in October 1858 and claimed to have been "wild" about the performance. She shopped at Novello's in London on June 8, 1859, and bought "She Is Far from the Land" and "God Save the Queen." Louisa took voice lessons in Paris with a violinist from the Italian opera. She went to performances at the Teatro San Carlo and the San Carlino in Naples, preferring the burlesques at the latter. Clearly her views contrasted those of Anne Boykin Jones.[23] These cases serve as a warning against using to broad a brush to paint the musical experiences of wealthy "elite" women.

Those who could afford to travel frequently made it a point to visit either New York or New Orleans to attend the opera. While visiting her aunt and uncle in New Orleans, Lizzie Randall wrote to her sister that their uncle came "in every morning to tell us that he has tickets or an opera box or something pleasant." She had at least two invitations to hear Verdi's *The Two Foscari*. Other operas included in Lizzie's sojourn in the Crescent City were Meyerbeer's "Prophet," Verdi's "Jerusalem," "Norma," and "Robert le diable" (with Madame Rosa DeVries in each). Her final comment on the operas is that "I have no time to tell you now half the enjoyment these operas have given us." She heard Jenny Lind and was thankful to have been "transported to the land of German tradition," in opposition to the French music she usually heard in New Orleans. Her only criticism of Lind was that she sang "Home! Sweet Home" "gaily and coquettishly . . . as if it were a good joke between herself and the audience." The professional singer transgressed the boundary of good taste, an offense of refinement and sincerity associated with gentility.[24]

Opera attendance was essentially mandatory as a marker of social aspiration by the 1850s. In his handwritten copy of Will H. Coleman's *Historical Sketchbook and Guide to New Orleans* (1885), New Orleans publisher Henry Wehrmann reproduced a chapter about antebellum opera. Coleman recalled that "not to be subscriber, or at least a regular attendant at the Opera, was tantamount to being ignored by society and looked upon as a person greatly lacking in taste; whilst, au contraire, a frequent and undeviating appearance, particularly on grand opera nights, tended greatly toward a kindly, hospitable reception into the best French society under the ancient regime."[25] The pointed reference to French society under the monarchy suggests that opera-goers in New Orleans saw themselves as part of that tradition.

The Importance of Place: Two Planter's Daughters

Mary Huger Lowndes and Penelope "Nellie" Ann Pugh were two planter's daughters of approximately the same age (born around 1830) who had their music bound into volumes before they married. Otherwise, their collections differ entirely. Perhaps no other single binder's volume illustrates the extent to which opera culture dominated the parlors of well-to-do urban southerners by 1850 better than that which belonged to Mary Lowndes. The daughter of a rice planter and a member of one of South Carolina's aristocratic families, she grew up in one of the largest houses in Charleston, at 51 East Bay St. Her impressive collection of technically advanced piano solos, most of which are based on opera melodies, also indicates the depth of training and practice that some southern women undertook (see Table 4.1). She was the niece of Harriet Lowndes (who sang Parisian chansons in the 1820s and purchased complete opera scores on her honeymoon in Europe in 1831) and the first cousin of Henrietta Aiken (whose extensive collection of both vocal and piano music evinces a talented and knowledgeable musician who studied in France). In fact, in 1848 Mary accompanied Harriet and Henrietta on one of their European sojourns, although Mary's music all came from US sellers (some imported from Paris, Leipzig, Berlin, and Mainz). Some of the compositions are quite lengthy, the type of pieces that drew the ire of commentators who advised young women to "let your playing be brief" when playing for your friends.[26] We do not know that Mary played them for friends in the formal parlor setting, but the women in her acquaintance would have been those most familiar with demanding arrangements of operatic literature, either as piano solos or renditions of arias as sung by Giulia Grisi and others.

Without a doubt, Mary played from this music. Her expensive copy of Thalberg's "Fantaisie pour le piano sur des thèmes de l'Opéra Moise de G. Rossini, op. 33" ($1.25) includes pedal markings in several places and fingering for some passages (see Figure 4.4). So, too, does her copy of Voss's transcription of *Les Huguenots*. In some measures, she needed assistance lining up the notes, and on page 48 her teacher (presumably) suggested she leave out tenths in one hand, opting for single notes instead. The fact of Mary performing this piano solo in her home, with people walking by and hearing her, and her acquaintances knowing she cultivated such repertory, fosters an aesthetic refinement that signifies a culturally superior position to those within and without her social circle. She did not perform it in public, as did Herminie Petit [Barbot], a professional prodigy

Table 4.1. Contents of SMB 32, Mary Huger Lowndes[1]

Page*	Title	Composer	Information
1/1	Fantasia on motives from Verdi's opera of Attila, op. 162	Verdi; arr. J. B. Duvernoy	"Mary H Lowndes"
2/15	Le Carnival de Venise	Leopold de Meyer	"Mary H Lowndes"
3/27	Fantaisie pour le piano pur des thèmes de l'opéra Moise de G. Rossini, op. 33	Rossini; arr., Thalberg	
4/49	Quadrille sur l'opéra de Giacomo Meyerbeer Le prophète	Meyerbeer; arr., J. Strauss	
5/57	Les quatres airs de ballet et la marche, de sacre de l'opéra Le prophète de Giacomo Meyebeer	Meyerbeer; arr., Garaudé	
6/67	Reminiscences de l'opéra Le prophète de Giacomo Meyerbeer, Duo brillante, op. 158	Meyerbeer; arr., Edouard Wolff	Piano duet
7/105	Les nationalités musicales—Six Esquisses (1'Écosses [schottische], la Russe [nocturne], Naples [tarantella], l'Angleterre [military march], l'Allemande [waltz], et l'Irlande [Irish tune]), op. 185	Kalkbrenner	
8/129	The celebrated duet in the opera of Linda di Chamounix	Donizetti; arr, Steyermarkische	"Marie H Lowndes / 1848"
9/137	Variations brillantes avec introduction & finale pour le piano sur l'air favori de célèbre Balfe "The light of other days" de l'opéra The Maid of Artois, op. 16	Balfe; arr., G.P. Manouvrier of New Orleans	"Mary H. Lowndes"
10/149	Choeur de Norma—Improvisation pour piano, op. 41	Donizetti; arr., Voss	"Mary H. Lowndes"
11/159	Les Huguenots, Fantaisie brillante, op. 66	Meyerbeer; arr., Voss	"Mary H. Lowndes"
12/177	Lucrezia Borgia, Fantaisie brillante, op. 86	Donizetti; arr., Voss	"Mary H. Lowndes"
13/191	Les Huguenots, Fantaisie brillante, op. 66	Meyerbeer; arr., Voss	Same piece as p. 159. "Mary H Lowndes 184[?]"
14/209	Pensées Italiennes—3 Cavatinas variées (No. 2, Anna Bolena), op. 16	Donizetti; arr, Rosellen	"Mary H Lowndes / 184[?]"
15/221	Fantaisie brillante pour le piano sur l.a Muette de Portici, op. 75	Auber; arr., Rosellen	"Mary H Lowndes / 184[?]"
16/241	Fantaisie Lucia di Lammermoor, op. 80	Donizetti; arr., Rosellen	
17/261	Decameron des jeunes pianistes. Collection progressive de Fantaisies, Variations, etc. (No. 9 "Souvenir d'Otello et de Bianca et Faliero"), op. 55	Rosellen; arr.	
18/269	Fantaisie brillane sur la rose de Péronne	Adam; arr., Rosellen	"Mary H. Lowndes"
19/283	Variations on a favorite cavatina in Donizetti's Opera Parisina, op. 18	Donizetti; arr., Rosellen	"Mary H. Lowndes"
20/293	Les charmes de Naples—3 Fantaisies pour le piano sur les opéras de Donizetti, op. 25 (No. 2 Roberto Devereux)	Donizetti; arr., Rosellen	
21/307	Fantaisie et variations sur l'opèra Il templario, op. 65	Isouard; arr., Rosellen	"Mary H. Lowndes" [Paris: Schlesinger]
22/323	Fantaisies, Variations, & Rondeaux pour le Piano Forte sur des motids favoris de l'opéra La sonnambula, op. 53/no. 2	Bellini; arr., Beyer	"Mary H. Lowndes / 1848"
23/339	Fantaisies, Variations, & Rondeaux pour le Piano Forte sur des motids favoris de l'opéra La sonnambula, op. 53/no. 3	Bellini; arr., F. Beyer	"Mary H. Lowndes / 1848"
/24355	Bouquet de Mélodies – Ernani de Verdi, op. 42/no. 9	Verdi; arr, Beyer	"Mary H. Lowndes"

1. Publication details and other information appear as an Appendix in CBA. The abbreviated table here illustrates the number of opera settings and the length of the arrangements.

Figure 4.4. Mary Lowndes's markings on Thalberg's "Fantaisie pour le piano sur des thèmes de l'opéra Moise de G. Rossini." Courtesy of The Charleston Museum, Charleston, South Carolina.

who played the same piece in Charleston in 1853.[27] Mary was not a professional musician, but an accomplished amateur.

Nellie Pugh belonged to the same aristocratic-planter echelon, but in rural eastern North Carolina at Liberty Hall, near Windsor. Everything about Nellie's binder's volume contrasts Mary's. She did not travel abroad, and thus her music resembles that of most other women who could afford a decently modern collection. Nothing singles it out as elite. Most of the volume consists of dance music for the piano, and waltzes by Francis H. Brown feature prominently. His works here date between 1842 and 1845, suggesting a narrow window of when they were purchased.[28] Musical oddities that would have appealed to a young teenager include the "Celebrated One Finger'd Study, Waltz," with several measures of right-hand glissandos performed by a single finger, and "3 Waltzes" that imitate a musical snuff box. It is possible to read this binder's volume as a testament to the widespread circulation of the latest music, including the growing popularity of the waltz, in remote areas.

Nellie's social status equaled that of Mary Randolph and Martha Dickinson, with whom her music bears more similarities. Even compared to these, however, her repertory was narrow. The first seventeen pieces in her binder's volume consist of songs in English, and the remaining twenty-eight piano solos are dances. She had no Italian or French opera, no songs by Schubert or even Abt. All of her music derives from English and American composers, and even the featured singers are native English speakers. Nellie's binder's volume illustrates the significance of place in this study: her location in an area far-removed from cities or towns with music sellers did not position her to acquire the latest opera-based literature. Her collection of waltzes would have suited the needs of herself and her acquaintances to dance at home.

Conclusion

The evidence of southern binder's volumes reveals seemingly contradictory information. Mary Lowndes and Nellie Pugh demonstrate that not all wealthy women owned the same music, and several others discussed in this chapter further confirm this conclusion. Mary Walker, the daughter of a Methodist minister, and Anna Johnson, the daughter of a Black barber and a formerly enslaved woman, both played technically challenging versions of familiar opera melodies. Kate Berry, whose family had a much higher disposable income, kept her music to simpler songs and dances, as did Nellie Pugh. Many women owned some different types of music. For example, at the South Carolina Female Collegiate Institute at Barhamville (where Bessie Allston also was a student), both Nannie McMorris and Sallie Doby include popular dances, excerpts from operas, and songs in their binder's volumes.

It is not merely financial worth that constituted the boundaries between operatic arias in original versions and watered-down arrangements of them, or Beyer's simpler transcriptions versus those in his op. 42. Presumably, as the daughter of a wealthy and prominent Tennessee politician, Amelia Haynsworth Gayle (1826–1913) could have owned any music she wanted, but nothing in her collection stands out as unusual. She lived some time in Washington, DC, where shops offered music from the latest publishers, and her family moved in a social circle that would have expected knowledge of the latest music. Amelia's music evinces an engagement with popular songs such as several from John Hewitt's *Songs of the Soiree* (1836), but it does not reflect an interest in European opera. Whether this was a personal preference or something else is unknown, but it illustrates the individual variation that exists even among a limited slice of the population, in this case wealthy planters' daughters.

Many southern women sang the operatic melodies of both bel canto and grand opera favorites. They walked a fine line between displaying their talent and sounding (and looking) too professional. Writing in 1860, at the height of the opera craze, Florence Hartley devoted a page and a half to repertory and the appropriate places to perform it. Significantly, she assures the reader that she does not recommend "poor music, or feeble, ephemeral compositions." This statement recalls descriptions of a repertory that has frequently been ignored on the basis that it is ephemera, but what she meant by "ephemera" and what today is classi-fied under that term—precisely all antebellum women's music—differs enough to warrant a reexamination of how musicologists define and value music.

Instead of "feeble" music, Hartley recommends balladlike pieces, which include compositions from "Home! Sweet Home!" to "When the Swallows Homeward Fly." She further observes that "there are many, in Italian, of great beauty, which, though they would not be selected for a concert room, or for brilliant display, are adapted for ladies."[29] Mozart's "O dolce concento/Away with Melancholy" fits this directive. This, indeed, is what many young women performed: simplified, translated, transposed versions of popular operatic arias. Others attempted more difficult music, but these tend to overwhelmingly belong to wealthier families.

Music teachers maintained the responsibility of preparing the young ladies, making sure they had fitting literature (which implies they were aware of etiquette rules such as Hartley's) and training their students to behave appropriately while performing. But they also capitalized on the need to be able to sing different repertories. When a Mrs. Murray visited Richmond, she advertised that, as a pupil of Professors Cooke and Walsh in London, she could assure the ladies who honored her with their patronage that they "will soon estimate the advantages of her style, either in the simple ballad or in the beautiful cantatas of Auber, Bellini, Donizetti."[30] Much lies between simple ballads and the arias of bel canto com-posers, and southern women seemingly embraced most of it. That none of the published music presumably went beyond the bounds of gentility suggests that musically gifted young women were given a wide berth.

Hartley's admonition does not mean that elite women, such as Mary Lowndes or Marianne Porcher Smith Alston overstepped the boundaries of good taste. Indeed, she was aware of the popularity of opera arias and duets, but also the dangers of performing it badly, merely because one wished to impress: "It is true that, to a person who loves music, the performance of one of the incomparable songs of Bellini, Rosini [sic], Flotow, or Mozart, is an actual delight—but, when attempted by a young amateur, it should be, like many other delights, confined to the private circle, and not visited upon society in general."[31] It was fine to prac-tice and be knowledgeable of the operatic repertory, but most could not sing it properly and should therefore avoid it in performance.

Advanced music could be left to those who had the money and leisure to pur-sue it, such as elite Charlestonians. They set the standards, moving in exalted social circles where European music and highly advanced skills formed part of their expected cultivation. Mary and her circle experienced these refinements firsthand. She accompanied the Aiken family on their journey overseas in 1848. They represent one segment of the uppermost class, and their music affirms their position: many of these families traveled to Europe, studied with influential musicians in Charleston, bought imported music when in the United States, had ample leisure time to practice, and played on fine instruments. They hardly fit the textbook model of middle-class white women in the parlor, yet they pursued the same general goals (musical accomplishment) and performed in the same basic place (the parlor) as did many women across the region.

A comparison of the contents provided in this chapter demonstrates the vast differences place can make in repertory choices, even among women of the same class. Mary's collection covers many of the composers that southern women studied after 1850, from Balfe to Verdi, and it evinces the popularity of Meyerbeer. Most studies of antebellum music in the United States acknowledged the appearance of bel canto opera, but few acknowledged French grand opera outside of New Orleans. Charlestonians' attraction to this style did not stem from New Orleans but rather firsthand experiences in Paris; *Le prophète* is the only opera Harriet Lowndes [Aiken] mentions in her 1857–58 travel diary.[32] Coleman makes clear that not knowing opera and not attending it cut one out of New Orleans society. Here, too, opera was used as a marker of distinction. And even though Mobile lacked the opportunities of New Orleans or Charleston, Octavia Le Vert sought them in London, Paris, and other performance venues in Europe.

Naturally, many southern women were not able to afford the experiences of Octavia Le Vert. Nonetheless, that women of lesser means across such a large region—one lacking a substantial rail system or even many decent roads—knew this repertory instructs us to broaden considerably our perspective as to what music American women played and sang in the 1850s. Granted, widely varying versions of operas were available in cities from Macon to Pensacola, and the costs were not so prohibitive that middle-class southerners could not attend. But one had to be in the right place at the right time, and given that many women were stranded on plantations scattered far and wide, or small farms frequently demanding their attention, or shop work to be done, it is unlikely that as many people who owned operatic music got to hear them performed professionally. Nonetheless, even those who couldn't "do" opera in public could use it in private to impress their peers or those above them in the social order. These women recognized its cultural cachet and spent hours perfecting its performance. Hartley acknowledged when she mentioned Bellini and Flotow: she wrote as if everyone who has need of her book knew this repertory. Her readers—the gentlefolk—understood its status and made it a point to stay up to date.

PART 3

Scientific Music and Professional Musicians

5

"Distinguished success . . . in teaching Music as a science"

Genteel Women Scientists

Standing at once outside and inside the performance of gentility through music is the training necessary to be able to render a composition naturally, unaffectedly, effortlessly. The process constituted a series of paradoxes that were continually suppressed by the development of a swirling spiral of etiquette rules. The education needed to accomplish this feat took years if one were to reach the highest levels, but such an aspiration was not required of, nor desired by, most: too much success and one risked being labeled a professional performer.[1] Nevertheless, southerners valued an academic stamp on musical training. Music teachers supplied this by offering their courses as a study in science.

One paradox lies in the authority that musical performance granted young women, usually the people with the least amount of authority in a given space. We might read music as a science being a type of agency because it could bestow a degree of control—of the room, of the listener's attention—for as long as the performer wished. This fact made it all the more necessary for etiquette writers to warn against overly-long compositions. Music as science also lends weight to girls' music practice. They must spend time perfecting the art much as any academician needed to master a subject.

Another social conundrum surrounded the teacher-pupil relationship. Genteel self-presentation through music required being taught by those in a culturally subordinate position. School teachers could only teach what they knew, and the limits of their understanding of gentility potentially circumscribed that of their students. This potentiality instilled the need for principals to ensure the quality of their staff, and for teachers themselves to remain above reproach. Women who taught music as a science could be held up as model. Presumably erudite and talented, they maintained their femininity. Had they not, they could not have been trusted to mold genteel young ladies. Many were also leaders of their own institutions or at least departments. Frequently, the women who taught in larger cities also had careers as professional performers. Their doing so initiated new concerns among elites about mixing with lower-class women who put themselves before the public gaze for remuneration. How these women negotiated the delicate balance between public gaze differed across the South, and the problem only began to dissipate with the onset of war.

Until now, southern women teachers have not been recognized, yet they arguably had a significant and commanding impact on music in the United States—their legacy as teachers, patrons, sponsors, performers shaped music in the latter half of the century, when many institutions were created (often under the auspices of such women). Because of their role in fashioning young women as well as their neglect by modern scholars, this chapter on working women musicians consists of three sections (instead of two). The first defines scientific music, examines how schools approached teaching music as science, and what the public thought about music, science, and gentility in combination. It focuses largely on Sarah Smith, a remarkable southern woman whose story reveals the intrinsic possibilities in research such as this. Section 2 closely examines specific people who taught in southern schools, from exotic foreigners to local familiars. The final section interrogates the circumstances surrounding the women who stretched the ideals of gentility, who took on more masculine roles, and how they fared in the public gaze.

Scientific Music

When the New York soprano Emma G. Bostwick toured the South in 1853, she chose a repertory that reflected the dual popularity of opera (Meyerbeer's "Robert, toi que j'aime") and more traditional songs ("Home! Sweet Home!"). The announcement of one concert in Nashville prompted a newspaper editorial that began with the question: which is better, to sing with art or with passion? The author veered in another direction, however, and concluded that "music is a science and no one who attempts to criticize it scientifically can succeed unless he understands it as such."[2] Art and passion added to the experience, but one first must comprehend music detached from these nebulous aspects; one must grasp the fundamental framework of the composition.

Nineteenth-century southerners understood "scientific" music in several ways. One was reading music from notation. In 1843, Ellen Lewis wrote to her sister Mary that "I play very much by ear as you know, but Mr. B[ode] has found it out and has begun to make me learn the Overture of Mr. Colhoun's book. Tell him that I play some of the hardest of 11 pages."[3] Prior to this, she had been playing by ear, perhaps learning popular pieces that her acquaintances knew. By the 1840s, this was unacceptable as a marker of gentility, and school catalogs justified music in the curriculum by emphasizing it as a science, which signifies intellectual pursuit.[4] Private institutions coveted the prestige of academic rigor, and describing music as a science made it sound less frivolous than some naysayers argued.[5] Parents wanted assurance that their daughters were truly taught—a nod to the sincerity inherent in gentility—and not mimicking someone else's performance or playing by rote. Another interpretation of scientific music was music of a certain pedigree, often performed in public concert halls by traveling European professionals. Either definition elevated a young woman's training, and therefore her refinement, above those who might learn to play by ear after hearing someone in church or at home.

More problematic, however, is the potential conflict between science and gentility: if music were to be a science, then music teachers were scientists as well as artists. Was it more agreeable to be a scientist than an artist? How qualified were these instructors to work with "ladies in the making,"[6] specifically to instruct them in the behaviors of gentility? What did they teach? What role did scientific repertory really play in gentility and in class definition? The fact that girls' schools boasted that their teachers taught music as a science indicates that the proper education of a young gentlewoman necessitated scientific music. Moreover, it argues that women of a certain class performed a scientific repertory. Which class and how scientific depended on numerous factors, but paying for an education constituted the first stipulation for this status. Scientific music and gentility went hand in glove.

Southerners' conception of "scientific music" and its place in private lessons or institutional curricula designed for gentlewomen fluctuated according to several factors, such as the social makeup of various institutions, the rigor of instruction (including theory, composition, and repertory), and particular details on the lives and careers of influential schools and teachers.[7] Music as science also constituted a way to make women's mastery of the art permissible. "Mastery" signifies a masculine level of achievement that women were not to surpass or even approach. The tension between science and accomplishment, between intellectual pursuit and gentility, grew throughout the antebellum period. By the 1850s, however, mastery of technically challenging compositions helped establish class distinctions. During the 1860s, society came to accept more physicality in music performance, erasing such lines between classes.

Scientific Repertory

Both men and women could teach music as a science. In 1850 the *Planter's Banner* described John Thuer as "Professor of Vocal and Instrumental Music, and lecturer on Elementary Principles and Science of the same" at the Thibodaux Female Institute (west of New Orleans).[8] Not only did Thuer teach how to play and sing music, but he also instructed a more academic understanding of it. Even private teachers, such as William Pratt in Alexandria (Virginia), advertised that "His system of instruction communicates, in an easy and familiar manner, the rudiments of the science as well as the more abstruse parts of the theory of Music, which tends to enlarge the mind, cultivate the taste, and facilitate the progress of his scholars."[9] Here the notice combines intellectual rigor with refined taste, the qualities inherent in ladylike behavior.

A concert review from 1843 exhibits the results of young women being taught music as a science by a proficient tutor.[10] It is all the more meaningful because the school was not located in a major cultural center but in Holly Springs, a small town in northwest Mississippi. The correspondent, "An Amateur," claims to have been surprised at the difficulty of the compositions chosen at the Holly Springs Female Institute's Examination Concert. It contrasted "those usually selected for such occasions . . . easy, simple, melodies, waltzes and marches, which . . . are not to be considered as a criterion of advancement in music as a science." The two music teachers, Mr. Morse and Miss Covington, had only arrived in Holly Springs that year, so the townspeople must have felt their impact immediately.

The writer credits the male teacher, Mr. Morse, with "musical taste . . . well matured and in accordance with the spirit of improvement which the great modern masters are making in musical compositions." (Miss Covington, the other music instructor, receives no accolades.) Luckily, Amateur provides the names of several of the selections, categorizing "scientific" music as understood in this place, at this time, by this social group. It is not the music that authors today label as the progressive music of the period (Schumann or Chopin), but rather composers whose works had sounded throughout the South since the 1820s. The "fine" and "difficult" pieces performed in Holly Springs in 1843 included opera overtures (from Boieldieu's *The Caliph of Bagdad* [1800], Rossini's *Il Tancredi* [1813], and Bishop's *Guy Mannering* [1816]). The students performed these "well and in good time" in spite of technically challenging fast passages that surprised the author in the degree of proficiency required of the young women performing them. Other scientific choices were Weber's embellished "last waltz," played "very much in the spirit and style of its great author, with pathos and eloquence": a "bold and brilliant" waltz by Walsh ("adapted to the fine bass of the grand pianno [sic], performed with much effect"); the widely disseminated variations set on Mozart's "O dolce concento," and difficult variations on "Aileen Aroon."[11] These and other scientific works demonstrated "a very considerable advancement in music." Amateur contrasts the scientific music heard in Holly Springs with others on the program, such as Herz's cotillions (possibly *Les coquettes*, op. 49). The dances did not qualify as scientific music.

The singers fared worse than the pianists, and Amateur blamed this unhappy effect on the expansive performance space. One or two singers "filled the room very well," but the rest, all the while singing "with taste," did not. The grand piano received special mention for its effective bass, but the mere mention of the instrument signified wealth and refinement, as did the "highly respectable" audience in attendance. Science and gentility had both been achieved.

Foreign-language opera belonged to a learned style and its appearance on early school programs contributed to their academic reputations. As its influence spread during the 1830s and 1840s, so too did its cachet. A year before the Holly Springs concert, one institution in Oxford (Mississippi) included the same type of scientific music. Here Miss Murphy (from Philadelphia) had her students perform (again) Boieldieu's Overture to *The Caliph of Bagdad*, Rossini's "Non più mesta" (from *La cenerentola*, possibly arranged as a rondo) and "Di tanti palpiti" (one of his most popular works in the United States), "The Huntsman's Chorus" (from *Der Freischütz*), and several other pieces with operatic associations, in addition to many ballads and songs such as "Long, Long Ago."[12] These programs depended on the operatic repertory as verification of scientific music, supplemented by challenging piano variations on popular tunes. The particular choices of compositions did not venture into new repertory, relying on the same melodies (often from the operas of Boieldieu, Rossini, Auber, and others) heard throughout the South.

The Columbia Female Institute, The Athenaeum, and Sarah Smith

Almost inevitably the schools that advertised scientific music stopped short of precisely defining scientific music. A noteworthy exception exists in the 1838 catalog of the Columbia Female Institute (Tennessee), which contains one of the most complete descriptions of how music would be taught and proves especially instructive in examining music's place in the curriculum as well as its status as a genteel virtue. Even though it acknowledges a commonly held belief that women abandoned their music once they left school, the author blamed this situation on the fact that they have been taught only "the manual execution of a few particular pieces, without acquiring the ability to read correctly, expressively, and with pleasure to herself, whatever is placed before her." This statement contrasts playing by rote with fluency in reading music and musicality, an interpretation underscored by another that assigns Sarah Ann Davis Smith (1811–72) the duty for "The Grammar of Music, the fundamental principles of the science, its technical terms, &c." Maintaining the banner of academia, students will have constant access to "the best books of reference" in scientific music. Assuring parents of its sincerity in this endeavor, the catalog advertises that music will be taught as both a science—"the principles of which require thorough study for their comprehension"—and as an art—"whose execution demands long continued, patient practice for its mastery." As proof of its ability to achieve scientific instruction in music, the catalog praises Smith's reputation for "distinguished success . . . in teaching Music as a science."[13] Given the expense of music, instrument upkeep, and the amply furnished, sizeable music room at her next school (the Athenaeum), the added income from long years of study served the Smiths well.

Music instruction and the philosophy behind it at the Columbia Female Institute are worth consideration on several accounts. Sarah Smith moved to Tennessee in 1837 to teach at the Institute, and she evidently had the running of the department. No other teacher is mentioned by name in the accounts of the curriculum, and this acknowledgment conveys the opinion that her contribution to the school's program outweighed that of her colleagues. No southern catalogs are more explicit about music as a science than this one. Of further note are the "thousands" of music titles she owned to supplement her teaching.

Sarah Smith fashioned a legacy in Columbia that lasted into the twentieth century and one that allowed her children to succeed her as teachers and musicians.[14] The success of her efforts varied. Former Athenaeum students Ellen Clifford Cabell and Henrietta Davis Smith recalled of Ellen O. Smith (no established relation to Sarah) that "her execution on the piano and the harp was highly pleasing, but yet could make no pretension of artistic accuracy on skill. Her knowledge of the elementary principles of music was accurate as far as it went, and sufficiently extensive to enable her to take pleasure in reading music by herself in the same manner as she could read books."[15] Ellen Smith acquired the ability to read music and to please others with it, and she could occupy her time by playing for herself. This level of accomplishment sufficed, even if her schoolmates in hindsight tinged their recollection with criticism.

Some institutions, such as the Athenaeum or the Burwell School, had rooms or outbuildings dedicated to music lessons. An advertisement for the Athenaeum pictures the music room, replete with grand piano, organ, and plenty of seats.[16] Most proprietors did not invest as much in their music facilities, though, and Smith's emphasis on this one, as well as using it in the advertisement for the school, testifies to its primacy at the Athenaeum. Similarly, the April 1861 inventory of the Columbia Female Institute (which Smith vacated in 1852) owned thirteen pianos, two harps, and three guitars, and a library of almost a thousand volumes. This amply furnished space functioned as a laboratory for the scientific study of music deemed necessary for refinement.

In the early days of the Institute, the entire student body participated in an "hourly practice of Vocal Music" (either hymn singing or "some cheerful song") to "exert a most salutary influence upon the pupils"; this encouraged a "happy frame of mind" and supposedly protected them from respiratory problems.[17] Voice class, in which all students participated as part of their physical exercise and as a way to bring the students into literal harmony with the school's codes of behavior, included solfege, as it did in other southern schools (such as the St. Louis Institute in New Orleans, under Eugenie Lavillebeuvre).[18] Margaret McLean Dale, a graduate of the class of 1861, had fond memories of her days there, especially when Carlo Patti (the brother of Adelina) joined the music class under the direction of Professor Hoffman.[19] Margaret Ulmer remembered when she moved to singing second and sat on the front bench, which could suggest gained proficiency or her desire to be seen.[20]

The building housed a long parlor for "recreations," including dancing. The health benefits of music are echoed by an anonymous diarist teaching in a girls' school (perhaps in Louisiana) in the mid-1830s where dance remained in the curriculum not only for its social importance but its advantages "physically speaking."[21] A similar justification kept dancing as part of regular exercise at the Burwell School.[22]

A good deal of music survives at the Athenaeum that probably belonged to the Smiths. Much of it dates from the years their son, Frank, directed the music program, but earlier choral books could have been used in the daily singing of hymns or in class voice.[23] One of these is *The School Singer, or The Young Choir's Companion*, by William Bradbury and Charles Walton Sanders (1845). Complete with a somewhat altered Guidonian hand for sight-singing, this book teaches rudimentary music and progresses to (not surprisingly) some of Bradbury's extended pieces. Among its contents are sacred and secular pieces, all of which would suit the "hourly practice of Vocal Music" for a "happy" mood. This psychological inducement echoes Halttunen's statement that sentimentalists linked good behavior to the "outpourings of right feelings from a right heart." People did not learn correct behavior by merely observing rules or ceremony but by following a sincere and true feeling.[24] Singing the right pieces together on a daily basis helped teach young women this aspect of gentility. It was not based on social status but natural sentiment, learned from respected sources. The words suited the exercise, and singing in harmony (both musical and spiritual) complemented it. Another book in the collection that might have been used at the Columbia Female Institute is John Cole's *Episcopalian Harmony* (Baltimore, 1811). Such a collection was eminently suitable for a school headed by the Episcopalian bishop of Tennessee (James Hervey Otey).[25]

Beyond voice class and the applied lessons in which women learned voice, piano, harp, or guitar, some institutions offered more advanced music studies.[26] Thorough bass appears in the curricula of several institutions.[27] Miss H. E. Hammarskold, a Swedish music teacher in Charlotte, included it among her advertised specialties in 1860.[28] Printed music from this period does not typically require being able to create an accompaniment from figures, although Henrietta Aiken's

music collection includes several manuscript vocal exercises that only have figures and a bass line.[29] Another practical use of this ability could have been the
performance of earlier printed songs with only the vocal and bass parts, handed
down through generations.

Moreover, the study of thorough bass implies instruction in basic harmonic
principles. The 1838 catalog of the Columbia Female Institute proclaims that
"much attention will be devoted to the study of its theory and general principles;
to the scales, intervals, positions and chords." These lessons portrayed music in
a more academic (scientific) light. Indeed, a front-page advertisement in the
Guardian (Columbia) almost ten years later spells out the music curriculum and
links the two together. Two extra courses follow the usual expenditures for music
lessons: Tuition in the Elements of Music, Preparatory to Taking Lessons on an
Instrument,—in classes $10.00; and Tuition in Thorough Bass and the Theory of
Harmony, in Classes, for advanced pupils only $10.00.[30]

The study of theory places music on an academic par with other subjects, such as
chemistry, and brings it in line with the sciences. Remarkably, in Columbia, "more
advanced young ladies will be instructed in . . . Musical Composition." Nineteenth-
century sources rarely name composition as a component of women's education,
although a few references suggest that some practiced it. Carrie Holt taught her
students how to arrange melodies for their own use and mentions having composed some songs herself.[31] An anonymous diarist from Pittsburgh living in Selma
(AL) wrote that "I think I was younger than the little girl who composed the verses
copied by Mrs. B. when I composed the song beginning with 'the lives.'"[32] Ann Sloman in Charleston taught her pupils to compose, too. Over a hundred southern
women published compositions before the Civil War, which suggests that some at
least studied composition."[33]

Sarah Smith and the Public Gaze

Teaching music in female institutes constituted a popular employment option for
antebellum women, but their positions often hung precariously on incidents beyond their control. It was inextricably tied to their own gentility. Sarah Smith felt
her reputation assaulted during a struggle in which she had no part when her husband, Franklin Gillette Smith, was charged with indiscretion with a student. He
promptly left the school in 1852, but townspeople rallied in his defense. As his wife,
Sarah was touched by the scandal, and her entry into the public debate provides
tangible evidence of the delicate balance between gentility and public display. In
her support, the *Herald* promised to "do all that is possible to insure the continued
prosperity of the Institute, or any other school over which you or she may preside."
Such high praise for a woman shows Sarah Smith a capable administrator, keen
businesswoman, and accomplished musician.

But the *Herald* went too far. They included her full name, breaking a cardinal rule of southern etiquette. A lady's first name was not to be published—it was against proper deference to her position as a lady. Smith took matters into her own hands and did the unthinkable: she wrote her own letter "To The Public." She asked the public to excuse her from writing a defense of her husband and continued "I trust that the same generous public will allow me to discharge the humiliating duty of defending myself, and that I may be permitted solemnly and publicly to protest against the use of my name in the newspapers of the day." She blamed the *Herald* editors for having "selected an arena where no lady wishes to appear, and where the blows of her champion, however well intended, can only end in her destruction. . . . I have never sought notoriety, nor can I conceive why the authors of that publication should present my name and conduct to the public gaze." She further noted that "She has, at least, the feelings of a woman and the pride of a mother, and shrinks from the thought that her daughter shall see that mother's name and conduct so ungenerously canvassed in the public papers."[34] Genteel white women shunned such attention, in part because it placed them on par with more "publicly accessible" women who could never be genteel.[35] An image (see Figure 5.1) published in *Graham's* in the same year as Smith's public embarrassment makes plain the discomfort a refined woman felt under the public gaze.

Figure 5.1. Thompson Westcott, "The Physiology of Dandyism," *Graham's*, 1852.

Such outright public action goes against very specific social customs that forbade women from overt public involvement. Sarah Smith's concern that she not be in "the public gaze" is a direct confirmation that women's names were not to be printed. I have made this point elsewhere by demonstrating the rarity with which southern women took full (identifiable) ownership of musical works they published prior to the Civil War. Granted, local people may have been able to identify those who simply published under the name "A Lady" (and similarly those who may have sung in semi-public venues), but the problem was not composing, it was publishing the name. A printed name exposed a woman to those who had not had her formal acquaintance, breaking the formalities symbolized most of all in the intricate calling-card culture of the period.[36]

In May, the *Guardian* announced the opening of a new school in Columbia: The Athenaeum, under the direction of "F. G. Smith and Mrs. Sarah Ann Smith." Sarah Smith is not listed as assistant or any other secondary title. Her considerable experience and reputation allowed her to establish a new institute in the same small town for the same prices—in direct competition with the Columbia Female Institute. A multibuilding campus, the new school was "even more ambitious than the massive, single building arrangement of the Female Institute or the Methodist college [also in Columbia]."[37]

Women like Smith elevated the music teacher from a junior member of faculty to stalwart member of the local community. This process did not reach fruition until after the war, but their efforts to do more than teach simple songs to southern girls established them as both well-regarded musicians and women of character—of gentility. Those who succeeded them reaped the benefits. One of Smith's daughters, Fanny Polk Smith [Hosea] (1840–1923), became a professional musician in Cincinnati. By 1880, Fanny Hosea was back teaching music at the Athenaeum. She later returned to Cincinnati and, in 1918, published *A Sonnet History of Music with Analytical Notes*, possibly the first published work by a woman that deals solely with music history. Her thorough training in music began at home with her mother. Hosea wrote about Guillaume de Machaut, troubadours, and many later composers, as well as a history of opera to Gluck.[38] For her, and many others, the science of music extended well beyond being able to sing "Home! Sweet Home!" in the parlor. It laid the foundation for monumental changes in self-perception and public approval.

Performance

In their schools, students learned not only the fundamentals of reading music but also how to perform according to the guidelines prescribed by the social class to which they corresponded or aspired. Courses and individual lessons worked together to enable young women to be competent technicians, to learn the correct repertory. One objective of being taught scientifically was proficiency in sight-reading. Performing a composition upon first sight, one of the highest achievements possible for these pupils, guaranteed a scientific education, which in turn conferred genteel status on the performer. Florence Hartley recommended against performing music that one had not previously studied.[39] Nonetheless, in diaries several southern women mention playing and singing pieces without having previously practiced them, verifying that they had been trained scientifically. Margaret Ulmer proudly records her playing of "Do They Miss Me at Home" from sight while at the Tuskegee Female Academy in 1858.[40] A simple strophic song (Margaret calls it "very easy") in compound meter, she may have sung and played it at the same time, a typical performance practice of the period.[41] Sight-reading offered another way to demonstrate superiority because playing difficult compositions came across as undignified, overly physical, and therefore ungenteel.[42]

In addition to the science of music as represented by notes on a page, institutions provided opportunities for young women to learn how to perform in the parlor. Socialization in the parlor could follow one of several forms, from learning the proper repertory to play or sing when calling on friends to more ambitious pieces at musical soirées with organized programs. Lavillebeuvre directed "Monthly Soirées," also called "Monthly examinations," at the prestigious St. Louis Institute in New Orleans in order to "rouse the public emulation, and ascertain their progress." By 1860, she taught night classes at the institute for those unable to attend during the day.[43]

In 1848 students at the Elizabeth Female Academy in Washington (Mississippi) gave their "Musical soirée," including a repertory more in line with what the writer from the *Holly Springs Gazette* expected, featuring "The Bluebells of Scotland," "Egyptian Rondo," an "Air Russo," and the "Swiss Boy."[44] In 1855 the *Musical World* reported that on 4 April, "young ladies" at the Judson Female Institute gave their third musical soirée of that session. Professor Julius Erickson selected thirty-two compositions, through which the students "displayed skill and good taste." Erickson, Professor Blanden, and five "lady teachers" taught music at Judson in this year, accommodating the 150 pupils (of a total 247) taking music lessons.[45] They had introduced "Music of a higher and nobler character," which points to scientific music even if it is not explicitly named, although the only composition mentioned is Stephen Glover's duet "Voices of the Night" (performed by E[lizabeth] Hunter and [Julia] Z[itella] Cocke). Zitella composed their alma mater, "L'envoi," in 1913.[46] Young ladies, lady teachers, higher and nobler music, and good taste are all indicators of gentility; the wording of this report assures its readers that the Judson Female Institute could be relied upon to produce genteel women, and music was one of its tools.

Extant programs from graduation exercises and other school productions rarely feature technically difficult music, yet other data proves that some of the same young women studied compositions that required expertise well beyond those programed in their semi-public performances at school. Bessie Allston's binder's volume includes robust, demanding piano music that was not appropriate for most performance situations—Hartley advises that "it is a great mistake to suppose that the best music is the most difficult of execution. The very reverse, generally speaking, is the case." Difficult music may be performed at musical soirées (occasionally called musicales). According to Hartley, these were occasions for performing piano pieces with "page after page of black, closely printed notes" to be "executed in the most finished style." Importantly, however, "they are not suited to general society." Such compositions are both appropriate and pleasurable for the musical soirée but not a mixed party.[47]

Musical events frequently warranted notice in local newspapers. At a Christmas event in 1855, students at the Orangeburg Female Seminary (South Carolina) performed overtures and marches, and sang songs (sentimental, pathetic, and humorous). A writer in the *Charleston Mercury* complimented their efforts in this "village."[48] A published account of a concert at the Kenansville Female Seminary, in the *Wilmington Daily Journal* of March 4, 1858, further contextualizes young women and the repertory in the female seminary:

> We had the pleasure of being present last night at a Concert given by the young ladies of the Female Seminary of this place. We say pleasure, because in fact it did afford us real pleasure to witness the triumphant success of the beautiful (I underscore for bachelors) young ladies of this excellent Institution on the occasion. . . . I will not undertake to discriminate where everything was performed so well, but will say that the performances of The Jenny Lind Polka, Katy Darling, The Twin Sisters, Fannie Gray (by two little girls,) Hard Times, and The Mocking Bird, afforded no peculiar delight on account of the fact, we suppose, that these are favorite airs of ours.
>
> The proficiency exhibited in the Musical Art by the young ladies on this occasion, paid a very high compliment to the [music teacher], the accomplished Mrs. Bailey.[49]
>
> —A.

As with almost every newspaper account of a recital such as the one at the Kenansville Female Seminary, the performers' collective beauty is the first item mentioned. The wording confirms that musical accomplishment was part of the training in which young women made themselves attractive to others, focusing on possible marriage partners. That these commentaries can be found throughout small towns and communities attests to the ubiquity of such training.

The lack of any special effect on the reviewer suggests that the author preferred something more scientific than "Katy Darling," "Hard Times," and "The

Jenny Lind Polka," all popular throughout the region. "Katy Darling" typifies such circulation. By the time of the Kenansville performance, southerners had been exposed to differing arrangements of this melody, and it is impossible to know which was performed here. Many publishers directed their versions to anticipated buyers, often by mentioning touring professionals as in an undated version as "Sung by Master Adams of Kunkel's Nightingale Troupe" (published by Mayo in New Orleans and Benteen in Baltimore). Waters (New York) offered "Katy Darling as sung by Wood's Minstrels," and Lee & Walker (Philadelphia) produced "Katy Darling . . . as sung by Mad: Henrietta Sontag." It belonged to both minstrel troupes and operatic sopranos.[50]

Schools did not always assign repertory; some students had their music sent from home, and thus the qualification for scientific music at school could be ignored. For example, a student at the Burwell School in Hillsborough, Sallie A. Mangum, wrote to her father requesting music on December 21, 1841:[51]

> dear Father I wish you would send me some music, I will write you the names of a few tunes that I want I wish you would send them by the post, and get a few New Tunes, These are the names of them White Sulpher Waltz, Saratogo Waltz, the Cinderilla Waltz, Copenhagen Waltz, the United states reel Mrs Mcleod reel the Russian dance with variations, the United states Marine March, Princess Victoria's March, and the Marseille's hymn, and I want you to send me some more reeles and Waltzes and Marches and a few Quadrilles. I wish you would send me Washingtons garden March, and Von Wibber last waltz.[52]

Sallie's dance music would have been useful at the Burwell School, where dancing in the parlor was a frequent occurrence.[53] The pieces themselves were famous ones, for the most part, and her letter exemplifies the types of music young women played for dancing in Hillsborough, scientific or not.

*   *   *

Female institutions provide ample evidence of the various social statuses and cultural positions that took part in the practice of scientific music as a necessary accomplishment in the performance of gentility. Music teachers tasked with its instruction varied in many ways, such as place of birth (ranging from foreign to local), training (conservatory to nearby church with an instrument), and commitment to education (career musicians or employed only while single). That such divergent paths all engaged in creating genteel women—ladies, for the most part— invites investigation into the backgrounds and circumstances of the teachers.

6

"Of that ilk"

Foreign Music Teachers and Genteel Pupils

Key questions for interpreting music in the United States during the nineteenth-century deal with the teachers rather than the pupils: where did they come from, what were their perceived social circles, and what qualified them to teach such a vast social array of the South's young women? The people involved in teaching the majority of musically literate Americans remain curiously anonymous, as does their preparation and instruction. However, recognition of highly influential pedagogues exposes trends in circulation, changing musical tastes, and demands of proficiency—and thereby yields a more accurate view of music practices. Those who taught in private lessons in a pupil's home theoretically transgressed a social wall because they were not on equal terms but occupied, if temporarily, a space reserved for those with approved standards of gentility.

Foreign teachers posed intriguing paradoxes. Their morals were suspect, but their Old World lineage bestowed prestige. Being able to say that one had studied with an Italian *maestro* or a *cantatrice* trained in France impressed most southerners, as can be shown by numerous descriptions in newspaper advertisements that point to these qualifications. A notice in the *Wilson Ledger* endorses the music teacher at the Richardsons' school as someone who has been "educated in Prussia, and understands music as a science and an art, which, unfortunately, cannot be said of many American teachers."[1] Her German training placed her above native-born teachers, although nothing is said of her actual talent. Sometimes perceived national tendencies for specific instruments or styles drove the attraction, even if the tutor hailed from the United States, as was the case in Natchez where Mrs. Armstrong, who had lived "with the Spaniards" for some time, taught a Spanish-style of guitar.[2]

In his *Musical Memories* (1908), George Putnam Upton observed retrospectively that foreign musicians saw the South as the most profitable region for their livelihoods, finding it "curious" that so many traveled south "as soon as they landed."[3] Why did so many foreign men come to the South to teach music? Perhaps the longer history of "scientific" music in cities such as Boston, New York, and Philadelphia caused many immigrant music teachers to seek their fortunes in the expansive South. The perceived authority of European culture worked to their benefit as many in the United States considered European music, and therefore European musicians, to be the epitome of sophistication. This being the case, studying with a foreigner added a perceived a degree of superiority to the accomplishment and could elevate one's own cultural standing.

The more esteemed schools tended to employ foreign men, often assisted by women with local connections. In New Orleans and a few other places, European women also symbolized a prestigious music education. Such preference can be seen in the hiring of a music instructor for the Raleigh Female Classical Institute in 1853. According to Harriet Person, a lady who was about fifty-years old had presented herself to Mr. Blake (presumably the principal) for a music position, but because she had no letter of introduction, "he sent her back." He soon thereafter hired Mr. Petricillia, "an excellent teacher, I recon you have seen his name in the papers."[4] Her observation attests to the attraction of a foreign name for the music instructor in female academies. Joseph K. Opl, from "Germany," also moved from a professional performer position (he led an orchestra in Richmond in 1841) to music professor to the Columbia Female Institute (Tennessee, in 1849).[5] While there he dedicated "La sensation" a "grande valse," to "Mademoiselle Sallie W[ard] Smith" (the director's twelve-year-old daughter) in 1849.

At the South Carolina Female Collegiate Institute at Barhamville, one of the largest music programs in the antebellum South, Principal Elias Marks depended on the prestige accorded European music instructors and hired mostly foreigners.[6] Several of the faculty also composed and published compositions, the majority of which survive in binder's volumes collected by students at the Institute. Sallie English Doby's collection includes arrangements by Felix Theodore Strawinski, including "When Other Friends Are Round Thee," published in Baltimore in 1846, and melodies from "The Child of the Regiment" (Donizetti) published in Baltimore and New Orleans and inscribed in pencil "To Miss Doby / from her Teacher / F. T. Strawinski." He similarly inscribed pages to another student there, Beaufort Sims.[7]

Private Music Teachers

Private music instruction constituted an alternative to school instruction. For some it was a way of demonstrating that parents could afford the costs of educating their children on a one-to-one basis (although the reality often meant a single person taught several children in the home). Occasionally, parents preferred their daughters to study with a particular musician, even if the young woman was in school somewhere else. Francis Levert desired that his daughter and ward study music privately, not at the Huntsville Female Seminary where they took other classes. He clipped a notice that read: "PROF. OAKES would inform his Patrons that he cannot receive the peoples in the Music Department at the Seminary, that are Pupils in English and French at other institutions." It continued to explain that Annie M. Kellogg (also at the Seminary) could not take English students from other places of study because teachers need to be "in command of students' time." Francis wrote that he hoped an exception could be made because he had a private music teacher for his daughter and Mary M. Withers. Kellogg replied saying this was not a problem since the teacher did not belong to another school, provided that Mary kept up with her schoolwork.[8]

In some cases, the teacher lived in with the family. Few women refer to men living in their homes to teach music, but a German male musician lived with the family of Letitia Burwell in southwestern Virginia and taught her music.[9] If the teacher were a woman, she could take the position of governess and instruct in music and other areas as the family desired. An advertisement in *The Sugar Planter* addressed this class specifically: "To Planters: A Lady of the highest respectability being about to relinquish her arduous duties as Principal of a Seminary, and Organist of a Church, proposes to become 'Preceptress' in some retired family in the country . . . [she can teach English, French, drawing, embroidery, and fancywork]. Also Music, which science she excels, having studied and practiced for twenty years under the direction of eminent foreign masters."[10] This woman carefully chose her words. She pointed directly to planters, called herself a lady and notes her character, and listed her qualifications (including study with foreign instructors). She avoided putting her name in print, further signifying her acquaintance with the refinement ethic of gentility. Notably, she added that she understands music as a science.

Many men taught music privately. In these circumstances, the potential for inappropriate male/female collaboration created risks because the rules of gentility carefully controlled interaction between the sexes. Whereas students sometimes visited the homes or studios of women teachers, male teachers almost always went to the homes of their students.[11] After he moved from Boston to New Orleans in 1842, Frederick Müller reported to Rebecca Valentine that "the teaching is done mostly by male teachers and the teacher is always required to visit the scholars."[12] His assertion that music instruction fell predominantly to men seems dubious considering that women teachers placed numerous advertisements in New Orleans newspapers. On the other hand, his tone suggests that he was unaccustomed to the rigidity of the social construction for male instructor to female student in the South, even though these expectations align with basic rules governing southern women's experiences around men. Seen through the lens of gentility, the South's rules for behavior did not translate into Müller's lived experiences elsewhere.

It comes as no surprise that guardians feared putting their young women into the hands of male musicians. Sarah Lois Wadley's confession that her piano teacher, Edward O. Eaton, "understands his profession, but I am not pleased with him in other respects" suggests an unpolished manner lacking in the coded behavior she associated with gentility. Ideally, as the paid lower-class teacher, he should have been honored to teach the planter's daughter. Eaton's interests, however, lay elsewhere. He soon moved to New Orleans to go to the opera "every night," and left teaching rural students because they repeatedly spread rumors of his intending to marry one or the other. Earlier that year, Sarah and her mother had visited a music teacher, Mrs. Cook, perhaps for the purpose of interviewing Cook as a potential instructor for Sarah.[13] The Wadleys engaged Eaton, rather than Cook, possibly because they preferred a male musician as a sign of refinement. Whatever the reason for hiring Eaton, a few months later Sarah took lessons with the Swedish organist Gustavius A. Gnospelius, who seems to have been unsatisfactory as well.[14] Sarah preferred Gnospelius (even if he missed lessons after an accident while drunk) to Eaton because "he manifests more interest in his employment," confirming that Eaton did not treat her according to the manner she expected.[15]

A common problem was unsuitable relationships or even contact with a student. Music lessons require an instructor to work one-on-one with a pupil, a delicate social situation that could contravene the rule that a woman did not meet with a man unchaperoned unless he was a family member. Presumably wealthy households always had someone available to watch over a young woman's music lesson, but those in reduced circumstances might not have had the luxury of auxiliary people to spend time overseeing an instructor's interaction with a pupil. Even worse, some students married their music teachers, thus realizing parents' worst suspicions.[16] Whether these particular relationships formed under the guarded eye of a chaperone remains unknown.

If male music teachers were problematic, foreign ones were even more so, and most of the men who taught music in the South came from Europe (or claimed to). Just before the war, in Macon parents could choose options such as Oscar Bristol from Prussia or Henrietta Swift from Georgia.[17] Immigrants accounted for forty of Mississippi's listed music teachers in 1860, including F. W. Miller, from Oren (Germany), and Francis Eberhardt Sr. and Jr., both from France. Of the thirty-five music teachers (men and women) in the New Orleans census of 1850, twenty-seven were foreign born, three were Creoles of color, and five were white men born in the United States.[18] These men represented, in different ways, Others. They differed in physiology, dress, language, and outlook from southern white men of Anglo (or in New Orleans, French) descent.

One of the most startling accounts of inappropriate interactions between a male teacher and female student took place in New Orleans in 1860. The *New Orleans Daily Crescent* reported that Thomas J. Martin, a free Black man, had seduced a "lady"—a white woman—in his capacity as her music teacher. Described as a "musician of some talent, a composer, and a proficient on the piano and guitar," Martin's refined demeanor had garnered him "admission into some of the most respectable families" in the city. Moreover, the paper claimed "good information" that he had "ruined other white girls."[19] The following day's news revealed the woman's name, Fanny Thayer, daughter of the actress Mrs. Ann Severs, adding that Martin and Fanny had been intimate for three years and shared a five-month-old child. Other women seduced by Martin included Miss Kate P—, who also bore a child by Martin, and Maria B—, a seamstress renting a room on Bacchus Street. His exploits were known in Virginia, as well. According to the article, "The Coffee-Colored Lothario," Martin had taught in New Orleans for almost twenty years by 1860. He also composed (and published) a relatively popular song, "Had I Never Known Thee," and several other pieces.[20] Whatever the questionable behavior of Martin, his story further documents musical interactions between Blacks and whites in the antebellum South.

Frederick Meerbach

Frederick W. Meerbach's experiences in western Virginia demonstrate the paradox between the dearth of gentility associated with a foreign teacher and the cachet accorded tutelage under a European musician. Born in Germany in 1814, Meerbach arrived in the United States by 1835, when he advertised as a "professor of Music" in Salisbury (North Carolina). By 1839, he had connections with the University of Virginia and in 1841 began offering music lessons in Charlottesville. These biographical facts somehow eluded one of his pupils there, Sara Agnes Rice, who left a colorful account of her lessons with Meerbach in the early 1840s. She claimed he had moved to Charlottesville in 1843 to teach Amélie Rives, whose socially prominent father (William Cabell Rives) had found him "somewhere in France, and promised him a large salary" to move to Charlottesville.[21] That he had been in the South for at least eight years seems to have escaped her notice, or Meerbach himself may have crafted the story that he was newly arrived from France to impress his students, all of whom were young women. (Amélie Rives might have put the story about that her father brought Meerbach to Virginia, enhancing her family's prestige.) The substantial cost of having such a foreign instructor solidified her position above those who simply learned music from their female relatives or perhaps a local woman.

Sara claimed that this "eccentric itinerant music teacher" would sometimes arrive at her home around midnight for her lessons. As the rules for having a chaperone required, her aunt "gladly" dressed to observe the ill-timed lesson. Sara constructed an identity for Meerbach that sparkled with incorrectness, severely criticizing his manner and lifestyle while simultaneously claiming that the Charlottesville coterie of students "prized him above rubies" because he constituted the "one pioneer apostle of classic music in all Virginia." He did not teach the repertory that typified American music in the 1840s, which Sara—incorrectly—described as the "Bonaparte Crossing the Rhine" and "Battle of Prague." (This iconic programmatic composition did live on through the century but hardly with the regularity writers since James Huneker have described.[22]) Rather, Meerbach, she claimed, brought them Beethoven and Liszt. Writing with retrospective surety, she remembered that "He was a brilliant pianist, a great genius; had studied with Liszt, early appreciated Chopin, adored Beethoven."[23] Part of her admiration must have been hindsight, as she was writing in 1909 and knew by then that music by these composers would come to dominate piano recitals in the late-nineteenth-century. That young women in Charlottesville were exposed to such composers in 1843–44 is highly irregular, as no evidence survives to corroborate that the women themselves played this repertory.

Meerbach did not meet with success as a piano teacher for most of the young women in Charlottesville: he lacked the gentility expected of such interactions. Sara's memoirs detail his method of delivery and mock his language and accent. She proclaims her own "keen" feeling for the "charm of music, even when it was beyond my comprehension," a statement that aligns with several qualities necessary for the performance of gentility. First, she has a natural, innate appreciation for music (which has been cultivated but is natural nonetheless). Second, in spite of this instinctive grasp of style, she is not too intellectual—she has only the correct amount of education that allows her to feel the music even if she does not understand it. Sara communicates that she manifests true, sincere feeling, remaining unencumbered by the masculine intellect of a bluestocking. Meerbach's playing allowed her to display her refined sentimentality, weeping as if on cue: "One day, happening to look up from his own playing, he detected tears in my eyes. He was enraged in three languages. 'Himmel! Zis is not bathétique! Zis is *scherzo*! Eh, bien! I blay him *adagio*.' And under shut teeth a sibilant whisper sounded much like '*imbécile*.'" This passage illustrates the ability of the German musician to evoke a deep emotional response from the young woman (which she obliged in return) but also shows his lack of gentility in calling her an imbecile. Even when Sara transported herself by her own playing, so that the "sweetness" of a "delicious passage might be long drawn out," Meerbach insulted her again. He reacted with vigor: "He literally danced! He beat time furiously with both hands. 'Ach! is it *you* yourselluf, know bedder zan ze great maestro,' and sweeping me from the piano stool he rendered the passage properly."[24] Throughout her description of Meerbach, Sara paints a picture of a gruff European man who would never be invited to become part of her own social circle yet bestows upon herself the attributes associated with gentility.

Meerbach's demeanor and behavior drove most of his students away, but Amélie Rives, Jane Page (Rives's cousin), Eliza Meriwether (the daughter of a local physician), and Sara Rice remained his pupils. This meant that the four girls' parents had to pay exorbitant prices for lessons ($8 per lesson at a time when a term's worth of piano lessons at St. Mary's, one of the most renowned institutions in the South, cost only $25).[25] All of the girls reportedly played very well, and Meerbach even desired that Sara travel to Richmond to play Thalberg's music for the pianist himself.[26] Not surprisingly, her aunt refused to let her go. Meerbach did not understand the lines between being an accomplished young lady and being an accomplished pianist. To put herself forward in such a manner would defy precepts of gentility, such as performing in front of an audience, playing difficult music, and essentially pushing herself into the public gaze in a mode that did not suit her social station.

Sara's association with Meerbach ceased soon thereafter, and by 1847 she studied with Powhatan Starke, who ran a singing school in the evenings. Here, young women gathered to learn pieces such as "Oft in the Stilly Night," "The Last Rose of Summer," and "Flow Gently, Sweet Afton"—a far cry from the Continental repertory Meerbach supposedly introduced in the area. These songs correctly displayed the women's gentility whereas Meerbach's selections did not. They had been vetted, circulated widely, and never demanded that the performer expose herself in an unladylike manner. Moreover, Meerbach's wish that Sara expose herself by playing for Thalberg would have placed her socially on par with Herminie Petit, who was destined for a professional career. Such display before the public gaze would be detrimental to her social position.

Gustave Blessner

Elite young women from across the South, such as Ann and C. E. McFaddin of Alabama, made long and tedious trips across several states to attend St. Mary's School for Girls in Raleigh.[27] During the 1840s, Mary North studied with music professor John Hill Hewitt at St. Mary's and, as his "best scolar," was preparing "the Parisienne" for exhibition in July.[28] Unexpectedly, she claimed that she intended to use music "to obtain a livelihood—as so many others in the United States 'have been obliged to do,'" but this seems an unlikely possibility since she belonged to a well-positioned and highly influential planter family with ties in both North and South Carolina. That she even expressed this desire suggests an attitude that differs from most in her social circle. On the other hand, she would be well-situated if she did pursue a career teaching the South's elite daughters, being an orphan in a prestigious family—a visitable connexion.

Rev. Aldert Smedes's "Rules for Behavior" at St. Mary's make plain the importance of knowing how to perform appropriately in the parlor, including music's role. He required attendance at musical soirées on Saturday evenings to help the girls attain "ease of manner in society," a key component of gentility.[29] (Mary Withers reported to her guardian Francis Levert that she partook of its compulsory musical soirées.[30]) At these gatherings, students displayed their musical accomplishments in a parlor setting that prepared them for similar activities when they returned to their homes. The following description of one such evening in April 1844 by William Hooper Haigh, a young lawyer from Fayetteville, details the performance of one such event.[31]

> After making our debut there—bowing here and there to teachers (because etiquette requires it)—then to pupils—the grand promenade was commenced. Soon however Blessner gave his musical signal . . . the first piece was magnificent, capable of thrilling even the most soules. . . . It was a composition of Blessner's dedicated to Misses [Henriette] Borden and [Laura] Washington, who performed it as a duet on the piano—accompanied by Mrs. Blessner & Miss Hundley on the harp & Blessner on the violin. After a number of vocal solos, all sang [the] "Vive le Compagnie" finale.[32]

William emphasizes the need for formality, for following the rules of etiquette required in the performance of gentility. He also displays an appreciation for Gustave Blessner (1808–1888), a violinist formerly in Musard's concerts in Paris."[33] Blessner composed several pieces while at St. Mary's, and the composition mentioned here is his "Montgomery Quick Step," published in Baltimore in 1844. A copy of the duet, dedicated to Henriette Borden and Laura Washington "of St. Mary's Hall, Raleigh," survives in the binder's volume of Lincoln County (North Carolina) native Sarah "Sallie" Virginia Burton.

Former student Ellen Brownlow described Blessner as "the very cleanest and neatest looking man of that 'ilk' I ever saw." Whether that means a foreigner or a musician is not discernable, but he obviously differed from other men in Brownlow's acquaintance. She clearly held expectations of foreigners/musicians (neither clean nor neat), and her remark places them beneath her socially. As Smedes typically employed Europeans in the antebellum period and these teachers worked closely with elite young women, it is reasonable to believe that pupils in the "best" schools expected foreign music professors, but the gender and social roles were somewhat confused. The professors, presumably of a lower social class, held sway over their pupils, reinforcing male/female gender roles, but the young women came from upper-class families, which inverted the power role.[34] On the other hand, being able to maintain respect for their instructors who were often beneath them socially was another sign of gentility.

Women Who Moved to the South

In almost every case of men and women teaching music in the same institution, the male instructor ranked first. Such was initially the case for Miss H. E. Hammarskold. Shortly after she immigrated to the United States in 1861, the *Charlotte Democrat* announced that she had graduated from the Royal Academy of Music at Stockholm and would begin "giving instructions on the Piano, in Singing, and in Thorough Bass" on the 28th of that month.[35] She soon moved to the Charlotte Female Academy when Robert Burwell hired her as a music assistant to Professor R. F. Hunt. A year later, only Hammarskold remained, now "in charge of the music department."[36] Her qualification as a graduate of the Royal Academy distinguished Hammarskold from other women music teachers and put her on par with men who claimed to have studied with the "best" professors, yet she lived the delicate balance between proper gentility and moving oneself higher socially by raising her status as a working woman.

In addition to foreign-born teachers, instructors in southern institutions also hailed from different parts of the United States, and each had her own reasons that led to a career in education. Northern women who traveled south in search of teaching positions have been documented by several scholars.[37] Their backgrounds varied: Emma Curtis came to the Louisburg Female Academy from Emma Willard's Troy Female Seminary, and Eliza Abbot journeyed from New Jersey to instruct pupils in music at the Prattville Female Academy (Alabama).[38]

Advantageous connections assisted some women in locating employment. When churches opened schools for young women, they often drew upon the daughters of local clergymen to fill the ranks of teachers. A logical practice, it also indicates that they had enough music education to be able to teach piano, voice, and sometimes guitar. The daughters or wives of male teachers frequently worked with them, and some instructors' daughters matriculated alongside the daughters of the elite. At the Holly Springs Female Institute, Mr. and Mrs. Kenno first had charge of the music department, succeeded by Rufus Beach and his daughter Eliza in 1839, and Professor John F. Goneke and his daughter (Miss M.) in 1842–43.[39] Emily Dunderale taught piano and guitar at the Richmond Female Institute and the Southern Female Institute at the same time (1855), while her father, John, taught piano and organ at the former.[40]

Carrie Holt: An Upper-class Canadian Moves South

Music teacher Carrie Holt provided an illustrative account of her move to Warrenton (North Carolina), a town with a long history of women's education, in her *Autobiographical Sketch of a Teacher's Life Including A Residence in the Northern and Southern States, California, Cuba and Peru* (1875). Her book describes the training a music teacher might have had before coming to the South in the early 1850s to teach privately or in schools. A native of Quebec, Holt attended school with the elite of the city, including some who eventually married aristocracy. She began music study at age seven in an Ursuline Convent and later studied with Stephen Codman, organist at Holy City Anglican Cathedral in Quebec City.[41] After six years there, she attended a boarding school in Montreal until age fifteen. Her life to this point was one of relative leisure, with extensive training in music.

Holt's self-described "thorny path" as a teacher began when her father died in 1852. That winter she made her "début as a teacher in a large boarding school in Warrenton," which she described as a "small inland country village, perhaps I ought to call it a town, at some distance from the railway," noting that a "'Sleepy Hollow' air . . . seemed to pervade the whole place." Holt was particularly critical of Daniel Turner, the proprietor of the school, whom she described as "a large unwieldy, pompous and illiterate man (the latter circumstance being apparently no disqualification for his election as Member of Congress) and totally unfitted for his post."[42] Her observations call into question Turner's ability to instill gentility in his pupils.

As Assistant-Teacher of Music, Holt taught piano alongside another "Mr. T.," who served as the Professor for piano and harp.[43] She did so on the "sweet-toned piano" in her own room, which she confessed was a luxury that she demanded of every position she took. At the end of the day, Holt and "Miss F." of New York sang and played together in her room: "whence in the deepening twilight, with a dear friend by my side, my wandering chords often evoked 'The light of other days.'"[44] With a confined range of nine notes, simple arpeggiated accompaniment, and strophic setting, Balfe's tuneful "Light of Other Days" was a staple of the repertory at this time.

As to other musical opportunities in Warrenton, Holt remarks somewhat surprisingly that Bochsa and Anna Bishop once performed there (which she attributes to a train possibly running off the tracks). Furthermore, having herself heard Bochsa before she came South, Holt found the Music Professor, Mr. T., the "superior" harpist. This being the case, the opportunity to experience well-performed music in Warrenton must have been at least decent, if the local harpist was on par with one of the most famous performers in the Anglo-American cultural sphere. Even more indicative of Holt's own musical accomplishment, she mentions later in her autobiography that she arranged "some simple airs as duets" for students in Madison (Florida), so she must have been competent in arranging music. She does not reveal whether or not she passed this knowledge to her pupils.[45] Taken together, Holt's experience vivifies music study in remote areas.

Holt left Warrenton in 1853 when Turner attempted to assign her more music students "out of school hours" without paying her more money. Presumably these would have been local girls who wished to study music but were not part of the regular student body. She initially moved to Charleston in 1854 to teach at a school on East Bay St., but when the woman for whom she had chosen to work sold the school, Holt took a position as governess in Georgia. She regretted this decision soon thereafter and moved on to another family in Jacksonville (Florida). Before 1860, Holt returned to Charleston as governess for the family of Archibald H. and Caroline Pinckney Seabrook at Rest Park Plantation near Beaufort. When the Seabrook family left to spend time in the North Carolina mountains, she chose to remain in town and began working for the Henry Lowndes family. This family removed to South Island at the mouth of the Santee River for the summers, but Holt found the conditions unbearable because of extreme heat, mosquitos, and her pupils' lack of interest in practicing.[46] Such moving around in over six years cannot have been easy for Holt, who never settled long in any location. Having been brought up to be a gentlewoman herself, she undoubtedly chafed against the situations in which she made her living.

Rural North Carolina: The Ubiquity of Music Instruction

An examination of the places where young North Carolinian women attended school—their locations, instructors, rules about music, and performances—provides a counterbalance to the standard assumption that only the rich could afford a formal education. When combined with the foregoing discussion of specific educators, it is possible to encapsulate the myriad socioeconomic backgrounds of teachers and students throughout the South. This framework illustrates how integrated music and genteel culture were across social divides. The majority of students in North Carolina did not qualify for elite status, contradicting a commonly held belief that only the wealthy attended boarding school.[47] Moreover, many residents had access to music teachers in small towns and communities, such as Scotland Neck, to which music teacher Eugenia Hanks journeyed from Emma Willard's "famous school in Troy, NY." In nearby Jackson, music also can be found among the curriculum for the female department at the Northampton School in 1835.[48] So, too, did Sparta, Lincolnton, Wadesboro, and Oxford. Such widespread music instruction confirms the significance placed on musical accomplishment in North Carolina before 1840. Wealthy families could not sustain such ventures alone; women of lesser means—the daughters of farmers and laborers—attended boarding schools alongside planters' daughters. Elite parents sent their daughters to the more prestigious schools, such as St. Mary's in Raleigh or Salem Academy, but the rising numbers of schools in rural areas signals a different clientele.

The teachers in these towns, some of which had populations of fewer than three hundred, rarely came from Europe. A few came from the North, such as Hanks or Emma W. Curtis, who traveled from Vermont with her two sisters to teach. She and the other faculty at the Louisburg Female Academy lived under the same roof as the students. In spite of being both a northerner and a working woman, Curtis married a wealthy local farmer, William Person Williams, in 1855.[49] Such action suggests that, in this area at least, lack of wealth or social status was not always a barrier to marriage, but marriage could (as in this case) put an end to a woman's teaching career.

Many institutions dotted North Carolina's landscape, and these served a representative population.[50] In rural areas, an overwhelming majority of young women in schools did not come from elite families but attended the same classes as wealthier local girls.[51] For example, amid "hundreds and hundreds of unused and unpopulated acres," in Robeson County, Presbyterians established Floral College in 1841 for the purpose of educating local young women. That this rustic landscape hosted three such schools testifies to the desirability of instructing young women in the manner seen elsewhere in the South. The students themselves were mostly North Carolinians or young women from bordering counties in South Carolina.[52]

In 1859, Catherine Jane McGreachy commented on her music lessons at Floral College: "Mr Johnson loves to give a girl the chance of splurging in her lessons. . . . I took my first lesson this morning. You may think of me any morning from 7 till 8 as thumping an old ding dong piano."[53] Catherine may have meant that the piano was in poor condition or that she preferred not to practice. Perhaps she had not grasped the importance of such exertion as it pertained to molding her into a lady or its role in instilling the qualities of gentility.

In sparsely populated northeastern North Carolina, the opportunity to attend school impacted the lives of young women from a variety of circumstances. The small town of Murfreesboro was home to the Chowan Baptist Female Institute, as well as an alternative school run by the Methodists. These two schools, one of which reportedly regularly offered instruction to over one hundred students, were located in a town that had a population of 466 in 1860. The young women who attended the Chowan Baptist Female Institute were local and came from families with incomes of significantly less than $10,000.[54] The regular course at the Chowan Baptist Female Institute cost $37 per year but the addition of music increased tuition to $83 in 1853–54. In 1853–54, M. C. Babcock was "pianist and organist," Susan J. Baker and Caroline D. Robinson both taught piano and voice, Mary E. Eldredge taught piano and guitar, and (in the Primary Department) Caroline D. Smith taught piano.[55] Of the thirteen instructors, five taught music. All of the women were unmarried. Babcock, Baker, and Eldredge had been in their present positions the previous year as well, when the other music teachers included Virginia Wood, M. A. Canes, and Emily Cushman. Babcock, too, may have given lessons, for the 1852 report to the Chowan Baptist Association assures its membership that "The Music Department has been placed under the care of a gentlemen teacher [Babcock], assisted by three lady colleagues, and is now furnished with seven new and superior instruments, together with a large and valuable Organ."[56] All of the musicians were pianists, two were also singers, and one played the guitar.

Unlike St. Mary's or the South Carolina Female Collegiate Institute and their foreign teachers of regional reputation, the music instructors at the Chowan Baptist Female Institute had connections closer to home—from households lacking musical backgrounds. A case in point is Susan Jane Baker (1826–1917), a member of the music faculty, born at Baking Mill, Gates County, to John B. Baker and Mary Burges. Susan grew up in a household that listed a $500 tax value in 1850 and which had declined to $300 by 1860. Yet by that year, Susan appears separately in the census as a "Teacher of Music," thirty-two years of age and worth $1800. Susan's musical education remains a mystery, but it clearly worked to her advantage. For her, musical education seems to have been to prepare for a career.[57] It also contributed to a genteel status, above her father's.

Chowan's catalog accorded pride of place to music by its being the first department described, and it informs that "Music is taught both as a science and as an art. . . . Musical Soirées are held at regular intervals, at which all the advanced students of music are required to perform."[58] Musical soirées, at both elite schools like St. Mary's and those serving a more diverse population, served to teach young women how to behave in polite society, in addition to the repertory suitable for parlor performance. Such instruction served a wide swath of society.

The Chowan Female Collegiate Institute had been founded to "establish for holy purposes;—to discipline mind;—instrumentally, to sanctify mind; and then direct its strengthened energies" because "transcendent talent, without moral culture, produces only evil." The catalog emphasizes that the work at Chowan is "extensive" because "Woman is a centre of mighty influences. With her is, chiefly, the governing power. Her influence . . . affects the character of the nation—affects the character of the world. Man moulds governments, but Woman moulds Man." Considering the heavy weight of the faculty toward music study, the subject must have had a meaningful impact on directing women in the molding of the character of her family.[59] Musical accomplishment assisted in defining and displaying the family's rectitude, while simultaneously confirming their genteel status and separating those who attained such accomplishment from those who did not. Christian Bell (1840–82) wrote to her father in April of 1854 that she was taking voice lessons but had not yet started practicing. In spite of a late start date, she wrote confidently on June 20 that her music will indeed please her parents.[60] Thus she intended to discharge the duty of pleasing someone else, a chief expectation of dutiful daughters.

The fact that women who did not come from planter families were taught this behavior underscores the fact that often those of lesser means instructed wealthier young women in how to be genteel. They also taught pupils from their own class. A flyer from the Wilson Female Seminary corroborates how young women, regardless of position, were expected to use musical accomplishment. Opened in 1860 on the Greenville Plank Road, just off of the Wilmington and Weldon railroad, this school also boasted regular musical soirées. Here, nineteen-year-old Lucy Maynard, the daughter of a Methodist minister in Franklinton, taught music and literature, and Mrs. C. D. Blackman taught vocal and instrumental music.[61] Its first bulletin states that the "Department of Fine Arts—Embraces Music, Drawing, Painting, &c., and offers complete provision for those graceful accomplishments which are always associated with the idea of the cultivated woman. This Department is distinct, and admits Parlor Pupils who may wish to pursue its studies only, without a regular connection with the school." The terms *parlor pupils* and *its studies* precisely assign these accomplishments to the parlor. And it was in this space—a stage that is neither public nor private—that young women from a variety of backgrounds demonstrated their inculcation in codes of genteel conduct that transcended the divide between the upper and middling classes, in the very least.

*   *   *

The line between professional and amateur was not to be crossed in the antebellum period, as many stories published in places such as *The Southern Literary Messenger* taught. The unknown author of "My First Serenade" contrasts how a blonde beauty's overly affected, masculine, almost professional performance brought displeasure to the writer, while the softer, more intimate, performance of Alegna Onerom pleased him immensely. The blonde who has performed in a private gathering is compared to a professional (Tedesco) and described in either masculine terms (hammering, retreating infantry, echelon motion, a volley of piano notes) or wanton ones (raptures, low wailing, lightly kissing, untamed, free). Emphasizing her lack of gentility, the writer adds that the drunken admirers gaped at her deep décolleté. This young woman had learned the accomplishments technically, but she did not acquire taste as she pursued them. Taste, a sense of decorum, and knowing not to display too ostentatiously are themes that run through most writings aimed at women. In stark contrast to the blonde, Alegna Onerom simply sat down and performed a French air. She won the heart of the author because she knew how to perform, that is, not to perform as a professional.[62]

7

"A remarkable accomplishment for one of the gentle sex"

Other Professionals

The emphasis on Sarah Smith's reputation as an educator and the foundational role she had in establishing music programs at both the Columbia Female Institute and the Athenaeum brings to the fore opportunities for southern women to craft their own careers. Those who deliberately put themselves before a public in the antebellum period risked much damage to their social standing. Most carefully guarded their gentility by retaining as much obscurity as possible, but others notably stood out for their place in the public gaze.

More cosmopolitan areas offered a wider range of possibilities for women than rural ones. Accordingly, a considerable proportion of the women examined in this section worked in Charleston, Mobile, Richmond, and New Orleans. Teachers who sought and reached renown, church musicians compensated for their duties, professional performers, and businesswomen constitute the bulk of new evidence presented here. This chapter concludes with the influence of the Salem Female Academy in preparing women for careers in music and their impact on the surrounding area.

New Orleans

Many women arrived from Europe to teach music, and several became institutions in their respective cities and towns. Renowned women teachers arrived in New Orleans, where elite families appreciated their expertise. French women were especially desirable because they not only brought Continental sophistication to their work but also spoke the language of the oldest families. One of the most influential was Jeanne Boyer. Decreeing herself a "professor of music," she held a salon in which the city's young musical prodigies, including a young

Louis Moreau Gottschalk, sought exposure.[1] Eliza Ripley described the space in which Boyer taught music as something of a modern piano studio. She recalled that in a city "dotted all over with music teachers," Boyer stood as the instructor "par excellence." She demanded much of her students. They had to learn pieces dedicated to Boyer by Strakosch and Émile Johns (a music seller), as well as "a dozen other bits a thousand times more difficult and intricate, like Gottschalk's 'Bamboula.'" Eliza's music, and that of her compatriots in Madame Boyer's studio, were "spotted with black pencil marks" because Boyer meticulously notated details of technique and expression in their scores.[2] One of Boyer's pupils, (Marie Antoinette) Virginie Borduzat, dedicated a piano composition entitled "L'étincelle" to her in 1852. Even though her father, a successful merchant, had died in 1841, Virginie still had the means to study music with one of the most prestigious teachers in the city.[3]

Women musicians born in New Orleans to French parents tended to remain in the city, undoubtedly because its size and cultural tastes supported a thriving industry. Louisianan Suzanne Eugenie Lavillebeuvre (1834–1912), "well known as standing at the head of the artists of Louisiana," succeeded Boyer and directed "the study of music" at the St. Louis Institution, Board and Day School, alongside Mr. Brocart, who taught singing. Her reputation as a musician prompted Grace King to model her character Madame Reveillière on her in *Monsieur Motte* (1888).[4] She composed "Reverie" in 1849, which a local newspaper declared to be the best musical composition by a lady Creole. A "delightful pianist" according to Eliza Ripley, Strakosch dedicated his "Caprice Russe" (1854) and "Flirtation Polka" (1849) to her.[5] Another local composer, Louise-Therese-Felicite-Thelcide Morphy (le Carpentier), known as "Thelcide Le Carpentier," "Telcide," or Mrs. [Thomas] Morphy (1808–85), composed and performed, as a vocalist, pianist, and harpist.[6]

Octavie Romey, like Boyer a French musician who had moved to New Orleans, also advertised herself as a "Professor of Music" in New Orleans in 1858. She claimed that to have been her title while in Paris, and it also followed a local trend, as seen with Boyer, Madame Letellier, and Belgians Madame Ed. Locquet and her sister-in-law Mme. Françoise Locquet (at the New Orleans Female Collegiate Institute).[7] In May of 1858, Romey taught piano at Mme. Desrayaux's school on Burgundy Street.[8] Boyer, Lavillebeuvre, Morphy, Romey, and others established themselves as professional women who instructed the elite of New Orleans—they could not have done so had they themselves not been genteel. They embody the complex and multifaceted musical practices of antebellum southern women in several ways. They taught, composed, published, and performed publicly. In these agentic acts, they intermingled with male and female professionals, all the while manipulating the musical practices of the elite in New Orleans.

Charleston and Mobile

Women professionals who became well known in larger cities—publicly lauded for their work immediately after the Civil War—tended to be foreign prodigies who purposefully crafted careers for themselves in an age when native-born women were less likely to do so. Nonetheless, many of these spent most of their lives in the United States. The following discussion focuses on women in Charleston and Mobile. Their stories illuminate music in two southern cities over 600 miles apart that differed dramatically in history, population, and social structures. Charleston was the epicenter of culture in the South, a city filled with an elite class that saw itself as aristocracy. Women in this group traveled to Europe to attend the opera, tour the sights, and study French in situ. They were particular about with whom they socialized, and they closely observed standards and behaviors that they set for themselves. These benchmarks seem to have been more clouded in Mobile, where Octavia Le Vert entertained politicians, foreign visitors, and actors as if on equal footing. But the women musicians who earned their livings in both cities followed remarkably similar paths, and this in turn sheds light on the complex web of performing gentility. After the Civil War, their efforts continued to impact musical events in both cities, further highlighting new interpretations of genteel womanhood.

If women musicians (other than singers) make infrequent appearances in the annals of performance before 1865, a few stand out for their impact on their communities and the unusual course of their careers. Most of those described included teaching, performance, and perhaps composition lessons or large-scale music endeavors among their activities. Marie Siegling, Ann and Elizabeth Sloman, Herminie Petit Barbot, and Maria Kowalewski were talented women whose names appear nowhere in general outlines of American music history, but their work significantly affected the musical cultures of their respective cities (Mobile and Charleston).

Women in Charleston had the opportunity to attend numerous concerts in which women performed as paid musicians; some of these made their homes in Charleston and taught there. Marie (Mary) Regina Siegling Schuman LeClerq provides an illuminating example of one southern-born woman's participation in professional music. Born in Charleston in 1824 to a highly successful southern music publisher (John Siegling) and a well-trained musician (Anna Mary Regina Schnierle), Marie Siegling debuted in New York (where she took lessons in 1842). She recorded that, while performing in Havana (where her father owned another publishing business) in 1844, she was labeled the "Charleston Jenny Lind."[9]

A composer herself, Siegling traveled to Europe to study with German composers (including her grandmother, Regina von Schröder Siegling in Erfurt), and while there met Eduard Schuman LeClercq, whom she married in 1850. According to her own memoirs, before she went to Europe she had been a popular teacher and held musical soirées, but news of her engagement made her "very unwelcome" in Charleston homes. Her lucrative career—and pursuit of a career as a composer—probably called into question the appropriateness of her acquaintance among Charleston's upper-class patrons.[10] Earning a substantial income blemished her gentility; Charlestonians permitted middle-class women to earn some money but not too much. Her European exposure mimicked those of the elite (Harriet Lowndes Aiken, for instance) but did not mirror them. Siegling did not lodge at the Hôtel Meurice or take an apartment in the Faubourg Saint-Germain, as the Aikens did. The fact that music was a professional interest, not a "mere" accomplishment or an acceptably feminine teaching endeavor, distinguished her. Siegling studied with professionals for the purpose of becoming a performer. As a rule, southern women did not perform in public, tour, or publish under their complete names, and certainly did not travel to Europe specifically to advance a career.[11]

Siegling left Charleston for Europe in 1850, but by at least 1851 a pair of sisters, Ann and Elizabeth Sloman, arrived to take her place as music instructors for Charleston's wealthy patrons. They offered lessons in piano, harp, and voice, bringing with them a measure of professional success as performing musicians, composers, and teachers. Indeed, all three of the daughters of English actor Elizabeth Constantia Whitaker Dowton and comic singer John Sloman became music teachers and composers. The career of one, Jane Sloman [Torry], is better known.[12] Elizabeth retired from acting before 1852 and as of May in that year lived in Charleston with her husband, who managed the St. Charles Theatre.[13]

Their two younger daughters, Ann Whitaker (1827–1915) and Elizabeth Constantia (1826-after 1915) made their debut as professional musicians (harp, voice, and piano) in Boston in 1844 at the Melodeon.[14] A review of this concert in the *Boston Evening Transcript* reported that Elizabeth "is without a peer" as a harpist, and both sisters performed well as pianists. Between three and four hundred people attended, indicating a degree of expectation for their performance.[15] An appraisal on October 12, 1844, was less than positive, preferring Anne's rendition of "Kathleen Mavourneen" over her "Una voce poca fa" but admiring Elizabeth's "Garland of Shamrocks" for surpassing beauty and great delicacy. The mixed genres presented in the recital reflected that heard in concerts and parlors across the South, and Anne was heralded as the successor to Jane.[16]

They performed at Charleston's Hibernian Hall in a concert of November 10, 1851 (their first concert in three years). The following March, Ann played "Grand Variations on the Prayer from "Moise in Egitto," Rossini, as a piano solo (possibly Thalberg's op. 33).[17] The Sloman sisters frequently programmed harp and

Figure 7.1. Elizabeth Sloman, *Godey's Lady's Book*, 1896.

piano duets, and on this night played Thalberg's "Grand Duo sur Norma" and a "Grand Duett for Piano Forte, on the March from Rossini's Opera of "Guillaume Tell" by Herz (a work the arranger performed with Louise Dulcken in London). Their status as professional performers is clear.

After several years of touring, Ann and Elizabeth Sloman took up residence in Charleston and offered music lessons. In 1852, they ran an advertisement in the *Charleston Courier*; the ad's striking simplicity seems calculated to draw attention to themselves (see Figure 7.2)[18] Whereas most teachers, such as Hammarskold, included at least a brief statement mentioning their qualities or training, the Slomans saw no need to do so. The straightforwardness connotes a level of professionalism. Their reputations assured, they saw no need to publish any other information.

Like her sister Jane, Ann composed. She also taught composition. One of her pupils in Charleston, William Capers, published "The Buchanan Polka" at age

· MUSICAL.
The MISSES SLOMAN, HARPISTS, PIANISTS
and VOCALISTS.
Residence, 28 Meeting-street.   F 2

Figure 7.2. Sloman Advertisement, *Charleston Courier*, May 7, 1852.

twelve, which he dedicated to "Governor" William Aiken.[19] On the sheet music, Capers claimed to be a "student of Miss Sloman's," and his "Rifle Regiment Polka" (before February 1862, dedicated to Col. James Johnston Pettigrew) confirms his connection with Ann (a student of "Miss A. Sloman"). He may have studied composition with her since he claimed on two publications that she was his teacher. Such tribute signifies an obvious respect for Ann, but it also signals that Capers expected something positive to be gained by associating himself with her. This was an unusual turn of events because it upsets the traditional male dominance/female submission standards of the antebellum period. The first reference to Ann as a composer appeared in the *Columbian Lady's and Gentleman's Magazine* in 1844 with her song "The Chain That Links My Heart" (listed in several newspapers from New York to Charleston).[20] She published other songs in this magazine, including three in 1846 (vols. 5–6): "The Midnight Wind," "Recall Me Not," and "Memory."[21] The Slomans remained in Charleston until at least 1864, but by 1870 they resided in New York City.[22]

Remunerated Church Musicians

Southern churches provided an alternative space for women to perform in public without damaging their reputations. As a church musician, author Augusta Evans often sang solos at her church and was a member of the Methodist choir at St. Francis Street for over twenty years. Several cities had women singers who performed regularly in sacred concerts. Many had paid women organists, and some had female singers who were remunerated for their services.[23] Sarah Ann Cooke moved from England to the United States in the late 1820s, and in the 1840s served as organist at St. James (Episcopal), Wilmington, where she also offered lessons on pianoforte and organ, and in singing.[24] Native-born Eliza "Lizzie" Adam Jones (1839–1911) played the 1845 Erben organ at St. Matthew's (Episcopal) in Hillsborough.[25] Jones was a local doctor's daughter who attended the Burwell School from 1848 until 1851, where she reportedly spent the majority of her time in music lessons in the "Brick House" (the detached music room).[26] After she left the Burwell School, Jones attended St. Mary's in Raleigh.[27] In 1855, Jones traveled to New York City and Brooklyn for further music study, returning home the next year.[28] Her father supported her music study, paying for her training in New York.

She settled back in her hometown to serve as organist in their church and held that position for decades.

Charleston could boast several such musicians. Mary Strobel, organist at St. John's (Lutheran), protested in 1837 that she earned significantly less than her male predecessor and ultimately quit the post in 1841.[29] Elizabeth Bacot served as organist at St. Michael's (Episcopal), from 1834 until 1862. When she took over the position it was expected that she would lead the choir, a task she relinquished because of the "limitation" of her vocal qualities. In the early 1840s, St. Michael's installed a paid quartet to sing instead of a choir (as did many churches). The leader—the soprano—received $200 in 1856 for her services. Such a substantial payment suggests that the singer was talented, and the church's need and respect for her great.[30] Second Presbyterian, which claimed the largest sanctuary in Charleston and (like St. Michael's) was deliberately built along the lines of St. Martin-in-the-Fields in London, had an all-male choir until 1852 when, under Dr. Honour, a new Henry Erben organ was installed and women were permitted in the choir. The new soundscape must have been significantly altered for those worshipping at Second Presbyterian, because prior to 1852 the men's choir had been accompanied by a solo cellist.[31]

None of these women impacted civic music in Charleston as much as Belgian pianist Herminie Petit [Barbot] (1842–1919). Her mother, Marie Petit ran a "School for Young Ladies" there during the 1850s, and her father, Victor, advertised a "solfeggi" class there in 1853.[32] When Adelina Patti performed in Charleston, Victor Petit accompanied her. A child prodigy who debuted before royalty, Herminie performed in such venues as the Théâtre Italien-Français (Brussels, February 1851), the royal palace before the court of William II (king of Holland, January 1851), and Niblo's Garden (New York, May 1852). When she was ten years old, Herminie accompanied Adelina Patti and in Charleston performed Gottschalk's "Le Bananier" and Thalberg's "Fantasie on Rossini's *Moses*." Furthermore, her playing was commended by Marie Pleyel and Sigismund Thalberg, among others and, in 1858, she performed the latter's "Grand Duette on Norma" with Thalberg himself.[33] This aspect of her upbringing contrasts sharply with that of Sara Pryor, who was not allowed to perform for Thalberg, and confirms her lower social status.[34] When Herminie's father died prematurely in 1856, she settled permanently in Charleston and taught in his place, as well as at Charleston's Orphan House School in the late 1850s.[35] Barbot supplemented her teaching income by being the organist at the Cathedral of St. John the Baptist and at St Mary's (Catholic) on Hasell Street.

Like Barbot in Charleston, Maria(h) Henrietta Dillon [Kowalewski, Poetz] moved from immigrant keyboard player to leading figure in Mobile music between about 1850 until her death at in 1897. Born around 1811 in Dublin, Ireland, her music studies began at a "Logiere College" in Dublin. She played organ at a church in Dublin at age twelve and performed in public at age fifteen; her repertory included Beethoven, Haydn, and Mozart. Her first compositions were a set of waltzes (composed at age sixteen), which were popular enough to have been arranged for ensemble performances in Dublin. At about this time, she became organist at St. James's Church, where she reportedly transposed a Te Deum at sight and earned a respected reputation based on this ability.[36] She married Dr. Kajetan Peter Kowalewski, who soon thereafter left Ireland for the United States. She and her mother subsequently joined her husband in Pensacola, where the women offered a singing school in "Wilhelm's new Vocal System" in 1838.[37] The extended family (including two sons) moved to Mobile in 1845. By 1846, she was organist at Christ Church (Episcopal), a position she maintained until her death.

Kowalewski's husband abandoned her, and on February 6, 1850, she was granted a divorce.[38] Surprisingly, the divorce did not keep her from being employed by Catholic churches in Mobile (or from marrying again). Her reputation as a teacher grew rapidly, to the point where (Miss) E. McCord of Mobile composed the "Hollywood Waltz" and dedicated it to "Madame Kowelenski" in 1852.[39] Male teachers composed many of these pieces for their female students, but only in a few circumstances did students dedicate works to women teachers. The waltz typifies the music young women, such as McCord, might have been taught by Kowalewski, and the dedication suggests a special attachment to her teacher.

Professionals on the Stage

Many women singers, such as Anna Bishop, Fortunata Tedesco, and Jenny Lind, performed on the stage in the antebellum South, and they were not treated with contempt.[40] Young women purchased sheet music with professionals' images on them and dropped their names in conversation as a signifier of refinement. Occasionally, professional women traveled through southern towns, perhaps giving concerts, and remained in the area because they married locally. Evidence of one such musician survives in one of Elizabeth Grimball's binder's volumes. In addition to Elizabeth's collection of difficult arias and piano solos (SMB 35), her other volume (SMB 22) has the same distinctive endpaper, but its contents—violin pieces—differ substantially.[41] The first work is "Fantaisie for piano and violin" by Weber; another is a "Concertante" by Herz/Burgmüller. These belonged to Aniela Niecieska (1827–89), supposedly the first female violinist to perform on the stage in the United States. She performed in Charleston in 1850, one week before Adele Hohnstock, another professional female instrumentalist, played a piano recital at Hibernian Hall.[42] Savannah newspapers knew her as "Mad'lle Angelique Gerard; being the daughter of a first marriage, she has elected to assume her own family name [Niecieska]."[43]

Elizabeth Grimball may have met Niecieska when the violinist performed in Charleston.[44] Evidence of interactions between elite families and touring musicians is scarce, and nothing has surfaced to connect Elizabeth and Niecieska. One of the Grimball sons possibly played the violin (one definitely played the flute), and the family could have invited her to their house when she was in town. Why her music remained in Elizabeth's binder's volume is unknown.

Niecieska's press reviews shed light on how professional women musicians, especially instrumentalists, might fit into genteel culture. The *Daily Chronicle & Sentinel* (Augusta) reported the following account of her life and how she happened to be a concert performer at this time (even though her mother was a countess). The article first extols that she "is a most exquisite performer on the violin," which surprised the writer because it was "a remarkable accomplishment for one of the gentle sex." Niecieska and her pianist sister performed "in public" for the noble purpose of supporting their "aged and exiled mother," and the fact that they had to do so "should meet with a warm response from every generous heart." The newspaper then reprinted an excerpt from the *Charleston Mercury* that explained:

> We have been informed that when M'lle Niecieska was quite a child, her extraordinary power[s] on the violin were displayed before a numerous assembly in NYC, where she attracted much admiration; but the delicate reserve of her mother withdrew her from before the public. Adversity did not then compel the sacrifice, and humbler industry supplied the means of support. Necessity now exacts the exertion, and this true-hearted daughter of the *Exile Nation*, with mature powers and masculine resolution, presents her claims to patronage before the justly discriminating taste and well known liberality of Charleston.[45]

The Charleston writer makes clear that Niecieska would not have performed in public except that she had to provide for her mother (and herself). She maintains her gentility with a "true-heart"—in spite of the fact that she attained "powers" as she matured and, even more surprisingly, she exerted herself with a "masculine" resolve.[46] Discerning and broadminded Charlestonians endorsed her; in other words, her character was vouched for, even though she earned money while in the public gaze.[47] Niecieska's romantic biography (living in exile with her countess mother) assisted in lifting her into an acceptable social position. She remained genteel.

Not all instrumentalists received such forgiveness. As a professional flutist, Amelia Siminski must have struck southerners as a curiosity. Hermann Schreiner accompanied Siminski in a concert in Wilmington in April 1854, where she performed the same types of pieces that young amateurs studied on piano, including Foster's "Eulalie," Truhn's "Scheiden and [sic] Leiden," and flute variations on "Lilly Dale" and "The Last Rose of Summer" (Siminski's arrangements).[48] Notably, these choices contrast those in her Richmond debut (January 27, 1854), which featured more opera-based selections.[49] For Virginia, she chose excerpts from *Lucrezia Borgia* and *Lucia di Lammermoor*. Why she changed her repertory for Wilmington is uncertain, since Schreiner played two piano solos on operas (*Lucia di Lammermoor* and *La fille du régiment*). It might connote uncertainty of the tastes in the less cosmopolitan city.

Southerners reacted with mixed reviews to Siminski's performances on an instrument not considered appropriate for women, and the contrast in reception illustrates diverging attitudes toward womanly behavior in places not too distant geographically but far-removed culturally. In Raleigh, commentators degraded her: "The Raleigh papers contain not an item of local intelligence, but the Editors are in raptures over Madame Siminski, who is playing on the flute, for the delectation of the people of the city of oaks.—The rascals talk as if they would all willingly be flutes if the Madame would only press them to her lips like she does the one she plays on."[50] The reporter in Richmond takes the higher road and does not venture into questioning the appropriateness of the instrument for women but instead comments on her dynamic range, "rapid and brilliant execution of difficult passages," and expressive tone.[51] Taken together, these two passages exemplify the world in which remunerated women musicians worked in the antebellum South. Southern women did not learn the flute—the affront to Siminski in Raleigh was not how they wished to be viewed. A Richmond critic with more progressive values looked past the irregularity and focused on the musicality. Such regional differences abound throughout the period. These examples verify that women instrumentalists who were not pianists found the profession socially complicated. Antebellum women musicians who appeared in concert almost always sang, although a few pianists (among them Adele Hohnstock) and Camille Urso (also a violinist) toured the region.[52]

Other Avenues: Businesswomen

Long before the Civil War necessitated the gradual acceptance of women supporting themselves in business ventures, publishing their compositions, and similarly self-determined sources of financial support, a few southern women followed a path to economic independence. Several sold music or musical instruments in the marketplace. Others took on crucial roles in civic musical organizations or local large-scale productions in which they would have been in a position to lead men as well as women. These entrepreneurs frequently came from musical families; they belonged to a social group that already used music as a means of support, not as an accomplishment. They promoted themselves as professionals who could assist in aspects of scientific music beyond teaching or performing as church musicians, and their impact on southern culture expanded as the century wore on. After it, women who entered trade advertised themselves openly, and men utilized their services.

The Sullys represent an early example of such a family. A Miss Sully in Richmond was the only woman listed on the program of the newly formed Richmond Sacred Music Society in 1841, where she played the organ and accompanied Rossini's quartet "The Prayer" and "Song of the Hebrew Captive" on the harp.[53] Her career began at a young age, almost certainly under the tutelage of her mother, Elizabeth Robertson Sully (1775–1851), who had a distinguished career as a musician.[54] Elizabeth Sully moved to Richmond, where she may have been the first woman to be described as "leading" a public concert in the United States.[55] In 1797, Mrs. Sully played a "Grand Sonata" by Steibelt in a concert at the Eagle Tavern in Richmond.[56] She also served as organist at the Monumental Church. At one point, James Evans had been elected as organist, but he magnanimously declined the post because Sully, the other candidate, had a large family to support.[57] Elizabeth took on a vital role in Richmond's concert life, working in both secular and sacred entertainments. Two of her daughters, Sally (1795–1860) and Charlotte (1809–76), also entered the music profession, although they followed the more traditional path of teaching.[58] A number of other musicians worked with Charlotte, including Sig. George (Eliza Harwood's teacher) and Meerbach (Sara Rice's uncouth instructor).

Isolated examples of women who formed unusual commercial relationships belie traditional notions of antebellum womanhood in the South. Here again, Sarah Smith stands out for extraordinary commendation by her employers. Before a list of testimonials on the efficacy of music instruction at the Columbia Female Institute in the 1838 catalog, a full paragraph positions Smith as an instrument broker, saying that "having been accustomed, in Virginia, to supply Musical Instruments" to her pupils, she maintained a connection with manufacturers and intended "to keep on hand at the Institute such instruments as her experience in the profession leads her to prefer before all others, and which she can safely recommend to purchases. The Piano Fortes, offered by Mrs. S., are from the manufactory of J. Chickering & Co., of Boston, and her Harps and Guitars from the house of ERARD, in Paris."[59]

Moreover, the author (almost certainly Smith herself) promised that "the instruments provided for the use of the pupils . . . will be kept in good order." This suggests that Smith will be procuring and looking after the instruments, even though accounts of tuners and repairers during this period all name men in this position, not women. Finally, the catalog assures parents that "a supply of the best modern music . . . embracing several thousand titles, is kept by Mrs. Smith, to which frequent accessions are received of all new publications of merit, both European and American." In other words, not only did Smith supply instruments made in Boston and Paris, but she also afforded the opportunity for amateurs (probably townspeople not enrolled at the school) and students to purchase the latest sheet music, including European prints. As demonstrated earlier, owning such material showed one's refinement and could position women above others within the same social circles. Smith's role in the attainment of gentility thus extended well beyond her occupation as teacher.

This is remarkable considering that when Smith arrived in Columbia, she was twenty-six years old and had been married to her second husband about one year. That a young woman had such established connections with major instrument manufacturers in 1837 might have contributed to Rev. Otey's high opinion of her and his confidence in her direction. The business acumen shown by Mrs. Smith necessitates a reevaluation of the roles southern women played in the practical need to earn a living. Her experience came in handy when the Smiths were forced from the Columbia Female Institute in 1852 and began their own school, the Athenaeum.

Smith came to Columbia with her husband. Harriet Whitaker (1812–73) made her place alongside her father, brother, and sons. The daughter of Wesley Whitaker, a piano maker of some renown who had set up shop in Raleigh in 1829, Harriet began her career using her father's music room on Hargett Street as an instructional space in the 1830s, when she would have been in her twenties.[60] Her brother was Lucius F. Whitaker (1828–1906), a professor of music by age twenty-one.[61] Harriet married her half-cousin John R. Whitaker and had eight children, including S. W. (b. 1831) and Thaddeus S. (b. 1844), also musicians.[62]

By 1850, Whitaker had moved to Wilmington, and in 1851, she advertised the "Wilmington Music School," at which she also sold pianos, piano and guitar music, and instruction books.[63] Like Sarah Smith, this account suggests teaching was only a portion of her income. These examples demonstrate that antebellum southerners not only hired women teachers but also went to women merchants to buy music and instruments. Moreover, Nancy Ping proposes that both Harriet's husband John and son S. W. worked in her store because both are listed as "clerk" in the 1850 US Census.[64] Although Harriet is not given an occupation, there is no doubt that she ran the business, much as her father had done in Raleigh. Indeed, another notice of 1855 locates "Mrs. H. Whitaker's Music Room" on Market Street across from the Episcopal Church, where she sold pianos ranging in price from $200 to $400.[65]

Whitaker returned to Raleigh by at least the late 1850s; an advertisement in early 1858 noted that the third session of "Mrs. H. Whitaker's Music School" would begin there, owing to the success of the previous two sessions.[66] She offered piano and guitar, and she added that she would take three to four young ladies as board-ers. Such young women must have been dedicated to music practice if they were willing to move to Raleigh and live with the principal of a music school—or they came to Whitaker with the intention of making music their livelihood. This offer also suggests that Harriet Whitaker was a businesswoman who earned money through a variety of means.

Whitaker's students' concerts measured the success of her teaching.[67] A descrip-tion of one of her Raleigh concerts appears in the *Newbern Weekly Progress* in June 1860, and "Horatio" (the reviewer) recounts "a concert given by the Music Students of Mrs. H. Whitaker . . . attended also by one of the largest and most refined audiences I have ever seen assemble for any purposes in that city. The young ladies who participated in the concert looked beautiful, sang charmingly, and performed admirably."[68] Unfortunately, Horatio does not record what they performed, but he assures his readers that the young women fulfilled the expec-tations of a genteel musical performance: physically they were "beautiful," their voices rendered the songs "charmingly," and their music performed "admirably." No one performed to excess, no one showed off. The audience, too, reflected gentility in their "refinement."

A Nascent Teachers' Institute:
Salem Academy and Louisa Van Vleck

Moravian music-making in North Carolina is well documented, and Salem Fe-male Academy, founded in 1772, contributes to this reputation for musical ex-cellence. Some of the most prestigious families sent their daughters here: Sarah Childress, wife of President Polk; Mary Morrison, the wife of General Thomas "Stonewall" Jackson; and Martha Martin, the wife of Stephen Douglass, figure among their alumnae.[69] Traditional Moravian views of music in culture resounded with those of upper-class (and middle-) southerners, even if they stemmed from different places: Moravians did not believe that music should be used solely for the benefit of the individual, it was for the good of the community.[70] Similarly, southern girls studied music in order to perform for someone else, not themselves. Moreover, both Moravian musicians and southern women should not play or sing too well in front of others because that would demonstrate conspicuous display, a characteristic shunned by both groups. The Moravians' educational philosophy suited the standards of gentility that southerners pursued.

Institutions from around the state sought women musicians who completed their studies at Salem, particularly the Moravians. In this regard, the Salem Female Academy mirrors the practical purpose of schooling found in northern schools, such as Troy. Of the twelve people teaching at the Greensborough Female College in 1860, eight were employed only to instruct in music and most had connections to the Moravians.[71] Their influence extended to aspects of the music instruction, as confirmed by letters of Louisa Cornelia Van Vleck (1826–1902). Born in Bethania (North Carolina), Louisa was one of several daughters in the musical family of Carl Anton Van Vleck and Christiana Susanna Kramsch.[72] Her sisters, Lisetta Marie and Amelia Adelaide (Amy), also made their livings as musicians.[73]

During the period in which Louisa taught in Greensboro, she wrote assiduously to her family and friends about the experience, frequently mentioning her good friend "Aug" (Augusta Hagen) in these documents. A typical entry concerns her overhearing Theodore Wolle (the music professor who took over the department from Hagen) and Aug playing a "long and difficult" duet and singing from a "new tune book."[74] Louisa confirms the emphasis on music at Greensborough Female College when she observes that "they are *very* thorough here."[75] She writes in April of 1855 that she is anxious about the upcoming commencement exercises and hopes that new music arrives in time to include it.

E. W. Lineback, the music professor at Salem in 1857, described Louisa's sister Lisetta as the "best Singer at first sight of any Lady he had ever known," emphasizing her mastery of the science. After reporting this news back to Lisetta, Louisa wrote that she had to finish the letter so she could practice piano examples for class and then sing some Methodist tunes with her "Alto singers." This practice reflects a tradition at Salem, where students had daily classes to sing chorales and hymns by memory.[76] It is all the more extraordinary because Louisa was hired to teach guitar, not piano or voice. She described the need for more music instructors, initially believing that Lisetta might be suitable, but she realized that their mother could not face the loss of another daughter. The dual roles facing women—loyalty to the family and her need to support herself—are firmly established in Louisa's understanding of women's functions.

When Louisa wrote to Lisetta that "being instructed in the right way of singing," students favored her above the other music teachers and that the students at Greensborough Female College frequently request a "Salem Teacher." This confirmed the Academy's reputation for well-trained graduates and an early training school for women who intended to have careers. Louisa ends the letter asking for her mother or sister to send her the latest *Harper's* and mentioning that she likes to practice two hours a day. That she had time to practice and to read magazines is remarkable, and that she felt the need to practice after so much applied music each day signals her devotion to music study as more than a mere accomplishment but rather as a career ambition.

Even more intriguing and telling are the letters from 1859. Louisa remarks that her students have done well in their sight-singing exams—both Wolle and Jones are pleased. The Moravians at the Greensborough Female College taught music as a science, proven by the students' exams. The instruction at Salem fully prepared them for positions in other schools, including some training in composition. Both Louisa and her sister Amy composed and sent compositions to the *Sentinel* for publication.[77] Louisa writes that she and Wolle tried some of her duets in March 1859, and one of the pieces performed for examinations in Greensboro was a guitar quartet that she had arranged ("Almack's Waltz").[78] Louisa Van Vleck found the instruction in Greensboro thoroughgoing, and her basis for comparison would have been Salem's excellent program.[79] She even describes the commencement exercises as a "greater affair" than those in Salem, which itself outshone many others.

Conclusion

Science and working women have been presented together to show music as more than an accomplishment. This might be a response to a growing acceptance of women teachers as well as music in the middle class. Several of the narratives developed here figure prominently later in this book, viewed through the perspective of changes in gentility wrought by the Civil War. Shifts in women's self-definition and cultural definition began before the war, however, and this cannot be ignored. None of these has been considered in the scholarly literature, but the foregoing discussion has shown that women began to make inroads into spaces defined by masculinity earlier.

The path into new arenas came partly through the combination of music and science in the pursuit of accomplishment. Those who preferred other types of music were not genteel. An unknown writer in Baltimore's *Daily Exchange* admitted in 1860 that not everyone preferred scientific music. He positioned Christy's Minstrels as its opposite, observing that their performances are "pleasing to the many who do not cultivate music as a science."[80] The many, the uneducated, the coarse, and the common: these had not cultivated music in the pursuit of refinement, they lacked the scientific training to employ music in the performance of gentility.

PART 4

The Civil War

8

"The female tribe as 'angels' on earth . . . is being . . . entirely dissipated"

The Parlor and the Civil War

On August 3, 1863, Henry Lea Graves of Covington, Georgia, wrote from Savannah to his thirteen-year-old sister Cora that he had not heard any new music since he had last seen her. He punctuates this by telling her that none of the ladies in Savannah was worthy of cultivating an acquaintance, a comment that concurrently emphasizes his sister's refinement and slights that of the women in Savannah. He asks Cora "to give me a list of all the music you have, both songs and instrumental music . . . you must to go Augusta and spend the winter and take some music lessons. I am afraid you are losing precious time. You ought to read a great deal and practice too. I had rather you were accomplished and poor when you are grown, than that you should be worth a half million and be a dunce."[1] His experiences in Savannah reinforced the idealized view that required women of his class to be able to spend time with male acquaintances by engaging conversation and appropriate musical performance. The implication of Henry's admonition to Cora is the assumption that she would need the same cultural ideals expected of women before the Civil War: gentility was not going out of fashion simply because the nation was at war. It remained a marker of social rank and had the ability to distinguish good company from bad. Yet Henry's remarks also suggest inevitable change brought by the conflict.

That Henry Graves, a planter's son from middle Georgia stationed in Savannah, should so carefully consider his sister's social position in August of 1863—a month after the battle of Gettysburg and the fall of Vicksburg—illustrates how the qualities associated with gentility persisted even as southerners faced deprivation, inflation, and the need to engage in physical labor outside their traditional positions. Music functions as a tool by which to gauge the war's effect on the role and performance of gentility as hostilities and politics altered social hierarchies. Boarding schools continued to inculcate antebellum social models as long as possible, but war often interrupted this process. Social interactions altered in ways unforeseen before the crisis. Music circulation reveals other aspects of war's influence on women, and a number of binder's volumes demonstrate shifts in women's musical practices across the region as they strove to maintain the cultural codes they learned from their mothers and grandmother—even though their lives differed considerably.

Maintaining Antebellum Expectations

Initially, southern music practice continued at the beginning of the Civil War as if nothing had changed. Schools still offered extensive musical opportunities and staged performances by their scholars on a regular basis. An inventory of the Columbia Female Institute (Tennessee) made in April 1861 includes thirteen pianos, two harps, and three guitars, in addition to a library of almost a thousand volumes.[2] Equally abundant, a month after the war began, Salem Female Academy held its final performance of the academic year on May 29, 1861. Over fifty young women performed, the sheer number of which implies that the war had not yet threatened their day-to-day existence. These closing exercises featured a few operatic excerpts, such as Miss L. Bird's performance of "Reminiscences of Norma" and the "Overture to Zampa" played as a duet by Miss. M. Siddal and Mary Glenn, but it primarily included parlor songs, dances, or piano or guitar adaptations of popular melodies. The exercises required three different sessions (at 9 a.m., 2 p.m., and 8 p.m.) in order to display all of the young women.[3] The war had no impact on their usual activities.

Many continued their music practices. A year into the conflict, Anna Cook of Milledgeville wrote in her diary that she wanted to spend her summer reading and practicing piano; however, she acknowledged that she might not be able to dictate how she spent her time: "our country's still in the midst of war with all of its terrors." This entry divulges both her desire to preserve normal activities and recognition of war's impact. She wrote from Marietta, one of several places she spent time, and though she may have moved about, it would be some time before the war touched the inner parts of Georgia. In August, her aunt gave her a piano for the family home. She found it "a great comfort," but in the same sentence records that she also prepared a dress for the Mantua maker.[4] Life as she knew it before the war essentially carried on, at least in its early years.

Anna and Catherine Johnson also kept up their music practice and purchased sheet music through the entire war. They maintained other antebellum social practices, such as sharing music with friends and entertaining men callers in the parlor. Indeed, both women may have performed music with white women, even during the Civil War. Anna's copy of "The Die Is Cast // The Lay of Pestal // Yes the Die Is Cast and Rest Troubled Heart" includes the name of Leila Bennett. Leila was a friend of the family: Catherine's diary (from the war years) mentions Leila and her sister Rose several times. Music was an interest the young women shared. On January 3, 1865, Catherine wrote that "Rose Bennett came in and asked for an [illegible]. I was seated at the piano when she came in." As a genteel woman, Catherine passed her time at the piano. She also mentions Leila in the same entry. That the women maintained social connections during the war can also be determined from "The Die Is Cast," which includes the date of Apr. 6, 1863, in Anna's hand on the top left and "Leila Bennett // Natchez Apr. 6th '63" on the top right, in ink. They also have the same squiggle underneath.[5] The only Leila Bennett I have been able to locate in Natchez was a white woman, a few years younger than Catherine. Whether this was a reference to war or to prohibitions on social mingling remains unknown, but the two women felt the need to comment on their situation.

"The Lay of Pestal" includes the text "Shall I be a slave," and one cannot fail to consider that the issues of the Civil War and the experiences of young free women of color might be on their minds when Anna added the notation "Y is the die so cast" to the title. She did not mark any others in such a way. Her family owned slaves. In December 1864, Catherine wrote "Why it [the war] was sent upon the land none can tell, it is a subject that baffles me completely."[6] In a book of verse by Anna that also contains Catherine's hand (Vol. 53, inside back cover), someone, presumably one of the two sisters, wrote about the "peasants" in the field—a phrase that reminds us that social class does not depend solely on race. The Johnsons identified with genteel society, like so many other southern women of relative means. Their father, William (d. 1850) had disapproved of his apprentices attending "darkey parties" and discouraged their socialization with enslaved men.[7] They may have supported the South's dependence on a slave-driven economy, thus belonging to a group of Black slaveowners whom J. H. Segars suspects had a love of homeland combined with the belief that their prosperity would be found in the South. This led even formerly enslaved people to remain loyal to the Confederacy. He proposes that these opinions prompted some people of color to support the Confederacy: southerners first, black second.[8] William's intentions seem to have been to distinguish his family from those beneath them socially—even if he and his wife had been enslaved themselves. He died eleven years before the war began, but Ann carefully guided the family along the path her husband began. They had risen socially, and part of the cultural capital they acquired was their knowledge of scientific music.[9]

Nora Gardner and The Parlor as Genteel Feminine Spaces

As the Civil War fractured the lives of many women, the code of gentility and its emphasis on sentimentality persisted. Access to materials became difficult as the war raged on, and some resorted to repurposing existing materials. A 1794

English-language version of Gluck's *Orfeo ed Eurydice* was repurposed as a scrap-book by a young woman in Virginia, for example.[10] Although the family had pre-served their copy of Gluck's *Orfeo* for decades, the tides of war cast the volume's potential for use in a new light. It became a material resource for the maintenance of genteel antebellum cultural performance, in this case as a scrapbook.

Regarding the preservation of culture, the print culture in this scrapbook func-tions similarly to printed sheet music: both often carried images, and teenage women kept favorite images—either those cut from magazines and journals or on sheet music—into a permanent book. Visual historian Susan Powell Witt interprets objects in the parlor as participants functioning in the cultural dis-course of the Civil War parlor, and this methodology provides a useful context for contemplating music collections of the same period. We can add music to this reading of the parlor as a "container for ideas about gender, class, and white-ness" and the place for the education of these ideas.[11] Doing so provides a fresh apparatus to evaluate the war's effect on the lives of unmarried women.

During the war, wealthy parents kept their daughters in school, often moving them to institutions farther from the scene of battle as needed. But schools not only provided physical safety, they also insured the pursuit of gentility. Here, schoolgirls continued to learn how to perform their culture—which was that of their mothers and grandmothers—in the parlor, understanding its role in finding marriage partners and suitable society.

The two binder's volumes belonging to Nora Lee Gardner (ca. 1845–1924), a planter's daughter from northwestern Tennessee, reveal how a dislocated young woman continued to collect music throughout the conflict and her efforts to maintain a way of life in spite of it. Nora added numerous inscriptions with dates, names, and places to her music; these document her peregrinations during the war, her attendance at several schools, and a social circle that extended on both sides of the border. They symbolize an active preservation of antebellum cultural ideals even as the war undid the familiar hierarchies that gentility reflected. Nora's binder's volumes record her desire to maintain life as it had existed before the war as well as the obstacles to doing so.

One of the most poignant notes in Nora's collection exists on the opposite page of "The China Rose Schottisch": "If Miss Nora ever peruses these lines let her remember those beautiful soul inspiring songs with which she favored me tonight and accept my sincerest thanks which in my fervor I was so negligent as not to offer. Yours truly,—, March 15th 1865." I have not been able to pinpoint where she was in March 1865, although her music notation puts her in Kentucky the following April. With this comment, the writer hints that Nora might see these lines when she goes through her music, and he asks her to remember the night when she sang beautiful and "soul-inspiring" songs that brought about fervent emotions, befitting a genteel young woman's duty to bring solace and comfort to the men in her company through musical performance. That the writer is male cannot be confirmed, but that Nora should be thanked for her singing implies a male point of view—she would have sung for him, as southern women were taught to do. This inscription confirms the desire to keep antebellum cultural structures in place even as anxieties arose concerning the roles of women in war. Witt summarizes the role of the parlor in war when she writes that the parlor stood as the "antithesis of the battlefield . . . a place of peace," finding that the parlor as discourse exhibited a set of ideas and practices which, taken together, organize both the way a society defines certain truths about itself and the way it deploys power.[12] Nora and her circle understood the parlor's place within the South's social framework and tried to maintain its meaning even through war by documenting her music collection. Kasson sees the parlor as a kind of "memory palace of culture," and Nora's wartime documentation supports this view.[13]

Nonetheless, the destruction of many parlors during the war meant the loss of the very space in which southern women constructed their femininity.[14] Nora Gardner's family attempted to sustain her position in social structure dependent on slavery by dispatching her to various places where she would remain safe and able to continue performing gentility by making music in the parlor. She managed to keep her collection together while moving across the region, another indication of the value she placed on it. She preserved not only her music but also the society through which she moved.

Those less favorably connected could not depend as surely on their maintenance, and self-supporting women found themselves in precarious positions. Circumstances frequently interrupted their existence and prompted or forced them to move from situation to situation. In December 1861, Olivia Stedman uprooted her large family and moved several counties away to teach. In the same year, Acélie (Aliza) Togno left her fashionable boarding school in Charleston to assume leadership of the South Carolina Female Collegiate Institute at Barhamville.[15] Carrie Holt left the South in March 1862.[16] Maria Kowalewski abandoned her flourishing music practice in Mobile and sought refuge in the North, not returning until 1867.

The war also affected the men teaching at girls' schools. Charles Chaky (de) Nordendorf (1839–84) served in the Austrian army until he came to Virginia in 1862, where he served the Confederacy as an engineer, but he also taught music, composed, and even published a music periodical after the war.[17] He moved frequently, living in Danville, Lynchburg, Petersburg, and Richmond. Carlo Patti left his position as a civic musician (and local favorite at the two women's institutions) in Columbia, Tennessee and fought for the South. Gustavious Gnospelius, the Savannah organist and erstwhile music tutor to Sarah Morgan Dawson, also joined the Confederate army.

Angelo Torriani ceased touring as a conductor of Italian opera and settled at the South Carolina Female Collegiate Institute as a singing teacher, where he trained Sally Isabella McCullough for a career on the stage.[18] Shortly before Union troops arrived in Columbia, Louisa Cheves McCord sent a carriage out twice a week over the course of several months to bring Torriani from the institute to teach singing lessons to Louisa and other young women who lived near the McCords.[19] He toured parts of the South in 1861 with an opera company, giving the proceeds of the concert to the Ladies Relief Association and similar organizations.[20]

Torriani's contributions to Louisa's voice instruction show how problematic it was for southerners to maintain normality in 1864. During this year, southerners found it increasingly challenging to find paper goods, and printed sheet music was no exception. As supplies for everything grew scarce during the war, so did the materials needed for music printing, evidenced by the old-fashioned music type in several Confederate imprints.[21] For more fortunate young women, manuscripts offered a one solution to the problem of limited printed music. Like Nora Gardner, Sarah Burton incorporated a handwritten copy of "Quadrille Le Prince-Impérial" in her binder's volume. Louisa McCord's binder's volume SMB 29 reflects these struggles. She wrote in her "Recollections" that "it was impossible to buy music in those days except a few popular songs composed at the time, so with few exceptions we used manuscript music."[22] Her binder's volume music confirms this with manuscript additions of seven pieces in the volume, plus *J. Concone's Exercises for the Voice with Piano Forte Accompaniment*, probably in the hand of Torriani.[23]

Even as the war drew to an end in the eastern theater, some young women remained dedicated to their music studies. Astonishingly, Mollie Ford took music classes every day during April 1865.[24] Perhaps it served as an escape, much as it had for Nora Gardner. At the revered South Carolina Female Collegiate Institute, Sophie Sosnowski opened the doors to those fleeing Sherman's sack of Columbia. William Orchard, one of the music teachers, may have stood up to Sherman's troops at the school, but another account credits the school's salvation to the intervention of Sophie Sosnowski, who ran the school at this time.[25]

Circulation and Repertory

Throughout the war, the same methods of music transmission that existed in the 1850s continued, including inheriting pieces from family members, receiving them from friends, and collecting music over a number of years. The sources of their acquisition, however, shifted to southern cities, taking advantage of the rapid expansion of a southern publishing industry in the 1850s.[26] The number of firms providing music expanded at an even faster rate in the early 1860s as these proprietors sought to supply music supporting the Confederacy. Frequently, music titles available in the North now appeared with a notice advertising that they had been "adapted" for southerners, such as "The Exotics: Flowers of Song Transplanted to Southern Soil" or "Gems of Southern Song." Publishers banked on the fact that copyright extended only to national borders, and since the Confederate States of America established themselves as a separate nation, northern copyrights did not apply.[27] This interpretation of the law allowed a raft of previously published music to appear anew.

Music publication at the beginning of the war proved profitable, and publishers like Blackmar served women's needs for sheet music. Antebellum inventory remains stocked alongside new material and patriotic compositions. Blackmar's 1861 New Orleans offerings listed on the back of "The Confederate Flag," (0013) carry the following categories: "Songs," Marches and Quick-steps," "Polkas & Schottisches," "Waltzes, Mazurkas, etc."; "Fantasies, Variations, etc.," but no collections. The categorization of genres is also instructive. Under "Songs," he includes a number of arias (such as "Ah! I Have Sighed to Rest" from *Il trovatore*, in Italian/English/French; "Ask Me Not Why" from *La fille du régiment*; and "Make Me No Gaudy Chaplet" from *Lucrezia Borgia*) as well as Schubert's "Ave Maria," Balfe's "Then You'll Remember Me," and Badarzewska's "Maiden's Prayer" (with text as "Each Hour of Life"). But these lists are not to be read as the complete music on offer at Blackmar's. Another printing of "The Confederate Flag," also in 1861, includes "Hear Me, Norma" (*Norma*); "It Is Better to Laugh Than Be Sighing" (*Lucrezia Borgia*); "Robert! Thou, Whom I Love" (*Robert le diable*); "Where Are Now the Hopes I Cherished" (*Norma*); as well as several songs, including Schubert's "Serenade"; "Softly Now the Stars Are Shining" by Buentivolio ("an exquisitely beautiful composition in the style of Schubert's Serenade, but in no sense a plagiarism"); and Reichardt's "Thou Are So Near, Yet So Far" in the series "Gems of German Song."[28]

Blackmar moved from New Orleans, where he was threatened with arrest for publishing "The Bonnie Blue Flag," to Augusta, where several others (for example, John Schreiner, George A. Oates,) maintained businesses during the war. The back page of Blackmar's 1863 printing of "The Confederate Flag" provides a sample of the musical items available in Augusta in that year and differs significantly from those of 1861. Its vocal music includes method books (for example, vocal methods by Lablache, Bassini, Concone, and Meignen), collections (*Ordway's Parlor Glees, Fireside Melodies, Temple Melodies, Wreath of School Songs, Zion's Harp* for Sunday School, *Tara's Harp* for seminaries, *100 Songs of Scotland*, and *100 Songs of Ireland*), and "Oratorios, Masses, Etc." (Haydn's *Creation* and Handel's *Messiah*).

Through the war, southern women continued to purchase sheet music. Louisa McCord (or her mother) paid $2.50 for Théodore Döhler's "Nocturne" (op. 24), an exorbitant price for a single piece of music. (By comparison, most songs of the 1850s could be had for about thirty-five cents.) This Chopinesque composition (with an arpeggiated left-hand part accompanying a melody with filigree ornamentation) was first published in 1838 by Mechetti in Vienna, but Louisa's version came out of Blackmar's Augusta operations. It must have been a popular work because it was sold from Virginia to Alabama. The Georgia edition also appears in the binder's volumes of at least two other southerners, Eva Thornton and Mary Glenn (who dated her copy "April 1864").[29]

Around 1863, southern women's purchasing choices dwindled significantly, judging from trends detected in binder's volumes and advertisements on the back of individual pieces. The blockade affected European imports; trade between Boston/New York/Philadelphia and southern sellers all but ceased, and even the materials needed to manufacture new music became scarce. As a result, the majority of women owned music that had been created nearby. For example, Letherea Henrietta Sheftall, the daughter of local attorney Mordecai Sheftall, purchased her music at Zogbaum's store in her hometown (Savannah); most of it was published in Augusta.[30]

The music sellers listed on Letherea's music have a decidedly eastern provenance, in contrast to the music of Tennesseans Nora Gardner and Alice Jenkins, which came from publishers in Cincinnati, St. Louis, Chicago, and Louisville; or Bessie Lamon's binder's volume, which was exclusively sold in New Orleans. The composers, types of music, and local favorites differed according to region, much as they had before the war.[31]

Confederate Music

Given the struggles of finding sheet music during the war, it comes as no surprise that binder's volumes created in the mid-1860s tend to blend music published in the North and South because many women simply added Confederate music to their existing collections. Since they performed music before, during, and after the war, few binder's volumes contain only Confederate imprints. Southern music sellers still had northern and even foreign publications in their stock in April 1861, and consumers necessarily purchased what could be had in local shops. Not surprisingly, music supporting the Confederacy can be found in almost all binder's volumes from the war years. Thus, the majority of these collections include music published in a variety of places across a number of years. Popular songs from the past and present still flourished, and dance music was always necessary. Opera never left the mainstream and remained a signifier of superior culture even as women proudly donned homespun dresses.

Six binder's volumes of Ann Beaufort Sims (1839–1920), compiled while she studied at the South Carolina Female Collegiate Institute, constitute the largest single music collection from the Civil War South identified to date. Born into a planter's family, she was the eldest of six daughters by Eliza Rebecca McMillan and Col. James Thompson Sims. That six volumes of bound sheet music belonging to a single young woman have survived is remarkable in and of itself, but the contents of this collection also evince a competent musician who exceeded expectations of genteel parlor performance. Beaufort, as she was called, sang and played both the piano and guitar, and she must have begun music lessons before the Civil War. At the beginning of the fighting, she was already nineteen. She remained at Barhamville during the war (suffering from ill health through most of it), even though she was older than the average student.[32] Her parents may have chosen school as a safe place to deposit their older daughters, as Nora Gardner's had done.

All of Beaufort's binder's volumes have strong ties to Columbia, such as her copy of Foster's "Gentle Annie" (1856), which came from William Ramsay's Piano and Music Store.[33] Some manuscript music in the hand of one of her instructors indicates she studied voice, practicing solfege as well as dynamics (see Figure 8.1). One large volume (SMB 13, more than two inches thick) could singly represent Sims's time at South Carolina Female Collegiate Institute. Its contents bear dates

Figure 8.1. Beaufort Sims vocal exercises. Courtesy of The Charleston Museum, Charleston, South Carolina.

between 1855 and 1861, came from Columbia, and include several works by Orchard, the English pianist who taught at the institute. Some works foreshadow the coming war, including Orchard's "The Orangeburgh March & Quick Step" and the "Governor's Guards Quickstep" (with the date "1860" written in pencil, as well as "April 15 1861"), or Edward Ripley's "Southern Rights Polka" (Siegling, 1857). Others belong to the war years, such as the popular "Maj. General Hampton's Quick Step," composed ca. 1864 by Orchard's daughter Lizzie.

In Natchez, the Johnson family appear to have bought whatever was available, including songs and piano solos that favored both the Union and the Confederacy (as did others): "Rosencrans' Victory March" (1863), "Stonewall Jacksons' Grand March" (1864), and "General Grant's Grand March" (1864). They also owned "Lincoln's Funeral March" and Meininger's "In Memory of the Confederate Dead" (published in 1866 in Kentucky). The presence of both Union and Confederate pieces in volumes such as these warns against drawing precise lines of intention based on inclusion in music collections. They serve as a reminder that within a large region, such as the South, individual variation provides a sharp counterbalance to overarching generalizations—none so keen as the availability of music in a specific area or the transmission of music across social circles.

Although it consists primarily of music published in the North, Lucy Brown's binder's volume typifies what a young woman in a rural area might have performed during the Civil War. Most of the music belonged initially to someone else, perhaps her mother or another family member, who passed it down to Lucy. After her marriage in 1867, she and her husband lived with her father-in-law, a blacksmith. Her story could be that of thousands of young women across the South and reminds us that even those in reduced circumstances before the conflict continued music practice as before.

Lucy's binder's volume comprises a diverse repertory, including easy settings of opera and antique songs, as well as more recent compositions by Francis Brown. With its dances and songs by Brown, it relates to that of Nellie Pugh, also from eastern North Carolina. However, whereas Nellie acquired her music at about the time it was published (in the 1840s), Lucy came to hers during the Civil War. Distinctly lower on both the social and economic scale, she nevertheless studied the same dance styles. She pursued gentility to the best of her circumstances.

That Lucy's binder's volume dates later can be shown by its Confederate publications, including "All Quiet along the Potomac To-night" and "Gen'l Morgan's Grand March" (C. L. Peticolas, 1864).[34] Like Lucy, Sarah V. Burton, of Ellerskie (Burke County, Georgia), incorporated a high proportion of dances and pro-South pieces in her binder's volume. Much of her music came from Schreiner's or Richards's in Macon, although one came from Norrell's in Augusta. Her Confederate imprints figure prominently in the ordering of her book: the "Secession

Quickstep" occupies pride of place as the first composition, and the fifth was "General Beauregard's Grand March," published in New Orleans but sold in Augusta at Oates's store.[35]

Letherea Sheftall's binder's volume also includes old and new music, even though she belonged to a much more prosperous family than Lucy. Letherea owned "The Beauregard Songster Being a Collection of Patriotic, Sentimental, and Comic Songs" by Hermann Schreiner, a collection of pieces with Confederate sentiments published in Macon in 1864. On the other hand, she also included popular prewar works, some of which had been around for decades. Her inclusion of older pieces follows the antebellum pattern of incorporating a variety of music that usually spans several decades into one volume. Older works were frequently reprinted. "Then You'll Remember Me" had circulated widely throughout the South since the 1840s: Blackmar released an imprint after he vacated New Orleans and moved to Augusta. Similarly, Badarzewska's "Maiden's Prayer" can be found in several antebellum binder's volumes in editions from Paris to New York, but Letherea's came from Schreiner in Macon. These examples demonstrate that rich (Letherea) and poor (Lucy) alike depended on old and new music during the war.

Targeted placement of Confederate music in binder's volumes can be seen in a few surviving examples, even if they do not exclusively consist of music published between 1861 and 1865. A deliberate organization differentiating Confederate-themed pieces and "others" can be seen in Lucy Hudson's binder's volume. Living in Cliff Cottage, Nashville, Lucy and her sisters were described by John Fitch in 1863 as "attractive in feature and manner, and possessed of many of those graceful accomplishments which mark the perfect woman."[36] This "perfect woman" performed physically imposing piano compositions that do not conform to antebellum ideals of deportment, such as not raising their arms above the waist (which only those who worked did). Her volume begins with five solos by Gottschalk, including his "Last Hope" of 1856—the outstanding example of sentimentality in the American repertory. She also played his "Bamboula" and "Banjo," two works with decided associations with Africa. "Bamboula" features in several binder's volumes, and Eliza Ripley recorded that several women in her circle performed it in New Orleans under the preparation of Jeanne Boyer.[37]

Someone assembled Lucy's collection according to music types because, as is the case in most binder's volumes, there is no attempt to follow a chronological or composer-oriented ordering. Rather, Lucy's binder's volume begins with large-scale piano works (by Wollenhaupt, Herz, and Ascher, in addition to Gottschalk), followed by mostly sentimental songs. It is an announcement of her ability to perform serious piano music, beginning with an American composer, and the songs with varying sentiments, including the humorous "I'll Love That Gal So Fat and Plump/She Makes My Heart Go Thump." Arrangements of a few operatic excerpts (from *La traviata* and *Il trovatore*) and dance-related pieces fill out the first part of the volume.

Beginning at #34, however, all of Lucy Hudson's music belongs to southern printers and carries decidedly Confederate themes, including "Inauguration March of Our First President" (1862), "Gen. A. Sidney Johnson's Grand March" (1861), the popular "Capt. John Morgan Schottish [*sic*]" (1862), and "Secession March. Sur le motif de Marseillaise" by Herz (1861).[38] Some of the pieces that occur earlier in the volume date from 1863 and 1864, so the grouping of Confederate pieces at the end carries special meaning. Few women went as far as Nannie Armistead (1850–1936), who proudly proclaimed her allegiance to the Confederacy with such signatures as "Nannie Armistead C.S.A. / August 2nd 1864" and "Windsor Castle, Henrico Co., Va., C.S.A. / April 1st 1865."

*　*　*

At the Salem Female Academy, the program of the "Musical Entertainment" on Mar. 26, 1864, was smaller in every way from the Closing Exercises of the Examination of three years earlier. Physically, the 1861 program measures 9.75 x 15.25 inches, but that of 1864 is less than half that size (9.25 x 6.25 inches). Instead of three separate events, the 1864 occasion required only one. The number of young women is thirty-three, but none performed twice. Confederate songs, such as "God Will Defend the Right" or those associated with the war, such as "Dear Mother, I've Come Home to Die," figure prominently, whereas only one title alludes to opera (the unnamed piano duet "Cavatina").[39] Located far from the war's action, the people in Salem still felt its affects.

Men commented on changes in women's behavior over the course of the war. Henry Graves, who had warned his sister in August to make sure she was accomplished, wrote to his mother from Savannah in November that "I am far from liking parties. . . . I find that my stock of sentimentalism constantly diminishes. The romantic light which clothes all the female tribe as 'angels' on earth, in my boyish imagination, is being . . . entirely dissipated."[40] The Civil War had dispelled many antebellum notions of what women could and should do. The parlor, the space where femininity had been constructed, was unfurnished, disheveled, and even burned. Alongside those actions, many accoutrements and behaviors of gentility disappeared.

9

"Many shades of caste and kind"

The Civil War and the Public Gaze

As the spaces in which women presented music changed, so too did society's attitudes toward women's musical performance in public venues. On the one hand, women attended operas, plays, and other types of theatrical shows as they attempted to preserve the cultural life of the previous decade. On the other, relatively secluded graduation recitals gave way to public benefits for soldiers and widows. Many professional women remained in the South throughout the war; several actively supported the Confederacy, but others seemed less interested in political aims and more focused on sustaining their careers. All of these changes inevitably brought significant transformation to the South's social hierarchies, including the gendered expectations of musical performance.

Changing Landscapes: Space and Place

As earlier chapters have demonstrated, southern women were no strangers to earning a living during the antebellum period. Many followed the path of music teacher; others found employment as organists or even businesswomen. During the Civil War, however, women who never expected to earn money were frequently forced to do so. We have seen that as early as 1843, such activity was approved for at least part of the middle classes, but for those of the "higher class," as Beaufort Sims categorized, it cannot have been.[1]

Emily Tillinghast wrote in her diary in 1861 that she had left school and had "scholars" to teach at church in Fayetteville. At this time, her father, an Episcopal priest, was away from home, serving as a chaplain in Pettigrew's 44th NC Brigade. She presumably had easy access to the church and may have needed an instrument there to teach music. Her devotion to practicing further supports this possibility. She bemoaned not being able to practice several times, such as when the "cavalry company came by" and "the ladies [of course] of the neighborhood congregated" in her centrally located house. A month later she had to cut short her practicing because a "servant" was sick, and she had to do her work. While staying with her aunt, Emily noted that her old piano sounded sweet when a Mr. Rose played for them, but hers (at home) sounded better.

The women in the Tillinghast family sought positions to support themselves during the war, as did many others. By August, a Mr. Hooper had engaged Emily's sister Eliza to teach, offering her $400, as opposed to another "gentleman" that would not reach that sum.[2] Olivia Stedman, another Fayetteville woman who moved in the same circles as the Tillinghasts (their daughters were friends), sought employment as a music teacher at Floral College to support her eleven children.[3] She had to move almost forty miles away to do so.

Several new schools opened during the war, an action which seems counterintuitive to what we know about difficulties in obtaining paper, sheet music, and even basic foodstuffs in the Confederate South. Sometimes these schools were in the homes of those who had room or needed paying boarders, such as the School for Young Ladies that Martha Person Mangum opened in 1863 in her mother's home in Orange County (North Carolina). She was the daughter of Willie Person Mangum, a two-time US Senator and one of the founders of the Whig party. Martha attended Sedgewick Female Seminary and the Burwell School before the war and used her training there to offer English and music in her own school when the war demanded she make her own way.[4] She discussed the idea of a school with her friend Emma Graves in Granville County, who had written to Martha about her own school on December 18, 1862. She also hired out her family's enslaved persons and talked of selling one of the family's plantations. Mangum received her teaching materials from W. L. Pomeroy, a merchant in Raleigh who wrote to her on February 12, 1863, saying that he hoped she would return the items she did not need because goods were scarce. Opening a school was not a benevolent act to offer a needed service to the community but a means by which she could support herself—something she had not thought would be necessary before the war.[5] Her training in music helped made this action possible. Moreover, Martha's assumption that her school would be populated from the local area suggests that she thought enough students would enroll so as to make the venture profitable. Many of these students would not have been members of the planter class, meaning that Martha would be employed by those formerly beneath her socially. Indeed, many women who had previously enjoyed the status and position of the upper classes turned to education as a means of support after the war.[6] Extensive training in music served them well in this regard, even if some young women truly hated teaching. Kate Foster wrote from Madison

Parish (Louisiana) in July 1865 that "I am not able to teach—the confinements of a school room would soon kill me." She had declared two years earlier, "I did the washing for six weeks, came near to ruining myself for life as I was too delicately raised for such hard work."[7] The training that this planter's daughter received had not prepared her to perform manual labor or support herself—Kate's education had been intended for a lady in the parlor.

Professional Performers

A number of performers who had established themselves in the South chose to remain at the onset of the war. In Charleston, Ann and Elizabeth Sloman advertised a concert at Hibernian Hall for February 8, 1863, in which they performed on the harp, piano, and "Alexandre Organ." Still influenced by the opera craze, Ann played excerpts from *Norma*, *Il trovatore*, *Lucia di Lammermoor*, and *Oberon* on the newly designed organ. The *Charleston Mercury* announced that Elizabeth would sing "Sumter" for the first time, which she had composed and dedicated to General Beauregard and the "brave sons of South Carolina." Admission to the concert was one dollar, and it included their father, John, singing "a Shakespearean Extravaganza called "The Lyfe and Death of Kynge Rychard the Thyrd," along with a Burlesque Song. The family offered similar entertainments later that year, the repertory typically being "Casta Diva," "Una voce poco fa," "The Last Rose of Summer," "Lorena," and "The Volunteer." They also performed "Marseillaise," which had become associated with the southern cause a few years earlier. On June 25, 1863, the *Charleston Mercury* announced their last concert as the "Slomans at Home," in which Ann and Elizabeth performed the Overture to *Fra diavolo*, in addition to the repertory listed earlier. A year later, when the Sloman family presented a "Grand Concert" on the anniversary of the battle of Sumter, the cost had risen to five dollars, the meteoric escalation in price reflecting wartime inflation.[8] A month later, however, they advertised a "complimentary benefit" in Augusta.[9]

The same month also saw the Queen Sisters (Laura, Fanny, and Julia Waldron) and Mr. and Mrs. Bates performing in Augusta.[10] Audiences especially requested Laura's "The Soldier's Grave," which she dedicated to the "Ladies of Savannah." They played to "well filled" houses in Savannah according to the *Daily Morning News*, November 18, and December 23, 1862. Indeed, the southern towns frequently hosted concerts and benefits by women throughout most of the war. Eloise Bridges, Lottie Estelle, Mrs. F. M. Bates of Wilmington, Carlo Patti and Company, and the Ella Wren Company each gave performances in Macon.[11] Lizzie Goldern sang in Columbia and Mrs. Jessie Clark in Atlanta.[12] Virginia Keeble performed in the farce "The Two Lovers" along with a Confederate Philharmonic Association concert in May 1861. In New Orleans, Madame K. W. Desrayaux held a Musical Soirée at the Institution to benefit Louisiana volunteers. The newspaper predicted "A most brilliant and agreeable affair may be expected, for among the pupils of that popular school there are many whose musical talents and acquirements are far above that of many professors."[13] Sometimes these were benefits associated with war needs, but others served different purposes, such as an 1862 concert in Atlanta to raise money for a library at Atlanta Female Institute—an act that demonstrates the insistence on preserving antebellum traditions even during war.[14]

Several women became famous as celebrities on the stage, such as Ella Wren and sisters Sally (Sallie) and Mary Partington. Women performers such as these appealed to soldiers stationed away from home and the civilians they left behind. Stephen A. Morgan, of Rivesville (now West Virginia) remembered the early days of the war in his journal of 1861: "Strolling over [Richmond] at night I occasionally strolled into the theater and tried to enjoy the poor performances or to see the fair face of Miss Ella Wren an actress."[15]

Wren toured widely in 1863–64, traveling to Macon and Augusta, and heading as far away as Montgomery.[16] Her repertory seems to have been limited to popular songs such as J. Recko's "Dying Camille, The Unknown Dead as Sung by Miss Ella Wren" (1863). Her name appears on several different publications, used by publishers to attract southern buyers. One such piece of sheet music, published and lithographed in Richmond by Dunn and Company, vividly illustrates Wren's impact and also exemplifies the type of music performed by such women during the war. Printed as "See at Your Feet a Suppliant One. As Sung by Miss Ella Wren in Balfe's Grand Opera of the Bohemian Girl," Wren's association with Balfe's popular music assured Dunn of success. Mary Eunice Copp's copy provides further insight into southern women's circulation practices during the Civil War. It is inscribed "From N L S to Miss Lizzy Hughes" but Mary's name also appears in this binder's volume.[17]

The English Partington sisters entertained audiences in Richmond during the war under the name the "New Richmond Company."[18] They proved to be a popular troupe that delved into different genres. Sallie (1834–1911) enjoyed a postwar reputation as the "toast of Richmond." Her performances in the *Virginia Cavalier* gained particular favor, and in 1863 George Dunn published a version of "The Southern Soldier Boy," using her performances at the Richmond New Theatre as a means of advertising it.[19]

Opera singers faced the same fate as other stage performers. After New Orleans fell in April 1862, Eugène Prévost found it impossible to mount successful opera seasons, and as a consequence, Bertha Ruhl moved to Richmond. On her way north, she serenaded prisoners in Columbia. Hailed as the "Southern cantatrice" (even though a native of Darmstadt), she performed regularly in the city until the end of the war.[20] An announcement in *The Sentinel* (Richmond) on December 22, 1864, encapsulates how professional performers worked during the war. The

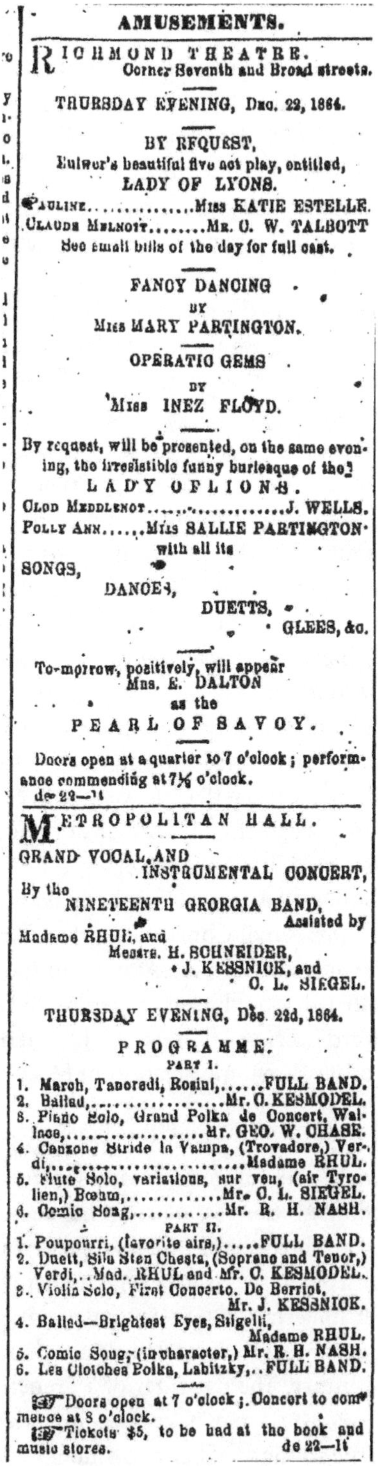

AMUSEMENTS.

RICHMOND THEATRE.
Corner Seventh and Broad streets.

THURSDAY EVENING, Dec. 22, 1864.

BY REQUEST,
Bulwer's beautiful five act play, entitled,
LADY OF LYONS.
Pauline..............Miss KATIE ESTELLE.
Claude Melnott........Mr. C. W. TALBOTT
See small bills of the day for full cast.

FANCY DANCING
BY
Miss MARY PARTINGTON.

OPERATIC GEMS
BY
Miss INEZ FLOYD.

By request, will be presented, on the same evening, the irresistible funny burlesque of the
LADY OF LIONS.
Clod Meddlenot....................J. WELLS.
Polly Ann......Miss SALLIE PARTINGTON.
with all its
SONGS,
DANCES,
DUETTS,
GLEES, &c.

To-morrow, positively, will appear
Mrs. E. DALTON
as the
PEARL OF SAVOY.

Doors open at a quarter to 7 o'clock; performance commencing at 7½ o'clock.
de 22—1t

METROPOLITAN HALL.

GRAND VOCAL AND
INSTRUMENTAL CONCERT,
By the
NINETEENTH GEORGIA BAND,
Assisted by
Madame RHUL, and
Messrs. H. SCHNEIDER,
J. KESSNICK, and
O. L. SIEGEL.

THURSDAY EVENING, Dec. 22d, 1864.

PROGRAMME.
PART I.

1. March, Tancredi, Rosini,......FULL BAND.
2. Ballad,....................Mr. C. KESMODEL.
3. Piano Solo, Grand Polka de Concert, Wallace,...................Mr. GEO. W. CHASE.
4. Canzone Stride la Vampa, (Trovadore,) Verdi,...........................Madame RHUL.
5. Flute Solo, variations, sur veu, (air Tyrolien,) Boehm,.............Mr. C. L. SIEGEL.
6. Comic Song,............Mr. R. H. NASH.

PART II.

1. Poupourri, (favorite airs,).....FULL BAND.
2. Duett, Sila Sten Chesta, (Soprano and Tenor,) Verdi,..Mad. RHUL and Mr. C. KESMODEL.
3. Violin Solo, First Concerto. De Berriot, Mr. J. KESSNICK.
4. Ballad—Brightest Eyes, Stigelli, Madame RHUL.
5. Comic Song, (in character,) Mr. R. H. NASH.
6. Les Clotches Polka, Labitzky,..FULL BAND.

☞ Doors open at 7 o'clock; Concert to commence at 8 o'clock.
☞ Tickets $5, to be had at the book and music stores.
de 22—1t

Figure 9.1. *The Sentinel*, December 22, 1864, featuring Mary Partington and Bertha Ruhl.

first listing features Mary Partington and the second, Bertha Ruhl (see Figure 9.1). The variety of music—entertainments offered for a single evening late in the war—confirms the need for and interest in attending such events even as the war drew close to Richmond. Ruhl offered Verdi's "Stride la vampa" from *Il trovatore* and Stigelli's popular "Brightest Eyes"—a perfect representation of the music sung by young women in parlors across the region: Verdi arias and parlor songs.[21]

Ruhl's concert repertory proves that gentility in the parlor as practiced by amateur musicians and professional performers cannot be defined by the choice of pieces a young woman learned, except for the fact that amateurs rarely performed their most difficult pieces in antebellum public appearances. When soldiers visited homes in Macon, they requested "Home! Sweet Home!" "Annie Laurie," and "The Girl I Left Behind Me," not bel canto arias.[22] These represent the type of music they expected their female acquaintances to sing. If amateur women did stretch the bounds of decorum, as they occasionally did (particularly in sacred concerts), their names did not appear in published reports. By the end of the war, however, distinctions between appropriate venues for amateur and professional women began to dissipate, paving the way for changes in performance—and therefore attitudes about gentility—during the Reconstruction.

As Sherman's army marched through South Carolina in March 1865, a number of locally celebrated musicians collaborated on a concert in Augusta for the "Columbia Sufferers." These included the Slomans, A. Hett, C. Atwell, G. B. Mitchell, W. D. Davis, and E. Clark Ilsley (director). Featuring a number of popular opera excerpts, popular songs, and burlesques, Miss Webber performed Wallace's "Grand Fantasia de Concert" on "Ben Bolt" and Ann and Elizabeth Sloman sang Arditi's duet "Tremarco Vil" and played the "Anvil Chorus" in a duet for organ and piano. The program continued with various other pieces for violin and piano, flute and piano, and then concluded with a chorus chosen to inspire those in attendance: "O, Hail Us, ye Free" from Verdi's *Ernani*.[23] Those highlighted at the beginning of the announcement were professional musicians, but Miss Webber may have been an amateur.

Some women may have prepared for a career as a performer or to work as one only until marriage, but too little information about them usually survives to determine which path they intended to follow. Modern scholarship has shown little interest in documenting American women who became professional performers, and narrowing the subject to southern women yields an even smaller amount of material.[24] Concert notices and other materials, however, prove that women supported themselves (sometimes in league with their husbands or other family members) throughout the nineteenth century. The daughter of a French hatter and his wife, Isabelle Coralie Leblond (1852–81), may have been intended for a professional career as a pianist, and, on the strength of her two binder's volumes, this likelihood is possible.[25] Elegantly bound in black with her name stamped in gold, Coralie's collection contains many works published in France imported to New Orleans by Benoit or Elie.[26] She played Rosellen's challenging arrangements of melodies from both *La traviata* and *L'Africaine*, as well as Schulhoff's flashy "Le carnaval de Venise" (op. 22) and several works of Gounod. The final two pieces in these books date from 1862, when Coralie was only ten years old.

Like Coralie LeBlond, Bessie Lamon in West Baton Rouge Parish owned two volumes of demanding piano music, purchased in the French Quarter of New Orleans, including some of the same pieces.[27] She was the daughter of a widowed school mistress, according to the 1860 census. Volume 2 is earlier, containing Ascher's "La cascade de roses," dated 1863, as well as Schulhoff's "Le carnaval de Venise," dated 1865, and his "Grand valses brillante." She dated her copy of Flora Byrne's "President Jefferson Davis Grand March" and Hünten's "Mélodies célestes" (op. 113), 1864. Bessie would have been between ten and twelve while working on these compositions, and others in her collection are equally challenging. Possibly, she studied music at the school where her mother worked, as did Lizzie Orchard, Bella Strawinski, and Fanny Smith. The idea of a girl, possibly ten years old, playing these piano pieces during the Civil War, in Baton Rouge, while her mother teaches school to earn their upkeep does not typify how this period is usually portrayed but reflects the necessity of a more thoroughgoing examination of women's practices.

Sallie Isabella McCullough (1847–80) of Columbia was a student at the South Carolina Female Collegiate Institute (Barhamville) in the early 1860s who deliberately pursued a life as a professional opera singer.[28] In school by age seven, Sarah McCullough belonged to the household of small-time Scotch "planter" Charles and Sarah. Whether she intended a career at this point can only be speculated, but, in the early 1860s, her intentions were apparently well known among her contemporaries. Described by schoolmate Bessie Allston as having a "big beautiful voice," McCullough studied voice with Torriani while at Barhamville, and his experience as an opera conductor and voice teacher benefited Sallie in her career. In her *Chronicles of Chicora Woods*, Bessie noted that McCullough lacked sophistication and was "big, sweet, simple" Sallie.[29] She does not mention if she heard McCullough after her time in Barhamville, but McCullough's career did flourish, if briefly, throughout the country.

Out of Slavery and into Professional Music: Ella Sheppard

Of the women discussed thus far in this book, none experienced a more dramatic change of course in her life's trajectory than Ella Sheppard. Born to Simon and Sarah Sheppard, both of whom were enslaved, she also entered the world in bondage. Her father purchased his freedom, but Harper and Phereby Sheppard refused to sell Sarah. To remove Sarah from any further disturbances that the family's dispersion might cause, the couple transferred her to another of their plantations in Mississippi. Ella saw her mother only one more time before the Civil War.[30]

With the money he had earned to free Sarah, Simon instead purchased the freedom of their daughter, Ella. During the 1850s, she attended a school for Black children in Nashville run by Daniel Watkins, a Disciples of Christ preacher. The Nashville city council closed the school in 1860. Looking for work, Simon Sheppard moved with Ella to an area of Cincinnati known as "Ragtown." The poor conditions resulted in permanent health problems for Ella, who remained thin (though tall) and physically weak for the rest of her life. While living there, Simon bought Ella an old piano because she had shown an aptitude for music as a young child. At age thirteen, Ella began studying music at the Wilberforce School but had to stop when her father died unexpectedly. With his death, the family had to sell everything to settle his affairs, including Ella's piano.[31]

Ella was then "adopted" by a Black photographer named James Presley Ball, who offered to pay for her music lessons in exchange for later repayment. He arranged lessons with Caroline Staub Rivé (1822–82), the same woman who composed and published two works in Nora Gardner's binder's volume. A French soprano from a German family, she had been a contemporary at the Paris Conservatory with Jenny Lind. She was on the faculty at the Glendale Female College and considered "one of the best-known music teachers" in the region.[32] (Her daughter, Julia Rivé-King crafted a career as a professional pianist.) While teaching at Glendale, she agreed to teach Ella Sheppard with the stipulations that Sheppard not tell anyone who her teacher was and, in Sheppard's words, to "enter through the back way to receive my lessons in the back room upstairs, from nine to quarter of ten at night."[33] She had twelve voice lessons with Rivé before having to cease study because Ball did not pay her tuition. Nonetheless, these music lessons and her ability to play the keyboard benefited her after the war when she earned her living as a professional musician.

Amateur Public Performances

With various professional women musicians touring the South, it stands to reason that southern women who would not dream of being so publicly exhibited nonetheless attended the performances and viewed the professionals from afar, just as they had done before the war. Dances, balls, operas, and other concerts proliferated during the war. The 1861 minutes of meetings held by the Société Dramatique de Bienfaissance [sic] de Thibodaux (about sixty miles west of New Orleans) describe a dance planned for October (including the names of young women invited and their responses) and a "Grand soirée musicale" in November, for which they sold tickets.[34] Other cities exhibited the same or similar patterns. Anita Dwyer Withers attended several concerts in Richmond, and her acquaintances even more.[35] On February 4, 1862, John Withers (Anita's husband), Lucy Duval, and Edmund Withers went to the African Church to hear the pianist known as Blind Tom play, among other items, Fischer's "Hornpipe" with right hand alone and "Yankee Doodle" with the left while he sang "Dixie." In Georgia, Anna Green Cook traveled from Marietta to Atlanta to attend Captain W. H. Barnes's concerts. Sallie Conley Clayton attended another of these in June 1861, and Caro Yancey heard them as well.[36] Gentlewomen did not forsake their appearance on such occasions, even at the end of the war. In March 1865, the rain prevented "the ladies" from attending a concert given by Professors Muller and Adams.[37]

A humorous and lighthearted account of homemade entertainments in Richmond toward the end of the war reveals how much had altered for the highest echelons of southern society. Constance Cary Harrison (1843–1920), one of the "Cary Invincibles," published several books and plays, and her *Recollections Grave and Gay* details life among a group of prominent Confederates during the later period of the war.[38] They called themselves the "Starvation Club" and organized to provide "a place for our soldier visitors to meet with us for dancing and chat . . . a desirable variation upon evening calls in private homes." These took place in the drawing-rooms of "the leaders in society." Thus, the club gathered as a substitute for their usual evening activities, which must have been restricted by the war, and as an opportunity to mingle with unfamiliar men, which the rules of gentility forbade.[39] It also provided an outlet for married women, who previously would not have participated in such revels.

In creating the Starvation Club, the women in Richmond served as agents in promoting social discourse, which in and of itself was not an innovative act, but the extent to which they took their activities differed from earlier behaviors. As proper gentlewomen, the Carys and friends initially offered dancing to piano accompaniment, but the male club members managed to pay for a small orchestra. All of this happened under the approval of Robert E. Lee, who requested that the women "look your prettiest, and be just as nice to them as ever you can be!" Here, again, they fulfilled their role of providing attractive visages for the male gaze.

As the war drew closer to Richmond, the Starvation Club still held cotillions. Their membership grew, as did their reputation. Constance reported that "all foreigners and general officers who visited Richmond were presented to our club, as a means of viewing the best society of the South." Even if they lacked many of the accoutrements of gentility because of the blockade, the members of the club maintained their station, their place on the social ladder. Their gentility was unquestioned.

Two colorful accounts of their gaieties warrant special notice. One was the production of the tableaux "Matrimony," which they portrayed in three scenes as "Mat, Rye, Money."[40] Their intent was clear: finding a husband. Constance stamps her account with all the trappings of her class, ensuring that readers in the early twentieth century remembered the Old South and people of her social class in their luxury and finery. For example, Frank H. Vizitelly, the English artist noted for his Civil War images, painted the backdrops. Hetty Cary appeared in "Rye" while someone played "Comin' Thro the Rye" on the piano. Constance performed "Money." As a "rustic maiden," she "perched coquettishly" on a garden fence against a scene "charmingly painted as an English thatched cottage wreathed in roses, with a glimpse of the Thames in the background." The war may have sent prices soaring, deprived them of their traditional social activities, and killed thousands of soldiers, but these elite women could have elaborately decorated sets for their theatricals. Moreover, the entire performance took place at the home of General Randolph, with Jefferson Davis, his cabinet, and "many more official people" in attendance. It borders on being a public spectacle, which implies that the Starvation Club members submitted themselves for the public gaze, and the descriptions left by Cary suggest that they enjoyed it.

Another noteworthy event was a performance of *The Rivals* in which Virginia Tunstall Clay [Clopton] played "Mrs. Malaprop," "dominating our little stage with the ease of a veteran actress."[41] But of course, she wasn't—or at least anything she had done earlier would not be described as such. Nonetheless, the group "played it two nights successfully before large audiences of our friends." Such performances run dangerously close to professional ones, yet the women's amateur status and their gentility, were not questioned. Halttunen reads parlor theatricals as a sign that the transparency of sentimental culture had been replaced by masks and sanctioned performance.[42] Playing as actors before a large audience removed both transparency and truth. Mary Lewis's sister Ellen recalled Virginia's wedding in 1843 by writing "Clem Clay is married to a Miss Tunstall and a very pretty young lady, she plays very well on both the Piano and Guitar and sings, she takes lessons from Mr. Bode."[43] Her impeccable pedigree—model of gentility as a young woman, wife of a senator, respected political hostess in both Washington, DC and Richmond—assured those in her company that their performances remained within the bounds of propriety and good taste precisely because of their social position.

Private Gatherings

In addition to the public entertainments southerners in Richmond attended, other less extravagant gatherings continued elsewhere. Anna Cook describes an evening late in 1863 in which she attended a "social winter's evening gathering" at

Dr. Benjamin White's house in Milledgeville. In this instance, the evening included both music and chemical experiments.[44] What the surgeon general of the Georgia State Troops demonstrated that evening is unknown, but that he took the time to entertain in such a manner demonstrates southern social life during the war: the need to maintain life as it was in the preceding decade in the face of the deprivations of war. In spite of the hostilities and difficulties, southern women earnestly attempted to follow the dictates of gentility. Anna illustrates other facets of this culture, too, when she writes that "I was introduced to a number of gentlemen" but had eyes only for a man courting her best friend. Romance, courting, and eventually marriage remained the goal of many young women. As late as March of 1865, Emmala Thompson Reed attended an "elegant supper" after a wedding in Richmond, and then sang songs with piano accompaniment. Afterward, others joined her in chorus.[45] Dancing also remained a favorite recreation during the war, although the space and attendees differed from earlier models. As morale dropped and fatalities rose, people from across the social spectrum gathered together with diminished expectations in maintaining distinction.[46]

Writing in 1934, Richard Dillard described an entertainment at a "big barn" in Centre Hill (Chowan County, North Carolina) that took place during his youth.[47] He called the gathering a "tableaux" in his "Civil War Incidents" in *Historical Reminiscences of Centre Hill*, and it exemplifies a type of music-making that mid-nineteenth-century southerners would have recognized. For the tableaux, Emma Womble portrayed Florida, Elizabeth Cochrane was Morning, Annie F. Parker (later Mrs. Dr. R. H. Winborne) was Night, and Annie Wesson sang "The Bonnie Blue Flag" and "The Hunter's Horn," the latter in recognition of the host, Dr. Winborne, a locally renowned fox hunter. Mary Isabella Parker (later Mrs. Dr. William T. Woodley) sang "appropriate selections" during the interludes, and Jane Simpson (later Mrs. Dr. Starkey Shape of Harrellsville) "beautifully rendered in pantomime. . . . 'They say I'm pretty.'" John G. Small loaned the piano used for the occasion.[48] Annie Wesson, a governess for William J. Holly at Bandon (another community on the Chowan River), later married another attendee, West R. Leary, a planter worth over $100,000 before the war. That a governess should wed a rich planter suggests that social lines were indeed being redrawn during the 1860s.

This gathering included people whose worth in the 1860 US census ranged from $100,000 (West Leary) to nothing (Mary Isabella Parker, head of household). The pianist is not named but surely played during the tableaux and accompanied the singers. All of the women were single at the time, which follows southern traditions that young marriageable women performed for those in attendance so that their accomplishments could be appropriately displayed. The cross section of society, however, differs from previous patterns. In addition to reflecting a rural gathering, it also suggests that the constraints brought on by the Civil War resulted in such a cross section of easterners coming together for a single event. Having the occasion in a "big barn" almost certainly resulted from the area's proximity to battle lines: nearby Winton (in Hertford County) was the first place in North Carolina to have been burned and decimated by Union troops, in February 1862. In this light, this event foreshadows changes in southern culture that would be felt immediately after the war, when necessity demanded that women take on new roles.

Musical Organizations

Musical associations, clubs, and societies that had formed before 1861 usually attempted to continue after the war began, with varying degrees of success. The needs of the army gradually dispersed the supply of talent at home, prompting organizers of benefits and related events to appeal to women for assistance. Such requests had to be carefully coded so as not to offend genteel citizens who could support the Confederacy while upholding following the behaviors appropriate to their social station. In Atlanta, Captain W. H. Barnes advertised in the *Southern Confederacy* as early as the fall of 1861 that he "Wanted: Recruits for the Atlanta Amateurs" to fill positions formerly held by men now fighting in the field: "The organization, known as the Atlanta Amateurs, was formed here last May, and, as all are aware, have, in every instance, responded to the call of their fellow-citizens, and with what success, I leave to our audience to determine. Many of our members, since we commenced, have left our association and gone to the defense of their country. *As these, one by one, left us, I called upon the ladies of our city to supply their places* [italics mine]." We can understand the case he makes for women stepping into men's roles more clearly than Barnes probably intended. Lifting the veil of revisionist history that painted a picture of elite women seemingly eager to be placed on a pedestal, accepting men's protection and bounty, his request for women to supply men's places proved more of a prediction than he intended.

The advertisement makes clear that this organization existed to raise money: "Over $4,000 has been procured by this pleasant method and distributed to the different companies and relief fund," meaning that amateur women will be treading a thin line between amateur, which was acceptable, and professional, which was less so—at least in 1861. Barnes pleads with readers to join him, noting it is not "discreditable to endeavor, in this pleasant manner" to do so. He knew that he was asking his women readers to transgress fundamental boundaries of gentility, so he attempts to persuade them with honor and duty. If that fails, the writer appeals to their vanity, noting the opportunity to display themselves to advantage: "I trust, therefore, that the ladies and gentlemen Amateurs of our city will . . . assist us. If there is honor in fighting the battles of our country in the field, it surely is not discreditable to endeavor, in this pleasant manner, to sustain our soldiery and assist their families. One is as imperative a duty as the other. Both must be performed. We have all the talent here that we could wish, and it only needs being brought forward, and where could it be displayed to better advantage, or for a more laudable cause."[49] Barnes widens the expectations of gentility, arguing that both the traditional view and a new one in response to the war weigh equally.

This shift in gender roles in the South during the war has long been recognized by scholars, but not in its application to music.[50] The idea of putting themselves on public display was not entirely unknown, but to do so with relative frequency was new. Barnes reassures women that there is no shame—no stain on their gentility—to put themselves on view in this way: "one is as imperative a duty as the other." In fact, he promises their talents could not be better "displayed," indicating that he understands the performance of gender in its usual guise (singing in the parlor) was now conscripted to an altogether different stage (in public). Unfortunately, we do not know who participated in most of these benefit concerts and cannot say for certain how it affected class divides or the effectiveness of his entreaty. That so many events took place suggests, however, that more people performed than had done so in the antebellum period.

Such ventures began early on, almost as if it were easier to perform songs and dances in public since women already did so in private and semipublic venues. In Milledgeville, the *Southern Federal Union* of August 6, 1861, announced that "the young Misses Concert and Tableaux" raised $52.05, which amount they turned over to the Ladies Relief Society. Torriani took a group of students from the South Carolina Female Collegiate Institute to Richmond for a concert tour in October of the same year. It was advertised as "Opera Excerpts in Concert: The Torriani Musical Amateurs from South Carolina" at the African Church.[51] We can only wonder who accompanied Torriani on this adventure—perhaps it included Sallie McCullough, the most famous singer from this institution, as well as elite planters' daughters and the progeny of school teachers.

Other concerts in Richmond (on December 17 and 19, 1861) raised money for those effected by the war: the first for the wives and children of the Richmond volunteers; the second a "Grand concert for the benefit of the wives and children of the Maryland volunt'rs, at the United Presbyterian Church . . . by ladies and gentlemen amateurs, assisted by able professors." A month later, the same group offered a "Grand concert for the benefit of the Kentucky volunteers (now at Manassas): at the Second Baptist Church."[52] The program on the 19th confirms the continued centrality of opera:

PART FIRST
  1. Overture—Orchestra
  2. Solo—Basso—Muller
  3. Aria from Lucia [di Lammermoor]—Donizetti

4. Grand Duo—Romeo e Giulietta—Bellini
5. Scena 'e Aria—Judith—Concone
6. Chorus—Ernani—Verdi

PART SECOND
1. Cavatina and Chorus—Tancredi—Rossini
2. Fantasia—Violoncello (by request)—Servais
3. Variations brillantes—Rode
4. Vespri Siciliani—Bolero—Verdi
6. Gipsy Chorus—Balfe[53]

Women gradually began to take on more roles in these organizations and not always under the guise of fundraising. On November 20, 1864, the *Daily True Delta* published an advertisement of an "Amateur Grand Concert" directed by a "young creole lady, assisted by a number of ladies and gentlemen of this city, in the parlor of the Opera House." Prior to this time, women did not take the lead—or at least were not credited with directing performances or, in the terminology of some writers, "getting up" concerts. Though the newspaper recognized the lady for directing this concert, it did not print her name. The concert in 1864 predictably programmed selections from *Il trovatore, Norma, Lucia di Lammermoor, La favorite,* and *Euryante.*[54] These events required rehearsals: Misses E. J. and H. A. Mills sent a handwritten invitation to Mesdames Wall and Dunbar on March 1862, for a musical rehearsal that evening at Hope Terrace. Such gestures show that the niceties surrounding gentility persisted in spite of conflict.[55]

*　*　*

The concerts of Lucie Inez Loening (née Palmer) (1842–1931) provide another signal that expectations in women's musical experiences altered as the war went on. According to her daughter's autobiography, Lucie was the daughter of a physician and planter, although the census lists him only as a physician. She attended school at the Sacred Heart Convent and apparently spoke French better than English. Her granddaughter, Olga Samaroff (born Lucy Mary Olga Agnes Hickenlooper, a talented concert pianist in her own right who married Leopold Stokowski), claimed that Loening performed a Beethoven concerto with orchestra at the French Opera House in New Orleans when she was fifteen (approximately 1857).[56] Samaroff relates a familiar trope: "In spite of her pronounced talent and her fine playing, no thought of a professional career had ever entered her head or those of her parents. Mayflower ancestors and southern traditions combined to place her among the women for whom at that time matrimony was the only desirable career. The stage, even the concert stage, was a dangerous and indecorous place quite beyond the pale for ladies of any social standing." That she played a Beethoven concerto in public promotes an alternative purpose, one that suggests a professional intention. Moreover, after Loening married at sixteen, she honeymooned in Europe, where she "often played for music-loving Ludwig I, of Bavaria." Her reputation as a pianist came to the notice of the king, which further contradicts her pretense against a professional career. Nevertheless, Samaroff perpetuates the idea that genteel women did not work in the 1850s, a concept that aligns more with descriptions of the Old South as reimagined in the early twentieth century.

As "Mme. L. Loening," she did indeed give concerts during the war. She performed arrangements by Thalberg and "Chopio" of "Norma, The Prophet, The Huguenots, William Tell, Bellesario, The Favorite, Anna Bolena."[57] Thus, Loening appears to have simultaneously broken the boundaries of women performing Beethoven works in public and to have been one of the first pianists to play Chopin publicly in the South. Following her lead in New Orleans, an increasing number of young women appeared on the stage, and some came treacherously close to being revealed by name. The *Daily Picayune* reported on May 19, 1864, that "gifted amateurs" participated in a concert given by Jacques Oliveira (violinist) and Mme. Loening (identified as the pianist at the Locquet Institute). Called "amateur debutantes," the paper listed the names as "Mesdemoiselles P—a, DeR. and P—r." Mlle. P—a played a fantasy on Don Pasquale "with an accuracy, ease and brilliance rare among lady performers on the piano."[58] She maintained her genteel status in spite of her public persona.

Conclusion

Some writers expressed frustration with the war's effect on women's culture, at least as they wished women's culture to be. An article from Mississippi in 1863 disagreed with the idea that women should be doing jobs that traditionally belonged within men's purview:

> Since the Hon. [congressman] Mr. Phelan . . . expressed his unbounded admiration of women plowing in the fields, the plowing women have become so proud, they refuse to speak to the non-plowers. If Mr. P. in company with a party of Richmond ladies, were passing a corn field in which several women were at their plows, do you think *he* would think of lifting his hat to *them*? Bless you, no: He would be too deeply absorbed in contemplating the beauties of some wild woodland scenery in the opposite direction to notice the rustic objects of his former admiration; objects admired only when "distance lends enchantment to the view." I think the sight should rather call forth one's pity, to see women doing men's work . . . Jay Bee.[59]

In addition to suggesting that what passed for civility in Mississippi would not suffice in Virginia, "Jay Bee" felt it better to ignore women working (which indeed followed antebellum dictates) and found it a pity that they had to do so.

Another example of change can be found in a report from Atlanta. In March of 1863, "Aliene" reported that "Society in Atlanta is unique, but agreeable, made up of a sort of Mosaic of many shades of caste and kind," suggesting a blending of social groups that might not have otherwise spent time together. Dancing continued as a popular pastime, and elite women of the upper classes let down their hair, so to speak, and joined in the communal exercise: "A few months ago . . . the pretty Puritans raised their white hands, and frowned from their pretty brows at the *mere idea* of dancing; indeed one of the fairest Georgians affirmed that she would not, at such a time, attend a soiree dansante; but the musical parties soon merged into 'hops,' and gay quadrilles replaced the dignified 'sonata, or monopolizing 'reverie.'"[60] That the *soirée dansante* became a "hop" and quadrilles replaced sonatas and "reveries" points to casual social interactions that heeded less to the rules laid out by Emily Thornwell and more to the practicalities brought by war and a desire for gaiety. (It also tinges with hyperbole, since sonatas had gone out of style decades before the war.) Henry Graves's advice to his sister that she learn the right pieces seems far-removed from the dances and other entertainments in Atlanta. The Atlanta event mirrors the mixing of social classes examined earlier in the barn entertainment in eastern North Carolina. Aliene's pointed use of "white hands" further suggests that the women to which she refers were indeed those who had never worked but who now mixed with many beneath their social status.

Southern women struggled to maintain their music practice in the face of deprivation. That some continued to use music to potentially improve their situation can be read as a testament to an enduring belief that things would eventually return to normal—or possibly even better. Malvina Sarah Black Gist (1842–1930) spent the final year of the war employed as a "treasury girl" signing currency. The daughter of a college bursar, she continued her music studies in spite of having to work.[61] She wrote in February that she "Took my lesson and paid Signor Torriani for my last quarter. He is gloriously handsome in the Italian way." Malvina also paid $200 for a new bonnet. Such expenditures substantiate her need to maintain the actions and displays of gentility. She eventually moved to Greensboro, North Carolina, and then to Richmond. She wrote from there on March 4, 1865, that "Johnny [her brother?] came through without a scratch, and so did my new Steinway."[62] Such happiness soon dissipated, however, and four days later she acknowledged: "[I] wish I had been taught to cook instead of how to play on the piano. A practical knowledge of the preparation of food products would stand me in better stead at this juncture than any amount of information regarding the scientific principles of music. I adore music, but I can't live without eating—and I'm hungry!" How she afforded or procured a Steinway piano is unknown.

Like Malvina, many young women of means saw their usefulness change from pleasure-giving entertainers in the parlor to manufacturers of goods over the course of the war. But, as Henry Graves warned his sister Cora, such transition did not mean giving up accomplishments, particularly music. Correspondence from "the Backwood of Mississippi" reported that, among other efficient uses of materials, "One lady has furnished fiddle strings for her musical friend, made out of her own hair."[63] Similar sentiments were echoed by a writer in Augusta's *Daily Constitutionalist* who praised southern women that now labored for the Confederacy in uncharacteristic ways:

> The women of the Confederate States—and no heroines of song or story outshine their peerless character—are giving heed to the things which make for the welfare of the army and the country. The rich are looking after their servants and directing their work—the making of cotton and woolen cloth. It is become the pride of the country matron, and even of the young ladies too. In almost every country place, and in the small towns and villages, we hear on every side the homely but not unpleasant whir of the spinning wheel, and the click and thud of the hand-loom. The fairest and the daintiest of the land are learning the mysteries of [dyes] and [color] setting and of warp and [weight].[64]

This commendation for the homespun dress, made popular in the song of that title by Carrie Bell Sinclair (1862), is a familiar trope in modern literature on Civil War music.[65] Indeed, two years earlier, the *Southern Confederacy* published an article that every young lady in Georgia lay aside the "abominable Yankee piano" and take up the spinning wheel.[66] The imagery almost reverses the phenomenon in Tolbert's observation that the piano replaced the spinning wheel, but the 1863 Augusta article stops short of undermining music's place in the definition of femininity.[67] The author specifically requests that these gentlewomen not only keep spinning but also maintain their musical skills: "All honor we say to the music of the spinning wheel, and especially to those who learn that while not forgetting their piano. They are fit to be the wives of heroes." The suggestion is that those who have the time to do both, spin and make music, receive the highest accolades. In other words, although the war brought unseen hardships for women of all economic classes, they were expected to contribute to the war effort and at the same time adhere to antebellum cultural codes by preserving gendered performance in the parlor. The reality of this position will be examined in the following chapter.

PART 5

Women Musicians in the Reconstruction Era

10

"She takes up music as a profession"

Career Women

In 1844, soprano Bertha Scheidler Ruhl (ca. 1839–99) moved from Frankfurt with her father, a conductor and singer, and began her US career singing opera in New Orleans. When the city fell to Union forces in 1862, she moved to Richmond. She performed for numerous events during the war and afterward found employment as music teacher and church musician. Times were difficult. Her husband (Peter) worked in a woolen factory, and by 1880, her nineteen-year-old daughter Nella also taught music. In spite of this, her obituary points to success: "In her time [Madam Ruhl] had been a great singer" including leading soprano at St. Paul's, Richmond. It continues: "For many years this lady has been a teacher of music and has gained a good reputation as such.—She has been a musical director and organist of church choirs and was enthusiastic in musical enterprises for benevolent objects."[1] Why Ruhl abandoned her career on the stage can only be imagined, but she refashioned herself as a church musician and teacher.

Sacred music and music education were prevalent remunerative options for women musicians before and after the war. The antebellum soprano who had been handsomely compensated at St. Michael's (Charleston) later returned to her position as lead singer in the choir. Teachers who spent the war years in the North, such as Maria Kowalewski, returned home (apparently with no resentment from those who stayed), but some left the South forever, such as the Slomans.[2] Others followed different paths. Nashvillian Alice Merritt Oates (1849–87) created a burlesque touring ensemble in 1868 (but changed its name to an "opera company" in 1871).[3] Lizzie Goldern, who gave concerts in Columbia during the war, continued doing so after it.[4]

Women had to rethink and rebuild themselves after the Civil War, a period when ideas of gender and class were in flux, and women like Maria Kowalewski in Mobile or Herminie Barbot in Charleston redefined women's sphere and influence after the war by linking domestic competence and control with a public persona.[5] Public performances took on a new meaning, and the repertory deemed appropriate for women changed significantly. Professional "lady" musicians challenged antebellum strictures about a woman's invisibility from the public gaze by embracing careers as wage-earning musicians while maintaining their genteel status in ways that differed from before the war. Ella Sheppard and other women of color crafted careers as professional musicians, on the stage or in their own communities.

Tensions surfaced when women started appearing in public performances and fund-raising event during the war. Once younger women tasted freedom from the restrictions of antebellum social rules—all devised to keep gentility carefully constructed and confined—their attitudes toward women's potential roles altered significantly. Victoria Ott discerns that after the war parents grew increasingly anxious over "fear of impropriety and the loosening of social restrictions" as regarded their daughters. She uses the example of Clara Solomon, whose mother found a letter that Clara had written to a soldier "too familiar and sentimental by elite standards."[6] Della Alston enraged her mother by writing a first-person response to an invitation from a man because first-person was too familiar, too intimate.[7] Conflicts arose between traditional understandings of gentility and the roles women could perform as young women from a wide variety of backgrounds (planters' daughters to newly freed women of color) actively sought music as a means of economic support. These shifting class boundaries influenced expectations of musical practice. Less wealthy women manipulated music as a form of cultural capital and transformed their social positions, gaining power within and beyond their own circles. Those beneath the elite transgressed upon the next level, as it were. Women with more economic means employed music in their efforts to constantly redefine gentility and reinforce class distinctions, even as traditional understandings of those distinctions altered.[8]

Gentility changed as the sentimental period ended. Halttunen locates the end of sentimental culture in 1856, supporting this date with dramatic changes in fashion and the rise in popularity of parlor theatricals.[9] Elite white women transformed their own racial and class identity around an evolved domesticity in this period. Like their middle-class neighbors, they consumed literature that redefined women's purpose and capabilities, establishing domesticity as the new aim of elite womanhood. All these things separated worthy women from those who were not and, in their view, "those who were not, of course, were the poor white and African American women" who worked as domestics, as farm laborers, or in factories. Poverty kept gentility beyond their reach.[10] Nonetheless, divisions between the elite and those immediately beneath them blurred significantly, as did other social boundaries further down the scale. A parlor in the home signified status, but not all parlors were equal.

They never would be equal, but aspiration to rise socially spurred women on as it had earlier. The difference was that now, to maintain their parlors or even their living, many more went to work. The practicalities of having to go to work in the 1860s struck some southern women as demeaning and difficult; for others it opened up the possibility of more respectability and recognition of endeavors they had already embarked upon. A number of women who trained assiduously in music before and during the war became wage-earning musicians shortly after it, even if a musical vocation (or any vocation) had not been their objective. On the other hand, pioneering women who always intended to sustain themselves as performing and/or teaching musicians took on leadership roles that were publicly acknowledged and sanctioned. Tensions between women who intended a career and those who fell into music as an unintended means of support rarely surface in postbellum literature because most of the surviving accounts of life during this period were published after 1900, and those doing the writing tailored their reminiscences to an idealized South.[11] By that time, elite women who had also been reduced to working glorified their efforts, such as Bessie Allston and her self-promoting *Chronicles of Chicora Wood* (1922) and *A Woman Rice Planter* (1913).

In spite of this skewed version of history, many middle-class women also worked. Their existence has been assumed but rarely explored by modern writers. The sources that provide firsthand data tend to be the handiwork of the planter class, not the middle-class women who were working before the war or those who sought careers after it. None of them features in modern scholarship of music history in the US, yet several touched the lives of all who heard them and became major forces of musical performance in their respective locales. Their biographies expand our knowledge of women and musical culture in the Reconstruction and beyond, and their performances reveal a preference for genres, styles, and composers that runs counter to the repertories described by authors of books on "American music," which base their conclusions largely on documentation from the North.

Carrying On

In the years immediately after the war some young women's lives carried on much the same as they had previously. Eva Eve, the plantation belle whose music figured in earlier chapters, and her husband moved to New York City when the fighting ceased. They remained there until the last Federal-dominated state government was overturned in 1877, returning at that time to Georgia.[12] Eva did not work upon their return. Similarly, Henrietta Aiken lost her piano during the war but never had to use her extensive musical training to support herself in the years following the South's defeat.[13]

Some southern planters continued to prosper as they had before the war, often because they had overseas investments and connections that sustained them financially. Ann and Carrie McFaddin of Alabama requested money for mourning attire and "a complete summer outfit," in addition to school fees while they attended St. Mary's in Raleigh. The totals for each girl in January 1869 were $643.64 for Ann and $494.81 for Carrie. Ann's totals included instrumental music and singing lessons, Carrie's $30 for music, unspecified.[14] Such sums confirm that although the South saw devastation and financial ruin, some of its constituents continued to maintain life as it was before the war, by whatever means possible.

Other antebellum practices persisted. Gifting continued, especially among family members, and whether this resulted from financial hardships, sentimentality for life before the war, or other reasons can rarely be determined. In the case of Basiline Prince, her mother's binder's volume was most likely a sentimental gift because the family maintained much of their wealth and position after the war. She marked it "Basiline Prince from her devoted Mother // Bath. Richmond County. Georgia 1868" and "Oct. 30th 1868" (presumably the date Basiline received it, at age thirteen).[15] The music, some of which came from Zogbaum's in Savannah, includes popular songs and dances, dating from the 1830s to the 1850s. Matthias Keller's "Bloomer Polka" and Thomas Valentine's variations on "Home! Sweet Home!" typify its contents. While a student at the Lucy Cobb Institute in Athens (which her maternal grandfather created in 1859), Basiline may have studied music with Sophie Sosnowski, who worked there after the war.[16]

Anna Cook's entries concerning social life in Milledgeville reveal that many antebellum and wartime activities continued uninterrupted. She attended a soirée at Dr. White's in early September 1865 but decided against going to another less than a week later (because she had cut her hair chin length in a pique of anger and subsequently felt too ugly to go out).[17] In the same year, her sister (Maddie) coached her in music lessons, and less than two years later she in turn taught her younger sister (Minnie). She frequently sang and played the piano to entertain herself and others, and on at least one occasion, music served to underscore a broken heart: in February 1867, as Anna played "Joys That We Tasted," a male friend asked her to play "Annie Laurie," which she attempted but could not perform because she was in love with the gentleman, who in turn favored one of her dearest friends.[18] All of these demonstrate that Anna's life as a genteel woman continued according to antebellum ideals after the Civil War.

Going to Work

The persistence of gentility in the postwar South underscores its application in new guises that arose out of financial necessity during the Reconstruction. The process of gentility adapted according to social change; it was not immutable across time. Anna's story outlines a trajectory that many southern women's lives followed throughout the mid-nineteenth century. Her father worked as superintendent of the Georgia Lunatic Asylum, but financially he belonged among the wealthier constituents of Milledgeville. After the Civil War, Anna's social status was slightly ambiguous, and in August of 1865, she was engaged to a planter who before the war ran a prosperous Alabama plantation but who was ruined, both financially and emotionally, after it. He died in 1867, and Anna soon thereafter married an alcoholic who had been treated at her father's institution. Such a seemingly disadvantageous marriage was better than none at all, at least to Anna, and she did not have to work to support her family.[19]

Other women followed different paths yet maintained their genteel status. In many instances, women whose families numbered among the wealthiest entered the workforce in the 1860s. As so many had studied music and music continued to be an expected accomplishment, it offered a subject for them to teach. Younger women were more likely to enjoy teaching, older women more often found it demeaning.[20] Some women of higher social status sought to earn money only as long as they had to. For example, after Eliza Fisk Harwood's husband died in the battle of Mechanicsville in 1863, she had five children to support. She returned to his family's land in eastern North Carolina and taught music.[21] Only a few years later, however, she returned to eastern Virginia, remarried, and ceased teaching. Similarly, Martha Mangum ran a school with her sister Sallie for only a few years.[22]

Numerous women who did not plan to support themselves balked at the need to do so and slipped back into more familiar patterns as soon as possible. Lucy Harvie Hull of Georgia chafed against having to work. She wrote retrospectively: "I had never thought of working before and my whole idea of life had been that I should marry, after having as good a time as possible 'in society.' I had a good and fairly well trained voice. . . . To teach was of course my first idea, but not in Augusta,—I could not *bear* that. All the other girls would be having such a good time and my life would be such a contrast; no, I could not bear that." The need to work mattered less than her reputation, and the idea that others would be engaging in social activities while she worked embarrassed her. She continued, "No such idea as 'the joy of the work' had occurred to me at that date; on the contrary, I felt very injured and oppressed, yet something of a heroine too. I was 'bravely going forth'—that was the phrase I hugged to my heart." Despite feeling sorry for herself, she finds agency and independence in setting out to earn money. This surge of unconventionality did not have a long-lasting influence, however. She taught only briefly (in faraway Memphis), married well, and moved to Savannah.[23]

Beaufort Sims, the talented music student at the South Carolina Female Collegiate Institute who owned at least six binder's volumes, opened a school sometime before her husband also created one in 1870.[24] Names and times on her copy of Czerny's *101 Exercises* suggest that she also taught piano lessons. Beaufort did not suffer these changes lightly. She wrote to Harriet Palmer that she felt they had no choice but to leave the United States and made plans to move to Brazil or Mexico. Taxation, she feared, would fall particularly heavily on "the higher class" and, worse, "the negro race are to be elevated." She felt she could not tolerate this idea but found she could not afford to move.[25] As one of those situated toward the top of the southern social hierarchy, the Civil War destroyed her expectations of her role in southern culture: her husband, the entity on which she had been taught to depend, was unable to fulfill his duty. In his failure of this trust, she had to refashion her own perceptions of self and society. Money she no longer had, but her social standing remained intact.

Antebellum-era schools that had closed during the war attempted to regain their positions in the local landscape, although the same faculty members often did not return. When the Columbia Female Institute (Tennessee) reopened in 1867, Mons. A. and Madame L. Esteve had charge of the music program.[26] A local paper noted that "More than ordinary attention is paid to the Fine Arts. Mons. A. Esteve . . . is the Director of that important department and Madame Esteve has charge of the vocal classes." When her husband died (by 1874) Madame Esteve was assigned sole control of the department.[27] She was not replaced with a male music professor.

Meanwhile, new schools emerged across the landscape, and if they maintained smaller faculties than seen in the 1850s, music study still continued to be a priority. *Branson & Farrar's North Carolina Business Directory of 1866–67* yields the following information concerning music in the state during the first year after the war. Under "Schools, Colleges, &c.," Mrs. M. S. Cushing ran a Music School in Wilmington; Margaret Bland offered Music Classes in Greensboro, as did Miss Miner in Hillsborough. Mrs. Taylor provided instruction in Music, Painting, and Drawing. The Jacksonville Academy of Music opened in 1866, and by 1871 Emma S. Pattison and Mary Porter both taught piano there.[28] When the Brownsville-Tennessee Female Institute announced its opening in 1867, the only people mentioned were its chief officer (a former president of Wesleyan College in Georgia) and the music teacher, John Wendel.[29] In the early 1870s, Annie W. Connor [Collin] was a student at the Brownsville school and wrote to her friend Eloise Gillespie that she was improving "imperceptibly" in her music but particularly enjoyed having a piano there.[30] This may have been a luxury for Annie that she did not have at home and her lessons a new experience altogether. Olivia Stedman, who sought work as a music teacher at Floral College, later lived with her daughter Olivia (1847–1922) who taught music in Fayetteville.[31]

William Hooper's correspondence with Marie J. Beattie reveals both the difficulties inherent in acquiring qualified faculty after the war and the bargaining power a quality education bestowed on women. He appealed to her to take the position of music teacher at the Wilson Female Academy (North Carolina). Her musical studies at Edgeworth Seminary in Greensboro, an institution boasting Moravian-trained musicians, had persuaded Hooper to overlook the fact that she was a Presbyterian. He also decried the "distressed state of the country + the prospect of all crops & 'hard times,'" a way of saying that he could not commit to a large faculty or high salaries. Unwilling to accept an insufficient salary, regardless of the reasoning, she declined his offer.[32]

Other women had to teach throughout the remainder of their lives. Mary Lewis, who spent her formative years at school in Paris and taught her younger siblings when she returned to Alabama in 1844, began teaching music out of financial necessity in the 1860s, and she continued to do so for many years.[33] Elizabeth Grimball taught music lessons after the Civil War to help support her family.[34] To name Adéle Petrigu Allston, the wife of former South Carolina governor Robert Francis Withers Allston and mother of Della, a professional music educator almost demands a suspension of belief—but she did. As a debutante in the 1850s, Della's gowns all came from Paris. Even at her wedding in 1863, she wore Brussels lace over a silk gown. After the war, however, Della operated a girls' boarding school. She maintained her upbringing and used it in her work: French was the exclusive language of instruction, thereby ensuring a new generation of women were taught the qualities of gentility as understood before the war.[35] Not all, however, chose to follow that path.

Professionals

Two commonly held views of nineteenth-century women concern the cult of domesticity and the doctrine of separate spheres. These ideas gained currency in the 1970s (at least) and served as foundations from which to observe aspects of women's cultural experiences. Since the 1990s, however, scholars have challenged the ubiquity of idealized domesticity for its reduction of women's interests and agency to an essentialist position of helplessness and shattered the binary of separate spheres with chronicles of women too numerous to be seen as exceptional.[36] Many women worked after the war, even those from the elite class.

Upper-class women who went to work because financial consequences of the Civil War forced them to do so constitute but one part of women's music in the Reconstruction South. Perhaps even more tantalizing are those who pursued careers as musicians and who forged new expectations of what it meant to be both genteel and leaders in their communities. After 1861, many more southern women deliberately created musical careers, and they applied the rules of gentility to the marketplace where women musicians asserted themselves as simultaneously businesswomen and genteel ladies. They redefined the rituals with more personal freedom than had been previously associated with gentility, all the while maintaining an antebellum worldview that placed marriage and motherhood in the forefront of a woman's duties.[37]

Some southern women who attempted to support themselves as solo musicians struggled. The most promising career lay in singing. A few met with success this way, such as Cora de Wilhout of Virginia (known as the American "prima donna") who performed in Balfe's *Bohemian Girl* in 1859.[38] Maintaining a career as a solo instrumentalist proved more difficult. In her later years, Lucie Loening expressed resentment about a musician's life. Unable to sustain a career on the stage, she taught at the Locquet Institute by at least 1870. She told her granddaughter, Olga Samaroff, that she gave up "the more interesting and lucrative career of a concert pianist" and became "doomed to the drudgery of giving piano lessons for the pitiful fees obtainable in the impoverished South." Loening later moved to Houston, Galveston, and finally San Antonio, where she taught Olga piano.[39] She manifested her bitterness over the lack of opportunities by conveying to her granddaughter the traditional view that marriage and not working was to be preferred above a career as a performer.[40]

Loening's experience contrasted those of other southern women, perhaps because she sought to make her mark as a touring pianist, which held fewer remunerative opportunities than other choices (educator, church musician, opera/concert singer). Several musicians in New Orleans succeeded in crafting careers, although they frequently appeared in multiple positions. Octavie Romey, for example, performed as a solo pianist with leading musicians in the city, and she also directed concerts, including "monster" ones featuring twenty-four women playing twelve pianos. She directed sacred women's choirs in New Orleans and composed a Mass that was performed in the Jesuit Church.[41] In late December 1865, she put together a benefit for widows and orphans at Odd Fellows' Hall, and she directed another one in April of the following year. As a piano soloist, Marguerite Elie Samuel's performances were praised as powerful and expressive.[42] She also published at least one composition for solo piano, "Vers le soir."

One of the most intriguing professional musicians emanating from the South was the opera singer Sallie Isabella McCullough. Her schoolmate Bessie Allston found her ungenteel because she sounded like an opera singer and was "big," but other writers described her in generous terms, such as one who wrote that she had a voice of "great compass and surpassing sweetness."[43] A *New York Times* writer described her as "a native of South Carolina, and a very beautiful woman. She was a singer by profession." *Godey's Lady's Book* described her much later as "a beautiful native prima donna."[44] This writer judged McCullough as a professional; Bessie Allston saw her as a schoolmate and measured her by social class. These standards differed. The *Times* article further commented that she "came of a good Southern family and the position of her husband and herself in the social circles of the Metropolis was secure."[45] This statement affirms her social status as different from the usual stage performer, but the fact that she sought a public career after attending the renowned South Carolina Female Collegiate Institute does not support the standards set for young women in the South.

Neither does the rest of McCullough's life. She left Barhamville and began a career as a singer as early as 1868, when her Parlor Opera Troupe performed the *Barber of Seville* in Memphis. She met the Neapolitan operatic tenor Pasquale Brignoli (1824–84) during a southern tour in 1869 and eloped with him to Montreal in 1870.[46] After they married, the two joined forces (and opera troupes) and sang together for the first time in Little Rock (not New York City, as claimed in the *Times* article). In Arkansas this troupe performed *Lucia di Lammermoor*, *Martha*, and *Il trovatore* in complete versions, one act from *Faust* (Gounod) and *Lucrezia Borgia* (Donizetti), as well as a sacred concert.[47] This substantial dose of opera constituted (reportedly) the first performances of that genre in Little Rock and, as would happen throughout her career, taxed McCullough's voice. The local paper nonetheless favored McCullough over the other singers, praising above all her southern roots. The troupe also sang in other cities in that region, including a well-reviewed concert in Memphis.

A review in the *Southern Musical Journal* of a Savannah performance in 1872 states that "the manager had evidently trusted everything to the magical name of *Brignoli* to attract a crowd. Madame Isabella McCullough Brignoli was the only member of the troupe worthy of notice . . . but her method showed a want of proper culture." (The writer grants that the hall itself would not do justice even to "a Nilsson."[48]) Indeed, her voice did not withstand the intense schedule and repertory she performed. In New York in 1866 (when she was about twenty-two), critics described McCullough's voice as "a good quality, but delicate in its texture and quickly exhausted"; by 1877, her Leonora was deemed "wretched, flat and weak."[49] At Brignoli's urging, she had misused her voice, and she turned to lighter fare in the mid-1870s. Most notably, in Boston she sang the role of Buttercup in *H.M.S. Pinafore* in November of 1878.[50]

A sensational divorce paraded McCullough's private life for all to see, but any negative reaction from it was overshadowed by her sudden death in 1880.[51] The first part of her obituary in *The Musical Record and Review* emphasized her southern origins.[52] The daughter of a minor planter whose mother ran the family's interests by the time she matriculated at the South Carolina Female Collegiate Institute, McCullough came from the middle classes. She must have realized while in school that she would have to support herself, and music allowed her to do so. The *Times'* writer's use of "good family" does not necessarily imply a rich one, and McCullough's family may have seen education at Barhamville as a means to a profession.

Other southern women musicians achieved a degree of success as performers after the war. The *Southern Musical Journal*, published in Savannah during the 1870s, provides a wealth of information about different types of musical events throughout the South and beyond, as well as articles on composers, performers, and all topics music-related. It serves as a gauge of musical activities and music education throughout the region and demonstrates the resiliency of musicians in the Reconstruction South. Savannah's Mozart Club is a case in point. In 1871, this club featured a male chorus and an orchestra of twenty; their associate members (defined as their audience in the 1850s) numbered 150. The next year, the orchestra had grown by four, but the associate members almost doubled. As they had done in the 1850s, women still avoided joining the chorus in 1874, although a number of women performed as soloists. Mrs. C. A. Clark, who became the paid soprano at Christ Church, performed several times in 1873–74. Among her repertory were "Casta diva," "Swiss Song" (with duets written by Eckhard), "Fra poco a me," "O luce di quest' anima," and the "Bolero" from Verdi's *Sicilian Vespers*.[53] Her repertory confirms the continued popularity of bel canto arias during the Reconstruction, another example of the persistence of genteel ideals.

The foregoing chapters have shown how difficult music formed a structural part of the southern woman's repertory by distinguishing those who could afford more time to practice and the better instructors from those who could not. After the war, much of the antebellum repertory could still be heard in recitals, and vestiges of the cultural capital accorded certain styles remained. The selections presented in Savannah by three women soloists (Clark, soprano; Mrs. D. A. [Josephine] O'Byrne; Miss M. Brooks) performed with members of the Mozart Club demonstrates this continuity. The discussion of the repertory in print, however, signals new ways of thinking about women, repertory, and appropriate public presentation. The author of a review in the *Southern Musical Journal*, reporting on Clark's "Casta diva," added the revealing comment that "This Cavatina has long been regarded as a sort of test piece for first class debutantes, in consideration of its extreme difficulty both in execution and in the intensity of emotional expression requisite especially of the andante movement. A fair success in a piece of this character being quite sufficient to establish the reputation of any vocalist."[54] This statement further confirms that antebellum upper-class young women sang bel canto arias. It might also suggest that only women of this class—or, of course, professional opera stars or concert singers—performed Italian opera in its original language and format. Both groups of women had to negotiate the technical demands of the area as well as portray the passionate feeling that accompanies it. And while stage performers had been praised for such abilities, young ladies had not. Such overt displays of emotion defied the careful training in gentility inculcated in women before the war, but it confirms the demise of sentimental culture and the signifiers of its replacement, such as parlor theatricals.[55] For her encore, Mrs. Clark sang Dempster's "Come over the

Figure 10.1. "The Nightingale's Trill," by Wilhelm Ganz, two versions of final measures.

Mountain," Benedict's "Skylark" ("too light" for her voice), and "The Nightingale's Trill," a performance that reportedly compared favorably with the Parepa's famous rendition. At least two publications included cadenzas on the final cadence, one in Paris (dedicated to Parepa) and one in New Orleans (published in the series *Songs and Ballads of Mlle. Parepa*) (see Figure 10.1). Either could have been Clark's choice, or she could have improvised her own.

From Lady Organist to Directress

Daniel Miller argues that the meaning of objects changes according to their manner and place of use, thus linking the materiality of an object to the materiality of the space in which it is sited.[56] A keyboard instrument in the home differed in meaning from one in church, all the more so if the performer were paid for performing on it. Before the war, women who served as church musicians ran the risk of transgressing their gentility in public display, but all of the examples investigated for this study negotiated the delicate balance by remaining hidden, either as subservient musicians or unnamed contributors. After the war, many continued in their antebellum positions. In Hillsborough, Lizzie Jones continued as organist of St. Matthew's, and in his centennial address Bishop Joseph Blount Cheshire acknowledged her service as "one noble woman . . . the faithful co-laborer . . . in creating the high standard of sacred music. . . . Omitting only the names of Bishop Green and Dr. Curtis, I doubt if any should be put on a level with hers."[57] Her impact on music at St. Matthew's was consequential enough for the new organ of 1883 to be called "Miss Lizzie's organ." After its installation, she wrote to a cousin that she had spent some seven hours in the church, mostly practicing. Such devotion to music makes a compelling case for the recognition that some women studied music as more than an accomplishment. Moreover, the bishop publicly acknowledged Lizzie Jones as simultaneously genteel (a noble woman) and a working woman (a co-laborer), calling her by name.

The soprano who led the St. Michael's choir (Charleston) in 1856 returned to her position when the church reopened after the war (1866) and was compensated with a salary of $150 per year and $212.50 by 1868, a substantial amount in the postwar economy. The quartet, consisting of "some of the best voices in the city," included Mr. and Mrs. E. H. Sparkman, who participated in services for many years, singing regularly.[58] The Sparkman family was a prominent one in Charleston; he was a bank president. Numerous references in the *Charleston Daily News* tell of Mrs. Sparkman traveling by steamer to various ports, confirming her place in the social order.[59] After a succession of male organists, Mrs. Harrison played at St. Michael's from 1874 until 1878.[60] St. Michael's was not alone, either. Grace Church on Wentworth Street (also Episcopal) had a paid quartet of singers, and Miss A. Groves was the leader.[61]

Before the Civil War, Herminie Petit Barbot established a name for herself in Charleston as a teacher, but, in the second half of the century, she increased her presence and garnered appreciation for her commanding role in the city's musical life. This professional organist who directed oratorios and operas in Charleston provides an example of how southern women negotiated ideals of gentility in the postwar South. In 1854, George Fitzhugh published his *Sociology of the South*, in which he proclaimed southern woman's lack of independence as her defining criterium: "So long as she is nervous, fickle, capricious, delicate, diffident and dependent, man will worship and adore her. Her weakness is her strength, and her true art is to cultivate and improve that weakness." He continued that the only right a woman held was for protection.[62] Herminie Barbot stands in opposition to such attributes; she had to support herself before marriage, but she continued to do so after it.[63] Before the war, she worked with her mother. After it, she took control of many aspects of sacred (and sometimes secular) music in Charleston. Even though she married, she maintained a degree of independence.

In the postwar period, Barbot supplemented her teaching income by playing the organ at the Cathedral of St. John the Baptist and at St Mary's (Catholic) on Hasell Street. The *Charleston Daily News* frequently lauded her work and praised not only her musicality but also her organization of Charleston's musicians. In 1873, it announced a concert of Haydn's *Creation*, describing it as a "pleasure by all lovers of classical music." The writer had attended rehearsals and predicted that the performance will "rarely if ever been excelled in Charleston." More to the point here, Barbot "had the direction and management of the undertaking from the beginning, and too much cannot be said in praise of her energy in promoting the love and practice of classical music."[64] Such wording signals a changing public face for remunerated women musicians: Barbot is praised for her energy and her ability to inspire both the love and practice of classical music in Charleston, which she accomplished through diligent work; most importantly, she was in charge. None of these attributes would have been interpreted as positive in terms of gentility before 1860. In fact, they implied the opposite.

Figure 10.2. Herminie Petit Barbot. Image from Willard, *American Women*.

Barbot's impact on Charleston's music was substantial, and her status as a lady never questioned. How her name and efforts appeared in print provide a gauge for how women were seen in the postwar landscape and how this contrasted antebellum expectations. Professional performers in the earlier period typically received brief mention in the press, but women on the stage (opera, church, or concert hall) are not mentioned as leading large-scale musical events. In this regard, she represents a new acceptance of working women after the war. The newspapers particularly praised her Christmas Day performances. In 1868, she accompanied Haydn's Imperial Mass in D, and, in addition to the highly praised (but unnamed) soprano soloist, a reviewer wrote that "The organ accompaniments were played by Mrs. Barbot, the organist of the church, who showed her management of her instrument as much good taste and judgment as musical knowledge and skill." In 1872, the *Charleston Daily News* reported that St. Mary's Church "always has good music, but Madame Barbot and her assistants on Christmas day excelled themselves," suggesting that she was in charge of others beneath her.[65] If male musicians were involved in this performance, she would have directed them—a crucial reversal in gender roles. That the Catholics in Charleston actively sought women organists, on at least one occasion, is shown by an advertisement in the same paper on October 15, 1872, that reads: "WANTED, A CATHOLIC LADY AS Organist at St. Peter's church. Apply to the Pastor." Barbot's success at St. Mary's may have encouraged the pastor at St. Peter's to seek out a woman for the organist's position. The desire for a "lady" encapsulates a newfound appreciation for and understanding of the contributions genteel women could make to society, although the possibility of offering her less money than a man might have induced the church to seek a woman.

Herminie's story takes on new attributes that are worth considering. One is that, in spite of being widowed with six children in 1887, "her marriage in no way interfered with her musical work," as one nineteenth-century author put it. Her obituary describes her in a like manner as "the best of wives, mothers, her marriage did not interrupt her music and her home has always been one of the city's musical centers." These statements hint that marriage could have been a problem for women musicians in the late-nineteenth century. Described in mixed-gendered terms as a "brilliant pianist with fine technique and great force [masculine] and delicacy of expression [feminine]," she did not do solo performances except as charitable contributions, another sign of her gentility. More unusual is Frances Elizabeth Willard's comment that "Her peculiar gift is in training and directing large musical forces. She has for years given cantatas, oratorios and operas with the amateurs of the city."[66] "Large musical forces" constitutes very different terminology to describe women musicians—language that accords Herminie Petit Barbot with control over sizable ensembles, the bulk of which must have been male. These began as early as the *Creation* performance in 1868.

Barbot's career in Charleston was not unique. She was but one of several women whose positions as music teachers grew into something more substantial after the war. A close examination of women's public musical activities in Mobile reveals significant changes that the war made in the possibilities available to women—or at least the opportunities that women seized when they arose, being that many of the same male musicians still lived and worked in the city during the Reconstruction. The example of Maria Kowalewski, Josephine Hutet Pillichody, and Fannie Sands, three women who worked together in Mobile during the early 1870s, encapsulates how women whose social status differed before the war but who joined together as remunerated musicians after it.

Maria Kowalewski supported herself in Mobile as a music teacher and organist after her divorce in 1850. She married again in 1859 (Nicholas G. Portz of the French Consul's office), but this union was short-lived as he went missing during the war.[67] She spent most of the war in New York and only returned to Mobile after it ended. Mobile city directories list her until her death in 1897; her residence was 450 Government Street, one of the most elegant streets in Mobile and known as "Mansion" or "Millionaire's Row" (where Octavia Le Vert had lived previously).[68] Though a professional woman, Kowalewski was known as a lady who lived in a fashionable district.

While she taught music and played the organ at the cathedral, Kowalewski took on a more public persona in Mobile's musical circles as an organizer and director of large events, including both operas and oratorios. As early as 1868, the *Mobile Register* included a review of an amateur production of Flotow's *Martha*, commenting that it had come together "under the direction of Madame Kowalewski Portz." Two years later, she is given credit for the artistic and, more amazingly, financial success of a performance of Haydn's *Creation*. For this concert, the reviewer praises her "unflagging zeal and industry" that led to no false notes in the chorus, and a neat, smooth, and precise orchestra. Kowalewski's zeal compares favorably to Barbot's energy. Moreover, "the triumph [of] the singers, the public and the beneficiary of the evening [was] mainly indebted to the talent and perseverance of Mad. Kowalewski Portz."[69] Such language praising the efforts of a woman musician in the South was unheard of before 1861, as previously women had been relegated to their own (solo) performances and rarely named unless they were touring artists.[70] Moreover, it attributes the precise playing of the orchestra, almost certainly a male-only group, to Kowalewski.

She continued to run large-scale events in the 1870s. In the *Southern Musical Journal* of March 1873, "Flute" reported that the Mobile Musical Association "gave their first concert under the management of that talented artist, Madame Kowaleuski-Poetz. It was a perfect success."[71] Moreover, a second concert was to be given a week later, and, even more surprisingly, she planned to revive the "Summer night Concerts" with twenty-four musicians.[72] Maria Kowalewski held no official position in the Mobile Musical Association—only men could be officers, and all business conducted was restricted to male members. An announcement placed by their president, I. I. Jones, in the *Mobile Register* on May 16, 1869, requests that gentlemen members come to a business meeting, and ladies and gentlemen to a rehearsal. Nonetheless, the press repeatedly credits her with the organization's work, whether it is programming, rehearsing, or performing. That a woman ran such an association speaks to the respect accorded Kowalewski in Mobile. Her social status remained as it was before the war, a music teacher and organist, but her role altered as she assumed a leadership role in an organization run by men. She did not suffer any negative reaction.

Another member of the Mobile Musical Association, Stephanie Lucy "Fannie" Durand Sands (1827–1878), also left her mark on music in Mobile, but before the war she did not receive payment for her assistance as an organist. She presided at the organ for a Sacred Concert on June 15, 1874, that was described by a correspondent in the *Southern Musical Journal*. Unexpectedly, she is credited there with "getting up" the concert with orchestral accompaniment. It began with a Bach Prelude by organ and orchestra, and the complete program was as follows:

PART FIRST

    Bach! [*sic*]—Prelude—Organ—Orchestra

    Kyrie—Solo—Chorus, Haydn

    Quis est Homo, Rossini

    Et Incarnatus—Tenor Solo, Mozart

    Fa cut Portem Va Cavatina, Rossini

    Alma Virgo—Solo Chorus, Hummel

    Le Berceuse—Organ Solo, Gottschalk

PART SECOND

    Inflammatus, Rossini

    Anthem—Quartette and Cho[rus], Schlesinger

    Aria—Soprano Solo, Rode

    Cantata—"St. Cecelia,"—Tenor Solo, Gajetano Capocci

    Ave Maria—Soprano Solo, Cherubini

    Heavens are Telling—Chorus, Haydn

Newspaper reviews of the keyboard players reflect the changes in reconstructed southern society. For this occasion, the writer ("Flute") describes Fannie Sands with masculine language that does not typify how anyone wrote about southern women until this point: "Madame Sands presided at the organ, and under her skillful management it seemed to be an immense thing of life, which, when animated by its mighty lungs, sounded out its combinations with an unmistakable firmness and accuracy, forming a foundation upon which the others could build up the most elaborate accompaniment." Before the war, words such as "mighty" and "firmness" would not have conjured positive images of women. The characterization of her fellow keyboard performer in this concert, Josephine Pillichody, contrasts that of Sands in that it typifies antebellum language: "Madame Pillachody [*sic*], ever ready to aid and assist in her lady-like and artistic manner, anything to bring out good music, presided at the piano, interspersing such delicate and elaborate runs, as were necessary to make a piece complete, with a feathery touch that the keenest imagination could not tell where the *material* ended, and the *immaterial* began." Flute recognizes Pillichody's feminine flourishes as "ladylike," being "delicate" and "feathery," but the writer also mentions her willingness to aid, which connects with antebellum expectations that women be useful and supportive.[73] She also did anything to make a piece complete, much like a wife was expected to complete her husband.

Flute continues by providing some background on how Fannie Sands came to be a remunerated musician in Mobile. This narrative could belong to numerous women in the Reconstruction South:

> Madame Sands should be proud of her success. Her case is but another one of those who once reveled in wealth, ease and luxury but are now forced to toil for home and comfort. Music was her delight; her devotion to her church caused her when rich and independent, to volunteer her services as organist at the Cathedral; her mansion was the gathering place for the best of music talent. She lost her husband; like thousands of others, she lost her property, and was reduced to her own personal efforts for her support. She did not stop to cry about it—if she did, no one knew it. She had a fond mother to care for; like a true, courageous woman, she dashes away the bitter disappointed hopes, she takes up music as a profession, and this is her debut.
>
> May her spirit encourage others to do likewise. God bless you, Lady Sands![74]

This enthusiastic accolade signals a dramatic shift in how society viewed women and work after the war, and it can also be read as a commentary on women and the public gaze. No longer did the dictates of antebellum gentility rule—Fannie Sands performed in public (a debut), her name was printed both in the program and newspapers, and she now had a profession. Even more striking is the fact that her move to this new social status was wholeheartedly applauded by the *Southern Musical Journal*.

Josephine Hutet Pillichody (1834–1905), the pianist in this performance, moved through a number of different social circles during her lifetime. Born in Albany, New York, Josephine had a career as a prodigy, accompanying Adelina Patti in a recital in New York at age twelve.[75] In 1857, she moved to Mobile with her husband, a modestly successful cotton merchant. She was not shown as working in the 1860 US Census, but in 1880 she is listed as a music teacher. After the war, she served as organist at Jackson Street Presbyterian Church, St. Francis Street Methodist Church, and twelve years at the cathedral. Her fame was such that she is the only composer mentioned by name in *The WPA Guide to Alabama: The Camellia State*, which claims (erroneously) that she wrote "the first recorded compositions" in Alabama.[76]

In a *Southern Music Journal* correspondence dated March 15, 1873, Flute writes glowingly of both Josephine Pillichody and Maria Kowalewski:

> There is one lady artist here, who is known in musical circles . . . as the "American lady Pianist"—Madame Pillachody [*sic*]. She is very successful with her pupils, and is a hard and constant worker, well deserving the ample patronage she receives—she is completing the musical education of some of the most finished of our young [lady] amateurs. Mobile is proud of having such talent here. One of her most charming characteristics is the cheerfulness with which she aids, gratuitously, all charitable entertainments, on the first invitation, [if] it is in her power to do so. Her particular forte is in the higher walks of music, where she shines as a true artist, but her gentleness of manner, cheerful temper and great patience, particularly adapts her to the instruction of children. Such a happy combination of character as she possesses is as rare as it is delightful in its influences.

Again, Pillichody "shines" as an example of ideal southern womanhood during the Reconstruction. She remains charming, patient, gentle, and cheerful; she volunteers her services for charitable events; she excels in teaching children; and she is a true (necessary for gentility) artist in a more highbrow repertory.[77] A major difference is the report that she works "hard." In previous decades if someone accidentally saw one of the women of the home working, the polite response was to turn away and ignore her. Less than ten years after the war ended, the *Southern Musical Journal* publicly acknowledges her efforts and congratulates her on them. She represents the beautiful but unnamed amateur who performed brilliant variations before the war and who after it adapted her cheerful and charming self to becoming a paid professional who plays "the higher walks of music." By the 1870s, someone with her qualities as a lady could perform in public without fear of public censure. She made enough of an impact in the South for the *Southern Musical Journal* in faraway Savannah to report her recovery from illness.[78]

As for Maria Kowalewski, she had assumed an even greater active role in creating events in Mobile by this time. Flute reports that "The Musical Association is doing wonders under the skillful guidance of the talented Madame Kowaleski-Potz [*sic*]. Entertainments are enjoyable and well attended. She displays a great taste in introducing more instrumental music into the programme. On the 26th inst., another of her concerts is to take place."[79] She added more instrumental music—not piano music but the instruments that women did not play. The Mobile Musical Association remained, in name at least, under the purview of the male-dominated governing board.[80] Nevertheless, Flute refers to the series as "hers."

In 1878, Kowalewski accompanied a commemorative performance of the Mozart Requiem in honor of Fannie Sands, former organist at the cathedral.[81] To mount such a work took substantial effort, and that they performed the requiem in honor of a working woman testifies to her significance to the community. The following year, Kowalewski and Mme Adelaide de V. Chaudron accompanied a sacred concert at Government Street Presbyterian Church. The performers included Sigmund Schlesinger, Josephine Pillichody, Ruth Dargan Huger, and Ellen "Nellie" Tarleton Bestor.[82] Like Herminie Barbot in Charleston, Maria Kowalewski began as a keyboard performer, altered the course and supported herself as a teacher and an organist in a prominent position (Christ Church Cathedral for fifty-two years.), and after the war essentially took control of amateur musical events in her city. Both women received laudatory statements in print, and their obituaries praised their work. Indeed, Kowalewski's properly sums up the manner in which women had the opportunity to make their own way without being dependent on men: "the lady was the architect of her own fortunes."[83]

"A well-furnished and cozy parlor" for Black Women

The end of the Civil War dramatically impacted musically literate Black women. Music was an integral part of the curriculum at the Avery Normal Institute, a school established in Charleston in 1865 for the purpose of training the area's young Black population for professional careers.[84] As it had done before the war, musical accomplishment formed part of the culture of gentility. Bishop Daniel Payne (1811–1893), a founder of the African Methodist Episcopal Church, confirmed this when he promised that "the free black middle class, like the white elite, cultivated a musical tradition, which would be continued at Avery."[85] Notably, Payne positioned the Black middle class alongside the white elite, not middle class. Mr. and Mrs. C. C. McKinney taught music at Avery; he had taught in Charleston's schools for free Blacks before the war. Music was part of the curriculum. Brooklyn-born Laura Williams Cardozo, who played the piano for the singers at the 1873 commencement exercises, came south with her husband when he returned to Charleston to teach after the Civil War.[86] The graduation concert in which they performed mirrored those in schools for white women.[87] Indeed, in 1883 Henry Ward Beecher complimented the music program at Avery for the "singing and comely appearance of the pupils," finding only Fisk University to be comparable.[88] That he chose to mention the physical as well as musical attributes further aligns this report with commentaries on white women's musical activities.

As noted earlier, Anna Johnson and Amanda Dickson grew up in houses with pianos.[89] Similarly, Rev. L. R. Nichols owned a piano, which stood in "a well-furnished and cozy parlor" along with six oil paintings (another material sign of gentility). Powers mentions one Black elite household in Charleston where the two sisters played the piano well enough to "solve the sweet mysteries of Shubert's [sic] and Bach's most difficult music."[90] Bach's music was rare in any American parlor, but merely naming the composer signifies cultural capital, similar to the invocation of opera stars.

Professional Black Women

In 1994, Ellen Norris authored one of the few music studies of the music of both Black and white southerners during the Reconstruction, documenting practices in education, church, and performance in Petersburg. She confirms that the repertory performed by Barbot in Charleston and Kowalewski in Mobile reflect southern preferences for the sacred music of Mendelssohn, Handel, and, above all, Haydn's *Creation*.[91] She also identified Black women organists and musicians in the area, such as Virginia M. Morgan and Mary E. Wallace at St. Stephen's Episcopal. As with white choirs, St. Stephen's Choir presented a concert at the Academy of Music in 1879 (reserving the better seats for whites, which implies a mixed-race audience). In the 1880s, payment for their woman organist was four dollars per month. Likewise, at First Baptist Church, Mrs. Elizabeth Smith ran a school for choristers during the 1870s.[92]

Other opportunities arose in Tennessee, particularly for the Fisk Jubilee Singers. The musicians at Fisk began concertizing in 1870; thus, the women who participated in them must have been trained prior to that time.[93] The American Missionary Association opened the "Fisk School" in 1866 as a Free Public School, with twelve hundred students (male and female) on its rolls and an average attendance of eight hundred.[94] In September of the next year, Fisk University opened. The 1869–70 Third Annual Catalogue lists Anna Ogden (wife of the school's president) as the Superintendent of Instrumental Music, Mrs. Leanora E. Aray and Miss Ella Sheppard as Teachers of Instrumental Music, and George L. White (Fisk's Treasurer) taught Vocal Music. Of these four, the only Black person was Ella Sheppard.

Piano and organ were both offered, but fees had to be paid in advance. "Pianoforte" with the use of an instrument was five dollars, but only four if the use of the instrument was not needed. "Cabinet organ" was available at the same rates, and vocal music classes (as well as gymnastics) were free. Fisk also offered a "Singing Class" with the objective of training men and women in the "true science and art of Church and Secular music, to correct prevailing evil habits, and to cultivate a purer taste in this much neglected branch of education." Acquired purity represented a necessary aspect of gentility. The natural style that students brought to the school was not only discouraged, it was named "evil." Fisk administrators advertised music as "science" in the same manner as Sarah Smith and others had done decades earlier. Members of the singing class became White's early choral group, which started giving concerts soon thereafter. Although not trained as a musician, he rehearsed the singers relentlessly, and the "purer taste" alluded to earlier probably was his work on pianissimo singing, careful tuning, and consistent vowel formation—all the hallmarks of European-styled choral singing as prescribed by Lowell Mason.[95] White worked to make the Fisk singers acquire the same choral sound prized by white choral directors associated with European classical (scientific) music, most notably espoused by those associated with the Handel and Haydn Society of Boston.[96]

First and foremost, among the members of the Fisk music department, the biography of Samuella "Ella" Sheppard warrants attention in this study. She served as the only Black faculty member in Fisk's earliest years: Assistant Director of the Fisk Jubilee Singers, their pianist/organist, and a music teacher for decades.[97] In the 1879 Nashville City Directory, Sheppard is listed as a Music Teacher; in the 1880 US Census, her occupation was Jubilee Singer. Both describe her career. How she came to such a career is a moving story of challenges, disappointments, and perseverance. In 1865, Sheppard then accepted a position at a Black subscription school in Gallatin (Tennessee).[98] She was only able to save six dollars for an entire term of teaching. Soon after her arrival in Gallatin, the school was burned—a fate suffered by many schools for Black children. When Ella sought admission to Fisk University, John Ogden allowed her to enroll if she could find work. Her studies at Fisk were somewhat erratic because of her poor physical health, and during the term after her first concert she was unable to attend class at all.

Sheppard earned money through her "music scholars"— Nashville children who wished to study with her, indicating that her reputation had spread—and odd sewing jobs to help pay her way through school until she was offered the "situation of assistant music teacher in the University." Undoubtedly, it was Sheppard's musical talent that brought her to the attention of White, who organized the singers at Fisk for a fund-raising concert in Nashville in 1867.

Ella Sheppard's part in the Fisk performances was considerable, and George White wrote in September 1869 that "if she is the right sort of stuff," he could successfully raise money for Fisk through concertizing. What that "stuff" meant to White is not clear, but Sheppard's demeanor, her ability to maneuver among white and Black audiences—in short, her performance of gentility, both through music and demeanor—allowed her to achieve success in spheres previously closed to southern Black women. She served as the accompanist for the Fisk concerts and sang soprano in the group. She also helped "drill" the singers, which validates her role as assistant director.[99] This woman, only twenty years old when the Fisk Jubilee Singers went on tour in 1871, had studied music (both piano and voice), had been hired as the only Black teacher at Fisk, accompanied the choral group, assisted in rehearsals, and taught her own music students on the side. These were remarkable achievements, inconceivable before the Civil War.

The parlor repertory dominated Fisk musicians' early performances. Their first concert included a variety of vocal works, mostly for chorus, including a "National Song and Chorus," abolitionist hymns such as "No Slave Beneath the Starry Flag" and "Are Ye Sleeping Maggie," as well as piano solos and duets.[100] One of the solos was "The Sultan's Polka," performed by Josephine Moore and Eliza Walker on piano and tambourine. It reflected the simple style of music sanctioned by writers such as Hartley for performance by genteel ladies. It did not approach the technical rigor demanded of more substantial works, which

Figure 10.3. "Gently Sighs the Breeze," by Stephen Glover.

during the antebellum period had been associated with professionals of lower social rank. Similarly, Glover's "Gently Sighs the Breeze" was best known as a duet popularized by images of Jenny Lind and Marietta Alboni on the cover (see Figure 10.4). Porter and Moore performed this song in the 1867 Fisk School Grand Entertainment. More complicated than "When the Swallows Homeward Fly" or "Home! Sweet Home!" it nonetheless signals antebellum gentility and, through the promulgation of the image of the two opera stars, constructed whiteness. Sandra Graham acknowledges the courage it took to present this repertory, but, when we consider the well-known image associated with "Gently Sighs," Porter and Moore's performance takes on an almost combative stance—daringly putting their faces in the place of Lind and Alboni.[101] Audiences would have expected operatic selections from well-trained musicians in the 1860s; however, they did not expect Black women to perform this scientific repertory.

Gabriel Milner sees the early Fisk performances as pointedly avoiding spirituals, the distinguishing marker of Black performativity, to emphasize virtuoso singing instead of racial difference, to define themselves "precisely in terms of its ability to transcend the racial designations confidently delineated by white writers." He reads their turn to spirituals soon thereafter with the dual purposes of meeting white northern expectations of a "quintessential American identity rooted in the soil" (and a "trope of redemption") to a liberating path of self-determination and economic security.[102] Kira Thurman's research on German audiences' reactions to the genteel qualities of the Fisk singers' repertory and sound further supports the mapping of antebellum ideals onto the performance of culture, even if the subject of the performance—Black gentility—was a novel notion in most of the United States.[103]

The young women of the group began their musical careers before the Civil War had ended, and several were from Tennessee.[104] Jennie Jackson (1852–1910) joined the Fisk Jubilee Singers in 1872 and reportedly had one of the best voices in the group; her mother initially forbade her performance in choirs, anticipating a solo career for her daughter. (Her admonition against singing in choirs suggests that she was acquainted with both a different repertory and the benefits of singing in another style.[105]) Jackson's signature piece was the spiritual "I'll Hear the Trumpet Sound," but audiences also demanded her performance of "Home! Sweet Home!" In this regard, she followed the traditions of other professionals, most notably Jenny Lind. Jackson left the Fisk Jubilee Singers in 1877 and later sang with at least four other groups, the last being her own Jennie Jackson DeHart Jubilee Club.[106]

Born enslaved in Lebanon (Tennessee), Maggie Porter (1853–1942) first attended Joseph McKee's Presbyterian mission school. She then matriculated at the Fisk Free Colored School at age twelve. As a teenager, she taught at several country schools. Her experience as a public school teacher mirrored those of Ella Sheppard: the Ku Klux Klan burned Bellevue, her first school, but she continued at two others.[107]

Porter was a member of all three of the Fisk troupes (1871–78) and pursued a European career until at least 1897. She sang the title role in costumed productions of William Bradbury's *Esther, The Beautiful Queen*, which also featured Jackson in a supporting role and Sheppard as organist. White audiences responded with mixed reactions to their performances. For some, it was impossible to erase expectations of Blackness with slavery: a reviewer in New Jersey thought his readers would best understand the performance by listing the characters—including "prices"—as they would have appeared in a slave auction.[108] Others saw the performances in a different light, and Juanita Karpf even argues that White's choosing of Porter, a darker-skinned soprano, for the title role was but one example of his "activist purpose" in staging *Esther*.[109] Writers frequently discussed the skin tone of the Fisk singers, as if that was a dominant feature of the group of musicians. The tenor of such reviews, of course, mentioned the music they heard, but the gulf between race and constructions of whiteness as defined by European-derived genres such as the oratorio remained.

Milner finds that the Fisk Jubilee Singers' early repertory, from "*Esther* to a mul-tiethnic mélange of polka and Irish jig" "situated the chorus within larger national currents."[110] The story of Esther is one of raising up persecuted people, a timely plot for newly emancipated slaves. The Fisk singers' influence spread, particularly the use of *Esther* among Black choral groups. This oratorio became a popular work in schools, community groups, and churches, sometimes used purposefully by the "'aspiring' strata of the black community."[111] All interpretations of the Fisk perfor-mance of Bradbury's work point to a desire to be seen as genteel by adopting the Eurocentric repertory associated with white Americans, but it can also be read as activist and feminist in light of its subject matter and plot.

A close-up from a photograph of the Fisk singers allows us to consider Shep-pard, Porter, and Jackson in their visual signification of class and culture—to view their performance of gentility (see Figure 10.4). Their clothing, jewelry, hairstyles, and stance declare them to be women of substance and taste, while their musical talents evince culture and education. Not only were they genteel, however. They crafted careers out of music and, like Kowalewski, became the architects of their own fortunes. Several of the women who sang with the Fisk Jubilee Singers formed their own groups, such as Walker's Famous Fisk Jubilee Singers (contralto Eliza Ann Nellie Walker [Crump], 1859–1941) or became pro-fessional concert singers (Marie "Selika" Smith Williams, 1849–1937, and Nellie Brown Mitchell, 1845–1924).[112]

Marie Smith, a coloratura soprano born in Natchez (only a few years after Anna Johnson), moved to Cincinnati early and studied music there. Known as

Figure 10.4. Ella Sheppard, Jennie Jackson, and Maggie Porter.

Marie Selika Williams, her career trajectory exemplifies the options Black women seized after the Reconstruction. On November 14, 1878, just two years after her concert debut, she performed in the White House's Green Room for an audience that included President Rutherford Hayes. Her performance included Verdi's "Ernani, involami," Moore's "The Last Rose of Summer," Harrison Millard's "Ave Maria," and Richard Mulder's "Staccato Polka." Her repertory corresponded to that discussed in Part 2, the sonic signs of gentility.[113] A writer in the *National Republican* praised the "celebrated colored prima donna" for her "remarkable power, sweetness, and versatility, and acknowledged her as the "Queen of Staccato." Combining power and sweetness in the assessment further demonstrates a change in the press's attitude toward both women and Black performers during the 1870s.[114] A review of the concert (published on the 16th) noted that "race prejudice may affect her success pecuniarily, but impartial critics will have to accord her a place among the greatest of sopranos in the country." Considering that the audience thunderously applauded her rendition of Verdi's formidable "Ah! fors e lui," Williams could indeed claim high status in music as a science.

Fisk was the first but not the only new school for Black southerners that featured a choir, and several groups, such as the "Jubilee Singers" from Norfolk, can be located throughout the South during the late-nineteenth century. The Hampton Singers organized in response to Fisk's success, although their style of singing differed. The women in the choir hailed from a broader geographic area than did those at Fisk, and many were formerly enslaved. Alice Ferribee and Rachel Elliott came from nearby Portsmouth and Sallie Davis from Norfolk. Maria Mallette, and Mary Norwood, however, traveled to Hampton from Wilmington, North Carolina, as did Lucy Leary.[115] The individual and collected histories of these Black musicians demonstrate their participation in scientific music practices as part of their training for careers.

* * *

The prospects and acceptance of seeking a career in music saw a substantial rise in respectability in the 1870s. Newspapers and other print materials confirm that women need not fear that a career as a professional musician might damage their social standing, at least not to the extent it had before the war. For example, music teachers occasionally expanded their options and became brokers of music and related items, much as Sarah Smith had done thirty years earlier. The *Southern Musical Journal* printed the names of all of its agents in the South in 1871, and among these are three women: Ella Baber in Macon, Grace Elmore in Abingdon, and Lena Postell in Marietta.[116] All of their names can be found as music teachers in newspapers and other media. That they appear so prominently in this notice, with their first as well as last names, signals a new acceptance of women in roles previously assumed to belong to men.

The prominent placement of women's names in print, either with their first names or simply the size and visibility of the print, points to a new perception of women's work. The slander dealt to Sarah Smith in 1852 is no longer an issue for women musicians after the war. Even when women had drawn attention to the names in the antebellum period, they remained veiled by using only their last names. Although the Sloman sisters' advertisement in 1852 (see Figure 7.2) broke with tradition with a simplicity that highlights their name and profession, Maria Kowalewski went considerably further in 1870 by not only adopting a similar visual effect but also by proclaiming herself a "Professor of Music" (see Figure 10.5).[117] The confidence exuded by this announcement indicates a woman who is sure of her position and reputation—to quote her obituary again, truly the "architect of her own fortunes." Indeed, throughout her entire life she exerted an

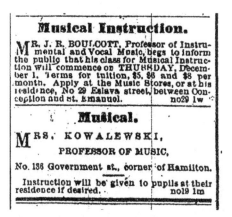

Figure 10.5. Kowalewski notice, *Mobile Register*, December 7, 1870.

independence that stood apart from her contemporaries. Perhaps Kowalewski's ability to pursue her own career is what Octavia Le Vert longed for when she wrote that English women were freer to engage in creative endeavors than she was. The Irish-immigrant-turned-Mobile-music-director contrasted sharply with the well-traveled and overtly public Madame. The former came through the system and evolved as women's position in society changed. The latter overstepped the boundaries of good taste, of the qualities of genteel culture, and suffered the consequences.

The public's approval of women musicians continued unabated. By the 1870s, the press referred to Barbot as a "Directress" in producing full versions of both Rossini's *Moses in Egypt* and Donizetti's *La fille du régiment*. The writer for one announcement acknowledges "her energy and undertaking the management and performing the arduous preliminary labor of this ambitious performance" of Haydn's *Creation*.[118] By 1885, the *Charleston News and Courier* featured a prominent advertisement for a "Grand Oratorio," Rossini's "Moses in Egypt," that "Will be given by Madame P. J. Barbot, Assisted by a large number of the best Musical Amateurs of Charleston, with full Chorus and Orchestra."[119] (See Figure 10.6). The surprising amount of white space in this printing highlights Barbot's name and role in the performance.

The Civil War proved a turning point in society's valuation of women, and with this came new ideas of the "lady." Many of the antebellum basic tenets remained intact: women remained subordinate to men in almost all situations. One striking exception exists in women who took control of musical performances, including male musicians. If, as Dianne Lawrence argues, material culture made and expressed cultural meaning in the nineteenth century, the physical destruction of many of the spaces that contained and defined gentility were destroyed by the war.[120] As women rebuilt these spaces, the practices that animated the culture

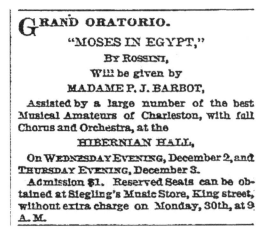

Figure 10.6. Barbot notice, for Rossini's "Moses in Egypt," *Charleston News and Courier*, November 29, 1885.

altered and the contextual meaning of materials subsequently differed from its former usage. The reconstructed spaces allowed for new realizations of the performance of gentility. The networks of meanings surrounding musical performance evoked power in ways hitherto unavailable to women. The manifestation of these post-war cultural mores is most visible in the new repertory they took on as soon as the war ended.

"Beethoven wrote it—that is enough"

Reconstructed Women Reconstructing Repertory

In June 1873, the young women at the Augusta Female Seminary in western Virginia opened their Commencement Exercises with a performance of Beethoven's Eroica Symphony on six pianos, two organs, and clarinet. The arrangement they used remains unknown but may have been an adaptation created by the music professor.[1] Its presence on the program can easily be misconstrued as something familiar to audiences in Augusta, a town west of Staunton but it was certainly not known in the area.[2] Did it represent the efforts of German musicians like Theodore Thomas, or even the journalist John Sullivan Dwight, to inculcate Beethoven's music among Americans? Maybe—the *Staunton Spectator* lauded the composer as if his works were standard repertory for the readers. He or she wrote, "It would be a work of supererogation for us to attempt to say anything in favor of the Symphony as a composition. Beethoven wrote it—that is enough," which not only validates the symphony as worthy of study but also implies that everyone reading the paper understands Beethoven's preeminence among composers. Southern papers had carried accounts of Beethoven's life and music for years, but to assume that subscribers in Staunton, at the southern end of the Shenandoah mountains (about forty miles west of Charlottesville), were familiar with his *oeuvre* is another thing entirely. The surety with which the anonymous author sanctions anything the composer wrote stands in stark contrast to the music that practically anyone in Staunton heard on a regular, or even irregular, basis.

This reviewer expressed an "unqualified admiration of the beautiful manner in which the young ladies executed this long and difficult composition," and credited the success to their music professor, John Koerber. His capacity as a "master in the science of music" enabled him to teach the students how to play at this level.[3] The use of the terms "long and difficult" ironically stand in opposition to the advice given in popular magazines and journals. "Mems for Musical Misses," a regular feature in *Harper's* cautioned young women to never perform "ugly music merely because it is the work of some famous composer and do not let the pieces you perform before people not professedly scientific or be too long."[4] Florence Hartley warned as late as 1860 that a young lady might choose to play a "brilliant, showy" piano piece in a mixed party, "but let it be short. It is better still to make no attempt at display, but simply try to please."[5] She also emphatically recommended avoiding the "loud, thumping style, and also the over-solemn style"—both of which might have crept into the Beethoven performance. Indeed, the account of the same concert in the *Richmond Whig* listed all four movements and complained of the symphony's length: "it was entirely too long, requiring over an hour in performance," and also affirmed that the young women performed the entire symphony.[6] Despite its length, the Staunton students again programmed the work (with the same instrumentation) in a benefit for the Memphis Orphans in December of that year.[7] The tension between the long-standing appreciation of music as a science and the difficulty associated with Beethoven's music encapsulates new ideas of gentility that arose after the Civil War.

Concert programs were not the only place sporting a newfound acceptance of Beethoven as part of women's repertory, beyond a few simple waltzes for piano. The *Staunton Spectator* had reported a week earlier (June 17, 1873) that Susan E. McGowan received two volumes of Beethoven for her "general excellence and deportment" at the Virginia Female Institute (in Staunton). Beethoven must have been part of her repertory, or least there was an expectation that it should be. This is a strange turn of events for young women who, ten years earlier, would never have been expected to play the Beethoven's sonatas, symphonies, or concertos.

In the same year, Anna Shields published a story that appeared in several North Carolina papers entitled "The Western Cousin," and she portrays the good taste and sensibility of the two main characters, Clara and her cousin Charles Easton, in part through music. Clara performs for him during his first visit to the east, choosing "the waltzes and polkas she at first thought suited to his comprehension." Discovering that he knew more about music than she had supposed, she moved from those simple dances "to give him rare musical treats in her exquisite rendering of Mendelssohn and Beethoven." Clara quickly learns that Charles plays the piano much better than she imagined, but he praises her initial choices: "the gentle kindness that prompted the fingers to play what was presumably suited to an ignorant ear, instead of trying to dazzle the country mind with a grand display of brilliant execution."[8] Those who had not been educated in scientific music—the ignorant country folk in this story—were not expected to enjoy the progressive music of Mendelssohn and Beethoven. Clara, however, could "exquisitely render" the music of these composers. Shields uses repertory as a sign of sophistication, as it had always been, but its substance had changed from Bellini to Beethoven.

Being assigned, taught, and awarded Beethoven's piano sonatas meant more than simply learning new pieces.[9] It signals a brash move toward a different type of music, one based on purely musical ideas and not outside influences such as poems, art, dances, favorite tunes, or operatic melodies. Nonetheless, the performance of his symphony by young women in Augusta, "pure unsullied triumphs of blushing maidenhood," elicited the question: "has the untried future aught in store, even for the happiest, to compare with them?" The young women continued to be seen in the antebellum perspective of young ladies exhibiting the ideals of gentility, even though their society's definition of that term had altered.

Before 1865, most southern women played piano music that was either meant for dancing, reflected patriotic sentiments, or was based on a favorite melody. It could be variations on "Home! Sweet Home!" or on something from Bellini's opera *Norma*, but it was a recognizable tune. They did not play instrumental pieces by Bach, Beethoven, or Schumann. Opera, yes. The German Classicists or Romantics, no. That they turned to this style around 1870 signals a sharp departure from the previous repertory and all that it represented, including their interpretation and application of genteel culture. The performance of Beethoven's music, and all of the other "new" composers whose music offered a distinct alternative to most of the repertory favored in the South, signified a new concept of what women musicians could perform, which in turn embodied expanded self-perception and public understanding. The music of Beethoven frames this discussion, but it serves as an umbrella encompassing the repertory that eventually coalesced into the canon (Beethoven, Schubert, Mendelssohn, Schumann, Chopin, and Liszt) that dominates recital halls even today.

Beethoven in the Antebellum South

The question of when southerners became aware of Beethoven and his music is multilayered. Before southern women began playing his music, they were aware of it from articles and announcements in antebellum newspapers, journals, and other media, such as "A Visit to Beethoven" in the *Columbian Lady's and Gentleman's Magazine* (1848).[10] Touring artists and local musicians introduced the instrumental works to audiences in larger cities on the routine circuit (Richmond, Charleston, New Orleans) and by the 1850s Beethoven's compositions could be heard with some regularity. Scores could be bought from importers and eventually American publishers, and women who traveled overseas could have purchased his music when they shopped in London, Paris, Berlin, Leipzig, Mainz, and Vienna. Musicians from Europe introduced his music through various other means. In 1853, the Philharmonic Society of Charleston informed the "Ladies and Gentlemen of Charleston" that Minna Mueller, Mrs. E. Hammarskold, and Mr. H. E. Vaas were forming a Musical Academy, by popular demand, to study "our greatest masters, such as Mozart, Beethoven, Haydn, Handel, etc."[11] That "our" greatest included only German composers signals a sentient approach to repertory and anticipates their persistent presence on concert programs in the latter half of the century.

Southerners learned about Beethoven and other composers in newspaper and journal articles from both the North and South. Several pianists (such as Gustav Satter, Otto Dresel, and Carl Wolfson) played his sonatas in the United States in the decade before the Civil War.[12] In fact, one writer for the *New York Times* chronicled in 1854 that William Mason "returns [from the Old Country] a thorough master of the modern German school of piano-forte playing. His touch is wonderfully vigorous, all his harmonies massive, and his effects finely wrought." The masculine language (master, vigorous, massive) stamps Mason's playing with an aesthetic that contrasts that of more familiar pianists who had toured the United States prior to this time, as the writer confirms: "One of his greatest recommendations is that he does not follow the THALBERG school. Thoughtful completeness rather than flippant brilliancy is his characteristic. His execution of Beethoven's Sonota [*sic*] in C sharp minor was in many respects admirable, and at once stamped him as a fine artist." This author also links the new approach to piano performance with the German school, foreshadowing an attraction to Leipzig that marks the 1860s and 1870s. That he played the "Moonlight" sonata also demonstrates a connection to Europe because audiences there favored the work, along with the "Pathétique." Moreover, Mason proposed to play Chopin the evening the review appeared, and the writer proclaimed that "not one performer in five hundred is capable of appreciating or rendering the solemn majesty of this great composer."[13] Although Chopin's music was less familiar in the United States than Beethoven's, in 1857, New Orleans native Ernest Guiraud (ca. 1840–92) won the Prix du Rome in Paris performing Chopin's first piano concerto.[14]

Beethoven's music was heard in several performances in the South before 1865. At Odd Fellows' Hall in New Orleans, in 1859, Miss Heywood sang the composer's concert aria, "Ah, Perfido" (op. 65), in an event that featured Signora Cairoll performing an aria from *La sonnambula*, as well as Heywood's rendition of "Auld Robin Grey."[15] Jullien conducted two performances in Charleston in 1854, incorporating a Beethoven symphony into the program.[16] In 1856, the pianist, composer, and conductor Gustave Collignon performed Mendelssohn's Piano Concerto in G minor, accompanied by his orchestra. By 1860, he had programmed Beethoven's symphonies 1–7 at least once in New Orleans, as well as the major overtures and some of the chamber works. Moreover, he included Mendelssohn's *Midsummer Night's Dream*, *Ruy Blas*, *Calm Sea*, and *Fingal's Cave* in his concerts.[17] Granted, the availability of these types of concerts was much higher in New Orleans than other southern towns and cities, but their frequency, variety of programming, and mere existence demonstrate that Beethoven's music was indeed known in the South.

The instrumental music also featured in several recitals, with soloists performing and others (frequently amateurs) assisting. German musicians impacted the
repertory to a degree, as shown by chamber music that formed a complete recital
in 1852, which included a septet by Hummel, Beethoven's string quartet in C minor, Robert Schumann's quintet in E-flat, and Mendelssohn's Octet. The only two
performers' names listed on the announcement are C[arl] Paulsackel (piano) and
T. Wohlien.[18] Thalberg and Vieuxtemps also performed some of this new repertory in concerts in New Orleans in 1858. They opened a matinee with Beethoven's
"Allegro, Andante and Variations from the Grand Sonata in A minor," and that
evening, Thalberg performed Chopin's funeral march and Mendelssohn's "Spring
Song," as well as solos on *Les Huguenots* and "The Last Rose of Summer."[19] The
announcement for this "Concert of Classical Music" makes the case that only
the German population of New Orleans knew of "the rich stores of harmony and
melody contained in the works" of Schumann, Beethoven, Mendelssohn, and
Hummel.[20] Writers increasingly labeled this repertory "Classical," another sign
of a need to distinguish it from more popular concerts.

The people who played Beethoven's instrumental works for public audiences
in the antebellum South were predominantly, if not exclusively, men. The masculine association with this repertory does not always appear in overt language,
but depictions of his music that described its "immensity" or that it is "not brilliant" but "profound" adopted terminology positively associated with men, not
women.[21] Nevertheless, a few women chose to perform his works, most notably
Lucie Loening. In 1859, Sophie Werner gave a concert (at age eleven) in Louisville,
Kentucky; since her father had reportedly studied piano with Chopin, Sophie
might have performed something of his in that concert.[22]

Compositions by Beethoven, Mendelssohn, Schubert, and Chopin could be
purchased in southern stores.[23] As early as 1840, George Oates advertised Chopin's "Three brilliant waltzes," and in 1841 his mazurkas, alongside sets of piano
variations on compositions by Meyerbeer and other popular composers.[24] In
1851, Oates announced a Beethoven sonata (unknown number) for sale and, in
1852, the 26th piano sonata (presumably "Les adieux," op. 81a). The other composers mentioned in Oates's advertisement can be found in numerous binder's
volumes, such as Voss, Beyer, and Duvernoy, thus Beethoven's sonata appears
as a regular and typical piece. Oates also advertised Beethoven's "sonatinas" in
Augusta in 1851.[25] In 1847, Peters & Webster in Louisville offered a "Grand Valse"
by Chopin, Mendelssohn's "Songs without Words," and Liszt's "Reminiscences of
Lucia di Lammermoor" for sale, in addition to the usual fare of arrangements by
Rosellen and Thalberg.[26] Nonetheless, the evidence of binder's volumes attests to
piano pieces based on popular melodies still holding sway.

If the latest editions of Beethoven's works were not available in local stores,
those who traveled extensively could have purchased them in more cosmopolitan

cities. In New York, Scharfenburg & Luis, and Breusing imported music from Simrock, Schott, Breitkopf, C. F. Peters, as well as French, English, and other European publishers. Had there been a demand for Beethoven's sonatas or Chopin's polonaises, they could have made them available, and southern women could have purchased them while seeking other titles. Furthermore, when women such as Harriet Lowndes, Sarah Crawford, or Louisa McCord toured shops in London, Paris, Brussels, Berlin, or other European cities, they might have seen these pieces and brought them back. Even if they did not intend to perform them, Beethoven or Chopin sheet music would have been a way to flaunt their knowledge of the latest music in Europe.

But they didn't. None of the antebellum amateurs that I have examined purchased this new repertory while abroad.[27] The reality remains that although southern women were aware of Beethoven's music, his stature among composers, and the respect accorded him by culturally educated Americans, their performance of his music did not stray beyond the simplistic waltzes, excerpts from *Christ on the Mount of Olives* (op. 85), and occasional renditions of "Adelaide." Beethoven, Chopin, Schumann, and to a large extent Mendelssohn and Schubert, remained a closed door to genteel women.

Beethoven during the Reconstruction

After the Civil War, southerners continued to learn about music by these composers through a variety of means, some imbued with a heightened sense of the theatrical. In early September 1865, the somewhat fanciful story, "Loves of Beethoven," ran in Columbia.[28] Perhaps the most colorful of these is a fictional account in both the *Augusta Chronicle* and the *Daily Constitutionalist* in July 1865 of Beethoven having been inspired to compose—or rather improvise—the "Moonlight Sonata": "Beethoven . . . drew open the shutters, admitting . . . moonlight." As the illumination hit on the composer and his piano, he declared: "'I will improvise a sonata to the moonlight!'"[29] Printed two months after Appomattox, this highly romanticized story hardly seems like the sort of reading one expects for defeated Confederates. On the other hand, the dreamy title (and opening movement) of the sonata suited the overly dramatic literary style of the period. It is no accident that the two sonatas favored in Europe, his "Pathétique" and "Moonlight," were also those being performed or described in the United States. Both were open to a literary interpretation that could easily find expression in the popular press.[30]

An article from New Orleans enlists Beethoven's sonatas for another purpose. Regarding the education of "fallen women," the anonymous author of "Social Riddle" believes: "It is right, for though vice makes one common level of morality between women, there must always be a distinction between the fallen creature, who reads Eugène Sue, and dashes off a *sonata* of Beethoven, and the fallen creature who can neither read nor play at all."[31] This writer confirms that musical accomplishments were not only something sought by the pure and sincere but also by others ("fallen" women) who emulated their gentility. It also tosses the composer's name about as if his piano sonatas were commonly known and emphasizes the genre with italics.

Credible accounts of both performances and compositions of the German masters appeared in print media, as when the *Richmond Whig* carried a report from Mrs. Horace Greeley's funeral that Albert J. Holden played Beethoven's "Funeral March" on the organ.[32] Philip Werlein, one of the most prominent publishers in New Orleans, took over a short-lived music magazine entitled *The Song Journal* in the mid1870s.[33] Among the composers whose music he printed was Robert Schumann: most of the *Album für die Jugend*, op. 68, appeared across several months in 1875–76.

Performances introduced more new music to southerners. Josefina Filomeno, a Chilean pianist and violinist who had studied in Paris, toured in 1868 and 1870, exhibiting a repertory and instrument that marked her as unusual. Not only did she play the violin, but her concerts also featured the Mendelssohn piano concerto in G minor and one by Beethoven (which remains unknown), both accompanied by full orchestra. An announcement in the *New Orleans Republican* declared that the Beethoven concerto was performed for the first time in that city. Since none of the references to performances of his concertos in New Orleans indicate which concerto, it is impossible to verify this claim. The announcement may simply represent an attempt to secure an audience.[34] If inaccurate, it might also have constituted political propaganda on the part of the Reconstruction politicians who wished to demonstrate their positive effects on southern culture.

Women had opportunities to hear this new repertory in cities across the region. Fourteen-year-old Marcus Epstein (1856–1947), a pianist from Mobile, performed a Beethoven piano concerto there in 1870, accompanied by full orchestra.[35] In the same month, Professor Rudolph Sipp gave a matinee recital in which he played Beethoven's Sonata in C-sharp minor (the "Moonlight"), Mozart's Concerto in C minor, and a Chopin Polonaise. The reviewer particularly admired the manner in which Sipp improvised on familiar melodies, modulating between them—harking back to the preferred antebellum style. This event formed part of an educational endeavor that amplified the introduction of potentially new repertory with a lecture on the history of music. Mr. Oriol, a gentleman, lectured on the "origin and history of music," and his character is vouched for in the column. The audience consisted entirely of women.[36]

After the war, pieces by Chopin and Liszt began to appear regularly on programs presented by women. Antoinette Fehringer, who claimed to have been a pupil of Liszt, arrived in New Orleans from Berlin to sing at the National Theatre in its first season (1866).[37] An advertisement on December 18, 1866, marks her first appearance: she sang in the main attractions and then played piano solos between them. The pieces she chose suited her audiences well by adhering to a familiar genre (virtuoso arrangements of operatic melodies) but by a new composer. Her first selection was Liszt's "Grande Valse Brillante . . . sur l'opéra de Faust" (S407). She performed two new works (for New Orleans) during the second intermission: Liszt's "Grande Fantaisie sur l'opéra Lohengrin" (unspecified section) and a nocturne by Chopin.[38] Her listeners may have first heard Chopin's works when performed by Marguerite Elie in her concert at Odd Fellows Hall in January.[39]

Recital Programs and School Repertory

After the Civil War, young women around the South were assigned an entirely new repertory that reflected the growing popularity of German music in the United States, and they returned to the sonata. Chopin's music also made a lasting impact on the repertory. These changes did not happen immediately but were part of a process that mirrored general tendencies throughout the country. Some southern musicians (mostly men) were aware of the latest currents and took on the mantle of incorporating unfamiliar music alongside old favorites, if not replacing them altogether. The path to making it acceptable for women amateurs involved overcoming barriers to a style of music associated with men. Its acceptance coincided, not incidentally, with the modifications to genteel culture after the war. The impetus for the new music, however, lay in those who studied it. Most of these young women fall into historian Jane Turner Censer's third generation, those born from about 1850—the most likely to seek and accept change.

The move to a different repertory took place with alarming speed, as shown in patterns of young women's public performances from the early 1870s. The program at a "Musical Soiree Given by Mr. Rob't S. Phifer & Pupils" (all women) on June 21, 1872, included an eight-hand performance of Mozart's Symphony #39 (3rd movement), Beethoven's overture to *Fidelio* (again eight hands), Robert Schumann's Sonata in G, performed by Annie Vogel, and, among others, Mendelssohn's Concerto in D minor, which featured Robert as soloist but his sister Minnie on the accompaniment.[40] He soon left Charlotte to take over the music department at the Roanoke Female College in Danville, not far from his wife's family.[41]

Phifer was not alone in bringing the music he learned in Leipzig to southern women students. The trend in this direction could be felt in various parts of the region throughout the early 1870s. For example, in 1871, Mollie Kean of Cumberland, Maryland took first place in the unusual category of music theory; the concert accompanying the festivities included Beethoven's "Adelaide" and

Mendelssohn's "Rondo capriccioso."[42] At the Peabody Institute, Mary Decker sang works by J. S. Bach and Robert Schumann, including "Er, der Herrlichste von allen" (from the *Frauenlieben und -leben* cycle). Catherine Johnson owned Beethoven's "March from Egmont," Schubert's "Der Wanderer," melodies from *Le prophète*, and "The Last Rose of Summer." At the Convent of the Sacred Heart in St. James Parish, Lillie Trust Gray carefully documented each of her student's piano assignments during the final three decades of the nineteenth century. The repertory up to 1874 corresponds to that seen in southern binder's volumes of the 1850s and 1860s. In that year, however, Gray apparently discovered Beethoven's piano music firsthand, for she assigned his sonatas op. 13, op. 27/2, and op. 28 to Maria Herbert within a few weeks of each other. By 1880, she taught Chopin's music as well.[43]

As was the case with other schools, the demands of the music curriculum at St. Mary's grew after the Civil War and clearly shows the move toward a more Germanic repertory in the United States. Will Herbert Sanborn was one of the music teachers responsible for this new direction in repertory. He arrived at St. Mary's School in 1879 at age twenty-six (resigning in 1881 to study in Leipzig). Under his direction, the program for the school's Commencement Musical and Literary Recital of 1880 far exceeds its antebellum literature. It included Chopin's Scherzo in B minor and Robert Schumann's "Nur ein lächelnder Blick"; the first part of this program ended with Josie Myers playing Mendelssohn's Concerto in D minor, with Eliza Smedes playing the orchestral accompaniment in a piano reduction. The second part began with four young women playing a piano reduction of Beethoven's Fourth Symphony on two pianos. Previous piano duet literature often included opera overtures but never symphonies. The change in repertory is striking.

A program from a concert presented at the Louisburg Female Seminary in 1855, just over eighty miles from Danville, highlights just how unusual this repertory was (see Figure 10.6). The young women presented typical dances, parlor songs, and choral pieces. Containing a few nods to opera, most of the compositions presented consisted of or were based on familiar melodies. The Louisburg event sounded nothing like the Roanoke Female College repertory of less than twenty years later.

Stock formulas could be easily learned; many of the more technically complicated variations sets of the 1850s rely on repetitive figurations in flat keys (often A-flat and D-flat). Once learned, such passages fall relatively easily under the fingers. But Chopin required a different preparation because the harmonic progressions followed less predictable patterns and could not be learned and simply reapplied in other compositions. Similarly, Beethoven's "Pathétique" introduces a piano style that challenges the performer in new ways. Even though it seems

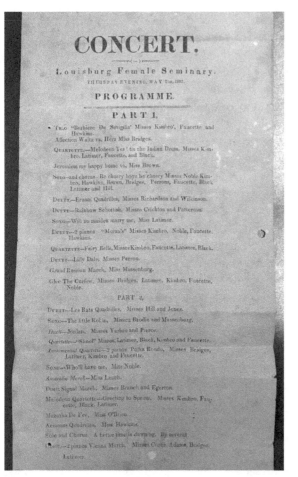

Figure 11.1. Louisburg Female Seminary program, 1855. Person Family Papers, Rubenstein Library, Duke University.

common enough today, the rising intervals in the right hand of the first theme constitute but one example of fingering that southern women were unaccustomed to using. The dramatic opening slightly resembles emotional introductions to variations sets (especially of operatic themes) and other pieces, but the unrelenting pathos of the movement, wherein this idea returns, differs substantially from the contemporary parlor repertory.

Several other binder's volumes testify to the addition of Beethoven, Chopin, Mendelssohn, and others to women's sanctioned repertory. Minnie Estel Cox (1865–1949), the daughter of a railroad watchman and a student at the Episcopal Female Institute in Winchester around 1879, owned Beethoven's "Pathétique," Liszt's arrangement of Schubert's "Erlkönig," Gottschalk's "Last Hope," and opera melodies in difficult transcriptions. All of these have fingerings that suggest she used the volume. In the early 1870s, while attending the St. Joseph Academy in Emmitsburg, Annie Rodissbaugh played all of the "Moonlight Sonata." The Appomattox Manor Music Collection from near Hopewell (Virginia) contains several binder's volumes and other music including music by Wagner, a complete print of Mendelssohn's *Songs without Words* (published by Walker in Philadelphia), Haydn's Military Symphony for two pianos, some difficult piano solos from the late 1860s, and a Chopin waltz.[44] One of the two binder's volumes that belonged to Felix Grundy McGavock (1832–97) contains Beethoven's piano sonata op. 27/2, in an edition published in 1860. The book bears the name "F. Grundy McGavock," who belonged to a powerful political family in Tennessee. His daughter Mary Louise McGavock must have received the book from him, for her name appears in pencil in large letters beneath his. Born in August 1857, she died before turning twenty-years old.

The foregoing examples of music by Beethoven, Chopin, and others elicits provocative questions and ideas, mostly pertaining to why these pieces, these specific composers, and this time. The attraction of two sonatas with picturesque titles (op. 13, the "Pathétique," and op. 27/2, "the Moonlight") could have corresponded to the popularity of similarly expressive named compositions, such as Wollenhaupt's "The Whispering Wind." Evocative titles connect Beethoven's piano pieces to the earlier favorites and can be seen as an extension of, rather than a break with, tradition. The popularity of Beethoven in France might have influenced French musicians in New Orleans (such as Collignon) to regularly offer his music there, although an article on *Fidelio* states that only the German music societies knew it well.[45]

Audiences and performers knew this repertory contrasted that of the antebellum period. One of the two understandings of scientific music in the nineteenth-century United States equates it with "classical" music, and after the war this became the more common one. This term appeared in nineteenth-century sources, such as an 1866 advertisement for "Classical Music" at Heroman's Book and Music Depôt in Baton Rouge. The listed choices, selected by Professor C. L. Doll, included the complete sonatas of Beethoven, Mozart, and Haydn; Mendelssohn's Song without Words; Thalberg's "L'Art du Chant," pour le piano; Bach's fugues, for piano; and the complete piano compositions of Chopin. Additional music by composers such as Henselt, Cramer, Clementi, Rosellen, Moscheles, Liszt, and other works by Thalberg were also available.[46]

Violinist Camille Urso, who moved to Nashville in the mid-century, commented in 1874: "It would be rash . . . to give programs composed purely of classical music to audiences untutored to it," but playing a few choice pieces would "elevate taste and the cause of good music." She herself included the Mendelssohn Violin Concerto and a Beethoven violin sonata on concerts at this time.[47] Classical music, as scientific music, entered the repertory in women's institutions. It began to replace earlier, less precise understandings of the term as instrumental music other than that on favorite melodies became the harbinger of real accomplishment.

Public Gaze

Alongside the increasing frequency with which women took the stage and tackled a new repertory came a public acceptance of their doing so. The printing of names and the terms employed to describe women in the press reflect acceptance of women's new role in society. It may have been a coincidence that a newspaper published the first names of young women musicians at the Belle Haven Institute in 1860, and the same performance included music by Beethoven and Chopin, but after the war it became much more commonplace. A concert report in the *Renaissance Louisianaise* in 1869 lists all of the works performed by young women at the Institut Saint-Charles, an important school in New Orleans that appears in several places in this study. This account is notable for several reasons. Unlike most antebellum publications of recital reviews, this one gives the first and last names of all of the pupils. This tendency can be found throughout the South in the years following the end of the war and marks a dramatic change from the demure "lady amateur," personified in Thornwell's Gentility, or the insult Sarah Smith felt when her full name appeared in print.

The Saint-Charles program maintained the repertory of the prewar period. Opera melodies dominate, either sung or played on the piano. *Robin des bois, La favorite, La reine de Chypre, Sémiramide, L'Africaine,* and others figure between French songs. Standing out among these is a "Sonnate, Beethoven, execute par Mlle Adélaïde Grima." The piano instructor, Désiré Delcroix, exhibited his students, as did the other teachers (Prévost, Mlles Capdevieille, Bringier, and Laudumiez).[48]

Another meaningful sign that gentility had changed exists in the fact that not only southern men, such as Robert Phifer, traveled to Leipzig to study. Some southern women did as well. Amy Fay's notable *Music Study in Germany* of 1880 represents the journey of one southern woman (she was born in Louisiana), but there were others. Eliza Smedes, daughter of the principal at St. Mary's in Raleigh, also traveled to Leipzig to study music for two years beginning in 1881. Will Herbert Sanborn was her music teacher at St. Mary's School in Raleigh; he was twenty-seven in 1880 and from Maine according to the census. He, too, made the journey to Leipzig to study (after his tenure at St. Mary's).

The value of such credentials can be perceived in an advertisement from the *Public Ledger* in 1867. It reads: "WANTED—A LADY FROM VIRGINIA, who has been taught by the best German Professors, desires to engage a few scholars to instruct in music on the piano. Will give lessons at the Virginia house."[49] This musician, a woman from Virginia, let her potential clients know that she had studied music with German—not simply foreign—professors. An 1874 advertisement in the *Southern Musical Journal* touts that the leader of the music department at Southern Female College, LaGrange (Georgia), H. Schirmacher, was a graduate of Leipzig and a pupil of Mendelssohn. He taught piano, organ, violin, and harmony. (Sallie C. and Alice M. Cox, the daughters of the school's president, taught piano and guitar.)[50]

Beethoven Not for Everyone

Not all southern women embraced the classical masters. Many women continued performing the same type of music after the war that their older sisters, friends, and others had learned: opera arrangements, variations on popular melodies, pretty piano pieces, and sentimental or comic songs. Predictably, many of those who adhered to the prewar favorites were older musicians themselves. For example, at the 1878 concert for the closing exercises at the Home School for Young Ladies in Athens, Sophie Sosnowski and her daughter Caroline oversaw the program. The repertory presented there harkens back to an earlier time: *La dame blanche*, Abt, Hewitt, *La semiramide*, and *Zampa*, although a few later works (arrangements of bel canto opera excerpts) appear here as well.[51]

In West Baton Rouge, Bessie Lamon (b. 1851) owned two volumes of demanding piano music but no Beethoven. Her collection included some of the same pieces seen in slightly earlier volumes from this area, such as Schulhoff's "Le carnaval de Venise," Thalberg's fantasia on "Home! Sweet Home!" and impressively substantial works by Hoffman, Wollenhaupt, Schulhoff, and Ascher. Bessie dated most of them in the late 1860s. Her music evinces serious piano practice and considerable expense on music. She also owned Gottschalk's "Berceuse" and Mendelssohn's "Spring Song" (on the front—inside the piece is called "Frühlingslied"), dated 1869. Alexandre Goria's rousing transcription of Bellini arias, published as his Fantaisie brillante sur des motifs de V. Bellini" represents the strength of her abilities. Bessie did not learn these pieces because she belonged to a rich planter's family and such accomplishments were expected. She was not wealthy: her mother (Mrs. C. E. Lamon) taught at St. Mary's Hall, and Bessie, like others before her, matriculated there because of her family connection. In this sense, she resembles Fanny Smith Hosea, Sarah Smith's daughter who became a professional musician, although whether Bessie used her music education toward a career remains unknown.

Coralie LeBlond's early years in New Orleans followed a path similar to Bessie's, and she, too, left behind a music collection that evinces real piano competency.

The contents of her first volume, a black volume with "Coralie Leblond" in gold on the front, contains eighteen difficult pianos works.[52] Most of her collection consists of French music, including Gounod. The final two pieces date from 1862, but others in the volume ("I would like to change my name" and "Champagne Charlie") were published between the end of the war and 1868. Only thirteen when the war ended, her music testifies to advanced pianism at a young age. She even married her music professor, local piano maker Aloysius J. Kirschenheuter.[53]

Some women preferred even lighter fare. Fredricka "Freddie" Knobloch of Charleston preferred a more modern collection of popular pieces. Lysander Thompson's "Pet Polka" and Rollin Howard's "Shew Fly!" typify the pieces in her binder's volume. (Her copy of "Charleston Galop" features an image of the composer, Miss Crawford, on the first page.) These sorts of songs are far removed from the music of Beethoven and Chopin, but they also differ from the genteel favorites featured in Sosnowski's program.

Other women collected music that reflects antebellum and wartime favorites. Opera excerpts remained in style for the remainder of the century. Annie Stuart Litchfield of Abingdon sang several items from the series *Gems of the Opera*, such as Rossini's "Una voce poco fa" and Verdi's "Caro nome," and French arias by Meyerbeer. Both Lulu Reynaud and Georgina Holmes owned a binder's volume that has the title *Souvenir of the Confederacy* on the outside, and both contain ninety-one publications. Lulu began and ended her collection with pro-Confederate pieces with perennial favorites like "Annie Laurie" sandwiched in between. Georgina's volume begins with Confederate imprints and seems to be a clearing out of Blackmar's inventory. All of the publications came from Blackmar's store, and several have later dates pasted over the originals.[54]

* * *

The *Southern Music Journal* reminded its readers that not everyone attempted the more demanding scientific music that it usually covered. Peregrine Pickle's humorous description of "Village Choirs" serves as an example of what choirs should avoid: "The old deacon who sings bass, and the spruce young grocery clerk who sings tenor, and the girl in white who sings soprano, and the girl in blue who sings alto, are at cross purposes with each other, and with the girl in yellow at the organ. The songs they sing are the songs our fathers sung, but the songs they would not have sung had they known how bad they were."[55] This could imply that women in the villages had fewer opportunities to attain the musical standards reached by those in cities, or it could be belittling the women (to keep them under their control like helpless children). The men have been assigned meaning and purpose through their careers; the women are all "girls."

Not all were treated this way, however, and the new postwar repertory reflects a decided turn to something different. Beethoven's music was known in the South before the Civil War, and many musically literate women were familiar with his name and reputation if not his music. Southern women who traveled in Europe had the opportunity to purchase Beethoven scores, and if there had been a sustained interest in the piano music, southern music sellers would have stocked it. European music teachers knew the music, too. The fact remains that his music, and to a lesser degree that of Chopin, did not enter the typical repertory until after the Civil War, when professionals and amateurs alike began programming his two best-known sonatas. This shift coincided with striking alterations in southern society that are best explained by new ideas of what women could and should do after the war.

Black women have not been included in this final section because to date I have been unable to locate materials, such as binder's volumes, that can be associated with a specific person. Perhaps the well-known migrations to northern cities after the war resulted in southern collections moving to northern archives, and these have yet to be identified because of the long neglect of women's ephemera in general. Nonetheless, evidence confirms that scientific music study continued. In the late 1860s and 1870s, Black women in Atlanta studied music at the Storrs Free School and Atlanta University. Similarly, in Louisiana, Straight College offered vocal music in 1870.[56] Private instruction also offered a means to a music education, but these have yet to be traced. Black women across the South also saw new opportunities for careers in music. Norris's study of musical practices in Petersburg exemplifies the possibilities that can be located in studies of individual places. The Odd Fellow and Masonic Hall offered musical entertainments as early as 1869, and events through the 1870s featured "grand" concerts. (The audiences for these occasions were mixed but seated separately.) Sometime before 1882, Virginia Morgan took the position of organist at St. Stephen's Church; she also served as an officer in the Chorannesse Literary and Social Club (1878), one of several music organizations in the city.[57]

Conclusion

Many fundamental aspects of southern women's culture transformed as a result of the Civil War and ensuing Federal occupation. The foregoing has shown how musical expectations and opportunities for women reflected these changes. Those who performed Chopin's Scherzo or Beethoven's sonata, op. 13 in recitals clearly transgressed Fitzhugh's 1854 conclusion that "woman naturally shrinks from public gaze, and from the struggle and competition of life."[58] After the war, women moved into the public gaze. The seeds planted in the mid-century bore fruit for years to come: the teaching of Moravians and the music tradition at Greensborough Female College; writer of music history Fanny Smith Hosea; professor and performer Ella Sheppard; touring Jubilee groups; successful professional pianist

Olga Samaroff; Black opera stars (such as Elizabeth Taylor Greenfield) born in the South; Eliza Smedes studying music in Leipzig; and Barbot and Kowalewski becoming directresses and pillars of the musical community in Charleston and Mobile.[59] After the war, the embryonic clubs of the antebellum period developed into full-fledged organizations for women's voices.[60] Even in less urban communities, southern women took on new roles. Rebecca Norfleet Hill, daughter of a wealthy antebellum planter, played organ at Trinity Church in Halifax County for a number of years.[61]

Black women, either formerly enslaved or free, continued to face entrenched obstacles to gentility as constructed by white southerners. As schools arose to educate Black children and young adults, the white majority continually worked to destroy them. Those that offered a curriculum beyond trade were particularly threatening to whites, and opposition to intellectually demanding courses of study remained fierce. Black students were advised to maintain an inoffensive stance to avoid inciting whites to violence. This potential for inflammatory display played a role in the development of the concert spirituals associated with the Fisk Jubilee Singers. Women like Ella Sheppard and Maggie Porter initially avoided the music they associated with the shame of the "dark past" of slavery in public performances, but the white men who controlled their affairs encouraged programming this material. Sheppard also realized that they held special meaning for their parents and recognized the positive attributes of faith inherent in their performance, as well as their financial impact on Fisk University. Graham incorporates Sheppard's assessment that spirituals resonated with Black singers (and others) in their cultural value in relation to both white and Black audiences.[62] The program of an 1882 ensemble including former Fisk singers illustrates the turn to a repertory more closely aligned with expectations of an all-Black choral group. Several spirituals, such as "Steal Away," intersperse with Foster songs ("Old Folks at Home"), and similar works.[63] As with Ann Battles Johnson aspiring to gentility by cultivating its rules of engagement in her daughters, the role of music in the lives of women like Sheppard and Porter resembled, but did not mirror, those of white women like Barbot or McCullough. It occupied a liminal space whose borders were being created as the South's social hierarchy underwent reconstruction. Amanda Dickson's life story evinces that a Black woman's constructed identity cannot simply be reduced to dichotomies of race, gender, or even class.[64]

New directions can be seen in other ways. Basile Barès (1845–1902), born enslaved in the household of piano and music store owner Adolphe Périer, journeyed to Paris on several occasions, and performed as a solo pianist at the World Exposition in 1867.[65] He also published several compositions, including at least two dedicated to white women. One of these, Delphine Dolhonde belonged to a prominent New Orleans family. Barès dedicated his "Delphine Valse Brillante" to her, some time before her marriage to Joseph Numi Augustin in 1870. In 1866, he honored Louise Hunt (1841–99, née Annie Louise Pitts in Georgia) with "La Coquette." How these dedications were received remains unknown, but their connection across race certainly differed from other traditions in the South.

These modified aspects of music practice signify changes in ideals of gentility. Women's agency in defining gentility becomes much more apparent as intentions to have careers through music become clear. Prenshaw writes that "the most oppressive and damaging result of the codification of subservience as the essential requisite of the lady was the injunction that she be silent."[66] Playing simple tunes in the highly controlled environment of the parlor, where etiquette manuals governed even the repertory, can be construed as a sort of silence: the performance constituted part of the background, either for dancing or polite discourse; or, when the focus fell on the musical entertainers, strict rules constrained the performance. Playing demanding works by Beethoven or Chopin, or Mendelssohn's Piano Concerto, in a public recital represented the opposite.

"This old piece of music keeps her name like a flower pressed in a book"

I return again to the 1909 *Times-Democrat* article on old music from New Orleans with which I began. The writer mentioned several women connected to compositions from the mid-nineteenth century and acknowledged that, although they be forgotten now, at one time their names meant something in the musical life of the city. One passage manifests the information that *Unbinding Gentility: Women Making Music in the Nineteenth-Century South* has sought to uncover and contextualize: "'La Reve,' published in 1843, was composed by W. V. Wallace and dedicated to 'Madame Coralie Frey, de la Nouvelle Orleans.' It is the dedication that localizes this 'Romance pour la Piano,' but the fair Madame Coralie Frey has gone her way into forgetfulness this many a year. Perhaps she sleeps in some tomb in the old St. Louis Cemetery, while this old piece of music keeps her name like a flower pressed in a book."[1] More than a century after these words were written, we can now better understand the performance of culture by women like Elizabeth Coralie Frey (ca. 1828–1937) through musical experiences mapped onto regional practices. Like flowers pressed into books (and some binder's volumes have them), the music played and heard by southern women reveals much about their values, education, and the challenges to their lives when social hierarchies broke down through the Civil War.

Ruth Solie uses the example from the novel *Elsie Dinsmore* as an example of the ubiquity of the young woman at the piano—Judith Tick cum Huneker's "piano girl" or Solie's own "girling at the piano"—observing that such activity was obviously required in 1868, before exploring the gulf between emblematic myth and firsthand reality. She finds the driving force behind "larger-scale cultural developments" to be domestic music-making.[2] The numerous examples presented in the first two chapters of this book corroborate Solie's thesis. Musicking belongs in a discussion of performative contexts. The synecdochical uses of "parlor music," "women's music," and even "American music" are inadequate. A history of women's music in the southern United States offers perspectives of class, social aspirations, and gender; and these differ substantially from composer-centric narratives.

The traditional view of telling music history as a series of composers and innovative styles has relegated much of women's music to a lesser, domestic, social culture. To a degree, this view aligns with nineteenth-century authors who interpreted women's practices the same way. The *Southern Musical Journal*, for example, published an essay entitled "Music at Home" in 1871, and its primary emphasis concerns the domestic use of music to ensure contentment in this avowedly feminine space: "There should be music in every house. A house without music is like Spring-time without birds. . . . The happiness of a family is not complete without music. . . . [Worship] is the highest use of music, but not the only one. We need it to refine the mind. We need it to awaken all those finer sentiments and emotions which respond to musical harmonies. . . . We need it to bind the members of the family into closer unity."[3] The attributes assigned in this excerpt fall directly under women's responsibilities. Moreover, the editors of the journal unabashedly connect the two with advertisements that appeared on several issues, beginning with its initial volume. Crockery, sewing machines, and pianos feature prominently on the first page of several issues, candidly letting the readers know what was expected of them (see Figure C.1).

Southern subscribers in 1871 would have understood that music, sewing, and cooking belonged to women's domain, but this public view was relatively new in the South: that the same women played the piano and did housework entered civic discourse only after the Civil War, at about the time that rules concerning the public gaze began to disperse. Before the war, few acknowledged openly that

Figure C.1. Advertisement from *Southern Musical Journal*, 1871.

women who could afford pianos had to do their own sewing or sweeping, although many did. Furthermore, the impact of the war on women's music—how it affected repertory, performance circumstances, and careers—has not been interrogated through gender until now. The period is too rich to reduce it to "repackaging familiar tunes" and engendering "communities of feeling," which treat all practices as one. As a counterbalance to the many books on "Civil War Music," *Unbinding Gentility* reveals many individual variations within women's lives that impacted their use of music before, during, and after the war.

Gentility was never homogeneous. The culture of gentility consisted of disciplined values, and only those within a social circle could decide who belonged and who did not. The ideologies of genteel culture meant following a specific set of attitudes that generated meaningful practices in the parlor and elsewhere. Performing gentility constituted gentility. Etiquette represented the most identifiable actions through which correctness could be expressed, and only those who participated in this conversation—who understood the rules of etiquette and flawlessly enacted them—belonged in the cultural circle. This dialogue between performer and audience established relationships that were verifiable through decoding the language and behaviors that marked one's group. The listener, or audience, is also a performer.

The performance of gentility is explicitly tied to gender: the expectations of genteel women were discussed widely in period literature. The parlor constituted the primary space in which society defined femininity and acted out the culture of gentility. Music played a substantial role on this stage. As antebellum sentimentality gave way perforce to redefined social hierarchies in the 1860s and 1870s, the way society viewed genteel women altered to adapt to new roles. These modifications can be detected in parlor theatricals, public performances, and different repertory preferences. Women's work was no longer contained by the "idle arts of gracious living"—the war dismantled that expectation and replaced it with one in which women took control over areas previously denied them.

Making a case for the influence and power of gentility does not deny other influences, nor does the recognition of broader frames of reference negate the significance of gentility.[4] Through an investigation of music as both ideal accomplishment and real practice in southern rural and urban communities, the myth of a simplified homogeneous narrative of women and music in the nineteenth century disintegrates. Such dissimilar people participating in music proves that a single, fixed signifier, such as social status, cannot sufficiently account for southern women's music practices. As a borderless ideal, gentility provides a more satisfactory explanation, and to this end, *Unbinding Gentility* replaces uniformity with a nuanced examination of a diverse representation of southern women and their musicking.

Notes

Introduction

1. "Old Musical Compositions that Link Present with Past," *Times-Democrat*, Oct. 31, 1909.

2. Eliza Ripley praises Rose Kennedy and her piano skills in *Social Life*. See *MSB*, 103–6. A portrait of Rose can be seen at Hémard, "New Orleans Nostalgia"; I have not been able to verify the current location of the image.

3. There are exceptions, and references will be made throughout to these.

4. See, for example, McInnis, *Politics of Taste*; Floyd and Bryden, *Domestic Space*; and Kelly, *Republic of Taste*.

5. Wilson, "Visual Culture," 30.

6. Crawford, *America's Musical Life*, 239.

7. Citron posits both the language and meaning inherent in the way we have described music in *Gender and the Musical Canon*, 57.

8. Private conversation with a donor who is still negotiating with the archive.

9. There are a few exceptions to this trend and particularly Cockrell's *Demons of Disorder*, which focuses on blackface performers. Others of note are Cockrell's other works listed in the Bibliography; Dunson, "Minstrel in the Parlor"; and more recent uses, Barnes, "The Faces of Racism" and "Yes, Politicians Wore Blackface."

10. Two recent dissertations have sought to correct this imbalance. Cooke's "Southern Women, Southern Voices" examines women lyricists and composers from the South, aiming at a different goal from mine here. Rumbley's "From Piano Girl to Professional" focuses on women's musical education at a seminary in Nashville from 1816 to 1920.

11. Several scholars, such as Katherine Preston and Julia Chybowski, have brought women's participation in musical practice to the public, but more needs to be done.

12. Weber, *Music and the Middle Class*, xxx.

13. Christopher Small introduced the term *musicking* to emphasize the process of making music rather than a static object in *Musicking*. I find it applicable to southern women's music in this period.

14. Solie, *Music in Other Words*, 1–2.

15. Kerrison, "The Novel as Teacher"; Harris, *Nineteenth-Century American Women's Novels*.

16. Previous literature related to women and music in the nineteenth-century United States typically deals with only a single part of the population. Race is a common divider: Epstein's *Sinful Tunes and Spirituals* and Southern's *Music of Black Americans* on one side; Tawa's *Sweet Songs for Gentle Americans* and Finson's *Voices That Are Gone* on the other.

17. On Black ephemera in archives, see Burroughs, *Black Roots*.

18. Halttunen, *Confidence Men*, 92.

19. *Ibid.*, 93, 101.

20. Bushman, *Refinement of America*. Linda Young's examination of gentility across the United Kingdom, United States, and Australia in *Middle-Class Culture* leads to similar conclusions.

21. Ibid., 18 and 209, and Young, *Middle Class Culture*, 10 and 43.

22. Young, *Middle Class Culture*, 201–2.

23. Halttunen, *Confidence Men*, 1 and 32.

24. Young, *Middle Class Culture*, 202.

25. Goffman, *Presentation of Self*, 22–30 and 70–76; Shamir, *Inexpressible Privacy*, 32; Sorisio, "Unmasking the Genteel Performer," 36; and Halttunen, *Confidence Men*, 93.

26. Lawrence, *Genteel Women*, 4.

27. Gatewood, *Aristocrats of Color*; Ackerman, "Theatre and the Private Sphere," 162, in Floyd and Bryden, *Domestic Space*; Phipps, *Genteel Rebel*; and Sorisio, "Unmasking the Genteel Performer."

28. Kasson, *Rudeness and Civility*, 34.

29. See Meyer-Frazier (*Bound Volumes*) and Scott (*Singing Bourgeoisie*) on the meaning and use of terms such as *parlor* and *drawing room*.

30. My work draws on ideas espoused by Pierre Bourdieu, but I have not adopted his theories wholeheartedly. Bourdieu, "Forms of Capital," 47. Jeanice Brooks first suggested that I investigate Bourdieu's work, and I appreciate her thoughtful advice.

31. Grier, *Culture and Comfort*, iii.

32. Cook, *The House Beautiful*, 48–49.

33. The question of a southern middle class, and when it moved from "middling" to "middle," is the basis of Wells's *Origins of the Southern Middle Class*.

34. McInnis, *Politics of Taste*, 8.

35. Prenshaw, "Southern Women Writers," 76–77.

36. Evans, *St. Elmo*, 114.

37. Lawrence, *Genteel Women*, 5–6.

38. Ibid., 4–5. Wells, *Origins of a Southern Middle Class*.

39. Hughes, *Victorians Undone*, 186, and "Discovering Literature."

40. Applying Bourdieu's terminology, Young interprets household inventories as evidence of habitus ("the structuring interaction of mentality with the material world"), which

thereby expresses how consumption asserted bourgeois standing. Bourdieu, *Distinction*, 1–2, 170, 56. See also Young, *Middle-Class Culture*, 201–2.

41. Halttunen, *Confidence Men*, 86 and 90.

42. These ideas are particularly inherent in Lawrence's *Genteel Women*, 6–7.

43. Witt, "Gendered Language of War," 8.

44. Lawrence cautions, however, that economic positioning cannot suffice as a boundary-defining tool because so many other factors figure in the antebellum understanding of gentility. Lawrence, *Genteel Women*, 4.

45. Southern historians have long sensed the "New-Englandization of women's history" (Clinton, *Plantation Mistress*, xv–xvi) or "Massachusetts Myopia" of American history (Urban, "History of Education," 133).

46. See the items under Preston in the Bibliography. Because many of the examples in this section were published under English translations of varying faithfulness to the original French or Italian, I have provided a list of original titles online.

47. Censer, *Reconstruction of White Southern Womanhood*, 275–76.

Chapter 1. Gentility, Music, and White Women

1. Eva Eve returned to Augusta in the mid-1850s. Composer A. Iverson of Columbus dedicated "When the Birds to the South" (printed in *GLB*, Oct. 16, 1838, 188) to Eve's aunt, Martha Deloney Berrien.

2. Kasson, *Rudeness & Civility*, 35–36.

3. Phipps, *Genteel Rebel*, 2; and Phipps, "'Their Desire to Visit.'"

4. Bushman, *Refinement of America*, xv.

5. O'Brien, *Conjectures of Order*, 4–7.

6. Virginia Shelton to sister Fannie, Mar. 7, 1851, Campbell Family Papers; quoted in Tolbert, *Constructing Townscapes*, 137.

7. See Bushman, "The House as Performer," in *Refinement of America*, 132; on the piano, 232.

8. *Holly Springs Gazette*, July 7, 1843.

9. Virginia Shelton to uncle, 16, 1851, Campbell Family Papers; quoted in Tolbert, *Constructing Townscapes*, 134–37.

10. Ibid., 137.

11. Kasson sees this in economic terms as well when he notes that those in the new urban middle class were "eager to acquire cultural capital and to set themselves off as quasi aristocracy from those below." *Rudeness & Civility*, 36; on readership, 53–57.

12. Young asserts that because of this, middle-class aspirants anxiously lived under the surveillance of those whom they assumed defined gentility. Young, "Extensive, Economical and Elegant," 203.

13. Young, *Middle-Class Culture*, 204.

14. Malnig, *Ballroom, Boogie*, 41.

15. Moreover, her well-known *Lady's Guide* derived from *Etiquette for Ladies; with Hints on the Preservation, Improvement, and Display of Female Beauty* (first published in Philadelphia in 1838), which contains many untranslated French terms and may have

originated with an unidentified French book. Grier, *Culture and Comfort*, 76. See also Ruth, *Social Culture*.

16. Chandler, "Belle of the Opera," 1.

17. Thornwell, *Ladies' Guide*, 97.

18. Mary Temperance "Tempie" Person (1839–1921). Person Family Papers. By comparison, the price of flour in 1860 averaged $5.60 per barrel. Kennedy, *Agriculture of the United States*, clxviii.

19. Thomas A. Person to Mary ("Tempie") and Sallie Person, Aug. 29, 1854. Person Family Papers.

20. Sallie and Mary "Tempie" Person wrote from Louisburg Female Academy to their father on Aug. 29, 1854, that they "have not taken any tune yet. Miss Emma [W. Curtis] puts in the first part of our instruction book. We got to go through before we take a tune which will be about three or four weeks." One of Tempie's pieces may have been "Lilly Dear," which she performed on a school concert on Nov. 29, 1855.

21. *Catalogue of the . . . Judson Female Institute* (Marion, 1855), 17; quoted in Jordan, *Ante-Bellum Alabama*, 38–39.

22. McInnis explores the intertwining of culture, politics, and rank in Charleston in *Politics of Taste*.

23. I explore why Henrietta's music remained unbound in *CBA*, 216–17. These other collections are also described throughout *CBA*.

24. Foreign music appeared in Charleston collections well before the 1850s, but in that decade the need and desire to differentiate the top of the social ladder from those beneath them peaked.

25. Mary Fenwick Lewis [MFL] to her sister, Aug. 11, 1844; quoted in Rohr, *Alabama School Girl*, 198. Southern women's associations with Paris run counter to the preferences for British culture described by Kilbride (*Being American in Europe*), see *CBA*, 9–10.

26. This option extended back into the eighteenth century; Harriet's aunt, Elizabeth Brewton Pinckney (d. 1857), attended Madame Campan's famous school for young women in Paris (Saint-Germain-en-Laye) for two years. Ravenel, *Life and Times of William Lowndes*, 60. On music at Campan's, see Geoffroy-Schwinden, "A Lady in Waiting's Account" and "Music as Feminine Capital."

27. Charles Izard Manigault to R. Habersham & Sons, Nov. 1, 1846; quoted in O'Brien, *Conjectures*, 112.

28. *CBA*, Part 2.

29. Rohr, *Alabama School Girl*, 52, 169, and 175. She probably meant Corneille's *Polyeucte*. MFL to mother, Apr. 17, 1844; quoted in Rohr, *Alabama School Girl*, 169.

30. MFL to Eliza (sister), June 5, 1844; quoted in Rohr, *Alabama School Girl*, 175.

31. MFL to mother, Feb. 25, 1844; quoted in Rohr, *Alabama School Girl*, 167–68.

32. MFL to Ellen Lewis (younger sister), Aug. 5, 1842; quoted in Rohr, *Alabama School Girl*, 42–43.

33. She never began harp lessons. MFL to her father, July 4, 1843; quoted in Rohr, *Alabama School Girl*, 19, 30, and 151. On the Calhoun (later Colhoun) family and their time in Paris, see Keith, *Colfax Massacre*, 30–36.

34. Rohr, *Alabama School Girl*, 205–6.

35. Mary Lewis (mother) to MFL, Mar. 31, 1843; quoted in Rohr, *Alabama School Girl*, 108; MFL to mother, Oct. 16, 1842, quoted in ibid., 71. Her sister began with Mrs. Bode, and wrote Mary such in 1844. She also played duets with Mary Coleman. Ellen and Ma to MFL, May 21, 1844; quoted in Rohr, *Alabama School Girl*, 179.

36. Mother to MFL, Oct. 9, 1842; Ellen L to MFL, Apr. 19, 1843; quoted in Rohr, *Alabama School Girl*, 67, 117.

37. Clement Comer Clay (John's father) was governor of Alabama and served in the US Senate; Clement Claibourne Clay (brother) served as US Senator for Alabama, 1853–61.

38. On Henrietta Aiken and Louisa McCord, see *CBA*.

39. She signed it "S M Crawford / Alexandria January 17th 1853." Most of Sarah's music does not have place names on it, so this seems to be especially significant to her. Ricordi (Milan) published the work, and Giuseppe Pugioli sold it in Alexandria.

40. Marie Louise (1830–62), daughter of Governor John M. Morehead, was a student at St. Mary's.

41. See Tatham, *Lure of the Striped Pig*, 23–24.

42. He listed his worth as $77,000 plus $40,000 in land in the 1860 US Census. Stewart's, "William T. Berry and His Fabulous Bookstore."

43. Details of John Stedman's death were reported in the *Wilmington Daily Journal*, Feb. 19, 1858.

44. Mrs. Kinney, wife of the Mississippi River steamboat captain received a copy of the "Lament of the Irish Immigrant" after her husband returned from a trip to St. Louis. Ostendorf, *Sounds American*, 165.

45. *Carolina Observer*, Nov. 4, 1861. See p. 176.

46. Fanny died before she could assume these duties. Engstrom, *Book of Burwell Students*, 60. The Burwell music room is one of the few antebellum spaces designated for music that still survive.

47. See also Mocha, *Poles in America*, 568. Bella was fourteen in 1860. His son, Thaddeus A., was the first Confederate casualty of the Civil War. Janta, "Early American-Polish Music," 87.

48. Lizzie Orchard published "Maj. General Hampton's Quick Step" during the war.

49. Volume 86, CPM (one of several in this family's collection). "We part forever" is probably "You Say We Part Forever," an arrangement of a melody from Auber's 1830 opera *Fra diavolo*.

50. These were passed down and across successive generations until the last Fanny Dickinson gave them to the Col. Hardy Murfree Chapter of the DAR. Volume 85 is the earliest, identified in the front cover as that belonging to "F. P. Dickinson."

51. "Aileen Mavourneen" never achieved the popularity of "Kathleen Mavourneen," which became the signature tune of the Irish soprano Catherine Hayes who toured the United States in 1851–53.

52. The repetitive names can be confusing: Fanny Priscilla Dickinson [Murfree] was the mother of Fanny Noailles Dickinson Murfree and Mary Noailles Murfree (1850–1922). Martha Elizabeth Dickinson is sister of Fanny Priscilla Dickinson. (Mary published under the name Charles Edbert Craddock.)

53. More information on Eliza and her music is presented in Bailey, "Binder's Volumes as Commonplace Books."

54. Maria Harwood's name is in one of Eliza's volumes. Many mothers taught their children music. For example, Mary Jane Anderson Lanier, an "accomplished musician," taught her son, Sidney, music. Starke, "Sidney Lanier as a Musician," 384–85.

55. See Bailey, "Binder's Volumes." Mary Maillard mentions that Julia served as an organist at Bruton Parish Church in Williamsburg, but I have not been able to corroborate this assertion. Maillard, *Belles of Williamsburg*, e-book.

56. Thornwell, *Lady's Guide*, 66. Further explanation of her concepts on taste can be found in *MSB*, 112–13.

57. Bushman, *Refinement of America*, 27.

58. On these women and others, see Bailey, *American Travel Literature*.

59. *GLB* 47 (1853): 375.

60. On the rarity of using one's name on music publications, see *MSB*, especially chapter 9.

61. Le Vert, *Souvenirs of Travel*, I, 70.

62. Satterfield, *Madame Le Vert*, 47–48.

63. Mrs. John K. "Passie" Ottley, in Alderman et al., *Library of Southern Literature*, 3223.

64. Satterfield, *Madame Le Vert*, 62.

65. Guterl, *American Mediterranean*, 14.

66. O'Brien, *Conjectures of Order*, 24.

67. Bremer and Howitt, *Homes of the New World*, vol. 3, 22.

68. Delaney, "Madame Octavia Walton Le Vert," 107.

69. Tawa, *Sweet Songs*, 44–45.

70. Ibid., 21. All of Tawa's examples in this regard come from the North, but there is no reason to assume similarly-situated southerners were lacking in these accomplishments.

71. See Bailey, "Sarah Cunningham's Music Book."

Chapter 2. Gentility, Music, and Women of Color

1. There are several studies of Black musicians performing from notated music: I refer the reader to Riis, "Cultivated White Tradition and Black Music"; Gable-Wilson, "Let Freedom Sing!"; Karpf, "An Opportunity to Rise"; and others cited later. King offers explanations for the dearth of material in *Essence of Liberty*, 34–35.

2. Myers, *Forging Freedom*, 8 and 12.

3. Intersections of minstrelsy and opera are described in Norris, "Opera and the Mainstreaming of Blackface Minstrelsy"; Dunson, "Minstrel in the Parlor"; and Graham, *Spirituals*.

4. Karl Hagstrom Miller addresses supposed distinctions between uncultivated and cultivated music in *Segregating Sound*.

5. Trotter, *Music and Some Highly Musical People*.

6. Chybowski, "Becoming the 'Black Swan'"; Moriah, "'A Greater Compass of Voice.'" Greenfield's musical education did not begin until she moved north while still young. Her voice, too, crossed what Stoever calls "the sonic color line" (*Sonic Color Line*, 111). See also Gable-Wilson, "Let Freedom Sing!"

7. Sorisio, "Unmasking the Genteel Performer," 25–26.

8. Trouillot's *Silencing the Past* finds application in the study of antebellum women—white and of color—and music in the United States, and parallels between his subjects and mine can be easily made.

9. This school closed in 1834. Ping, "Music in Antebellum Wilmington," 67.

10. American Almanac Collection (Library of Congress) (1838–1861). *Metropolitan Catholic Almanac and Laity's Directory* (Baltimore: F. Lucas, 1854): 364. King, *Essence of Liberty*, 92; Gerdes, "To Educate and Evangelize," 189; and Morrow, "Our Convent," 46. On Baltimore, see Graham, *Baltimore*; on music instruction among them, see "Colored Schools," *Catholic Mirror*, Mar. 26, 1853.

11. Gerdes, "To Educate and Evangelize," 189; information from the Archive of the Oblate Sisters of Providence.

12. Morrow, "'Our Convent,'" 37.

13. Morrow, "Oblate Sisters of Providence," 343, 345.

14. "Some Correspondence," *Weekly Anglo-African*, Aug. 13, 1859; quoted in Morrow, "Oblate Sisters of Providence," 347.

15. Ross, *Great New Orleans Kidnapping Case*, 29. Henriette Delille and the Sisters of the Holy Family may have offered music lessons to young free women of color.

16. Leslie, *Woman of Color*, 120. See also Davis, *Black Catholics*, 189. On the Sisters of the Holy Family, see Detiege, *Henriette Delille*; and Hart, *Violets in the King's Garden*. I wish to acknowledge Sierriana Terry, who brought Delille and the Sisters of the Holy Family to my attention.

17. An 1842 bequest from Marie Justin Camaire, a free woman of color in the city, created the school. Lovato, "Households and Neighborhoods," 22–23; and Mitchell, *Raising Freedom's Child*, chap. 1.

18. On Lambert, see Sullivan, "Composers of Color," 54, 58–62; Gushee, "Black Professional Musicians,"

19. Kinzer, "Tio Family," 89; and Trotter, *Music and Some Highly Musical People*, 348.

20. Bazanac is listed in the Lambert household on the 1850 US Census. The 1869 city directory lists Duhart at the same address as the Bazanacs, 347 St. Claude. Bell, *Revolution, Romanticism, and the Afro-Creole Protest Tradition*, 125.

21. See, for example, Edmund Dédé's "Mon pauvre coeur." Kein, *Creole*, 185. On the practice identified in the twentieth century as *plaçage*, see Clark's *Strange History of the American Quadroon*, 148–59.

22. Nathan's carefully crafted will and assistance from a white friend enabled Susan and her children to inherit a considerable estate. Alexander, *Ambiguous Lives*, 78–79. See also Nash, *Forbidden Love*.

23. Day (ca. 1801–1861) was a highly successful businessman who at one point was a stockholder in the State Bank of North Carolina. Wealthy North Carolinians sought out Day for his beautiful woodworks as well as his architectural designs. She and two brothers later attended Wesleyan Academy in Wilbraham, Massachusetts. See also Barfield and Marshall, *Thomas Day*.

24. *Moravian Records*, XI, 5879–5880.

25. McInnis, *Politics of Taste*, 7–8; see also Pease and Pease, *Web of Progress*. Several scholars address the significance of place in the lives of free people of color. In addition to the writers cited later, see King, *Essence of Liberty*, and Lebsock, *Free Women of Petersburg*.

26. Fitchett, "Traditions of the Free Negro," 144–47.

27. Powers, *Black Charlestonians*, 22 and 79.

28. Myers, *Forging Freedom*, 4 and 25.

29. Reynolds speculates that Martha Inglis may have hired a music tutor for her children, either a free Black teacher or a European governess. Either could be the case and can be supported by isolated examples from around the South. Reynolds, "Wealthy Free Women of Color," 134–36, and 146–47. According to Robert Harris, there was one Black music instructor in Charleston listed in the 1850 census. Harris, "Charleston's Free Afro-American Elite," 305.

30. Young, *Middle-Class Culture*, 209. Ross echoes these ideas when he writes of educated men and women "whose scrupulous manners and dress reflected a commitment to the values of respectability" held by many upper- and middle-class whites. He also argues that the gentility of two women involved in the kidnapping, "mulatresses" Louisa Murray and sister Ellen Follin, affected the way in which reporters wrote about them. Ross, *Great New Orleans Kidnapping Case*, 98–99.

31. William Johnson diary, William Johnson Papers.

32. "Miss Venena Miller" or "Miss V. Miller." These items previously belonged to Lavinia Miller McCrary, Anna Johnson's older cousin and godmother.

33. The US 1860 census has J. Wannemaker, 25, of Bavaria, Teacher of Music, just above the listing for the Johnson family.

34. He is the subject of books and two articles: Ben E. Bailey's seminal 1985 article, "Music in the Life of a Free Black Man of Natchez," and Cockrell, "William Johnson: Barber, Musician, Parable" in *American Music*. On Lavinia McCrary, see King, *Essence of Liberty*, 48.

35. *L'abeille*, Apr. 7, 1853; quoted in Baron, *New Orleans*, 99.

36. Account Book, William Johnson Papers, p. 64. Bailey put forth the idea that this was a white man willing to teach music to young children of color. "Music in the Life," 9. Gould transcribed many of the Johnson family materials in *Chained to the Rock*.

37. The 1850 Mississippi State census, in Ostendorf, *Sounds American*, 136.

38. King, *Essence of Liberty*, 2.

39. The Johnson copy of "The Swinging Polka" is in the boxes of loose music in LSU; Eva's has been pasted into her binder's volume.

40. Leslie printed this image on musical works in several issues of his *Gazette* in 1857.

41. Catherine Johnson Diary, Nov. 1, 1864, William Johnson Papers, Vol. 31.

42. Myers, *Forging Freedom*, 116. Myers makes the important qualification that "free" itself is a problematic term, as people of color were restricted by many official and unofficial practices.

43. Case, *Leaders of Their Race*, 6–7, and 69. "Belle" is a problematic term, but its use on the sheet music clearly signifies a stylish, genteel young lady (at least for the other four cities).

44. Gould, *Chained to the Rock*, xxii.

45. Leslie, *Woman of Color*, 44, 65, 90, 360–61. On the Sayre-Hunt children and Dicksons. See also Schultz, "Interracial Kinship Ties," 146–47.

46. Myers, *Forging Freedom*, 160 and 162. Myers discusses the likely nature of the relationship between the slave and master.

47. Receipt Book 1, SCSVP, B2/F1/D1 at LCP.

48. Since the only child of this union named Sarah (Ann) was not born until May of 1839, "Miss Sarah" must refer to Sarah Martha Sanders, not their child Sarah Ann (as Myers suggests). Myers, "Negotiating Women," 186, 191n.

49. One of her daughters, Mary, gave piano recitals in Philadelphia after the children were sent there by Cogdell in the 1850s. James Garcia appears in the 1830 city directory as a music teacher and may have also instructed the Inglis children.

50. Myers, *Forging Freedom*, 160.

51. One of the daughters was described as a "fairly competent pianist." In 1858, Richard made provisions to his will and left his daughter Sarah Ann a music box from Geneva and a new opera glass (among other items); she and her sister Cordelia received the piano. Cordelia married William H. Chew. She died in Philadelphia in 1879.

52. Herz, *My Travels in America*, 87–88, and 93. He stayed at a hotel (the St. Charles) run by another woman of color. Some venues in New Orleans allowed anyone who could afford to pay admission to attend concerts, but this was apparently not the case here. Henrietta Amantine Mercier Soulé (1811–59) was the wife of Senator Pierre Soulé. Amantine participated in amateur concerts of Herz's music (his *William Tell Overture* arranged for eight pianos, sixteen pianists) on at least two occasions. Lott, *From Paris to Peoria*, 79.

53. See, for example, Clark, *Strange History of the American Quadroon*.

54. Floyd, "Black Music and Writing Black Music History," 116.

55. Wells repeats these assertions in *Women Writers and Journalists*, 5 and 52.

56. I am most grateful to David Garcia for suggesting this line of analysis to me in his response to my paper, "Interrogating the Musical Practices of Women of Color in the Antebellum South," at the workshop, Music and the Construction of Race in Early America, University of Pennsylvania, October 2019.

57. The tendency of free women of color to not marry or not remarry and as such retain real property was another way of asserting agency. See King, *Essence of Liberty*, 55–57.

58. More information is available for later in the century. See Shaw, *What a Woman Ought to Be*.

59. "Eight Things That Do Not Look Well," *Southern Cultivator* 1 (Nov. 22, 1843): 191–92.

60. Myers, *Forging Freedom*, 155.

61. Hartley, *Ladies' Book*, 178–79.

62. Hartman, *Wayward Lives*, xiii.

Chapter 3. Melody

1. Why they remain popular has yet to be interrogated fully, but Tony Horowitz's *Confederates in the Attic*, which begins with Civil War reenactors, might hold valuable clues. Among the many books on this music, see Luper, *Civil War Music*; McWhirter, *Battle Hymns*; Finson, *Voices That Are Gone*; Tawa, *Sweet Songs*.

2. Moreover, the audience for minstrel shows in the United States was essentially male. Cockrell, *Demons of Disorder*, 56. A few volumes include isolated examples of dialect, but not many.

3. On these respectable groups, see Cockrell, "Of Soundscapes and Blackface," 63–65.

4. On Harwood, see Bailey, "Binder's Volumes," 453–56. On Herz, see Lott, *Paris to Preoria*, 55–104.

5. See Wilson, "Impact of French Opera in Nineteenth-Century New York"; Preston, "The 1838–40 American Concert Tours of Jane Shirreff" and *Opera on the Road*. On purchasing, see Preston, "Music in the McKissick Parlor," 17.

6. These sonatas bear the same opus number as his Grand Concerto but are distinct pieces.

7. Variation sets had been heard in the United States since at least the eighteenth century. A particularly popular and representative example is Donald Ross's working of "Auld Langsyne."

8. These may be defined as compositions not based on a preexisting melody, not associated with a dance, and not the abstract works entitled sonata, concerto, or sonatina. They often evoke a single mood or emotion.

9. Housewright writes that Chopin, Liszt, Mozart, and Mendelssohn played in Pensacola but provides no date or source material. *Music & Dance in Florida*, 169.

10. The Horners' Roman Catholic roots in Fauquier County (Virginia) extend back into the eighteenth century. *Records of the American Catholic Historical Society*, 275–77. Volumes printed for pedagogical purposes often incorporated a substantial amount of sacred music, and these served as sources for religious music for musical families. A manuscript of sacred music in John Thuer's hand, dated 1837, also survives in the Thomas Butler and Family Papers, but this was not necessarily performed in the parlor.

11. *Daily Picayune*, Jan. 16 and 25, 1842; quotes in Kimball, "Northern Music Culture," 55–56.

12. *Richmond Whig*, Apr. 29, 1853.

13. *Courier*, Apr. 25, 1853.

14. Hindeman, "Ante-Bellum Charleston," 636–37.

15. The finder's aid for this volume includes publication data: https://scrcguides.libraries.wm.edu/repositories/2/archival_objects/19227.

16. Hartley, *Ladies' Book*, 179. Mark Knowles finds a southern gravitation "toward more aristocratic forms of amusement" promoted dancing especially in that region. *Wicked Waltz*, 6.

17. An anonymous binder's volume, UNC Music Library, Old Series XCVII, contains a number of compositions purchased in Savannah, which points to an owner somewhere in that area. On Kneass, the author of "Ben Bolt," see Krohn, "Nelson Kneass."

18. In addition to Eliza Harwood, Mary Ann Boyers (Nashville), Virginia Reeves (Hickman Co., Tennessee), and many other women owned this work. A Sheet Music Consortium search of the "Cinderella Waltz" yields over 19,000 copies. The opera was performed in New Orleans in 1833. Mahan, *Showboats*, 5. On piano adaptations of Rossini works, see Gallo, "Selling 'Celebrity.'"

19. I place it earliest because the sheet music in the book contains different versions of her name: Eliza Fisk and Eliza F. Harwood (which she eventually settled on), and none

of the pieces bears a date later than 1837. See Bailey, "Binder's Volumes as Commonplace Books." Eliza's books are privately held; a relative of the current owner has recently suggested to me that there are more binder's volumes that belonged to Eliza.

20. Preston deduces that women sometimes purchased music after hearing singers in concert locally. *Emily's Songbook*, 15.

21. MFL to mother, Sept. 30, 1842; quoted in Rohr, *Alabama School Girl*, 62.

22. She especially noticed the movement of men while dancing: "gentlemen don't dance here, they walk." MFL to mother, June 22 1843; quoted in ibid., 150.

23. Composed by Adolphe-Clair Le Carpentier, published by Lee and Walker in Philadelphia, n.d. The Jackson/Prince copy was sold at Zogbaum's in Savannah.

24. I explore the use of such pictures to cultivate cultural refinement in "Binder's Volumes."

25. September 1851, "Mems for Musical Misses," *GLB*: 489.

26. Lehuu argues that *Godey's* created a space for women's culture and finds its figures, as visual texts, imposed conformity even if they juxtaposed dialectically opposed advice. Lehuu, "Sentimental Figures," 74–75, and 89.

27. Knowles, *Wicked Waltz*, 34–36.

28. John Berkeley Grimball Diaries, 1832–83, Series 1. See also John Berkley [*sic*] Grimball Papers. Grimball's brother, Berkley J. (1833–99), owned a collection of eight volumes of *The Apollo*, treble melodies for flute bound in 1837 (Charleston Museum, SMB 175).

29. Published in 1848, but Eva must have used it later because she was only seven in 1848.

30. Housewright, *Music & Dance in Florida*, 195. Second journal, Aug. 23, 1852; quoted in O'Brien, *Evening When Alone*, 177.

31. Waltzes in five began to appear in the 1840s, with Pietro Saracco's "Five-Step Waltz," Elias Howe's "Waltz in Five-Four," and another by Christian Nolff.

32. In the collection of Anne Ehlen. Published by Willig; dedicated to Miss Achsah Carroll.

33. Ripley, *Social Life*, 151. See also Ostendorf, *Sounds American*, 159.

34. *Biennial Report of the Superintendent . . . 1896-'97 and 1897-'98*, 691.

35. Knowles discusses the role of religion and the second Great Awakening on dance, citing several authors. Knowles, *Wicked Waltz*, 6–10.

36. Quoted in Housewright, *Music and Dance in Florida*, 185.

37. Ibid., 199–201. She also confirms that they used her mother's music, as others described here did.

38. Pease and Pease, *Family of Women*, 61.

39. Mary J. Withers to Francis J. Levert, Apr. 30, 1858, Susanna Claiborne Withers Clay, Box 1, Le Vert Family Papers. Another of Francis's nieces, Helen Withers, wrote to him about the lack of a piano in 1859: "We do not practice now for they have left the piano at Millwood." Apr. 10, 1859, Helen Withers to FJL. Box 3, SHC.

40. Cheer, *Great Lablache*, 372. The music, however, is found in an opera by Guilio Aláry, *Le Tre Nozze*, in which Sontag and Lablache appeared in 1851. C. T. deConiel arranged the "Polka aria, or, Sontag polka" for harp in 1852. Other prints include only Sontag on the cover.

41. On Elssler, see Hutchinson, *Fanny Elssler's Cachucha*. On Taglioni, see Sowell et al., *Icônes du ballet romantique*.

42. Exoticism and related imagery on sheet music have been discussed by several authors, including Hijar "Pin Up, Piano, Parlor"; Brooks, "Pocahontas"; Dunson, "Minstrel in the Parlor." The literature on minstrelsy and representations of African Americans in this period is voluminous. See, for example, Norris, "Opera and the Mainstreaming of Blackface Minstrelsy."

43. July 10, 1841, Pettigrew Family Papers.

44. Ostendorf, *Sounds American*, 156–67; Stoutamire, "Music in Richmond," 274.

45. Rohr, *Alabama School Girl*, 52. Nineteenth-century critics ranked Cerito with Fanny Elssler and Marie Taglioni. On Elssler in Charleston, see Pease and Pease, *Ladies, Women, and Wenches*, 56–57. She married Arthur Saint-Léon (also a dancer and named on the cover of SMS 656, "S. Leone") in 1845 and remained with him for six years, which coincides with the date of 1848 on Henrietta's copy of "La Siciliana, Ballo Nazionale" (SMS 656). She challenged governmental authority dancing with the political implications of "La Siciliana," see *CBA*, 111.

46. This set exists in collections belonging to Eliza Harwood in Williamsburg and Sarah Cunningham in Savannah, but their economic circumstances did not equal that of the Draytons.

47. Scott et al., *The Beauties of Sir Walter Scott*, 1826.

48. Second journal, Sept. 11, 1852; quoted in O'Brien, *An Evening When Alone*, 214.

49. Housewright, *Music & Dance in Florida*, 137.

50. Nash, *Ladies in the Making*, 49–50; and *MSB*, 73–74.

51. Jennings, "Grand Opera in Kansas City," 679.

52. Cryer, *Love Me Tender*, 73–74.

53. In 2017, a search of the Sheet Music Consortium yielded over 18,000 results for "Home! Sweet Home!" http://digital2.library.ucla.edu/sheetmusic/index.html.

54. Siegling's version in Old Series XIII. Charles Hamm's *Yesterdays* accurately describes the vocal repertory, but his insightful assessment seems not to have had the impact on later research that it should.

55. Melpominé Stella Bringier to Amède Bringier, Feb. 18, 1858, Louis A. Bringier Papers.

56. Carrie may have been related to Maggie Mallett; Mary lists her as a lady of quality in her binder's volume. In 1856, Firth, Pond and Co. printed the same setting by Coppock, here dedicated to "Miss Julia Waterbury of Williamsburgh" (in a binder's volume belonging to Maggie Uhlinger).

57. The date is 1864 on the music, but that looks like an addition.

58. Meyer-Frazier discusses Sarah Burton of Raleigh in *Bound Music*, 77. The two women might be related, or possibly the same person. Carrie Mallett's copy was part of a series entitled "Parlor Album Songs" (#9). Caroline McNairy had one printed copy and one manuscript version of the same.

59. Tawa, *Sweet Songs*, 6.

60. The quadrilles from the opera include dance instructions, printed in Philadelphia in 1845.

61. This is in her manuscript volume (in several hands), recently acquired by the Belmont Mansion.

62. Sarah Ann Foster's manuscript book, dated 1812, exemplifies this earlier period of binder's volumes. Handwritten sources are more common in the late-eighteenth and

very early-nineteenth centuries, but volumes consisting only of manuscript material are unusual for affluent young women of the 1830s.

63. *Yazoo Democrat*, Dec. 11, 1858.

64. Sarah Lois Wadley, "Diary," Aug. 10, 1860, 55.

65. Housewright, *Music & Dance in Florida*, 175. Aiken Rhett Collection, SMS 456.

Chapter 4. Opera as Cultural Capital

1. In the following discussion, "European opera" indicates that in French, Italian, and German. English opera had long been a staple in the United States and continued to do so well into the nineteenth century, as Preston argues in *Opera for the People*.

2. This is taken from the end of Act I, "Das klinget so herrlich." Fernando Sor popularized the melody as "O cara armonia" in 1821, but it soon appeared as "O dolce concento" or "Away with Melancholy." The English version appeared in London in the early 1790s; American imprints date from 1797 onward. A simpler version of this song occurs in Sarah Ann Foster's book.

3. *City Gazette and Commercial*, Feb. 12, 1823.

4. Fisher et al., *Best Companions*, 48. Only a year younger than Harriet Lowndes, Emma married at a slightly older age but still in the 1830s (Joseph Allen Smith Jr. in 1838).

5. Whether by Emma's choice, her parents', or the binder's is unknown. Most of the sheet music came from Siegling's shop in Charleston.

6. The contents of Emma Huger's binder's volume are given in *CBA*, 39–43.

7. Paisiello's aria can be found in several identified binder's volumes from the 1820s and does not mark Emma's as unique. Butler locates performances of Paisiello's music in Charleston as early as 1801 and Mozart in 1802. Butler, *Votaries of Apollo*, 234–35 and 337n58.

8. Ibid., 191–92. Overtures by these men could be heard in Charleston between 1805 and 1817, and Gilfert even composed a set of variations on a theme from Dalayrac's popular opera *Nina*.

9. Sola moved to England in 1817. Some of Sola's pieces (compositions or arrangements) can be found in American collections, either imported from Europe or published by such firms as Riley in New York and Willig in Philadelphia. The Weber chorus saw repeated use, including a manuscript copy belonging to Margaret King (Georgia).

10. Advertisement in *Charleston Courier* May 12, 1843.

11. On the intermingling of celebrity, marketability, and Rossini's works, see Gallo, "Selling 'Celebrity.'"

12. *Courier*, Dec. 19, 1837.

13. Unless otherwise noted, when I refer to opera here, I intend operas that did not originate in English.

14. Preston, "Between the Cracks," 350. See also Wilson, "Impact of French Opera."

15. Quoted in Housewright, *Music & Dance in Florida*, 189.

16. Rerestler sold the latter in his music store in Augusta, importing it from New York.

17. Eva served as a bridesmaid at Ruth's wedding in 1858, and in October 1863 married Ruth's widowed husband (Charles Colcock Jones, the last antebellum mayor of Savannah). Rozier, ed., *Granite Farm*, 114.

18. Young, "Extensive, Economical, and Elegant," 215.

19. On the influence of European pianists in the United States, see Lott, *From Paris to Peoria*.

20. Mary Mather played advanced operatic arrangements, such as *Lucia di Lammermoor* from *Italian Gems from Donizetti's Operas* (arr., Le Carpentier), but I have not been able to identify her social position. She probably was the daughter of William George Mather (a wealthy planter) or his son George (a physician) in St. James Parish, Louisiana. Some of her music came from Paris via Benoit and Grünewald in New Orleans.

21. This teacher could have been "the celebrated musician Mr. Stradelli" of New York, whose appointment as music instructor was noted in the *Wilmington Journal* on Apr. 11, 1856.

22. Anne Boykin Jones Diary, 1851, pp. 43 and 150. More curious is her attitude toward Queen Victoria (whom Harriet never mentions) and the king of Belgium. Anne writes as if she expected to run into the queen, meet the royal family in the street, or find them at home while visiting residences. For example: "We shall miss seeing the Queen altogether, unless by some chance we should meet with her in Scotland, where she is at present at Balmoral." While in Brussels, the family visited the royal palace "but *did not see the King*"—underlined as if this were a surprise. (p. 52)

23. More information on Louisa's time abroad available in *CBA*, 173–90.

24. Lizzie Randall to sister Mary, Mar. 11, 1851, LSU.

25. Henry Wehrmann Scrapbook, 1838–1939, folder 2, 134–35. The Théâtre d'Orléans put on two complete grand operas and two opéras comique each week.

26. Thornwell, *Lady's Guide*, 109.

27. *Charleston Courier*, Nov. 23, 1853.

28. See Coolidge, "Francis Henry Brown." The contents of her volume are in Appendix A.

29. Hartley, *Ladies' Book*, 188.

30. *Daily Dispatch*, Mar. 24, 1853.

31. Hartley, *Ladies' Book*, 186–87.

32. Harriet Lowndes Aiken, Travel Diary 1857–58, Aiken-Rhett Papers.

Chapter 5. Genteel Women Scientists

1. On the problems inherent in singing like an opera singer, *MSB*, 128–36.

2. *Nashville Union*, Jan. 13, 1853. She also sang similar programs in New Orleans and Mobile on this tour. Baron, *New Orleans*, 362; and *Music* (1850): 431.

3. Ellen L [Huntsville, AL] to MFL [Paris] Apr. 19, 1843; quoted in Rohr, *Alabama School Girl*, 117. Ellen's assignment of the book to Meredith Colhoun (her guardian in Paris) provides a rare glimpse of southern elite men owning music, if indeed that is what she meant.

4. Golding presents an interesting corollary to this idea in chapter 1, "Music as Science: Edinburgh, 1837–1865," of *Music and Academia*.

5. Southern schools demanded more rigor than many have assumed, and their offerings were designed to be on par with those at men's institutions. Farnham, *Education of the Southern Belle*, 26–27.

6. This term is taken from the book of the same name by Ann Strudwick Nash.

7. Tolbert, *Constructing Townscapes*, 129.

8. *Planter's Banner*, Nov. 7, 1850.

9. *Alexandria Gazette*, May 9, 1837. Pratt taught piano, guitar, flute, cello, and voice.

10. *Holly Springs Gazette*, July 7, 1843.

11. The piece that circulated as "Weber's Last Waltz" belongs not to Carl Maria von Weber but to Carl Gottlieb Reissiger (op. 26, no. 5).

12. The complete program appears in Mayes, *History of Education in Mississippi*, 94.

13. *Catalogue of the Columbia Female Institute, Columbia, 1838*, 20–21. On Smith's biography and influence in Columbia, see Bailey, "Sarah Smith."

14. She and her husband listed over $200,000 of combined worth in the 1860 Census.

15. Cabell and Smith, *Children of the Rectory*, 12.

16. An image of this room is available in Bailey, "Sarah Smith," 161.

17. *Catalogue of the Columbia Female Institute, Columbia, 1838*. The Institute had not procured an organ when it opened, but the catalog mentions that there is a platform in the study hall for its placement, when acquired.

18. *Daily Picayune*, Oct. 27, 1855. She also taught harp, piano, and singing.

19. Dale, "Columbia Institute Years Ago," May 30, 1930; Columbia Female Institute Hanging File, Maury County Archives.

20. Mar. 15, 1858, Margaret A. Ulmer diary.

21. July 21, Anonymous Diary, Mss. 533, LSU Hill Valley Mississippi Collection.

22. *MSB*, 73.

23. Binder's volumes indicate what individual students studied, but they do not usually reveal voice class repertory. In 2015, I examined twelve boxes of music materials at the Athenaeum, ranging in date from early editions of Handel operas to late-nineteenth-century concert bills. I thank Michelle Meinhart, who introduced me to this collection.

24. Halttunen, *Confidence Men*, 93.

25. This edition is older than most in the Athenaeum's collection, but two early editions of Handel operas suggests that these may have been among Sarah Smith's "thousands" of pieces of music.

26. The one binder's volume now in the Athenaeum collection belonged to Kate H. Brantley. It includes Gottschalk's "Marche de nuit" and French vocal music, in addition to a more traditional English repertory. The music predominantly came from New Orleans and Vicksburg and was bound in 1856 in New Orleans.

27. According to Siepmann, by the nineteenth century "thorough bass had become effectively a forgotten art," *Piano*, 45. See also Steib, *Reader's Guide*, 168. Chapman argues a different view in "Thoroughbass Pedagogy."

28. *Charlotte Democrat*, Sept. 17 and 24, Oct. 8, 1861.

29. For an example of Henrietta's vocal exercises, see *CBA*, 145.

30. Guardian, Nov. 15, 1846.

31. Holt, *Autobiographical Sketch*, 10.

32. Selma Plantation Diary, Dec. 9, 1835; quoted in O'Brien, *Evening When Alone*, 122.

33. See *MSB*, chapters 7–9. While at the Madison Female Seminary, Holt "arranged some simple little airs as duets" to provide them appropriate material for semipublic performances. Holt, *Autobiographical Sketch*, 10–11.

34. *Guardian*, March/April 1852, 188–92.

35. Sorisio, "Unmasking the Genteel Performer," 25–26.

36. Halttunen discusses this code in *Confidence Men*, 102–17.

37. Tolbert, *Constructing Townscapes*, 146.

38. Another of Sarah's daughters, Sallie Ward Smith (1837–1910), sat for a portrait with her harp; both remain in the parlor of the Athenaeum.

39. Hartley, *Ladies' Book*, 57 and 189.

40. Mar. 4, 1858, Margaret A. Ulmer diary.

41. Carey North also mentioned sight-reading "Sleeping I Dreamed of Love," *MSB*, 46–47.

42. On the importance of keeping the body in order, see Kasson, *Rudeness & Civility*, chapter 4, "Venturing Forth: Bodily Management in Public," 112–46.

43. *Times-Picayune*, Oct. 27, 1855; and other announcements in 1854–55. On evenings, *Times-Picayune*, Apr. 26, 1861.

44. *Mississippi Free Trader*, Apr. 26, 1848.

45. "Where the Music-Teachers Are, and What They Are Doing," *New York Weekly Review* 5 (1854/55): 75.

46. Willis and Moran, *Musical World* 11–13 (1855): 189. Erickson published the "Resignation Polka" when M. P. Jewett left the post of principal at Judson. "Editor's Armchair," *Ladies Repository* 24 (1856): 119. Manly, *Judson College*, 202.

47. Hartley, *Ladies' Book*, 189 and 288.

48. *Charleston Mercury*, Jan. 1, 1855.

49. *Wilmington Journal*, Mar. 5, 1858.

50. Ping analyzes the appeal of "Katy Darling" in "Music in Antebellum Wilmington," 46. Arrangers (William Iucho, William Dressler, and Charles de Janon) also provided instrumental versions. Grobe's version wins pride of place, at least in name, for his "Vox Populi: A Tip-Top Selection of Popular Melodies and Brilliant Variations," op. 289 (1852), which Mary Hunt of Jonesville (North Carolina) included in her binder's volume. He transposed the tune to C major and includes several typical techniques for variations, including alternating triplets between hands, scales in a "vivace e brillante" section, and finale with the hands spread apart by several octaves.

51. The proprietors of this school are the same Burwells who owned Elizabeth Keckley.

52. Sallie A. Mangum to Willie P. Mangum, Dec. 21, 1841, Willie Person Mangum Papers.

53. Engstrom, *Book of Burwell Students*, 65–66.

Chapter 6. Foreign Music Teachers and Genteel Pupils

1. *Wilson Ledger*, Dec. 2, 1860.

2. Ostendorf, *Sounds American*, 137 and 159.

3. Upton, *Musical Memories*, 254; see also *MSB*, 57.

4. Harriet Person to mother, Aug. 24, 1853, Person Family Papers.

5. His name occurs in the household of Frank Smith in the 1850 US Census. In 1841, Opl led the Richmond Sacred Oratorio Society in an oratorio concert that also included

Signor George (formerly at Norfolk but in Petersburg at this time; he taught Eliza Harwell in the 1830s) and Miss Sully on the organ and harp. Richmond *Whig*, June 9, 1840.

6. Cohen, *Barhamville Miscellany*, 46, 149; *MSB*, 85. At least two, Mary Mills and Miss A. Bluxome, were from the United States. Bluxome may have been Mary A. Bluxome, elder sister of Georgiana, a music teacher in Wilmington in 1860. Another sister, Serena, taught nearby at the Columbia Female Academy. See *MSB*, 81–89.

7. Strawinski was in the United States by 1838, when he bought a Martin guitar in New York City. Gura, *C. F. Martin*, 61.

8. This clipping is attached to a letter dated Sept. 27, 1854, to Francis J. Levert. Letter, Levert Family Papers, Box 2.

9. See *MSB*, 55 and 98.

10. *Sugar Planter*, Oct. 18, 1858.

11. For example, Ann and Elizabeth Sloman taught at their residence on 280 King St. in Charleston (*Charleston Courier*, Jan. 5, 1852). On locations in Macon, see Mahan, *Showboats to Soft Shoes*, 52.

12. Frederick F. Müller to Miss Rebecca Valentine, July 9, 1842, LSU. Müller also wrote that he intended to have "social music" added to the curriculum in public schools in New Orleans. Her name is difficult to discern from the address. Much more information on Müller is available in Kimball, "Northern Music Culture," 19–47.

13. Wadley, "Diary," 53, May 29, 1860, and 35, Jan. 26, 1860.

14. Since 2010, new information has come to light that Gnospelius immigrated from Sweden in 1850 and became the organist at Christ Church, Savannah (not German, as in *MSB*, 59).

15. Wadley, "Diary," 81, Nov. 17, 1860. Eaton was habitually drawn to New Orleans, especially the theater, and eventually moved there. He composed several pro-South pieces during the war.

16. Several of these are documented in *MSB*, 63.

17. Mahan, *Showboats to Soft Shoes*, 52–53. For more examples, see *MSB*, 57.

18. Ostendorf, *Sounds American*, 136. Furvelle De Pontis, McDonald Reponey, and P. A. Rivarde appear as "mulattos" in the census. Rivarde composed "When Love Is Kind" (published in New York in 1869) and "Entreat Not" (published in Chicago, 1883). Composer C. B. Hawley studied with him. Such lists rarely include all people teaching music, and women's names are the most likely to be omitted.

19. *New Orleans Daily Crescent*, June 25, 1860.

20. In all, authorities connected Martin sexually to at least thirty white women and received a prison sentence for his transgressions. See also Sullivan, "Composers of Color," 71–72.

21. *Carolina Watchman*, Aug, 13, 1835. William Cabell Rives served as Minister to France 1849–1853, and Amelie was the goddaughter of Queen Marie-Amélie.

22. Quoted in Tick, "Passed Away Is the Piano Girl," 325; and Hohl Trillini, *Gaze of the Listener*, 190.

23. Pryor, *Reminiscences*, 47–49.

24. Ibid., 50. St. Mary's (see later) advertisement in *Richmond Enquirer*, Mar. 15, 1844.

25. *Catalog of the Greensborough Female College, Greensboro,* 1847.

26. Pryor, *Reminiscences,* 50–51.

27. Tuition statement and letter, Rev. Aldert Smedes to Dr. G. Drake, May 1, 1869. Johnson-McFaddin Papers, SHC, 2489-Z. J. B. Averitt describes the school as "perhaps the most popular [girls'] school in the South." Averitt, *Old Plantation,* 98.

28. Mary to William S. Petigru, June 23, 1843, James Louis Petigru Papers, folder 91.

29. *Manual of St. Mary's,* 1857. *North Carolina Standard,* Nov. 22, 1843. The Southern Collegiate Institute in Jackson had similar soirées, alternating Saturday evenings on etiquette instruction. *New Orleans Weekly Delta,* Oct. 30, 1848.

30. Mary was the daughter of John Wright Withers, therefore the niece of Eliza Ann Ward Withers, Francis's wife. Mary J. Withers to Uncle, Nov. 3, 1854, Levert Family Papers. Mary affirms St. Mary's reputation across the region by writing that it "is greatly superior in looks, gravity, [and] more intelligent girls."

31. Blessner arrived at St. Mary's in the early 1840s and in 1844 performed as a soloist at a party given by Governor John Morehead. Murray, *Wake, Capital County,* 341. On Haigh, see Fox-Genovese and Genovese, *Master Class,* 144.

32. William Hooper Haigh diary, Sept. 6, 1844, 134, 259–60.

33. "Grande Vocal and Instrumental Concert," *Charleston Courier,* Feb. 19, 1840. Ellen Brownlow noted in her 1907 memoirs of Blessner, "our German Music Master," was a composer, pianist, and violinist. Brownlow, "St. Mary's in the Forties," 16. Murray's sources indicate he was born in France. *Wake: Capital County,* 341. See Blessner and Ping-Robbins, *Anthology of Music.*

34. Brownlow also wrote of Blessner's wife, whom she only names as "Mrs. Blessner." This Englishwoman taught piano and painting at St. Mary's in the Music Room with her lap dog in attendance. She created the artwork that graced her husband's "The Flowers of the South," which has an image of St. Mary's on the first page and is dedicated to the young ladies there.

35. *Charlotte Democrat,* Jan. 22, 1861. According to the 1860 census, an H. M. Hammarskold, age twenty-two, lived in a household headed by Charles Hammarskold; her occupation is given as a "Teacher of Music." Nine other Swedes lived with the Hammarskolds, including an H. E. Hammarskold (female), age fifty.

36. *Charlotte Democrat* advertised their positions at the school, Sept. 17 and 24, and Oct. 8, 1861; *Charlotte Democrat,* Aug. 19, 1862. Burwell had moved his school from Hillsborough to Charlotte. Any connection between Miss H. E. Hammarskold and Mrs. Emelie Hammarskjöld (née Holmberg, 1821–54), also a graduate of the Royal Academy in Stockholm and a singer who toured the South, has yet to be established. According to Stanton, women were given "access" to the Royal Academy only in 1854 and had "profitted" by this "privilege." *Woman Question,* 205. The *Svenskt biografiskt handlexicon* of 1906 states that "Again, she was called organist at St. Peter's Church in Charlestown and founded a Philharmonic Society in the city." Hofberg et al., "Emilie Augusta Kristina Holmberg." This must have been the keyboard player, not the vocalist.

37. Most aptly in Farnham, *Education of the Southern Belle,* 2.

38. Evans, *Conquest of Labor,* 89.

39. Mayes, *History of Education in Mississippi,* 48–50.

40. *Richmond Whig,* Oct. 12, 1855. Da Costa taught music, as did Meerbach, at the Southern Female Institute. Sarah Sully, whose mother took part in most Richmond musical events earlier in the century, taught harp alongside Dunderale at the Richmond Female Institute.

41. Holt, *Autobiographical Sketch,* 5–6. Codman (ca. 1796–1852), an Englishman, was a former student of William Crotch. On the Mordecais in Warrenton, see MacDonald, *Education of the Heart*; Nuermberger, "Notes on the Mordecai Family"; Falk, "Warrenton Female Academy"; and Hanft, "Mordecai's Female Academy."

42. Holt, *Autobiographical Sketch,* 7.

43. The 1850 US Census lists John T. Brandt of Sweden as the only music teacher at the academy.

44. Holt, *Autobiographical Sketch,* 8. This popular song by Balfe can be found in several binder's volumes, including that which belonged to Anna Roulhac, daughter of a Raleigh merchant.

45. Ibid., 8–10.

46. Ibid., 13–19. Notably, she found that the only child to enjoy music and to make suitable progress was the boy, probably William Aiken Lowndes (1856–63).

47. On North Carolina's demography, see Cecil-Fronsman, *Common Whites.*

48. *Star,* June 21, 1837. Scotland Neck was not incorporated until 1867; the school for young women opened in the 1830s. On Jackson, *Star,* June 23, 1835. See also Coon, *North Carolina Schools,* 183–84.

49. Both Curtis and Hanks came from Emma Willard's school in Troy. Curtis was Tempie Person's teacher. See also Hill, *Person Place.* The 1860 census does not list Emma as working.

50. On distinguishing between types of schools in the South, see Farnham, *Education of the Southern Belle,* 11–32. My research contradicts Case's findings (*Leaders of Their Race,* 4 and 20) that most of the attendees in the South were the elite.

51. One student had been left at the school and her parents never returned. Smedes took her in, and she became a music teacher there.

52. Thomas, *Robeson County,* 56. Catherine Jane McGreachy Buie Papers; quoted in ibid., 106. See also Rable, *Civil Wars,* 161–66, note 33. See also Tyner, *Robeson County.*

53. Buie Papers; quoted in Thomas, *Away Down Home,* 106. The 1848 catalog at Floral College lists both vocal and instrumental music.

54. This conclusion is shown by a comparison of the students' names and US Census data. Several of the school's catalogs list the names and hometowns or counties of the students. The school was known by several names during the nineteenth century.

55. *Chowan Baptist Female Institute Catalogue, Murfreesboro,' 1853–54,* 18 and 22.

56. Wheeler, *Minutes of the Forty-fifth Annual Session of the Chowan Baptist Association,* 17.

57. She was part of the reorganization of the music department at Chowan in 1851, with only two other music teachers (Miss S. A. Johnston and Miss C. W. Stevenson). *Catalogue of Chowan Female Collegiate Institute, Murfreesboro,' 1850–51,* 25. Her death certificate lists her as a "retired music teacher."

58. At chapel, the young women may have sung from the *Baptist Hymn Book,* which was recommended in 1852 by Pritchard Jordan, chairman of the Committee on Hymn

Books, to the newly created Southern Baptists. Wheeler, *Minutes of the Chowan Baptist Association, 1847*, 18. That the Baptists had a large organ for daily chapel services in rural northeastern North Carolina is surprising, for the use of instruments in church was not agreed upon by all at this time.

59. *Catalogue of Chowan Female Collegiate Institute, Murfreesboro,' 1853–54*, 20.

60. Letters of Christian Bell to her parents, Apr. 20, and June 1 and 20, 1854. Major Bell Papers.

61. Lucy's father's prospects increased substantially between 1850, when he was a merchant with $3000, and 1860, when as a preacher his total value was around $20,000. In spite of this income, Lucy still taught. In the 1860 US Census, she is listed among his household as a teacher of music, Latin, Greek, and painting. Broadside #-260, Rubenstein Library, Duke University. Laura Vaughan, another member of this household, is listed as a teacher of English and "ornamentals."

62. Since recounting this story, "My First Serenade," *Southern Literary Messenger* 14, no. 8 (1848): 482–83, in *MSB* (18–19), I have since discovered that "Alegna Onerom" refers to Angela Moreno Mallory, wife of the Confederate Secretary of the Navy, spelling her name backward. Her father was Don Francisco Moreno, "Father of Pensacola," and the official representative of the King of Spain in Florida for over fifty years.

Chapter 7. Other Professionals

1. Her husband, Gabriel, ran a school for "young gentlemen." Starr, *Gottschalk*, 44.

2. Ripley, *Social Life*, 10 and 150–51.

3. She published "L'étincelle / Polka da salon" in 1851.

4. *Daily Picayune*, Feb. 25, 1854.

5. Mme. E. Deron (who had attended a seminary at St. Denis, France) ran the Institute and taught harp and piano in its early days. *Daily Picayune*, May 3, 1854; *Daily Picayune*, Feb. 25, 1854; and *Chronique*, Jan. 4, 1849. King, *Memories of a Southern Woman*, 61. See also Reinders, *End of an Era*, 191; and Ripley, *Social Life*, 149. Only the Reed publication carries the dedication of the latter to Lavillebeuvre.

6. Morphy receives a brief mention as a composer ("another creole woman") in Reinders, *End of an Era*, 192. Eliza Ripley mentions her in *Social Life*. Her son, chessmaster Paul Charles Morphy famously played against Duke Karl of Brunswick, Count Isouard at the Théâtre Italien on Oct. 21, 1858, while Rosina Penco sang the title role in *Norma*. Golombek, *Chess: A History*, 142.

7. *Times-Picayune*, Apr. 26, 1861.

8. *Times-Picayune*, May 12, 1858. Romey also published "Marseillaise et Bonnie Blue Flag / Grand Fantaisie de Concert" in 1864. On Desrayaux, see *L'abeille*, Apr. 30, 1853.

9. A more extensive account of Siegling can be found in *CBA*, 117–19; on her published compositions, see also *MSB*, 142 and 155. On musical life in Havana, see also Holt, *Autobiographical Sketch*.

10. Schuman LeClerq, *Memoirs of a Dowager*.

11. A notable exception was Marguerite Elie, daughter of the New Orleans publisher, who studied with Rossini and Auber at the Royal Conservatory in Paris. Baron, *Concert Life*, 209–10.

12. The eldest, Jane (1824–1906), features in Tick's *American Women Composers*. Her compositions were sold in Charleston by Samuel Hart in 1843. *Charleston Courier*, Nov. 10, 1851. The British Library owns a copy of *A Biographical Sketch of Jane Sloman, the Celebrated Pianiste* (Boston, 1841).

13. Wemyss, *Wemyss' Chronology*, 130–31 (1852). In 1840, Elizabeth and John Sloman performed at St. Charles Theatre in New Orleans and in Vicksburg. *Times-Picayune*, Jan. 31, 1840; *Philadelphia Inquirer*, Jan. 30, 1840. John is first mentioned in Charleston in the *Courier*, Feb. 24, 1843.

14. *Boston Daily Bee*, Oct. 4, 1844.

15. *Boston Evening Transcript*, Oct. 7, 1844.

16. *Daily Atlas*, Oct. 12, 1844.

17. Grobe's set does not appear to have been published before 1857.

18. *Charleston Courier*, May 7, 1852.

19. Aiken was governor of South Carolina in 1856–58, overlapping Buchanan's presidency. 1857–58.

20. See, for example, *Charleston Courier*, Jan. 3, 1844. At this time, her father could be found touring various small southern towns around Columbus, Georgia, and into Alabama.

21. *Columbian Lady's and Gentleman's Magazine* 1 (1844). Her other songs in that volume are "Go and Forget" and "Wo's Me, Wo's Me." Many of the contributions to this magazine are by women.

22. Cooke, "Southern Women, Southern Voices," 70.

23. Ayres, *Life and Works*, 162. Kimball mentions a few in "Northern Music Culture," 54–55.

24. Watson, *Wilmington, North Carolina*, 167.

25. I wish to thank John Druesedow for generously sharing his research on Jones and on the organs at St. Matthew's.

26. *Burwell School Catalogue, Hillsborough, 1848–51*.

27. She was confirmed at St. Mary's in November 1853. *St. Matthew's Episcopal Church Vestry Minutes, Hillsboro, N.C., 1824–1884*. Ellen Weig, church historian at St. Matthew's, speculates that Jones may have studied organ with Mary Jane DeRosset, wife of Moses Ashley Curtis (rector at St. Matthew's 1841–47 and 1857–72). Weig, "Lizzie's Organ," 2–3. I appreciate Ms. Weig's assistance in researching Jones's connections with St. Matthew's.

28. Engstrom, *Book of Burwell Students*. Weig explains the various connections Jones may have had while in New York in "Lizzie's Organ," 3–4.

29. Pease and Pease, *Ladies, Women, and Wenches*, 57. In nearby Beaufort, Marian Verdier served as organist at St. Helena's Episcopal Church until she left in 1830, receiving a silver service for her work; She played a melodeon until a new organ arrived in 1829. After the war, the church went back to using the melodeon because Union soldiers had dismantled the organ. *History of the Parish Church*, 170–71.

30. Williams, *St. Michael's*.

31. Ibid.

32. His solfege tutor survives in 1005.02.03, Box 11/069a, Barbot Family Papers, SCHS.

33. The next year she performed with her father and H. W. Greatorex. Hindman, "Ante-Bellum Charleston," 664–65, 683, 732.

34. Thalberg wrote to Marie Petit about Herminie's potential career in 1857 and 1858. Barbot Family File, 11/68/4, SCHS.

35. Oberneufemann, "Invisible Lines," 63. See also Willard and Liverman, *American Women*, vol. 1, 1897.

36. Johann Bernhard Logier arrived in Dublin in 1809. A composer, teacher, and publisher, Logier was one of the inventors of the chiroplast, a device that held the hands in "correct" positions for piano practice. Mendelssohn (with whom she was reportedly friends) figures among her early repertory, but this is doubtful given that she is reported to have played his music when he was only sixteen. Obituary, *Mobile Register*, Oct. 21, 1897. See also Robert, "Madame Kowaleski."

37. *Pensacola Gazette*, May 6, 1843.

38. *Alabama Legislative Acts*, 101.

39. E. McCord, "Hollywood Waltz" (Mobile: W. D. Synder, ca. 1852).

40. Biddlecombe probes the juxtaposition of prima donna and public persona regarding Lind in "Jenny Lind."

41. Her name is not on the cover but appears on the inside, as does the date 1842.

42. Hindman, "Ante-Bellum Charleston," 628 and 631. Niecieska's performances predate those of Camille Urso, who settled in Nashville during the mid-century.

43. *Savannah Daily Republican*, Dec. 4, 1849.

44. Her first husband was violinist/composer J. P. Temple. As newlyweds, they performed together in Augusta. *Daily Chronicle & Sentinel*, Dec. 17, 1850.

45. Ibid., Dec. 20, 1849.

46. With her first husband and pianist, E. C. Sofge, Niecieska performed solos, concerts, duets, and trios by DeBeriot, Artot (including his "Souvenir de Bellini"), Viotti, Labitsky, Herz, and others. *Daily Chronicle & Sentinel*, Apr. 17, 1850.

47. Several newspaper accounts of her performances exist in Augusta and Savannah newspapers between 1849 and 1850: *Savannah Daily Republican* Dec. 4, 1849; Dec. 7, 1849 (accompanied by a "Full German Orchestra"); *Friend of the Family*, Dec. 15, 1849; *Daily Chronicle & Sentinel*, Apr. 17, 1850; and *Daily Morning News*, Apr. 17, 1850.

48. *Daily Journal*, Apr. 8, 1854.

49. *Richmond Whig*, Jan. 2, 1854.

50. *Daily Journal*, Mar. 23, 1854.

51. Performance at Metropolitan Hall; *Richmond Whig*, Jan. 27, 1854. Siminski also performed in Athens (Coulter, *College Life*, 224) and gave a concert shortly after Urso in Macon in 1854 (*Musical World* 9 (1854): 42).

52. The Swiss-born clarinetist Margaret [Margreta] Knittel (1788–after 1821) performed in Charleston in 1820 and advertised to teach piano, single and double flageolet, Spanish guitar, flute, and violin. Hindmann, "Ante-Bellum Charleston," 192. Knittel's repertory in Charleston included works by Solère, Mozart, and herself; her interpretation of concertos by Bernhard Crusell brought her acclaim. Ellsworth, "Clarinet in Early America," 93 103, 125n. See also Weston, "Out of Purdah"; and Wichmann, "Europäische Instrumentalistinnen."

53. *Richmond Whig*, Apr. 2, 1841. The 1856 city directory (p. 262) includes the names of those in Richmond Sacred Music Society; no women's names appear.

54. See, for example, Stoutamire, "Music in Richmond," 115. Elizabeth was born in Scotland, per 1850 US Census; she was 75, Sarah 53, and Charlotte, 41. She had married Matthew Sully, "of the circus," in Scotland in 1792, and they immigrated to the United States shortly after 1800. Their musician-daughters were born in Charleston, where Elizabeth and Matthew both worked in entertainment. He died in Augusta in 1812, and his death certificate describes him as a comedian.

55. Ibid., 119.

56. Sonneck, *Early Concert Life*, 59.

57. Stoutamire, "Music in Richmond," 123.

58. Charlotte taught voice at Mrs. Mead's School in 1844, alongside other music instructors, Miss C. E. Poiteaux (piano), E. B. Barber (piano), and E. E. Ulmo (guitar). *Mrs. Mead's School Catalogue, Richmond, 1844*, 3. In 1856, both Sally and Charlotte Sully are listed as "professor of music" in the city directory at the same address. Charlotte is still a music teacher (unmarried) in 1869 and 1874.

59. *Catalogue of the Columbia Female Institute, Columbia, 1838*, 20–21.

60. Murray, *Wake: Capital County*, 339; Amis, *Historical Raleigh*, 72. One of Wesley's pianos is now housed in the Executive Mansion, Raleigh.

61. Lucius eventually moved to Marion, Alabama, where he taught music.

62. Because of her marriage to a near relation with the same last name, "Mrs. Whitaker" also refers to Harriet. Ping incorrectly asserts that all of the compositions attributed to L. H. Whitaker were in fact the work of Mrs. Whitaker ("Music in Antebellum Wilmington," 88).

63. *Wilmington Journal*, Dec. 12, 1851.

64. Ping, "Music in Antebellum Wilmington," 88.

65. *Wilmington Journal*, Jan. 24, 1851. Whitaker was in Wilmington in 1855 (Watson, *Wilmington, North Carolina*, 167).

66. *Semi-Weekly Standard*, Jan. 30, 1858.

67. In late 1859, Whitaker publicized that her students would perform a concert at the end of the term; The advertisement did not run until later: *Semi-Weekly Standard*, May 2, 1860.

68. *Newbern Weekly Progress*, June 12, 1860.

69. Fries, *Historical Sketch*, 20–21, and 23. Sarah's music collection survives in the Polk home, Columbia, Tennessee.

70. Knouse, *Moravian Music*, 19.

71. On the makeup of the music faculty, see *MSB*, 78–80.

72. Louisa's father died in Greeneville (Tennessee) in 1845, where he had been the president of a women's college. Her mother moved the family back to Salem. Knouse, notes to "A Loving Home's."

73. Amelia, or "Amy," was particularly noted for her musical work in the community. See Leinbach, *Regiment Band*, 232n. *SMJ* 2 no. 6 (1873), includes a copy of Amy's "Carolina March" (Brainard, 1866).

74. Letter to her sisters, Van Vleck Family Papers.

75. Letter of Aug. 15, 1858, to mother and sisters, from Louisa, Van Vleck Family Papers.

76. Knouse and Crews, "Moravian Music," 217. While a student at Salem in 1838, Louisa Gist wrote to her father, planter William Gist, that she participated in singing school every Wednesday. Letter to father William from Louisa Gist, student at Salem, Apr. 10, 1838. Archives of Rose Hill Plantation, South Carolina. Louisa also attended the South Carolina Female Collegiate Institute at Barhamville.

77. Some of their works are listed in *MSB*, 140.

78. Louisa and three current students—Mittie Bethel (who would become part of the faculty in 1860), Sophie Lindsey and Pattie Sherrod—performed the waltz.

79. Letter to her sisters, 1859, Van Vleck Family Papers.

80. *Daily Exchange*, Aug. 1, 1860. An earlier discussion of musical taste, vis-à-vis scientific music, declared ultimately that elevated music reigned over simplistic ballads. *Courier*, Feb. 6, 1846, and June 24, 1847.

Chapter 8. The Parlor and the Civil War

1. Georgia Archives, "Confederate Diaries," VI, 297. In 1880, Cora (Cordelia, Cornelia) was single and living in Henry's household. Their mother, Sarah Ward Dutton Graves, had been a teacher at the Troy Female Seminary (New York) and moved to Covington, Georgia, to teach in 1834. Graves Family Papers, SHC.

2. J. O. Church, trust deed to Thomas J. Kelly, Apr. 10, 1861, recorded in Office of Maury County, TN, Register, Volume II, Book N, 497–98.

3. Salem Program, May 29, 1861, CMLS C.I. Broadsides 3247–2, VHMC.

4. Cook, *Journal of Milledgeville Girl*, June 23, 1862.

5. Johnson Music Collection, Box 2, Folder 2. Another reference to Leila Bennett occurs in Catherine's diary on Nov. 19, 1864: "Leila was up hear [*sic*] Monday she seemed in high spirits." Additionally, the Johnson music includes a binder's volume that belonged to Aggie Stockton (unknown) and parts of a collection of music published in single volumes. The only Agnes Stockton I have located in Natchez (in the 1850 census) was white.

6. Jan. 1, 1865, Catherine Johnson Diary.

7. King, *Essence of Liberty*, 31; reference from Davis and Hogan, eds., *Barber of Natchez*, 54–68, 241.

8. Barrow et al., *Black Confederates*, 4.

9. Solie discusses the importance of "upward mobility" and its place in a new society based on wealth, rather than birth, in *Music in Other Words*, 94–95. Its purpose among people of color is a new area where this idea should also be applied.

10. In addition to contextualizing Nora Gardner's music collection in detail, Bailey, "'Remember the Beautiful Songs,'" provides the contents of her binder's volumes and a map of her travels during the war.

11. Witt, "Gendered Language of War," 8–9.

12. Ibid.," 19.

13. Kasson, *Rudeness and Civility*, 174–76, and "Genteel Performance in Hall and Parlor," 173–81.

14. Witt observes this sentiment in the works of a Confederate officer writing in 1864. Witt, "Gendered Language of War," 143.

15. She continued to employ teachers, according to Louisa McCord, including Strawinski and Orchard, and later Angelo Torriani. Some of Togno's own music is in the Hughes Collection, CNU.

16. Holt, *Autobiographical Sketch*, 20–21. Holt's constant change in positions reflected her own disposition to seek new opportunities in California, Cuba, and Peru.

17. *Weekly Fireside*, Nordendorf's publication of music, began publication in 1871. Abel, *Singing the New Nation*, n42.

18. He had conducted some performances of the Italian Opera Company when it was in Columbus, GA, 1860.

19. Smythe, "Recollections," 50 and 53. A neighbor whose daughters also studied lessons with Torriani took him back to the school.

20. *Charleston Mercury*, Oct. 27, 1861.

21. Bernath, *Confederate Minds*, 91. Several writers on music refer to these difficulties as well. See also McWhirter, *Battle Hymns*; Abel, *Singing the New Nation*; Hoogerwerf, *Confederate Sheet-Music Imprints*. Additionally, many libraries and other archives have "Confederate imprints" singled out.

22. Smythe, "Recollections," 50.

23. See Part 3 of *CBA*, including an image from this manuscript (202).

24. Mollie Ford to Brother Frank. Captured mail collection, Diggs, section 5, VMHC.

25. Mary Maxcy Leverett to her son Milton, Feb. 24, 1864, printed in Taylor et al., eds. *The Leverett Letters*, 386–87. On the principals at the institute, see *MSB*, 82. See also White, "Madame Sophie Sosnowski."

26. On music publishing during the war, see Abel, *Singing the New Nation*, 225–75.

27. Wright explores the influence of music publishers in Britain at about the same time in "Novello, John Stainer, and Commercial Opportunities."

28. Alexander Reichardt (1825–85) was a Hungarian tenor noted for his performances of Schubert's lieder. See Johnston, *Musical Life of Nineteenth-Century Belfast*, 139.

29. Mary Glenn's copy is in the HSMC, Duke University (confo300).

30. On the Sheftall family, see Proctor, et al., eds. *Jews of the South*, 62–78. Her father, Mordecai, was a lawyer.

31. See, for example, Chassaignac's *Mélodies* (1862), a collection containing predominantly French titles. Lemmon, "Eugene Chassaignac."

32. Sims, "I Must Learn to Paint."

33. Among its many pieces, SMB 13 includes Foster's "Old Folks at Home," which is not unusual by itself, but the imagery that accompanies the song is noteworthy. It served as an advertisement for the Georgia Southern and Florida Rail Road, with a train crossing White Springs on the front and a detailed map of the entire Suwanee River route on the back. It lacks the composer's name.

34. The contents of Brown's binder's volume are listed in Appendix B (online).

35. This is the march by E. Heinemann (1861), not the work by the same title by Virginia Cowdin.

36. Fitch, *Annals of the Army of the Cumberland* (1863), 473; quoted in Horn, "Dr. John Rolfe Hudson," 336.

37. Ripley, *Social Life*, 151.

38. Her copy of "My Maryland, My Maryland" was published in New York. Candace Park owned "Capt. John Morgan Schottish" (1863).

39. CMLS C.I. 3247-3, VMHC.

40. Georgia Archives, "Confederate Diaries," VI, 307.

Chapter 9. The Civil War and the Public Gaze

1. See "Music in Families," *Holly Springs Gazette*, July 7, 1843.

2. Tillinghast Diary, entries for 1861: 5, July 30; 6, Aug. 29. An acquaintance of Mary Stedman, Emily later taught at the school for deaf children in Morganton; two of her brothers were deaf.

3. *Carolina Observer*, Nov. 4, 1861. Her husband had died in 1858.

4. See, for example, an advertisement in the *Semi-Weekly Standard*, Feb. 20, 1863. Martha was the sister of Sallie Mangum, whose request for music is noted on p. 107.

5. Willie Person Mangum Papers, W. L. Pomeroy to Martha P. Mangum, Feb. 12, 1863; Emma Graves to Martha P. Mangum, Dec. 18, 1862; O. N. Allen to Martha P. Mangum, Dec. 8, 1862; Sally A. (Mangum) Leach to Charity A. Mangum, Apr. 12, 1862.

6. Martha even served as the Postmaster in Flat River in 1873. *NC Register of Officers and Agents*, v. 1. 826.

7. Kate D. Foster Diary, July 18, 1865; Nov. 15, 1863.

8. *Charleston Mercury*, Feb. 2, 1863; June 25, 1863; Apr. 11, 1864.

9. *Daily Constitutionalist*, May 25, 1864.

10. Ibid., May 28, 1864.

11. Dannett, "And the Show Went On," 107-8, 112, and 114; Fife, "Confederate Theater."

12. Hines, *Musical Activity in Norfolk*, 50-51; *Southern Confederacy*, Aug. 27, 1862.

13. *Daily Crescent*, Jan. 20, 1862, Morning.

14. Fife, "Theatre during the Confederacy," 189-90.

15. Stephen A. Morgan Journal, Nov. 29, 1861; quoted in Moore, "Confederate Journal," 201-216.

16. Wren to Montgomery per the *Southern Illustrated News*, Jan. 25, 1864. On her tour of Georgia, see Fife, "Theater during the Confederacy," 195-96.

17. Mary (1833-1910) was the daughter of a Yankee merchant, who had married an insurance agent in 1855. The name Fanny M. Dickens occurs elsewhere in the volume.

18. Dannett, "And the Show Went On," 107-8.

19. She performed with John Wilkes Booth and helped perpetuate the conspiracy that he had not died in 1865. The performance was advertised in *Clipper* 25 (Feb. 25, 1878): 374. A card with her image in blackface can be seen on the websites "Minstrel Banjo," http://minstrelbanjo.ning.com/photo/katie-partington-as-topsy?context=popular; and Stephen Railton, "Uncle Tom's Cabin and American Culture," http://utc.iath.virginia.edu/. Another sister, Kate, infamously portrayed Topsy from *Uncle Tom's Cabin*, in blackface, in New York in the 1870s. I am grateful to Fiona Palmer for her assistance with images of the Partington family.

20. For more details on Ruhl's performances during the war in Richmond, see Stoutamire, *Music of the Old South*, 229–33.

21. *Sentinel* (Richmond), Dec. 22, 1864. In 1870, L. F. Whitaker, professor of music taught at the St. John's School (Oxford) with his assistant, Miss E. G. Hubard, who "for four years had been a pupil of the renowned singer Madame Ruhl." *Southerner*, Dec. 22, 1870.

22. Fife, "Theatre during the Confederacy," 191. Other documentation in Thompson, *Bugle Resounding*, 109–11.

23. *Augusta Chronicle*, Mar. 16, 1865.

24. Preston's work on women who performed in opera troupes constitutes a notable exception to this prejudice.

25. Baron reports that her granddaughter said she had been a concert pianist and composer at age fourteen. *Concert Life*, 135. The catalog record for LeBlond's collection says that she studied in Paris and was acquainted with many other mid-nineteenth-century musicians in New Orleans.

26. The last page of Vol. 1 is a handwritten index, in pencil; upside down on the back cover someone has written "478 St. Charles." The lettering on the cover of Vol. 2 (bound by Reichert on Royal Street) is smaller than on Vol. 1.

27. Her copy of the "Carnaval de Venise" came from Gabici's store, where the Johnsons bought their music.

28. Cohen, ed., *Barhamville Miscellany*, 137. Pringle, *Chronicles of Chicora Wood*, 180–81. See also Jennings, "Grand Opera in Kansas City," 683.

29. Pringle, *Chronicles of Chicora Wood*, 180–81. See *MSB*, 126–28.

30. Pike, *Jubilee Singers*, 50–51; Ward, *Dark Midnight*, 4–5.

31. Pike, *Jubilee Singers*, 50–51, 56; and Ward, *Dark Midnight*, 7.

32. Pike, *Jubilee Singers*, 52. Rivé was also a singer, and her song, "The Music of the Foot-Fall," includes an image of the composer on its cover. Published in Cincinnati, Dec. 15, 1865. Caroline and her husband, Léon Rivé, moved to New Orleans in 1850. After their three children died in a cholera epidemic, the couple moved to Baton Rouge and then Louisville (Kentucky), before settling in Cincinnati. Bryan, *Papers of Jane Addams*, 193.

33. Quoted in Ward, *Dark Midnight*, 72. See Ammer, *Unsung*, 69–72, for additional information on Julia Rivé-King.

34. E. Dansereau, "Minutes for Société Dramatique de Bienfaissance de Thibodaux," 1861; LSU. Ephemera, Box 6, LSU.

35. She did not accompany her husband much at this time because she suffered pleurisy, pneumonia, and miscarriage in February 1862.

36. Cook, *Journal of a Milledgeville Girl*; Davis, *Civil War Atlanta*, e-book "A Southern soldier leaves for war"; Clayton, *Requiem for a Lost City*, 44.

37. *Nashville Daily Union*, Mar. 3, 1865. This circumstance echoed Gertrude Clanton Thomas's comment that she did not attend a performance because of rain. *MSB*, 8. Adam is the same instructor who wrote on Nora Gardner's music.

38. "Cary Invincibles" refers to women from the same extended family, including Hettie and Jennie Cary, at whose home "Maryland! My Maryland" originated. See *MSB*, 177–78; and Davis, *Maryland, My Maryland*.

39. These excerpts are taken from Harrison, *Recollections*, 150 and 173–77.

40. Parlor theatricals often consisted of several parts whose titles formed such puns. See Halttunen, *Confidence Men*, 174. See also Cobrin, "Dangerous Flirtations," and Lewis, "Tableaux Vivants."

41. Anita Withers and husband called on them Nov. 1, 1860 (his diary). Virginia's portrait appears in *MSB*, 99.

42. Halttunen, *Confidence Men*, Chapter 6, "Disguises, Masks and the Parlor Theatricals: The Decline of Sentimental Culture in the 1850s."

43. Ellen L to MFL, Apr. 19, 1843; Rohr, *Alabama School Girl*, 117. She had the same music teacher as the Lewis girls.

44. Cook, *Journal of a Milledgeville Girl*, 43 (Dec. 12, 1863).

45. Emmala Thompson Reed Journal, VMHC; quoted in Oliver, *A Faithful Heart*, 227. Here, she comments on false friends who now see them as too common.

46. See Jabour, *Scarlett's Sisters*, 271, on gaiety during war.

47. Centre Hill was located in an isolated part of the county near the Chowan River. It is now known as Tyner, an unincorporated community about twenty miles from the county seat of Edenton (population in 1860: 1,504).

48. Dillard, "Civil War Incidents" #4. Jane Simpson probably sang "They Say She's Pretty" by Alfred von Rochow (1862), altering the words perhaps for humor. Phipps's "Hunter's Horn" dates from the early 1820s, thus rendering its performance during the Civil War something that required explanation.

49. *Southern Confederacy*, Oct. 20, 1861.

50. Drew Gilpin Faust asserts such repositioning of southern women's roles in *Mothers of Invention*. In *MSB*, I follow a similar argument in women becoming composers as a vehicle to be useful in the war effort. See Faust, *Mothers of Invention*, 26; Whites, *Civil War as a Crisis*, 121; and *MSB*, 160–64.

51. Stoutamire, "Music in Richmond," 197.

52. *Richmond Whig*, Dec. 17, 1861; *Richmond Examiner*, Dec. 19, 1861; *Richmond Whig*, Jan. 16, 1862.

53. Program from #39, Dec. 19, 1861, 1862: 27, Broadsides CMLS, VMHC.

54. *Daily True Delta*, Nov. 20, 1864.

55. Mss2 M6255 a 1 (CMLS), VMHC.

56. Stokowski, *American Musician's Story*. This event is undocumented. She also wrote that Lucie studied piano with French musicians from New Orleans. Lucie Palmer married George Loening and later Lorenzo Grünewald, of the music-publishing family.

57. *Daily Picayune*, Jan. 23, 1864. Chopin left two extended transcriptions of operatic melodies, but they were not those listed in the *Picayune*.

58. *Daily Picayune*, May 19, 1864.

59. *Southern Confederacy*, May 3, 1863. Correspondence from Breeze Hill, Mississippi, Apr. 23, 1863.

60. "Aliene" writes in *Southern Confederacy*, Mar. 24, 1863, Atlanta Correspondence of the *Charleston Courier*.

61. John Blair Black listed his occupation as bursar in the 1860 US Census; in 1850 he gave it as "Clerk."

62. Waring, "A Confederate Girl's Diary," 273, Feb. 6, 1865; Letter from home, Mar. 4, 1865. When she purchased the new Steinway is unknown, and the thought of moving it to Richmond in March 1865, just over a month from the end of the war, defies practical consideration.

63. *Southern Confederacy*, May 3, 1863. Correspondence from Breeze Hill, MS, Apr. 23, 1863.

64. *Daily Constitutionalist*, Mar. 15, 1863, "She Layeth Her Hands to the Spindle."

65. Several writers have commented on this particular song. See, for example, Mc-Whirter, *Battle Hymns*, 84.

66. "Something We Like," *Southern Confed eracy*, Aug. 25, 1861. This paper also republished "She Layeth Her Hands to the Spindle" on Mar. 21, 1863.

67. Tolbert, *Constructing Townscapes*, 137.

Chapter 10. Career Women

1. *Spirit of Jefferson*, Mar. 8, 1899. They traveled from Savannah to New Orleans. He went on to St. Louis and then to Cincinnati, becoming the first leader of its Leidertafel. *Deutsch-amerikanische Geschichtsblätter*, 360; Mersman, *Whisky Merchant's Diary*, 340.

2. Kowalewski's return was announced in the press (*Mobile Register*, Oct. 12, 1868). At this time, she taught voice and instrumental music at her home on 136 Government Street, corner of Hamilton. On the Slomans, *Charleston Courier*, Mar. 18, 1867.

3. Preston, *Opera for the People*, 48.

4. *Columbia Enquirer*, Dec. 10–13, 1865.

5. Censer, *Reconstruction of White Southern Womanhood*, 6.

6. Ott also includes the example of Jane Sivley's mother, who told her "without good manners you will never show off to a good advantage" and to act "more dignified and graceful" at social events. Ott, *Confederate Daughters*, 114; quoted from Ashkenazi, *Diary of Clara Solomon*, 137; and mother to Jane Sivley, Nov. 4, 1863, Sivley Family Papers.

7. Pringle, *Chronicles of Chicora Wood*, 144; quoted and described in Pullum-Piñón, "Conspicuous Display," 159–60.

8. Young explores these ideas further in *Middle Class Culture*, 20–21, and 31.

9. Both served as masks: the 1850s and 1860s saw the acceptance of the "mask of fashion"; it was in this period that "polite hypocrisy" achieved "cultural legitimacy." Halttunen, *Confidence Men*, 165–67.

10. Edwards, *Scarlett Doesn't Live Here*, 182–83. Sims also addresses this inequality and the social distance between white and Black women and its continuation after the war in *Power of Femininity*, 6–7.

11. Among many writers, see Prenshaw, "Southern Ladies," 77.

12. On this period, see Foner, *Reconstruction*; and Downs, *After Appomattox*.

13. Her mother sold some jewels in 1867 to obtain funds to buy Henrietta a Chickering piano. Marie H. Cottonet to Harriet Lowndes Aiken, Oct. 13, 1867, HLA Personal Correspondence, Aiken Collection.

14. Rev. Aldert Smedes, St. Mary's Raleigh, to Doctor G. Drake, May 1, 1869; Room and board, and tuition statement, St. Mary's. Jan. 16–June 7, 1869. Johnson McFaddin Papers.

15. See accounts in the Jackson and Prince Family Papers.

16. du Bellet, *Prominent Virginia Families*, 119; Rutherford, "History of Athens and Clarke County." Rutherford gives the opening date as 1858. Basiline later took over the workings of the alumnae association. See also their roles in Confederate postwar society: Graham, *History of the Confederated Memorial Associations*, 42.

17. Cook, *Journal of a Milledgeville Girl*, 87, Sept. 2, 1865; and 90, Sept. 6, 1865.

18. Sept. 16, 1865, 91; Feb. 15, 1867, 100; and Feb. 22, 1867, 103.

19. Case examines how women (Black and white) adapted their social role in light of changes in southern culture after the war throughout, *Leaders of their Race*. On white women specifically, see also Censer, *Reconstruction of White Southern Womanhood*, 128–38.

20. Ibid., 175.

21. Skinner Family Papers, SHC.

22. Parham, *Mangum Family Bulletin*, 32.

23. Lucy Hull Baldwin Papers, SHC, "Autobiography," 15. Her later desires including writing a book; she crafted plays from Dickens's books.

24. Alice Galliard Palmer to Harriet R. Palmer, Aug. 10, 1870; quoted in Towles, *World Turned Upside Down*, 659. Her sister Babe became a Treasury Girl during the war and later (with another sister) tried to restore the Barhamville school, unsuccessfully. Brackman, *Civil War Women*, 97.

25. Quoted in Culpepper, *All Things Altered*, 210.

26. *Nashville Union*, July 4, 1867.

27. *Columbia Herald*, Apr. 7, 1871; *Herald and Mail*, Oct. 9, 1874.

28. *SMJ* 1, no. 2 (1871): 25. This list of schools is far from complete.

29. Advertisement in *Memphis Daily Appeal*, Aug. 21, 1867.

30. Letter of Jan. 22 [no year], Annie W. Connor Collin and E[loise] C. Gillespie Correspondence, Annie W. Connor Collection. Letters of 1873 to L. C. Gillespie from J. E. Bright mention payments for board and tuition that year.

31. Olivia Stedman Hall was married to William, a dry goods clerk.

32. Letter, Dec. 11, 1867, William Hooper Papers, SHC.

33. Rohr, *Alabama School Girl*, 205–6.

34. John Berkeley Grimball Diaries, 1832–83, Series 1, SHC.

35. "Accounting Book 1866–1868," Allston Family Papers; Pringle, *Chronicles of Chicora Wood*, 143, 187–88.

36. Elbert, "Introduction," in *Separate Spheres No More*, 1. See also Rotman, "Separate Spheres?" 666–74; Kerber, "Separate Spheres, Female Worlds," 43–63; and Davidson, "Preface: No More Separate Spheres!" 443–63.

37. Ott, *Confederate Daughters*, 101–2.

38. Young et al., *History of Macon*, 188. In the fall of 1859, she sang with Strakosch and his Opera Troupe in Macon, after returning from a European tour. She also performed as part of W. M. Fleming's Company in *Romeo and Juliet* and *Shrew* in Ralston Hall in January 1856.

39. *National Cyclopædia of American Biography*, 96.

40. Stokowski, *American Musician's Story*. Ammer, *Unsung*, 80; Hinson, *Pianist's Bookshelf*, 177.

41. Baron, *New Orleans*, 134.

42. Ibid., *New Orleans*, 402–4.

43. Quoted in Dougan, "Pasquilino Brignoli," 107. On how southern ladies should sing, see *MSB*, 126–36.

44. Parkes, "Great Singers of This Century," *Godey's Lady's Book* 132 (1896): 634.

45. "A Tenor's Divorce Suit," *New York Times*, Feb. 17, 1879. Earlier she had been described as "a southern songstress." *Evening Tribune*, June 4, 1868.

46. This tour included performances in Richmond, Norfolk, Raleigh, Charleston, and Savannah. See Jennings, "Grand Opera in Kansas City," 681–83.

47. They performed approximately the same repertory in Mobile, also in 1870. Brown, "A History of Theatrical Activities," 91.

48. *SMJ* 1, no. 4 (1872): 52.

49. *New York Times*, Apr. 23, 1866; quoted in DiGaetani, *Opera and the Golden West*, 109.

50. *Musical Record and Review*, 194. See also *Salt Lake Herald*, May 14, 1899, 11.

51. "A Tenor's Divorce Suit," *New York Times*, Feb. 17, 1879.

52. *Musical Record and Review*, 85.

53. *SMJ* no. 5 (1873): 5; no. 6 (1874): 4; no. 7 (1874): 5; no. 10 (1874): 5.

54. Report on the Mozart Club performance of Jan. 15, *SMJ* no. 5 (Feb. 1873): 5.

55. See Halttunen, Chapter 6, "Disguises, Masks, and Parlor Theatricals: The Decline of Sentimental Culture in the 1850s," in *Confidence Men*, 153–90.

56. Miller, *Material Consumption*.

57. Cheshire, *Historical Address*, 32.

58. Williams, *St. Michael's*, 215–16, and 326.

59. For example, *Charleston Daily News*, Nov. 23, 1867.

60. Williams, *St. Michael's*, 327.

61. Way, *History of Grace Church*, 133, and 139–41.

62. Fitzhugh, *Sociology for the South*, 214.

63. According to the 1880 Census, her husband was a bookkeeper.

64. *Charleston Daily News*, Mar. 8, 1873.

65. Ibid., December 26, 1868; Dec. 27, 1872.

66. Willard, *Woman of the Century*, 53.

67. He may have drowned in 1863; the authorities never located his body. Maria filed a petition in the Wills and Probate Records on Sept. 4, 1863, to claim her inheritance, which was substantial for the period ($20,000). She held on to most of this money for the duration of the war, and in the 1870 Census, she is listed as a Music Teacher, head of household, worth $15,000 and $1000 in real estate. She never dropped the "Kowalewski" and later in life used it exclusively, perhaps because her reputation had been made under that name.

68. Delaney, *Story of Mobile*, 68.

69. *Mobile Register*, May 19, 1868; May 22, 1870.

70. Katie Estelle, who ran the Petersburg Theatre in 1864, may have taken advantage of wartime necessity to establish herself in a management position. *Southern Illustrated News*, May 7 and June 11, 1864.

71. "Flute" may have been Thomas Cooper De Leon (1839–1914), the managing editor of the *Mobile Register* and the manager of the Mobile Theatre. Flora and Vogel, eds., *Southern*

Writers, 123. The Mobile Musical Association included such members as the Mobile Musical Association that included several leading musicians, including Dr. George Lingen, a cellist; Professor Peter Gass; Fannie (Mrs. James) Sands; and Louise Parker (Mrs. Daniel Geary).

72. Correspondence, *SMJ* 2, no. 6 (1873): 6.

73. Ellis discusses descriptions of women pianists in print with regards to gendered language in "Female Pianists and Their Male Critics," 367–78.

74. *SMJ* 3, no. 10 (1874): 10.

75. Her father taught music at the Albany Select Family School. See, for example, the announcement in *Albany Evening Journal*, Mar. 26, 1841. Robert, "Madame Josephine Hutet Pillichody"; quoted in Brown, "History of Theatrical Activities," 113. Her husband's name appears usually as "Pillichody" in official documents, although the account here spells it differently.

76. Federal Writers' Project, *The WPA Guide to Alabama*, "Music."

77. Levine explores the topic of how nineteenth-century audiences and writers viewed musical styles in *Highbrow, Lowbrow*; see also Broyles, *Music of the Highest Class*.

78. Dec. 20, 1873, *SMJ* 3, no. 4 (1874): 7.

79. *SMJ* 2, no. 7 (1873): 6. The writer further remarks that "the good people of our city are in the midst of Lent, and amusement of all kinds are, consequently, at a low ebb."

80. In 1868, for example, Israel I. Jones served as president, Leon Provost as musical director, and Lavitsky on piano. *Mobile Register*, Dec. 6, 1868.

81. Brown, "History of Theatrical Activities," 112.

82. *Evening Register*, Feb. 11, 1879.

83. Obituary, *Mobile Register*, Oct. 21, 1897.

84. Drago, *Charleston's Avery Center*, 110.

85. Quoted in ibid., 33. Bell, *Revolution, Romanticism, and the Afro-Creole Protest Tradition*, 125, 127; Gehman, *Free People of Color*, 74. Bell describes secret schools for free blacks that moved frequently to avoid detection.

86. Graduation program, Avery Institute, Fourth Anniversary, March 1873; quoted in Drago, *Charleston's Avery Center*, 66–67. Forbes, *African American Women*. Cardozo's husband, Rev. Francis Louis Cardozo, was described as a "Charleston free negro" educated at the University in Glasgow. See Webster, *Freedmen's Bureau*, 134; and Brock, *Thomas W. Cardozo*, 185.

87. The similarities between the two support scholars such as Powers and Fitchett, who describe common features between the two seemingly disparate groups. Fitchett, "Traditions of the Free Negro," 144–47; Powers, *Black Charlestonians*, 178.

88. Quoted in Drago, *Charleston's Avery Center*, 110.

89. Leslie, *Woman of Color*, 65.

90. Powers, *Black Charlestonians*, 178.

91. Foreign men led these events. Norris, "Black and White Communities," 117.

92. Ibid., 131–35.

93. An excellent place to begin is Graham's *Spirituals and the Birth of a Black Entertainment Industry*. The accompanying web materials contain biographical and other details on numerous musical groups formed by people of color after the Civil War. See also Thurman, "Singing the Civilizing Mission."

94. This number seems unusually large but is mitigated by the fact that on the eve of the Civil War, Nashville was home to the largest concentration of Black people in Tennessee.

95. On Mason, see Pemberton, *Lowell Mason*.

96. Lovett, *African-American History*, 160. Other important sources are Pike, *Jubilee Singers* (1873) and Marsh, *Story of the Jubilee Singers* (1876).

97. See also Ward, *Dark Midnight*, 124; Graham, *Spirituals*, 26–32; and www.pbs.org/wgbh/amex/singers/peopleevents/pande04.html.

98. Ward, *Dark Midnight*, 72. Gallatin was also the home of Nora Gardner.

99. Pike, *Jubilee Singers*, 53.

100. Program provided in Ward, *Dark Midnight*, 83; and Graham, *Spirituals*, 23.

101. Graham, *Spirituals*, 24–25.

102. Milner, "Tenor of Belonging," 401.

103. Thurman, "Fisk Jubilee Singers," 462–65.

104. The website accompanying Graham's *Spirituals* includes information on many singers of the Fisk ensemble and others of the same period.

105. Pike, *Jubilee Singers*, 61.

106. A favorite with Europeans, some troupe members later claimed it was her jet-black complexion that attracted followers. http://www.blackpast.org/aah/jackson-jennie-1852-1910#sthash.5Cfc9ZHl.dpuf.

107. http://www.pbs.org/wgbh/amex/singers/peopleevents/pande02.html. It was not Handel's but Bradbury's.

108. Milner, "Tenor of Belonging," 409; taken from the *Newark Evening Courier*.

109. Karpf, "An Opportunity to Rise," 245.

110. Milner, "The Tenor of Belonging," 404.

111. Abbott and Seroff, *Out of Sight*, 53.

112. Minnie Tate (1857–99) was a contralto born in Nashville to free Black parents.

113. In the years following her performance at the White House, Williams continued to tour nationally performing for all-Black audiences. She toured Europe and the West Indies. See Southern, *Biographical Dictionary*; Kirk, *Music at the White House*, and *Musical Highlights*.

114. *National Republican*, Nov. 14, 1878.

115. Shipley, "Music Education at Hampton," 106. The Hampton Singers also performed *Esther* (1893), but the evening prior to their concert they sang "weird plantation spirituals." Karpf, "Opportunity to Rise," 255. On other groups, see Graham, *Spirituals*.

116. *SMJ* 1, no. 3 (1871): 36.

117. *Mobile Register*, Dec. 7, 1870.

118. *Charleston Daily News*, Mar. 8 and 11, 1873.

119. *Charleston News and Courier*, Nov. 29, 1885, for concerts on Dec. 2 and 3.

120. Lawrence, *Genteel Women*, 6.

Chapter 11. Reconstructed Women Reconstructing Repertory

1. Michelle Meinhart discovered Frank Smith's arrangements of Wagner choruses for his students and the local band in Columbia, Tennessee. I added to her findings by locating some of the students' parts in the Maury County Archives, and together we located

Smith's own scores marked with notations and other physical evidence of his adaptations for the Athenaeum students. It probably represents a widespread practice of reworking what was becoming known as classical music for amateur performances.

2. The Augusta Female Seminary became Mary Baldwin University. By the early twentieth century, all of the music teachers came from or studied in Germany. Waddell, *Mary Baldwin Seminary*, 49 and 73.

3. *Staunton Spectator*, June 24, 1873.

4. "Mems for Musical Misses," *Harper's* (Sept. 1851): 489.

5. Hartley, *Ladies' Book*, 189.

6. *Richmond Whig*, June 20, 1873.

7. Ibid., Dec. 25, 1873.

8. *Wilmington Journal*, Nov. 14, 1873.

9. The announcement does not specify sonatas, but publishers offered them in a two-volume set at this time. Moreover, two books' worth must have included at least a few of the sonatas.

10. Mrs. St. Simon, transl., "A Visit to Beethoven: From the German of Ludwig Restrab," *Columbian Lady's and Gentleman's Magazine* 9 (1848): 540–47.

11. *Charleston Courier*, Jan. 4, 1853.

12. Chan, "Beethoven in the United States," 171.

13. *New York Times*, Oct. 13, 1854. On gendered piano repertory, see Ellis, "Female Pianists," especially 363–66, and on gendered critique, 367–78.

14. *Semi-Weekly Courier*, Sept. 12, 1957. See also Weilbacher, "Guiraud," 19n.

15. *New Orleans Crescent*, Apr. 27, 1859.

16. *Charleston Courier*, Mar. 25, 1854. The early performance of a symphony in Charleston is well documented, as are performances of his choral music.

17. Baron, *Concert Life*. Ruhl sang on some these programs. Collignon dedicated his "La Pervenche Valse" to Amantine Soulé. An announcement in the *Daily Picayune*, Sept. 12, 1866 (p. 5) claims that for fifteen years Collignon had been in charge of the music department at the Young Ladies' Institute (a day and boarding school on Carondelet St. run by Miss S. S. Hull), teaching alongside Mme. Boudousquié.

18. *Daily Picayune*, Oct. 15, 1852.

19. *Daily True Delta*, Feb. 28, 1858.

20. *Times-Picayune*, Oct. 5, 1852.

21. "Beethoven," *Musical World and New York Musical Times*, Dec. 25, 1852. Beethoven as masculine has long been a topic, and I do not need to rehearse the extensive bibliography covering the subject here. See, for example, *The Cambridge History of Nineteenth-Century Music*, 130 and 144; and McClary, *Feminine Endings*, 17–18.

22. *Louisville Daily Courier*, Mar. 8, 1859.

23. This, in addition to a number of questionable works, is attributed to Beethoven.

24. *Charleston Courier*, Nov. 19, 1840; and July 15, 1841.

25. *Charleston Courier*, Feb. 8, 1851; and Feb. 12, 1852 (see also Feb. 8, 1851, with a different advertisement); *Augusta Chronicle*, Mar. 15, 1851.

26. *Louisville Daily Democrat*, Nov. 1, 1847.

27. One of Emilia Carriere's volumes includes Beethoven's "Pathétique" and a waltz by Chopin. The nameplate on the cover bears the date 1861, and both pieces came from Parisian publishers. Emilia belonged to a wealthy New Orleans family, and her continued acquisition of French publications during the war suggests that she may have refugeed abroad.

28. *Daily Phoenix*, Sept. 5, 1865.

29. *Augusta Chronicle*, July 9, 1865; and *Daily Constitutionalist*, July 9, 1865.

30. Chan, "Beethoven in the United States," 174–75.

31. *New Orleans Times*, Feb. 13, 1870.

32. *Richmond Whig*, Nov. 5, 1872.

33. The *Song Journal* began as a Whitney publication (Detroit), but in Volume 4 Werlein (New Orleans) claims ownership (although the journal continued to be printed in Detroit).

34. See, for example, the *New Orleans Republican*, May 31, 1870; and June 2, 1870; *L'abeille* Feb. 20, 1870. See also Baron, *New Orleans*, 410–11.

35. *Mobile Register*, May 19, 1870.

36. *Times-Picayune*, May 1, 1870. Sipp also performed duets with Filomeno in recitals.

37. She performed at the Victoria Theatre (Berlin) in December 1866. Dacus, "German Opera," 11n.

38. *New Orleans Times*, Dec. 18, 1866.

39. No titles given; *Times-Picayune*, Jan. 9, 1866. Earlier that same year, Joseph Pozanski (brother of the violinist I. B. Pozanski) introduced audiences in Augusta to Chopin's music with his "Fantasie impromptu." *Daily Constitutionalist*, Apr. 12, 1866. On Elie's repertory in New Orleans, see Baron, *Concert Life*, 211–15.

40. The venue was his father's house. Phifer Family Papers, SHC.

41. On this couple and their music collections, see *MSB*, 10–12.

42. *Intelligencer*, June 30, 1871.

43. Box 6 of the Johnson music collection; Lillie Trust Gray Papers.

44. One work is dated Feb. 13, 1872.

45. *New Orleans Times*, Feb. 6, 1870. On such titles, see Johnson, "Beethoven and the Birth of Romantic Musical Experience in France," 29–30. Chan credits the Germanians with bringing Beethoven's music to Richmond. "Beethoven in the United States to 1865," 125.

46. *Baton Rouge Tri-weekly Gazette & Comet*, Apr. 10, 1866.

47. Ammer, *Unsung*, 37.

48. *Renaissance Louisianaise*, July 4, 1869.

49. *Public Ledger*, Feb. 5, 1867.

50. *SMJ* no. 10 (July 1874): 18.

51. Sosnowski and Schaller Families folder, South Caroliniana Library.

52. The end of the volume includes a handwritten index in pencil, as well as "478 St. Charles" on the back cover.

53. The couple apparently divorced because each later remarried, Coralie in 1877. The Annual Examination of students at the Institution of the Sisters of St. Joseph in August

1874 included Alice LeBlond (1861–75), Coralie's sister, in a quartet performing "La Caravane." *Morning Star and Catholic Messenger*, Aug. 2, 1874.

54. Andrea Cawelti of the Houghton Library graciously brought this collection to my attention.

55. *SMJ* no. 4 (Jan. 1872): 50.

56. Jewell, "'Black Ivy,'" 73–83; Comminey, "History of Straight College," 29, 87–88.

57. Norris, "Music in Black and White Communities," 131, 134, 184–86.

58. Fitzhugh, *Sociology for the South*, 214.

59. The Lady Orchestra Troupe of New York, a group of twenty-one musicians, performed in Savannah in 1872. *SMJ* no. 8 (May 1872): 115.

60. Another such group was the Mendelssohn Musical Association in Petersburg, organized by organist and pianist Antonia Dickson (from Scotland) in 1879. Norris, "Music in Black and White Communities," 180. Protestant denominations approved women's missionary groups early on, and later these proved to be outlets for all female-gatherings. Sims, *Power of Femininity in the New South*, 8–12.

61. Censer includes her as an example of the second generation. *Reconstruction of White Southern Womanhood*, 185. See also Smith, *Smiths of Scotland Neck*, 118.

62. Graham, *Spirituals*, 18, 30–31, 45–47.

63. Concert announcement of the Nashville Ideal Jubilee Singers, *Tennessean*, May 18, 1882.

64. On these ideas, see Higginbotham, *Righteous Discontent*.

65. Collins, "Music of Basile Barès."

66. Prenshaw, "Southern Ladies," 78.

Conclusion

1. "Old Musical Compositions That Link Present with Past," *Times-Democrat*, Oct. 31, 1909.

2. Solie, *Music in Other Words*, 85–87.

3. "Music at Home," *SMJ* 1, no. 3 (1871): 34.

4. Lawrence, *Genteel Women*, 4–5.

Bibliography

Collections

Aiken-Rhett Collection, Charleston Museum, Charleston, SC

Allston Family Papers, SCHS, Charleston, SC

Anne Catherine Boykin Jones Diary, 1851, SHC, UNC, Chapel Hill, NC

Annie W. Connor Collection, Memphis and Shelby County Room, Memphis Public Library, Memphis, TN

Appomattox Manor Music Collection, from the Eppes Family, SWEM, College of William & Mary, Williamsburg, VA

Blanche Herminie Petit Barbot Family File, 11/68/4, SCHS, Charleston, SC

Campbell Family Papers, Rubenstein Library, Duke University, Durham, NC

Captured mail collection, 1862–1865, presumably compiled by John Fletcher Diss, VMHC, Richmond, VA

Catherine Jane McGreachy Buie Papers, Rubenstein Library, Duke University, Durham, NC

Columbia Female Institute Hanging File, Maury County Archives, Columbia, TN

Confederate Collection, Boston Athenaeum, Boston, MA

Eggelston-Roach Papers, Hill Library, LSU, Baton Rouge, LA

Elijah Dunbar Correspondence, 1850, 1851, Hill Library, LSU, Baton Rouge, LA

Emily R. Tillinghast Diary, Tillinghast Papers, Rubenstein Library, Duke University, Durham, NC

Graves Family Papers, 1818–1939, Rose Library, Emory University, Atlanta, GA

Historic American Sheet Music, Rubenstein Library, Duke University, Durham, NC

Hughes Collection, Christopher Newport University, Newport, VA

Jackson and Prince Family Papers, SHC, UNC, Chapel Hill, NC

James Louis Petigru Papers, SHC, UNC, Chapel Hill, NC

John Berkeley Grimball Diaries, 1832–83, SHC, UNC, Chapel Hill, NC

John Berkley [sic] Grimball Papers, Rubenstein Library, Duke University, Durham, NC

Kate D. Foster Diary, 1863–77, Rubenstein Library, Duke University, Durham, NC
Lemuel Parker Connor Collection, Hill Library, LSU, Baton Rouge, LA
Lester Levy Sheet Music Collection, Johns Hopkins University, Baltimore, MD
Levert Family Papers, SHC, UNC-CH, Chapel Hill, NC
Lillie Trust Gray Papers, Hill Library, LSU, Baton Rouge, LA
Louis A. Bringier Papers, Hill Library, LSU, Baton Rouge, LA
Lucy Hull Baldwin Papers, SHC, UNC, Chapel Hill, NC
Manigault Family Papers, SHC, UNC, Chapel Hill, NC
Margaret Ann Ulmer Diary, SHC, UNC, Chapel Hill, NC
Mobile Archives, Mobile, AL
Person Family Papers, Rubenstein Library, Duke University, Durham, NC
Pettigrew Family Papers, 1776–1926, SHC, UNC, Chapel Hill, NC
Polk Papers, NC Dept of Archives and History, Raleigh, NC
Sarah Lois Wadley Papers, 1849–1886, SHC, UNC, Chapel Hill, NC
Sivley Family Papers, SHC, UNC, Chapel Hill, NC
Skinner Family Papers, 1705–1900, SHC, UNC, Chapel Hill, NC
Smythe, Louisa McCord. Recollections of Louisa Rebecca Hayne McCord (Mrs. Augustine T. Smythe), Daughter of David J. and Louisa Cheves McCord. Typescript, South Caroliniana Library, Columbia, 1928.
Sosnowski and Schaller Families folder, South Caroliniana Library, USC, Columbia, SC
Thomas J. Butler and Family Papers, Hill Library, LSU, Baton Rouge, LA
Van Vleck Family Papers, Archie Davis Moravian Archives, Salem, Winston-Salem, NC
William Hooper Haigh Papers, SHC, UNC, Chapel Hill, NC
William Johnson Music Collection, Hill Library, LSU, Baton Rouge, LA
William Johnson Papers, Hill Library, LSU, Baton Rouge, LA
Willie Person Mangum Papers, NC Dept of Archives and History, Raleigh, NC

Newspapers and Magazines

L'Abeille (New Orleans)
Albany Evening Journal (NY)
Alexandria Gazette (VA)
Baltimore Clipper
Baton Rouge Tri-weekly Gazette & Comet
Boston Daily Bee
Boston Evening Transcript
Carolina Observer (Fayetteville, NC)
Carolina Watchman (Salisbury, NC)
Catholic Mirror (Baltimore)
Charleston Courier
Charleston Daily News
Charleston Mercury
Charlotte Democrat

Chronique (New Orleans)
Clipper (New York)
Columbia Herald (TN)
Daily Atlas (Boston)
Daily Chronicle & Sentinel (Augusta)
Daily Dispatch (Richmond)
Daily Exchange (Baltimore)
Daily Journal (Wilmington, NC)
Daily Morning News (Savannah)
Daily Phoenix (Columbia, SC)
Daily Picayune (New Orleans)
Daily Southern Augus (Norfolk, VA)
Deutsch-amerikanische Geschichtsblätter (Chicago)
Evening Tribune (Mobile)
Frank Leslie's Gazette of Fashion and the Beau Monde (New York)
Fraser's Magazine (London)
Friend of the Family (Savannah)
Godey's Lady's Book (Philadelphia)
Goldsboro Star
Graham's Magazine (Philadelphia)
Guardian (Columbia, TN)
Harper's (New York)
Herald [and Mail] (Columbia, TN)
Holly Springs Gazette (MS)
Intelligencer (Wheeling)
Jeffersonian Republican (Charlottesville, VA)
Louisville Daily Democrat
Memphis Daily Appeal
Mississippi Free Trader (Natchez)
Morning Herald (Columbia, TN)
Musical Gazette (Boston)
Musical Record and Review (New York)
Musical World (New York)
Nashville Union
National Republican (Washington, DC)
Newark Evening Courier
New Orleans Crescent
New Orleans Times
New Orleans Weekly Delta
New York Musical Gazette
New York Musical Review and Gazette
New-York Review and Athenaeum Magazine
New York Weekly Review

North Carolina Standard (Raleigh)
Pensacola Gazette
Philadelphia Inquirer
Planter's Banner (Franklin, LA)
Public Ledger (Memphis)
Renaissance Louisianaise (New Orleans)
Richmond Enquirer
Richmond Whig
Salt Lake Herald (Salt Lake City)
Savannah Daily Republican
Semi-Weekly Standard (Raleigh)
Southern Confederacy (Atlanta)
Southerner (Tarboro, NC)
Southern Illustrated News (Richmond)
Southern Musical Journal (Savannah)
Star (and North Carolina Gazette) (Raleigh)
Sugar Planter (West Baton Rouge)
Tarborough Southerner (Tarboro, NC)
Weekly Anglo-African (New York)
Weekly North Carolina Standard (Raleigh)
Wilmington Journal (Wilmington, NC)
Wilson Ledger (Wilson, NC)
Yazoo Democrat (Yazoo City, MS)

Sources

Abbott, Lynn, and Doug Seroff. *Out of Sight: The Rise of African American Popular Music, 1889–1895.* Jackson: University Press of Mississippi, 2009.

Abel, E. Lawrence. *Singing the New Nation.* Stackpole Books, 2000.

Alderman, Edwin Anderson, Joel Chandler Harris, and Charles William Kent, eds. *The Library of Southern Literature: Biography.* New Orleans: Martin & Hoyt Co., 1909.

Alexander, Adele Logan. *Ambiguous Lives: Free Women of Color in Rural Georgia, 1789–1879.* Fayetteville: University of Arkansas Press, 1991.

Amis, Moses Neal. *Historical Raleigh from Its Foundation in 1792: Descriptive, Biographical, Educational, Industrial, Religious; Reminiscences Reviewed and Carefully Compiled.* Raleigh: Edwards & Broughton, 1902.

Ammer, Christine. *Unsung: A History of Women in American Music.* Contributions in Women's Studies, no. 14. Westport, CN: Greenwood Press, 1980.

Ashkenazi, Elliott, ed. *The Civil War Diary of Clara Solomon: Growing Up in New Orleans, 1861–1862.* Baton Rouge: Louisiana State University Press, 1995.

Averitt, James Battle. *The Old Plantation: How We Lived in [sic] Great House and Cabin before the War.* Tuscaloosa: University of Alabama Press, 1901.

Ayres, Brenda. *The Life and Works of Augusta Jane Evans Wilson, 1835–1909.* Abingdon: Routledge (Ashgate), 2012.

Bailey, Ben E. "Music in the Life of a Free Black Man of Natchez." *The Black Perspective in Music* 13, no. 1 (1985): 3–12. https://doi.org/10.2307/1214790.

Bailey, Brigitte. *American Travel Literature, Gendered Aesthetics, and the Italian Tour, 1824–1862*. Edinburgh: University of Edinburgh Press, 2018.

Bailey, Candace. "Binder's Volumes as Musical Commonplace Books: The Transmission of Cultural Codes in the Antebellum South." *Journal of the Society for American Music* 10, no. 4 (2016): 446–69. https://doi.org/10.1017/S1752196316000353.

———. *Charleston Belles Abroad: The Music Collections of Harriet Lowndes, Henrietta Aiken, and Louisa Rebecca McCord*. Columbia: University of South Carolina Press, 2019.

———. "The Multifaceted Music Career of Sarah Smith." *Tennessee Historical Quarterly* 75, no. 2 (Summer 2017): 160—82.

———. *Music and the Southern Belle: From Accomplished Lady to Confederate Composer*. Carbondale: Southern Illinois University Press, 2010.

———. "Sarah Cunningham's Music Book: A Manuscript Collection of Music for a Young Girl of Scottish Descent in Savannah, ca. 1840." *Early Keyboard Journal; Athens, GA* 25–26 (2010): 7–27.

Bares, Basile. hnoc.tamretail.net. "Music of Basile Bares." https://hnoc.tamretail.net/SelectSku.aspx?skuid=1004562.

Barfield, Rodney, and Patricia Phillips Marshall. *Thomas Day: African American Furniture Maker*. Raleigh: North Carolina Office of Archives and History, 2005.

Barnes, Rhae Lynn. "The Faces of Racism: A History of Blackface and Minstrelsy in American Culture." National and online radio programming, February 8, 2019. https://www.backstoryradio.org/shows/the-faces-of-racism/.

———. "Yes, Politicians Wore Blackface. It Used to Be All-American 'Fun.'" *Washington Post*, February 8, 2019, sec. Perspective.

Baron, John H. *Concert Life in Nineteenth-Century New Orleans: A Comprehensive Reference*. Baton Rouge: Louisiana State University Press, 2013.

Barrow, Charles K., J. H. Segars, and R. B. Rosenburg. *Black Confederates*. New Orleans: Pelican Publishing, 2016.

Bashford, Christina, and Roberta Montemorra Marvin. *The Idea of Art Music in a Commercial World, 1800–1930*. Woodbridge: Boydell Press, 2016.

Battle, Rev. A. J. *Piety, the True Ornament and Dignity of Woman*. Marion, AL: Dennis Dykous, 1857.

Bell, Caryn Cossé. *Revolution, Romanticism, and the Afro-Creole Protest Tradition in Louisiana, 1718–1868*. Baton Rouge: Louisiana State University Press, 1997.

Bellet, Louise Pecquet du. *Some Prominent Virginia Families*. Lynchburg: J. P. Bell Co., 1907.

Bernath, Michael T. *Confederate Minds: The Struggle for Intellectual Independence in the Civil War South*. Chapel Hill: University of North Carolina Press, 2010.

Biddlecombe, George. "Jenny Lind, Illustration, Song and the Relationship between Prima Donna and Public." In Bashford and Marvin, eds. *The Idea of Art Music*. Woodbridge: Boydell Press, 2016, 86–113.

Biennial Report of the Superintendent of Public Instruction of North Carolina for the Scholastic Years 1896-'97 and 1897-'98. Raleigh: Guy V. Barnes, 1898.

Blessner, Gustave, and Nancy R. Ping-Robbins. *Anthology of Music*. Wilson, NC: Regan Press, 1985.

Bourdieu, Pierre. *Distinction: A Social Critique of the Judgement of Taste*. Translated by Richard Nice. London: Routledge, 1986.

———. "The Forms of Capital." In Richardson, J. *Handbook of Theory and Research for the Sociology of Education*. Westport, CN: Greenwood, 1986.

Brackman, Barbara. *Civil War Women: Their Quilts Their Role*. Concord, CA: C and T Publishing Inc., 2010.

Bremer, Frederika, and Mary Howitt. *The Homes of the New World: Impressions of America*. New York: Harper and Bros., 1853.

Brock, Euline W. *Thomas W. Cardozo: Fallible Black Reconstruction Leader*. Athens, GA: Southern Historical Association, 1981.

Brooks, William. "Pocahontas: Her Life and Times." *American Music* 2, no. 4 (1984): 19–48. https://doi.org/10.2307/3051561.

Brown, Edward Devereaux. "A History of Theatrical Activities at the Mobile Theatre: Mobile, Alabama, from 1860–1875." MA thesis, Michigan State College, 1952.

Brownlow, Ellen. "St. Mary's in the Forties." *The Saint Mary's Muse* 12 (1908): 21.

Broyles, Michael. *Music of the Highest Class: Elitism and Populism in Antebellum Boston*. New Haven: Yale University Press, 1992.

Bryan, Mary Lynn MacCree, ed. *The Selected Papers of Jane Addams. Vol. 1 Preparing to Lead, 1860–81*. Urbana: University of Illinois Press, 2003.

Bryan, Thomas Conn. *Confederate Georgia*. Athens: University of Georgia Press, 2009.

Burroughs, Tony. *Black Roots: A Beginners Guide to Tracing the African American Family Tree*. New York: Simon and Schuster, 2001.

Bushman, Richard Lyman. *The Refinement of America: Persons, Houses, Cities*. New York: Vintage, 1993.

Butler, Nicholas Michael. *Votaries of Apollo: The St. Cecilia Society and the Patronage of Concert Music in Charleston, South Carolina, 1766–1820*. Columbia: University of South Carolina Press, 2007.

Cabell, Clifford, and Henrietta Davis Smith. *Children of the Rectory; Memoirs of Ellen O., Clifford Cabell, and Henrietta Davis Smith*. Nashville: W. T. Berry, 1860.

Campbell, Gavin James. *Music and the Making of a New South*. Chapel Hill: University of North Carolina Press, 2004.

Case, Sarah H. *Leaders of Their Race: Educating Black and White Women in the New South*. Urbana: University of Illinois Press, 2017.

Cecil-Fronsman, Bill. *Common Whites: Class and Culture in Antebellum North Carolina*. Louisville: University Press of Kentucky, 2014.

Censer, Jane Turner. *The Reconstruction of White Southern Womanhood, 1865–1895*. Baton Rouge: Louisiana State University Press, 2003.

Chan, Anne Hui-Hua. "Beethoven in the United States to 1865." PhD dissertation, University of North Carolina at Chapel Hill, 1976.

Chandler, Joseph P. "The Belle of the Opera: Essays upon a Woman's Accomplishment, Her Character and Her Mission." *Graham's Magazine* 34, no. 1 (1849): 1–7.

Chapman, David. "Thoroughbass Pedagogy in Nineteenth-Century Viennese Composition and Performance Practices." PhD dissertation, Rutgers University, 2008.

Cheer, Clarissa Lablache. *The Great Lablache.* Bloomington, IN: Xlibris, 2009.

Cheshire, Rt Rev. Joseph Blount. *An Historical Address Delivered in Saint Matthew's Church, Hillsboro, NC, on Sunday, August 24, 1924: Being the One Hundredth Anniversary of the Parish.* Durham: Christian and King, 1925.

Christensen, Thomas. "Public Music in Private Spaces." In *Music and the Cultures of Print.* Robert Chartier and Kate Von Orden, eds. New York: Garland, 2000, 67–94.

Chybowski, Julia J. "Becoming the 'Black Swan' in Mid-Nineteenth-Century America: Elizabeth Taylor Greenfield's Early Life and Debut Concert Tour." *Journal of the American Musicological Society* 67, no. 1 (2014): 125–65.

Citron, Marcia J. *Gender and the Musical Canon.* Cambridge: Cambridge University Press, 1993.

Clark, Emily. *Strange History of the American Quadroon: Free Women of Color in the Revolutionary Atlantic World.* Chapel Hill: University of North Carolina Press, 2015.

Clay-Clopton, Virginia. *A Belle of the Fifties: Memoirs of Mrs. Clay, of Alabama, Covering Social and Political Life in Washington and the South, 1853–1866.* New York: Doubleday, 1905.

Clayton, Sarah Conley. *Requiem for a Lost City: A Memoir of Civil War Atlanta and the Old South.* Macon, GA: Mercer University Press, 1999.

Clewell, John Henry. *History of Wachovia in North Carolina: The Unitas Fratrum or Moravian Church in North Carolina during a Century and a Half, 1752–1902, from the Original German and English Manuscripts and Records in the Wachovia Archives, Salem, North Carolina.* New York: Doubleday, Page & Company, 1902.

Cobrin, Pamela. "Dangerous Flirtations: Politics, the Parlor, and the Nineteenth-Century Victorian Amateur Actress." *Women & Performance: A Journal of Feminist Theory* 16, no. 3 (November 2006): 385–402. https://doi.org/10.1080/07407700600958085.

Cockrell, Dale. *Demons of Disorder: Early Blackface Minstrels and Their World.* New York: Cambridge University Press, 1997.

———. "Of Soundscapes and Blackface," in Stephen Johnson, ed. *Burnt Cork: Traditions and Legacies of Blackface Minstrelsy.* Amherst: University of Massachusetts Press, 2012.

———. "William Johnson: Barber, Musician, Parable." *American Music* 32, no. 1 (2014): 1–23.

Cogan, Frances B. *All-American Girl: The Ideal of Real Womanhood in Mid-Nineteenth-Century America.* Athens: University of Georgia Press, 2010.

Cohen, Hennig, ed. *A Barhamville Miscellany; Notes and Documents Concerning the South Carolina Female Collegiate Institute, 1826–1865, Chiefly from the Collection of the Late Henry Campbell Davis.* Columbia: University of South Carolina Press, 1956.

Collins, Peter. *Music of Basile Barès.* Vol. CRC2835. Historic New Orleans Collection. Centaur, Presto Classical.

Comminey, Shawn Christopher. "A History of Straight College, 1869–1935." PhD dissertation, Florida State University, 2003.

Cook, Anna Maria Green, and James C Bonner. *The Journal of a Milledgeville Girl, 1861–1867.* Athens: University of Georgia Press, 1964.

Cook, Clarence. *The House Beautiful: Essays on Beds and Tables, Stools and Candlesticks.* New York: Scribner, Armstrong, 1878.

Cooke, Mary Lee. "Southern Women, Southern Voices: Civil War Songs by Southern Women." DMA dissertation, University of North Carolina at Greensboro, 2007.

Coolidge, Arlan R. "Francis Henry Brown, 1818–1891, American Teacher and Composer." *Journal of Research in Music Education* 9, no. 1 (1961): 10–36. https://doi.org/10.2307/3344392.

Coon, Charles L. (Charles Lee). *North Carolina Schools and Academies, 1790–1840; a Documentary History.* Raleigh, Edwards & Broughton, 1915.

Coulter, E. Merton. *College Life in the Old South.* Athens: University of Georgia Press, 2009.

Cox, Karen L. *Dixie's Daughters: The United Daughters of the Confederacy and the Preservation of Confederate Culture.* Gainesville: University Press of Florida, 2003.

Crass, David Colin, Bruce Penner, and Tammy Forehand. "Gentility and Material Culture on the Carolina Frontier." *Historical Archaeology* 33, no. 3 (1999): 14–31. https://doi.org/10.1007/BF03373620.

Crawford, Richard. *America's Musical Life: A History.* New York: WW Norton, 2001.

Cryer, Max. *Love Me Tender: The Stories Behind the World's Favourite Songs.* Sydney, Australia: Exisle Publishing, 2008.

Culpepper, Marilyn Mayer. *All Things Altered: Women in the Wake of Civil War and Reconstruction.* Jefferson, NC: McFarland, 2014.

Dacus, H. Edward Jr. *German Opera and Operetta at the New Orleans National Theatre, 1866–1878.* DMA dissertation, Louisiana State University, 1999.

Dale, Margaret McLean. "Columbia Institute Years Ago Recalled by Alumnae Writing," May 30, 1930. Columbia Female Institute Hanging File. Maury County Archives, TN.

Dannett, Sylvia G. L. "And the Show Went on . . . In the Confederacy." *Maryland Historical Magazine* 61, no. 2 (1966): 105–19.

Davidson, Cathy N. and Jessamyn Hatcher, eds. *No More Separate Spheres!* Durham: Duke University Press, 1998.

Davis, Cyprian. *The History of Black Catholics in the United States.* New York: Crossroad, 2016.

Davis, Edwin Adams, William Ransom Hogan, and William Johnson. *The Barber of Natchez [i.e. William Johnson], Etc. [With Extracts from Johnson's Diary. With Plates, Including a Portrait.* Baton Rouge: Louisiana State University Press, 1954.

Davis, James A. *Maryland, My Maryland: Music and Patriotism during the American Civil War.* Lincoln: University of Nebraska Press, 2019.

Davis, Robert Scott. *Civil War Atlanta.* Charleston: Arcadia Publishing, 2011.

Dawson, Sarah Morgan. *A Confederate Girl's Diary.* Boston, New York: Houghton Mifflin, 1913.

Delaney, Caldwell. *Remember Mobile.* Mobile: Gill Printing and Stationery Co., 1948.

———. *The Story of Mobile.* Mobile: Gill Printing and Stationery Co., 1953.

Detiege, Audrey Marie. *Henriette Delille, Free Woman of Color: Foundress of the Sisters of the Holy Family.* New Orleans: Sisters of the Holy Family, 1976.

DiGaetani, John Louis, and Josef P. Sirefman. *Opera and the Golden West: The Past, Present, and Future of Opera in the U.S.A.* Rutherford, NJ: Fairleigh Dickinson University Press, 1994.

Dillard, Dr. Richard. "Historical Reminiscences of Centre Hill 'Civil War Incidents' #4," n.d. Bound Pamphlet, Durham: Duke, Rubenstein Library.

Dougan, Michael B. "Pasquilino Brignoli: Tenor of the Golden West." In *Opera in the Golden West*, 97–112, n.d.

Downs, Gregory P. *After Appomattox: Military Occupation and the Ends of War*. Cambridge: Harvard University Press, 2015.

Drago, Edmund L. *Charleston's Avery Center: From Education and Civil Rights to Preserving the African American Experience*. W. Marvin Dulaney, ed. Revised edition. Charleston, SC: The History Press, 2006.

Dunson, Stephanie Elaine. "The Minstrel in the Parlor: Nineteenth-Century Sheet Music and the Domestication of Blackface Minstrelsy." PhD dissertation, University of Massachusetts Amherst, 2004.

Edwards, Laura F. *Scarlett Doesn't Live Here Anymore: Southern Women in the Civil War Era*. Urbana: University of Illinois Press, 2004.

Elbert, Monika. *Separate Spheres No More: Gender Convergence in American Literature, 1830–1930*. Tuscaloosa: University of Alabama Press, 2000.

Ellis, Katharine. "Female Pianists and Their Male Critics in Nineteenth-Century Paris." *Journal of the American Musicological Society; Richmond* 50, no. 2–3 (Summer 1997): 353–85.

Ellwsorth, Jane Elizabeth. "The Clarinet in Early America, 1758–1820." PhD dissertation, Ohio State University, 2004.

Engstrom, Mary Claire, and Historic Hillsborough Commission. *The Book of Burwell Students: Lives of Educated Women in the Antebellum South*. Hillsborough, NC: Historic Hillsborough Commission, 2007.

Epstein, Dena J. *Sinful Tunes and Spirituals: Black Folk Music to the Civil War*. Urbana: University of Illinois Press, 1981.

Evans, Augusta J. *St. Elmo.* New York: Grosset & Dunlap, 1866.

Evans, Curtis J. *The Conquest of Labor: Daniel Pratt and Southern Industrialization*. Southern Biography Series. Baton Rouge: Louisiana State University Press, 2001.

Falk, Stanley L. "The Warrenton Female Academy of Jacob Mordecai, 1809–1818." *North Carolina Historical Review* 35, no. 3 (1958): 281–98.

Farnham, Christie Anne. *The Education of the Southern Belle: Higher Education and Student Socialization in the Antebellum South*. New York: New York University Press, 1994.

Faust, Drew Gilpin. *Mothers of Invention: Women of the Slaveholding South in the American Civil War*. Chapel Hill: University of North Carolina Press, 2004.

Federal Writers' Project. *The WPA Guide to Alabama: The Camellia State*. New York: Trinity University Press, 2013.

Fife, Iline. "The Theatre during the Confederacy." PhD dissertation, Louisiana State University, 1949.

Finson, Jon W. *The Voices That Are Gone: Themes in Nineteenth-Century American Popular Song.* New York: Oxford University Press, 1997.

Fisher, Eliza Middleton, Mary Hering Middleton, and Eliza Cope Harrison. *Best Companions: Letters of Eliza Middleton Fisher and Her Mother, Mary Hering Middleton, from Charleston, Philadelphia, and Newport, 1839–1846.* Columbia: University of South Carolina Press, 2001. .

Fitchett, E. Horace. "The Traditions of the Free Negro in Charleston, South Carolina." *Journal of Negro History* 25, no. 2 (1940): 139–52. https://doi.org/10.2307/2714595.

Fitzhugh, George. *Sociology for the South; or, The Failure of a Free Society.* Richmond, VA.: A. Morris, 1854.

Flora, Joseph M., and Amber Vogel. *Southern Writers: A New Biographical Dictionary.* Baton Rouge: Louisiana State University Press, 1980.

Floyd, Janet, and Inga Bryden. *Domestic Space: Reading the Nineteenth-Century Interior.* Manchester: Manchester University Press, 1999.

Floyd, Samuel A. "Black Music and Writing Black Music History: American Music and Narrative Strategies." *Black Music Research Journal* 28, no. 1 (2008): 111–21.

Foner, Eric. *Reconstruction: America's Unfinished Revolution, 1863–1877.* New York: Harper & Row, 1988.

Forbes, Ella. *African American Women during the Civil War.* New York: Garland, 1998.

Fox-Genovese, Elizabeth, and Eugene D. Genovese. *The Mind of the Master Class: History and Faith in the Southern Slaveholders' Worldview.* New York: Cambridge University Press, 2005.

"Frederick W. Meerbach (Jan. 17, 1814–ca. 1893) | Students of the University of Virginia, 1825–1874." https://uvastudents.wordpress.com/2014/04/16/frederick-w-meerbach-17-jan-1814-ca-1893/.

Fries, Adelaide Lisetta. *Historical Sketch of Salem Female Academy.* Salem: NC: Crist & Keehln, Printers, 1902.

Gable-Wilson, Sonya R. "Let Freedom Sing! Four African-American Concert Singers in Nineteenth-Century America." PhD dissertation, University of Florida, 2005.

Gallo, Denise. "Selling 'Celebrity': The Role of the Dedication in Marketing Piano Arrangements of Rossini's Military Marches." In Bashford and Marvin, eds. *The Idea of Art Music,* 18–38.

Gatewood, Willard B. *Aristocrats of Color: The Black Elite 1880–1920.* Fayetteville: University of Arkansas Press, 1990.

Gayle, Sarah Ann Haynesworth, Sarah Woolfolk Wiggins, and Ruth Smith Truss. *The Journal of Sarah Haynsworth Gayle, 1827–1835: A Substitute for Social Intercourse.* Tuscaloosa: University of Alabama Press, 2013.

Geoffroy-Schwinden, Rebecca Dowd. "A Lady-in-Waiting's Account of Marie Antoinette's Musical Politics: Women, Music, and the French Revolution." *Women & Music; Lincoln* 21 (2017): 72–100.

———. "Music as Feminine Capital in Napoleonic France: Nancy Macdonald's Musical Upbringing." *Music and Letters* 100, no. 2 (2019): 302–34. https://doi.org/10.1093/ml/gcz047.

Gerdes, Reginald M. "To Educate and Evangelize: Black Catholic Schools of the Oblate Sisters of Providence (1828–1880)." *U. S. Catholic Historian* 7, nos. 2/3 (1988): 183–99.

Goffman, Erving. *The Presentation of Self in Everyday Life*. Edinburgh: University of Edinburgh, 1956.

Golding, Rosemary. *Music and Academia in Victorian Britain*. Music in Nineteenth-Century Britain. Burlington, VT: Ashgate, 2013.

Golombek, Harry. *Chess: A History*. New York: Putnam, 1976.

Gould, Virginia Meacham, ed. *Chained to the Rock of Adversity: To Be Free, Black & Female in the Old South*. Southern Voices from the Past. Athens: University of Georgia Press, 1998.

——. *Henriette Delille*. Strasbourg: Éd. du Signe, 2012.

Graham, M. Louise Benton. *History of the Confederate Memorial Associations of the South*. [New Orleans]: Confederated Southern Memorial Association, 1903.

Graham, Sandra. *Spirituals and the Birth of a Black Entertainment Industry*. Urbana: University of Illinois Press, 2018.

Grier, Katherine C. *Culture & Comfort: Parlor Making and Middle-Class Identity, 1850–1930*. Washington, DC: Smithsonian Institution Press, 1997.

Gura, Philip F. *C. F. Martin & His Guitars, 1796–1873*. Chapel Hill: University of North Carolina Press, 2003.

Gushee, Lawrence. "Black Professional Musicians in New Orleans c. 1880." *Inter-American Music Review*, 1991, 53–63.

Guterl, Matthew Pratt. *American Mediterranean: Southern Slaveholders in the Age of Emancipation*. Cambridge: Harvard University Press, 2013.

Halttunen, Karen. *Confidence Men and Painted Women: A Study of Middle-Class Culture in America, 1830–1870*. New Haven: Yale University Press, 1982.

Hamm, Charles. *Yesterdays: Popular Song in America*. New York: Norton, 1983.

Hanft, Sheldon. "Mordecai's Female Academy." *American Jewish History* 79, no. 1 (1989): 72–93.

Harris, Robert L. "Charleston's Free Afro-American Elite: The Brown Fellowship Society and the Humane Brotherhood." *The South Carolina Historical Magazine* 82, no. 4 (1981): 289–310.

Harris, Susan K. *Nineteenth-Century American Women's Novels: Interpretative Strategies*. Revised edition. New York: Cambridge University Press, 1992.

Harrison, Mrs. Burton. *Recollections Grave and Gay*. New York: Scribner's, 1912.

Hart, Mary Francis Borgia. *Violets in the King's Garden: A History of the Sisters of the Holy Family of New Orleans*. New Orleans: Hart, 1976.

Hartley, Florence. *The Ladies' Book of Etiquette: And Manual of Politeness: A Complete Hand Book for the Use of the Lady in Polite Society: Containing Full Directions for Correct Manners, Dress, Deportment, and Conversation . . . and Also Useful Receipts for the Complexion, Hair, and with Hints and Directions for the Care of the Wardrobe*. Boston: Cottrell, 1860.

Hartman, Saidiya. *Wayward Lives, Beautiful Experiments: Intimate Histories of Social Upheaval*. New York: WW Norton, 2020.

Hémard, Ned. "New Orleans Nostalgia: Joe and Rose Kennedy at the Ball." *New Orleans Bar Association*, August 10, 2016. https://www.neworleansbar.org/uploads/files/Joe%20 and%20Rose%20Kennedy%20at%20the%20Ball%208_10_16.pdf.

Herz, Henri. *My Travels in America*. Logmark Editions. Madison: State Historical Society of Wisconsin for the Dept. of History, University of Wisconsin, 1963.

Higginbotham, Evelyn Brooks. *Righteous Discontent: The Women's Movement in the Black Baptist Church, 1880–1920*. Cambridge: Harvard University Press, 1993.

Hijar, Katherine. "The Pin-up, the Piano, and the Parlor: American Sheet Music, 1840–1860." *Imprint* 30, no. 2 (2005).

Hill, Michael R. *The Person Place of Louisburg, North Carolina*. Raleigh, NC: Division of Archives and History, 1980.

Hindman, John Joseph. "Concert Life in Ante-Bellum Charleston." PhD dissertation, University of North Carolina at Chapel Hill, 1972.

Hines, James R. *Musical Activity in Norfolk, Virginia, 1680–1973*. PhD dissertation, University of North Carolina at Chapel Hill, 1974.

Hinson, Maurice. *The Pianist's Bookshelf: A Practical Guide to Books, Videos, and Other Resources*. Bloomington: Indiana University Press, 1998.

Hofberg, Herman. "Emilie Augusta Kristina Holmberg." In *Svenskt biografiskt handlexikon*, 1:509, 1906. http://runeberg.org/sbh/a0509.html.

Hoffschwelle, Mary S. "Women's Sphere and the Creation of Female Community in the Antebellum South: Three Tennessee Slaveholding Women." *Tennessee Historical Quarterly* 50, no. 2 (1991): 80–89.

Hohl Trillini, Regula. *The Gaze of the Listener: English Representations of Domestic Music-Making*. Amsterdam: Rodopi, 2008.

Holt, Carrie. *An Autobiographical Sketch of a Teacher's Life*. Quebec: James Carrel, 1875.

Hoogerwerf, Frank W. *Confederate Sheet-Music Imprints*. Brooklyn: Institute for Studies in American Music, Conservatory of Music, Brooklyn College of the City University of New York, 1984.

Horn, Stanley, F. "Dr. John Rolfe Hudson and the Confederate Underground in Nashville on JSTOR." *Tennessee Historical Quarterly* 69, no. 4 (2010): 330–49.

Horwitz, Tony. *Confederates in the Attic: Dispatches from the Unfinished Civil War*. New York: Pantheon Books, 1998.

Hosea, Fanny Polk. *A Sonnet History of Music, with Analytical Notes*. Cincinnati: Steinhauser Print Co., 1918.

Housewright, Wiley L. *A History of Music & Dance in Florida, 1565–1865*. Tuscaloosa: University of Alabama Press, 1991.

Hughes, Kathryn. *Victorians Undone: Tales of the Flesh in the Age of Decorum*. Baltimore: John Hopkins University Press, 2018.

Hutchinson, Ann, ed. *Fanny Elssler's Cachucha*. London: Diane Pub. Co., 1981.

Jabour, Anya. *Scarlett's Sisters: Young Women in the Old South*. Chapel Hill: University of North Carolina Press, 2009.

Janta, Alexander, Justine Chopin, and F. Yaniewicz. "Early XIX Century American-Polish Music." *Polish Review* 6, no. 1/2 (1961): 73–105.

Jennings, Harlan. "The Early Days of Grand Opera in Kansas City, Missouri, 1860–1879." *Opera Quarterly* 15, no. 4 (1999): 677–96. https://doi.org/10.1093/oq/15.4.677.

Jewell, Joseph Oscar. "'Black Ivy': The American Missionary Association and the Black Upper Class in Atlanta, Georgia, 1875–1915." PhD dissertation, University of California, Los Angeles, 1998.

Johnson, James H. "Beethoven and the Birth of Romantic Musical Experience in France." *19th-Century Music* 15, no. 1 (1991): 23–35. https://doi.org/10.2307/746296.

Johnston, Roy. *The Musical Life of Nineteenth-Century Belfast.* Burlington, VT: Ashgate. 2017.

Jordan, Weymouth T. *Ante-Bellum Alabama: Town and Country.* Tuscaloosa: University of Alabama Press, 1957.

Kallberg, Jeffrey. *Chopin at the Boundaries: Sex, History and Musical Genre.* Convergences. Cambridge: Harvard University Press, 1998.

Karpf, Juanita. "'In an Easy and Familiar Style': Music Education and Improvised Accompaniment Practices in the U.S., 1830–80." *Journal of Historical Research in Music Education* 32, no. 2 (2011): 122–44.

———. "An Opportunity to Rise: Reinterpreting Esther, The Beautiful Queen." *Black Music Research Journal* 30, no. 2 (2010): 241–71.

Kasson, John F. *Rudeness & Civility: Manners in Nineteenth-Century Urban America.* New York: Macmillan, 1990.

Kein, Sybil. *Creole: The History and Legacy of Louisiana's Free People of Color.* Baton Rouge: Louisiana State University Press, 2000.

Keith, LeeAnna. *The Colfax Massacre: The Untold Story of Black Power, White Terror, and the Death of Reconstruction.* New York: Oxford University Press, 2009.

Kelley, Bruce C., and Mark A. Snell. *Bugle Resounding: Music and Musicians of the Civil War Era.* Columbia: University of Missouri Press, 2004.

Kelley, Mary. *Learning to Stand and Speak: Women, Education, and Public Life in America's Republic.* Chapel Hill: University of North Carolina Press, 2012.

Kelly, Catherine E. *Republic of Taste: Art, Politics, and Everyday Life in Early America.* Philadelphia: University of Pennsylvania Press, 2016.

Kennedy, Joseph Camp Griffith. *Agriculture of the United States in 1860: Compiled from the Original Returns of the Eighth Census, Under the Direction of the Secretary of the Interior.* US Government Printing Office, 1864.

Kerber, Linda K. "Separate Spheres, Female Worlds, Woman's Place: The Rhetoric of Women's History." *Journal of American History* 75, no. 1 (1988): 9–39. https://doi.org/10.2307/1889653.

Kerrison, Catherine. "The Novel as Teacher: Learning to Be Female in the Early American South." *Journal of Southern History* 69, no. 3 (2003): 513–48. https://doi.org/10.2307/30040009.

Kilbride, Daniel. *Being American in Europe, 1750–1860.* Baltimore: Johns Hopkins University Press, 2013.

Kimball, Warren Keith. "Northern Music Culture in Antebellum New Orleans." PhD dissertation, Louisiana State University, 2017.

King, Grace. *Memories of a Southern Woman of Letters*. New York: Macmillan, 1932.

King, Wilma. *The Essence of Liberty: Free Black Women during the Slave Era*. Columbia: University of Missouri Press, 2006.

Kinzer, Charles E. "The Tio Family: Four Generations of New Orleans Musicians, 1814–1933." PhD dissertation, Louisiana State University, 1993.

Kirk, Elise K. *Musical Highlights from the White House*. Malabar, FL: Krieger Pub. Co., 1992.

——. *Music at the White House: A History of the American Spirit*. Urbana: University of Illinois Press, 1986.

"Knittel, Margaret–Sophie Drinker Institut." http://www.sophie-drinker-institut.de/knittel -margaret.

Knouse, Nola Reed, and C. Daniel Crews. *Moravian Music: An Introduction*. Winston-Salem: Moravian Music Foundation, 1996.

Knowles, Mark. *The Wicked Waltz and Other Scandalous Dances: Outrage at Couple Dancing in the 19th and Early 20th Centuries*. Jefferson, NC: McFarland, 2009.

Krohn, Ernst C. "Nelson Kneass: Minstrel Singer and Composer." *Anuario Intermericano de Investigacion Musical* 7 (1971): 17–41. https://doi.org/10.2307/779859.

Lavina, Javier, and Michael Zeuske, eds. *The Second Slavery: Mass Slaveries and Modernity in the Americas and in the Atlantic Basin*. Zürich: Verlag Münster, 2014.

Lawrence, Dianne. *Genteel Women: Empire and Domestic Material Culture, 1840–1910*. Manchester: Manchester University Press, 2015.

Lebsock, Suzanne. *The Free Women of Petersburg: Status and Culture in a Southern Town, 1784–1860*. New York: WW Norton, 1984.

Lehuu, Isabelle. "Sentimental Figures: Reading Godey's Lady's Book in Antebellum America." In *Culture of Sentiment: Race, Gender, and Sentimentality in Nineteenth-Century America*, 73–91. New York: Oxford University Press, 1992.

Leinbach, Julius Augustus. *Regiment Band of the Twenty-Sixth North Carolina . . . Edited by Donald M. Mccorkle. Reprinted from Civil War History, Etc.* Donald McCorkle, ed. Winston-Salem: Moravian Music Foundation, 1958.

Lemmon, Alfred. "Eugene Chassaignac." Know Louisiana. http://www.knowlouisiana.org/ entry/eugene-chassaignac.

Leslie, Eliza. *Miss Leslie's Behaviour Book: A Guide and Manual for Ladies as Regards Their Conversation; Manners; Dress; with Full Instructions and Advice in Letter Writing; Receiving Presents; Incorrect Words*. Philadelphia: T. B. Peterson and Brothers, c1859.

Leslie, Kent Anderson. *Woman of Color, Daughter of Privilege: Amanda America Dickson, 1849–1893*. Athens: University of Georgia Press, 2010.

Levander, Caroline Field, and Robert S Levine. *Hemispheric American Studies*. New Brunswick: Rutgers University Press, 2008.

Le Vert, Octavia Walton. *Souvenirs of Travel*. New York: Derby & Jackson, 1859.

Levine, Lawrence W. *Highbrow, Lowbrow: The Emergence of Cultural Hierarchy in America*. Cambridge: Harvard University Press, 2002.

Lewis, Robert M. "Tableaux Vivants: Parlor Theatricals in Victorian America." *Revue Française d'études Américaines*, no. 36 (1988): 280–91.

Lott, R. Allen. *From Paris to Peoria: How European Piano Virtuosos Brought Classical Music to the American Heartland*. Oxford: Oxford University Press, 2003.

Lovato, Frank Joseph. "Households and Neighborhoods among Free People of Color in New Orleans: A View from the Census, 1850–1860." MA thesis, University of New Orleans, 2010.

Lovett, Bobby L. *The African-American History of Nashville, Tennessee, 1780–1930: Elites and Dilemmas*. Fayetteville: University of Arkansas Press, 1999.

Luper, Albert Thomas. *Civil War Music*. Iowa City: State University of Iowa Press, 1958.

MacDonald, Edgar E. *The Education of the Heart: The Correspondence of Rachel Mordecai Lazarus and Maria Edgeworth*. Chapel Hill: University of North Carolina Press, 2012.

Mahan, Katherine Hines. *Showboats to Soft Shoes; a Century of Musical Development in Columbus, Georgia, 1828–1928*. Columbus, GA: Columbus Office Supply Co., 1968.

Maillard, Mary, ed. *The Belles of Williamsburg: The Courtship Correspondence of Eliza Fisk Harwood and Tristrim Lowther Skinner 1839–1849*, n.d., e-book.

Malnig, Julie. *Ballroom, Boogie, Shimmy Sham, Shake: A Social and Popular Dance Reader*. Urbana: University of Illinois Press, 2009.

Manly, Louise. *History of Judson College*. Atlanta: Foote & Davies Company, 1913.

Marsh, J. B. T. *The Story of the Jubilee Singers: Including Their Songs*. London: Hodder and Stoughton, 1903.

Matthews, Catherine Taylor, J. Tracy Power, Frances Wallace Taylor, eds. *The Leverett Letters: Correspondence of a South Carolina Family, 1851–1868*. Columbia: University of South Carolina Press, 2000.

Mayes, Edward. *History of Education in Mississippi*. Washington, DC: Government Printing Office, 1899.

McClary, Susan. *Feminine Endings: Music, Gender, and Sexuality*. Minneapolis: University of Minnesota Press, 1991.

McInnis, Maurie Dee. *In Pursuit of Refinement: Charlestonians Abroad, 1740–1860*. Columbia: University of South Carolina Press, 1999.

———. *The Politics of Taste in Antebellum Charleston*. Chapel Hill: University of North Carolina Press, 2005.

McWhirter, Christian. *Battle Hymns: The Power and Popularity of Music in the Civil War*. Chapel Hill: University of North Carolina Press, 2012.

Merish, Lori. *Sentimental Materialism: Gender, Commodity Culture, and Nineteenth-Century American Literature*. Durham: Duke University Press, 2000.

Mersman, Joseph J. *The Whiskey Merchant's Diary: An Urban Life in the Emerging Midwest*. Columbus: Ohio University Press, 2007.

Meyer-Frazier, Petra. *Bound Music, Unbound Women: The Search for an Identity in the Nineteenth Century*. Monographs and Bibliographies in American Music, No. 25. Missoula, Montana: College Music Society, 2015.

Miller, Daniel. *Material Culture and Mass Consumption*. Oxford: Wiley-Blackwell, 1997.

Miller, Karl Hagstrom. *Segregating Sound: Inventing Folk and Pop Music in the Age of Jim Crow*. Durham: Duke University Press, 2010.

Milner, Gabriel. "The Tenor of Belonging: The Fisk Jubilee Singers and the Popular Cultures of Postbellum Citizenship." *Journal of the Gilded Age and Progressive Era; Normal* 15, no. 4 (October 2016): 399–417. http://doi.org/10.1017/S1537781415000560.

Mitchell, Mary Niall. *Raising Freedom's Child: Black Children and Visions of the Future after Slavery*. New York: New York University Press, 2010.

Mocha, Frank. *Poles in America: Bicentennial Essays*. Stevens Point, WI: Worzalla Publishing Company, 1978.

Moore, George. "A Confederate Journal." *West Virginia History* 22, no. 4 (1961): 201–16.

Moriah, Kristin. "'A Greater Compass of Voice': Elizabeth Taylor Greenfield and Mary Ann Shadd Cary Navigate Black Performance." *Theatre Research in Canada/Recherches théâtrales au Canada* 41, no. 1 (2020): 20–38.

Morrow, Diane Batts. "The Oblate Sisters of Providence: Issues of Black and Female Agency in Their Antebellum Experience, 1828–1860." PhD dissertation, University of Georgia, 1996.

———. "'Our Convent': The Oblate Sisters of Providence and Baltimore's Antebellum Black Community." In *Negotiating Boundaries of Southern Womanhood: Dealing with the Powers That Be*, Janet L Coryell, ed., 27–47. Columbia: University of Missouri Press, 2000.

Murray, Elizabeth Reid. *Wake, Capital County of North Carolina*. Raleigh: Capital County Publishing Co., 1983.

Myers, Amrita Chakrabarti. *Forging Freedom: Black Women and the Pursuit of Liberty in Antebellum Charleston*. Reprint edition. Chapel Hill: University of North Carolina Press, 2014.

———. "Negotiating Women: Black Women and the Politics of Freedom in Charleston, South Carolina, 1790–1860." PhD dissertation, Rutgers University, 2004.

Nash, Ann Strudwick. *Ladies in the Making (Also a Few Gentlemen) at the Select Boarding and Day School of the Misses Nash and Kollock, 1859–1890, Hillsborough, North Carolina*. [n. p.] Hillsborough, 1964.

Nash, Gary B. *Forbidden Love*. Boston: Henry Holt and Company, 1999.

Newman, Nancy. *Good Music for a Free People: The Germania Musical Society in Nineteenth-Century America*. Rochester: University Rochester Press, 2010.

Norris, Ethel Maureen. "Music in the Black and White Communities in Petersburg, Virginia, 1865–1900." PhD dissertation, Ohio State University, 1994.

Norris, Renee Lapp. "Opera and the Mainstreaming of Blackface Minstrelsy." *Journal of the Society for American Music* 1, no. 3 (August 2007): 341–65. https://doi.org/10.1017/S1752196307070113.

Nuermberger, Ruth K. "Some Notes on the Mordecai Family." *Virginia Magazine of History and Biography* 49, no. 4 (1941): 364–73.

Obernuefemann, Kelly. "Crossing Invisible Lines: Social Interaction between the Free Women of Antebellum Charleston, South Carolina across Class and Race Lines." https://www.researchgate.net/publication/35498502_Crossing_invisible_lines_social_interaction_between_the_free_women_of_antebellum_Charleston_South_Carolina_across_class_and_race_lines.

O'Brien, Michael. *Conjectures of Order: Intellectual Life and the American South, 1810–1860*. Chapel Hill: University of North Carolina Press, 2004.

O'Brien, Michael, ed. *An Evening When Alone: Four Journals of Single Women in the South, 1827–67*. Charlottesville: University Press of Virginia, 1993.

Oliver, Robert T. *A Faithful Heart: The Journals of Emmala Reed, 1865 and 1866.* Vol. 108. Columbia: University of South Carolina Press, 2004.

Orr, N. Lee. *Alfredo Barili and the Rise of Classical Music in Atlanta.* Atlanta: Scholars Press, 1996.

Ostendorf, Ann. *Sounds American: National Identity and the Music Cultures of the Lower Mississippi River Valley, 1800–1860.* Athens: University of Georgia Press, 2011.

Ott, Victoria E. *Confederate Daughters: Coming of Age during the Civil War.* Carbondale: Southern Illinois University Press, 2008.

Pappacena, Flavia, Audrey Gay-Masuel, Bruno Ligore, and Marie Taglioni. *Souvenirs: Le manuscrit médit de la grande danseuse romantique*, 1st ed. Saint-Denis-sur-Sarthon: Editions de Grenelle sas, 2017.

Parham, J. L. *Mangum Family Bulletin.* Huntsville, AL: By the author, 1980.

Pease, Jane H., and William H. Pease. *A Family of Women: The Carolina Petigrus in Peace and War.* Chapel Hill: University of North Carolina Press, 1999.

———. *Ladies, Women, and Wenches: Choice and Constraint in Antebellum Charleston and Boston.* Chapel Hill: University of North Carolina Press, 2017.

———. *The Web of Progress: Private Values and Public Styles in Boston and Charleston, 1828–1843.* Athens: University of Georgia Press, 1991.

Pemberton, Carol Ann. *Lowell Mason: A Bio-Bibliography.* Westport, CT: Greenwood Press, 1988.

Phi, Alpha Delta. *The Alpha Delta Phi, 1832–1882.* [Boston:] By the fraternity, 1882.

Phipps, Sheila R. *Genteel Rebel: The Life of Mary Greenhow Lee.* Baton Rouge: Louisiana State University Press, 2003.

———. "'Their Desire to Visit the Southerners': Mary Greenhow Lee's Visiting 'Connexion.'" In *Negotiating Boundaries of Southern Womanhood: Dealing with the Powers That Be,* Janet L Coryell, ed., 215–33. Columbia: University of Missouri Press, 2000.

Pike, Gustavus D. *The Jubilee Singers, and Their Campaign for Twenty Thousand Dollars . . . With Photographs by Black.* London: Hodder & Stoughton, 1873.

Ping, Nancy Regan. "Music in Antebellum Wilmington and the Lower Cape Fear of North Carolina." PhD dissertation, University of Colorado, 1979.

Powers, Bernard E. *Black Charlestonians: A Social History, 1822–1885.* Fayetteville: University of Arkansas Press, 2016.

Prenshaw, Peggy Whitman. "Southern Ladies and the Southern Literary Renaissance." In *The Female Tradition in Southern Literature,* 73–88. Urbana: University of Illinois Press, 1993.

Preston, Katherine K. "The 1838–40 American Concert Tours of Jane Shirreff." In *American Musical Life in Context and Practice to 1865,* 173–202. New York: Routledge, 1994.

———. "Between the Cracks: The Performance of English-Language Opera in Late 19th-Century America." *American Music* 21, no. 3 (2003): 349–74.

———. "Music and Musicians at the Mountain Resorts of Western Virginia, 1820–1900." In Richard Crawford, R. Allen Lott, and Carol J Oja. *A Celebration of American Music: Words and Music in Honor of H. Wiley Hitchcock,* 154–73. Ann Arbor: University of Michigan Press, 1990.

————. *Music for Hire: A Study of Professional Musicians in Washington, 1877–1900.* Hillsdate, NY: Pendragon Press, 1992.

————. "Music in the McKissick Parlor." In Slobin, Kimball, Preston, and Root, eds. *Emily's Songbook, 14–21.* Recent Researches in the Oral Traditions of Music 9. Middleton, WI: A-R Editions, 2011.

————. *Opera for the People: English-Language Opera and Women Managers in Late 19th-Century America.* AMS Studies in Music. New York: Oxford University Press, 2017.

————. *Opera for the People: English-Language Opera and Women Managers in Late 19th-Century America.* New York: Oxford University Press, 2017.

Pringle, Elizabeth Waties Allston. *Chronicles of Chicora Wood.* New York: C. Scribner's Sons, 1922.

————. *A Woman Rice Planter.* New York: Macmillan, 1913.

Pryor, Sara Agnes Rice. *My Day; Reminiscences of a Long Life.* New York: Macmillan, 1909.

Proctor, Samuel, Louis Schmier, Malcolm H. Stern, eds. *Jews of the South: Selected Essays from the Southern Jewish Historical Society.* Mazal Historical Collection. Macon: Mercer University Press, 1984.

Pullum-Piñón, Sara Melissa. "Conspicuous Display and Social Mobility: A Comparison of 1850s Boston and Charleston Elites." PhD dissertation, University of Texas at Austin, 2002.

Rable, George C. *Civil Wars: Women and the Crisis of Southern Nationalism.* Urbana: University of Illinois Press, 1991.

Ravenel, Harriott Horry Rutledge, *Life and Times of William Lowndes of South Carolina, 1782–1822.* New York: Houghton, Mifflin and Co., 1901.

Records of the American Catholic Historical Society of Philadelphia. American Catholic Historical Society of Philadelphia, 1903.

Reinders, Robert C. *End of an Era: New Orleans, 1850–1860.* New Orleans: Pelican Publishing, 1964.

Reynolds, Rita. "Wealthy Free Women of Color in Charleston, South Carolina during Slavery." PhD dissertation, University of Massachusetts, Amherst, 2007.

Riis, Thomas. "The Cultivated White Tradition and Black Music in Nineteenth-Century America: A Discussion of Some Articles in J. S. Dwight's Journal of Music." *Black Perspective in Music* 4, no. 2 (1976): 156–76. https://doi.org/10.2307/1214503.

Ripley, Eliza. *Social Life in Old New Orleans: Being Recollections of My Girlhood.* New York: D. Appleton, 1912.

Robert, Kate Ayers. "Madame Josephine Hutet Pillichody," n.d. Mobile Archives Office. Mobile Public Library.

————. "Madame Kowaleski," November 18, 1935. Mobile Archives Office. Mobile Public Library.

Rohr, Nancy M., ed. *An Alabama School Girl in Paris, 1842–1844: The Letters of Mary Fenwick Lewis and Her Family.* Huntsville: Silver Threads Publishing, 2001.

Ross, Michael A. *The Great New Orleans Kidnapping Case: Race, Law, and Justice in the Reconstruction Era.* New York: Oxford University Press, 2014.

Rotman, Deborah L. "Separate Spheres?: Beyond the Dichotomies of Domesticity." *Current Anthropology* 47, no. 4 (2006): 666–74. https://doi.org/10.1086/506286.

Rozier, John, ed. *The Granite Farm Letters: The Civil War Correspondence of Edgeworth & Sallie Bird.* Athens: University of Georgia Press, 1988.

Rumbley, Erica Joy. "From Piano Girl to Professional: The Changing Form of Music Instruction at the Nashville Female Academy, Ward's Seminary for Young Ladies, and the Ward-Belmont School, 1816–1920." PhD dissertation, University of Kentucky, 2014.

Ruth, John A. *Social Culture: A Treatise on Etiquette, Self, Culture, Dress, Physical Beauty and Domestic Relations, Together with Social, Commercial and Legal Forms.* Springfield, MA: King-Richardson Co., 1902.

Rutherford, Mildred Lewis. "History of Athens and Clarke County," 1923. Clarke County Archives, Georgia.

Samuels, Shirley C. *The Culture of Sentiment: Race, Gender, and Sentimentality in Nineteenth-Century America.* New York: Oxford University Press, 1992.

Satterfield, Frances Gibson. *Madame Le Vert: A Biography of Octavia Walton Le Vert.* Edisto Island, SC: Edisto Press, 1987.

Schultz, Mark R. "Interracial Kinship Ties and the Emergence of a Rural Black Middle Class, Hancock County, Georgia, 1865–1920." In *Georgia in Black and White: Explorations in Race Relations of a Southern State, 1865–1950,* 141–72. Athens: University of Georgia Press, 1995.

Schuman-LeClercq, Mary Regina [Siegling]. *Memoirs of a Dowager.* Charleston, SC: Mary Siegling Schumann-LeClercq, 1908.

Scott, Derek B. *The Singing Bourgeois: Songs of the Victorian Drawing Room and Parlour.* Aldershot, Hants, England: Ashgate, 2001.

Scott, Walter, Thomas Moore, and Gentleman of Philadelphia. *The Beauties of Sir Walter Scott and Thomas Moore Esquire: Selected from Their Works with Historical and Explanatory Notes.* Philadelphia: Ash & Mason, and T. Desilver, 1826.

Shadle, Douglas. *Orchestrating the Nation: The Nineteenth-Century American Symphonic Enterprise.* New York: Oxford University Press, 2018.

Shamir, Milette. *Inexpressible Privacy: The Interior Life of Antebellum American Literature.* Philadelphia: University of Pennsylvania Press, 2013.

Shaw, Stephanie J. *What a Woman Ought to Be and to Do: Black Professional Women Workers during the Jim Crow Era.* Chicago: University of Chicago Press, 1996.

Shipley, Lori. "Music Education at Hampton Institute, 1868–1913." *Journal of Historical Research in Music Education* 32, no. 2 (2011): 96–121.

Siepmann, Jeremy. *The Piano.* Milwaukee: H. Leonard, 1998.

Sims, Anastatia. *The Power of Femininity in the New South: Women's Organizations and Politics in North Carolina, 1880–1930.* Columbia: University of South Carolina Press, 1997.

Sims, Edwin Thomas. "'I Must Learn to Paint': The Life of Sarah Adeline Sims." *Proceedings of the South Carolina Historical Association,* no. May (2015): 125.

Sisters of the Holy Family. *The Sisters of the Holy Family of New Orleans, Louisiana: 1842–1987.* New Orleans: The Sisters, 1987.

Slobin, Mark, James W. Kimball, Katherine K. Preston, and Deane L. Root, eds. *Emily's Songbook: Music in 1850s Albany.* Recent Researches in the Oral Traditions of Music 9. Middleton, WI: A-R Editions, 2011.

Small, Christopher. *Musicking: The Meanings of Performing and Listening.* Middletown, CT: Wesleyan University Press, 1998.

Smith, Claiborne T. *The Smiths of Scotland Neck: Planters on the Roanoke.* Baltimore: Gateway Press, 1976.

Solie, Ruth A. *Music in Other Words: Victorian Conversations.* California Studies in 19th-Century Music 12. Berkeley: University of California Press, 2004.

Sonneck, O. G. *Early Concert-Life in America (1731–1800).* Leipzig: Breitkopf & Härtel, 1907. https://catalog.hathitrust.org/Record/001454762.

Sorisio, Carolyn. "Unmasking the Genteel Performer: Elizabeth Keckley's 'Behind the Scenes' and the Politics of Public Wrath." *African American Review* 34, no. 1 (2000): 19–38.

Southern, Eileen. *Biographical Dictionary of Afro-American and African Musicians.* Westport: Greenwood Press, 1983.

———. *The Music of Black Americans: A History.* New York: WW Norton, 1997.

Sowell, Madison U., Debra Hickenlooper Sowell, Francesca Falcone, and Patrizia Veroli. *Icônes du ballet romantique: Marie Taglioni et sa famille.* Rome: Gremese, 2016.

Stanton, Theodore. *The Woman Question in Europe: A Series of Original Essays.* New York: Putnam's Sons, 1884.

Starke, Aubrey H. "Sidney Lanier as a Musician." *Musical Quarterly* 20 (1934): 384–400.

Starr, S. Frederick. *Louis Moreau Gottschalk.* Urbana: University of Illinois Press, 2000.

Steib, Murray. *Reader's Guide to Music: History, Theory and Criticism.* New York: Routledge, 2013.

Stewart, David Marshall. "William T. Berry and His Fabulous Bookstore: An Early Nashville Literary Emporium without Parallel." *Tennessee Historical Quarterly* 37 (1978): 36–48.

Stoever, Jennifer Lynn. *The Sonic Color Line: Race and the Cultural Politics of Listening.* New York: New York University Press, 2016.

Stokowski, Olga Samaroff. *An American Musician's Story.* New York: WW Norton, 1939.

Stoutamire, Albert. "A History of Music in Richmond, Virginia from 1742 to 1865." PhD dissertation, Florida State University, 1960.

———. *Music of the Old South: Colony to Confederacy.* Rutherford, NJ: Fairleigh Dickinson University Press, 1972.

Sullivan, Lester. "Composers of Color of Nineteenth-Century New Orleans: The History behind the Music." *Black Music Research Journal* 8, no. 1 (1988): 51–82. https://doi.org/10.2307/779503.

Tatham, David. *The Lure of the Striped Pig: The Illustration of Popular Music in America, 1820–1870.* Barre, MA: Imprint Society, 1973.

Tawa, Nicholas E. *Sweet Songs for Gentle Americans: The Parlor Song in America, 1790–1860.* Bowling Green, Ohio: Bowling Green University Popular Press, 1980.

Taylor, Mrs. Thomas, Mrs. A. T. Smythe, and Miss M. B. Poppenheim, eds. *South Carolina Women in the Confederacy.* South Carolina Daughters of the Confederacy. Columbia: The State Company, 1903.

The British Library. "The Middle Classes: Etiquette and Upward Mobility." https://www
.bl.uk/romantics-and-victorians/articles/the-middle-classes-etiquette-and-upward
-mobility.

The History of the Parish Church of St. Helena, Beaufort, South Carolina: Church of England, 1712–1789, Protestant Episcopal, 1789–1990. Beaufort, SC: The History Committee, 1990.

The National Cyclopædia of American Biography: Being the History of the United States as Illustrated in the Lives of the Founders, Builders, and Defenders of the Republic, and of the Men and Women Who Are Doing the Work and Moulding the Thought of the Present Time. New York: James T. White and Co., 1893.

Thomas, Maud. *Away Down Home: A History of Robeson County, North Carolina.* Charlotte: Delmar, 1982.

Thompson, David B. "Confederates at the Keyboard: Southern Piano Music during the Civil War." In Kelley and Snell, eds. *Bugle Resounding.* 106–18.

Thompson, William M. *The Charleston South Carolina Second Presbyterian Church at 200: A History.* Charleston: William M. Thompson, 2009.

Thornwell, Emily. *The Lady's Guide to Complete Gentility: In Manners, Dress and Conversation, in the Family, in Company, at the Pianoforte, the Table, in the Street, and in Gentlemen's Society; Also a Useful Instructor in Letter Writing, Toilet Preparations, Fancy Needlework, Millinery, Dressmaking, Care of Wardrobe, the Hair, Teeth, Hands, Lips, Complexion, Etc.* Philadelphia: Derby & Jackson, 1838.

Thurman, Kira. "Singing the Civilizing Mission in the Land of Bach, Beethoven, and Brahms: The Fisk Jubilee Singers in Nineteenth-Century Germany." *Journal of World History* 27, no. 3 (September 2016): 443–71. DOI: 10.1353/jwh.2016.0116/.

Tick, Judith. "Passed Away Is the Piano Girl: Changes in American Musical Life, 1870–1900." In *Women Making Music,* Jane Bowers and Judith Tick, eds., 325–48. London: Palgrave Macmillan UK, 1986. https://doi.org/10.1007/978-1-349-09367-0_13.

———. "Women as Professional Musicians in the United States, 1870–1900." *Anuario Interamericano de Investigacion Musical* 9 (1973): 95–133. https://doi.org/10.2307/779908.

Tolbert, Lisa C. *Constructing Townscapes: Space and Society in Antebellum Tennessee.* Chapel Hill: University of North Carolina Press, 1999.

Towles, Louis Palmer. *A World Turned Upside Down: The Palmers of South Santee, 1818–1881.* Columbia: University of South Carolina Press, 1996.

Trotter, James M. *Music and Some Highly Musical People: Containing Some Chapters on: I. A Description of Music. II. The Music of Nature. III. A Glance at the History of Music. IV. The Power, Beauty and Uses of Music; Following Which Are Given Sketches of the Lives of Remarkable Musicians of the Colored Race. with Portraits, and an Appendix Containing Copies of Music Composed by Colored Men.* Boston: Lee and Shepard Publishers, 1878.

Trouillot, Michel-Rolph. *Silencing the Past: Power and the Production of History.* Boston: Beacon Press, 1995.

Tyner, K. Blake. *Robeson County in Vintage Postcards.* Charleston: Arcadia Publishing, 2005.

Upton, George P. *Musical Memories: My Recollections of Celebrities of the Half Century, 1850–1900.* Chicago: McClurg, 1908.

Urban, Wayne J. "History of Education: A Southern Exposure." *History of Education Quarterly* 21, no. 2 (1981): 131–45. https://doi.org/10.2307/367687.

Waddell, Joseph Addison. *History of Mary Baldwin Seminary (Originally Augusta Female Seminary) from 1842 to 1905.* Staunton, VA: Augusta Printing Corp., 1905.

Ward, Andrew. *Dark Midnight When I Rise: The Story of the Jubilee Singers, Who Introduced the World to the Music of Black America.* New York: Farrar, Straus, and Giroux, 2000.

Waring, Malvina Sarah Black Gist. "A Confederate Girl's Diary." In Taylor, Smythe, and Poppenheim, eds. *South Carolina Women in the Confederacy*, 272–87.

Watson, Alan D. *Wilmington, North Carolina, to 1861.* Jefferson, NC: McFarland, 2003.

Way, William. *The History of Grace Church, Charleston, South Carolina; The First Hundred Years.* Durham, NC: Seeman Printery, 1948.

Weber, William. *The Great Transformation of Musical Taste: Concert Programming from Haydn to Brahms.* Cambridge: Cambridge University Press, 2008.

———. *Music and the Middle Class: The Social Structure of Concert Life in London, Paris and Vienna between 1830 and 1848.* 2nd ed. Music in Nineteenth-Century Britain. Aldershot, Hants, England: Ashgate, 2004.

Webster, Laura Josephine. *Operation of the Freedmen's Bureau in South Carolina.* Charleston: Nabu Press, 2010.

Weig, Ellen. "Lizzie's Organ: A Gift from the Ladies Sewing Society." Presented September 15, 2013 at the St. Matthew's Church Adult Forum, Hillsborough, NC. Typescript.

Weilbacher, Daniel O. "Ernest Guiraud: A Biography and Catalog of Works." DMA dissertation, Louisiana State University, 1990.

Wells, Jonathan Daniel. *The Origins of the Southern Middle Class, 1800–1861.* Chapel Hill: University of North Carolina Press, 2004.

———. *Women Writers and Journalists in the Nineteenth-Century South.* Cambridge: Cambridge University Press, 2011.

Welter, Barbara. "The Cult of True Womanhood: 1820–1860." *American Quarterly* 18, no. 2 (1966): 151–74. https://doi.org/10.2307/2711179.

———. *Dimity Convictions: The American Woman in the Nineteenth Century.* Athens: Ohio University Press, 1977.

Wemyss, Francis Courtney. *Wemyss' Chronology of the American Stage, from 1752 to 1852.* New York: W. Taylor & Company, 1852.

Weston, Pamela. "Out of Purdah: Three Early 19th-Century Female Virtuosi." *Clarinet* 31, no. 1 (2003): 90.

Wheeler, S. J. *Minutes of the Chowan Baptist Association Held with The Church at Mt. Tabor, Hertford County, N.C., May 13–15, 1847.* Raleigh: Recorder Office, 1847.

———. *Minutes of the Forty-Fifth Annual Session of the Chowan Baptist Association Held with The Church at Bethlehem, Hertford County, N.C., May 15–18, 1851.* Raleigh: Recorder Office, 1851.

White, Mary Harriet. "Madame Sophie Sosnowski, Educator of Young Ladies." *Georgia Historical Quarterly* 50, no. 3 (1966): 283–87.

Whites, Leeann. *Civil War as a Crisis in Gender: Augusta, Georgia, 1860–1890*. Athens: University of Georgia Press, 2000.

Wichmann, Jannis. "Europäische Instrumentalistinnen des 18. und 19. Jahrhunderts." http://www.sophie-drinker-institut.de/knittel-margaret.

Willard, Frances E., and Mary A. Livermore. *A Woman of the Century: Fourteen Hundred-Seventy Biographical Sketches Accompanied by Portraits of Leading American Women in All Walks of Life*. Buffalo: Moulton, 1893.

Willard, Frances Elizabeth, and Mary Ashton Rice Livermore. *American Women: Fifteen Hundred Biographies with over 1,400 Portraits; a Comprehensive Encyclopedia of the Lives and Achievements of American Women during the Nineteenth Century*. New York: Mast, Crowell & Kirkpatrick, 1897.

Williams, George Walton. *St. Michael's, Charleston, 1751–1951*. Columbia: University of South Carolina Press, 1951.

Wilson, Jennifer C. H. Jones. "The Impact of French Opera in Nineteenth-Century New York: The New Orleans French Opera Company, 1827–1845." PhD dissertation, City University of New York, 2015.

Wilson, Michael J. "Visual Culture: A Useful Category for Historical Analysis?" In *Nineteenth-Century Visual Culture Reader*, 26–33. New York: Routledge, 2004.

Withers, John, and Jennette Green. *Lt. Col. John Withers, Civil War Confederate Officer: In His Own Words: American Civil War Journal of Assistant Adjutant General for Jefferson Davis: Records of Civil War Life, Battles, History*. Bakersfield, CA: Diamond Press, 2011.

Witt, Susan Powell. "The Gendered Language of War: Picturing the Parlor in Civil War America." PhD dissertation, Stanford University, 2009.

Wright, David. "Novello, John Stainer and Commercial Opportunities in the Nineteenth-Century British Amateur Music Market." In Bashford and Marvin, eds. *The Idea of Art Music*, 60–84.

Young, Ida, Julius Gholson, and Clara Nell Hargrove. *History of Macon, Georgia*. Macon: Lyon, Marshall and Brooks, 1950.

Young, Linda. "'Extensive, Economical and Elegant': The Habitus of Gentility in Early Nineteenth Century Sydney." *Australian Historical Studies* 36, no. 124 (2008): 201–20.

———. *Middle Class Culture in the Nineteenth Century: America, Australia and Britain*. Basingstoke : Palgrave Macmillan, 2003.

Index

CANDACE BAILEY is a professor of music at North Carolina Central University. She is the author of *Music and the Southern Belle: From Accomplished Lady to Confederate Composer* and *Charleston Belles Abroad: The Music Collections of Harriet Lowndes, Henrietta Aiken, and Louisa Rebecca McCord.*

MUSIC IN AMERICAN LIFE

The University of Illinois Press
is a founding member of the
Association of University Presses.

University of Illinois Press
1325 South Oak Street
Champaign, IL 61820-6903
www.press.uillinois.edu